DATE DUE

Peacock Displayed

Thomas Love Peacock at seventy-two
Portrait by Henry Wallis
(National Portrait Gallery, London)

Peacock Displayed

A Satirist in his Context

Marilyn Butler

Routledge & Kegan Paul
London, Boston and Henley

First published in 1979
by Routledge & Kegan Paul Ltd
39 Store Street,
London WC1E 7DD,
Broadway House,
Newtown Road,
Henley-on-Thames,
Oxon RG9 1EN and
9 Park Street,
Boston, Mass. 02108, USA
Set in Bembo by
Computacomp (UK) Ltd, Fort William, Scotland
and printed in Great Britain by
Redwood Burn Ltd
Trowbridge and Esher

British Library Cataloguing in Publication Data

Butler, Marilyn
Peacock displayed.
1. Peacock, Thomas Love – Criticism and interpretation
I. Title
823'.7   PR5164   79-40541

ISBN 0 7100 0293 9

Contents

Preface

In England, at least, Peacock has his devoted readers. Most of them are not professional students of literature; they are nevertheless a formidable band, if casual sampling is anything to judge by. A clever writer attracts admirers of his own kind. While writing this book, I encountered an eminent economist who could recite Peacock's satirical poems of the 1820s, *The Paper Money Lyrics*, and an eminent philosopher who remembered the longest word in Peacock, from *Headlong Hall*. Appropriately, John Fowles has written a novella in *The Ebony Tower* in which Peacock is made to stand for a modern intellectual's cult-figure – humane, intelligent and balanced, and an ancient master of language.

But perhaps even for the élite the appeal of Peacock is generally more basic than this. He is attractive for many of the same reasons as Jane Austen. His *oeuvre* is similar in extent, and hence knowable: for her six books, he offers seven, and on the whole they are shorter. He has a similar wit and precision of phrase. Even more than hers, his humour breathes high spirits and the urbanity that comes from carefully weighing a subject. 'We have recorded, as historical evidence, that the most incorruptible republicans were austere and abstemious; but it is still a question whether they would not have exercised a more beneficial influence, and have been better men, if they had moistened their throats with Madeira, and enlarged their sympathies with grouse.' As with Jane Austen, the mastery of language, especially of dialogue, is matched by the ability to create a fictional world of unusual clarity and charm. Five of

Peacock's satires, from *Headlong Hall* in 1816 to *Gryll Grange* in 1860, are set in country houses, in a green and sunny landscape. The other two, *Maid Marian* and *The Misfortunes of Elphin*, evoke a mythical romance past. It is no wonder that Bruce Richmond, the first editor of the *Times Literary Supplement*, likes the word coined for their spirit – Pavonian – which serves to emphasise that Peacock's world is both unique and self-contained. Pavonians and Janeites alike are under the spell of a very old and universal kind of fantasy.

But Peacock's career and his attitudes are also extraordinarily different from those of Jane Austen. He is much more consciously aware of his times, and of the writer's part in them. Indeed, the period of revolutionary upheaval which he spans, from his birth in 1785 to his death in 1866, is an extraordinary one for the intellectual. Books, articles, comment, are widely circulated and greedily read, as never before and seldom since. The careers of Rousseau and Tom Paine epitomise an age of powerful innovatory ideas and of vehement controversy. In the France of the Revolution, and in the England of the Reform Bill, the press emerges as a fourth estate of the realm, to give a voice to a potent mass force never before identified – public opinion. For all his apparent frivolity, opinion as a contemporary phenomenon – 'the tumult of voices' – is Peacock's subject. It is no accident that almost all his writing is concentrated in two short periods of intense controversy. More than half his *oeuvre*, including *Headlong Hall* (1816), *Melincourt* (1817), *Nightmare Abbey* (1818) and *Maid Marian* (nearly completed in 1818) emerges directly from the threatened revolution which in England followed the end of the Napoleonic Wars. Two more books, *The Misfortunes of Elphin* (1829) and *Crotchet Castle* (1831), together with a spate of articles and the *Paper Money Lyrics*, are a part of the intellectual upheaval that brought about the Reform Bill. There is nothing prosy or eccentric about Peacock's involvement in political controversy, nor about his involvement in controversy of other creative writers. The literature of his day was profoundly politicised; the clash of ideas was also a struggle to command opinion. Coleridge, one of the writers Peacock selected as an antagonist, was never a pure Bible scholar, nor a pure philosopher, but he was, like Hazlitt, Cobbett, and Peacock himself, a commentator, a polemicist, an engaged intellectual. Neither the fluctuations of political opinion at the time, nor amorphous movements of ideas, like Romanticism, liberalism, and the religious revival, existed independently of one another, or of underlying social change. This is why Peacock's career has such special fascination. Individually he had little or no influence on events (but then literary people are always inclined to exaggerate the influence of other *litterateurs*). He did write about key subjects at key times, and with a degree of seriousness, and intelligence, that illuminates them still.

I am indebted to the scholars of different disciplines who shared their expertise with me, including Mr William Boyd, Mr Michael Brock, Mr Howard Colvin, Mr Karsten Engelberg, Miss Angela Leighton, Mr H. C. G. Matthew, Mr W. E. Thomas and Mr Robert Wokler. More of my students than I can name discovered Peacock for themselves, and disputed his qualities in the true style. Mrs Anne Piper lent me the unpublished essay of her uncle, Bruce Richmond. At different stages, Mrs Christina Colvin and Father Illtyd Trethowan generously gave their time to reading the whole text. My husband and my sons have goodhumouredly submitted to a domestic trial resembling the inundation of Gwaelod. Finally, though belatedly, my gratitude goes to Peacock himself (*Audisne haec, Amphiarae, sub terram abdite?* – 'Do you hear these things, Amphiaraus, hidden under the earth?'), the most re-readable of authors and tantalising of personalities.

St Hugh's College, Oxford   M.S.B.

Chapter 1

'A Strain too Learned': Introduction

> Let his page
> Which charms the chosen spirits of the time
> Fold itself up for the serener clime
> Of years to come.
>
> Shelley on Peacock:
> 'Letter to Maria Gisborne'

The modern age ought to be a propitious one for Peacock, more apt than any since his own. It would be odd if he could not find readers in a period which has hailed Evelyn Waugh and Anthony Powell, and knighted P. G. Wodehouse. Civilised comedy must be a minority taste, especially if it appears a little cynical and *dégagé*, but there are moments in history when the minority may add up to a sizeable multitude. It was of all people Dr Leavis, and in the grim postwar year of 1948, who depicted Peacock and the modern Peacockian in the most flattering terms. 'In his ironical treatment of contemporary society and civilization, he is seriously applying serious standards, so that his books ... have a permanent life as light reading − indefinitely re-readable − for minds with mature interests.'[1]

And yet, despite that readability which brings those who have found him back again, Peacock has not been a writer to generate much warmth in his following. A note of reserve has always been heard, even in the most favourable accounts of his art. As a sceptic, he quickly fell foul of early Victorian religiosity. James Spedding, a very intelligent contemporary admirer, noted his merits, but found them always stopping short of what he could praise without qualification – 'an understanding very quick and bright, – not narrow in its range, though wanting in the depth which only deeper purposes can impart.'[2]

We no longer require our writers to wear their religion or other deeper convictions openly on their sleeves. An interesting case study which should have some bearing on changing attitudes to Peacock is the critical reputation of Jane Austen. In the nineteenth century her ironic manner aroused distaste in the zealous Charlotte Bronte and the feeling Mark Twain. In the twentieth century she is admitted to the pantheon, but – interestingly – not at the expense of such Victorian criteria as seriousness and sincerity. An age which thinks of itself as more sophisticated in aesthetic matters is no longer deterred by a light ironic surface, provided the profundities are not too far underneath. We have more in common with the Victorians than we sometimes think. Though tastes affecting style or literary modes may have varied considerably in the post-Romantic period, the taste (perhaps ultimately a middle-class one) which demands a serious outlook on life has been more constant.

Peacock, unlike Jane Austen, has never persuaded the world of his seriousness. Critical commentary on him has been remarkably uniform in the nineteenth and twentieth centuries. A modern may not set out his worries quite as Spedding does: he achieves a very similar effect by insisting that Peacock is, after all, only a *minor* writer. With two partial exceptions,[3] the books that have been written to commend him since 1900 – for example by J. B. Priestley, Howard Mills, Carl Dawson, Felix Felton – have been unanimous on the point, that it is useless to look for a consistent meaning. A few sophisticated spirits have actually rejoiced in the notion that, unlike Godwin, Wells, 'and similar tedious persons', he has an inability to take sides.[4] More usually, the note heard is of honest complaint: 'One commonly finishes a volume with the wish that Peacock would, like Bernard Shaw, prefix a preface to make certain just what he wants the whole thing to mean.'[5] There seems indeed to be a growing tendency to react to Peacock's supposed perversity with downright impatience:[6]

> Peacock is not a novelist of ideas as (say) Aldous Huxley is, and the ideas in the novels are as much a part of the pageant as the

characters themselves. For the truth of the ideas, Peacock seems to care very little; it is their quaintness, their picturesqueness, their absurdity that catches his eye ... What we appear to be offered is the reassertion of commonsense over wild intellectualism, a two-sides-to-every-question geniality, steering all sharp exchanges towards the safety of sport.

Here, then, is a formidable consensus – that if Peacock believes in anything, he has not shown what.

The accessibility of any writer depends on a number of factors, not all of them under his own control. For one reason or another – incompetence or deliberate exclusivity being among them – he may not labour to make his meaning clear. He may use symbols or allusions that a reader will have to learn before comprehending him. In a more literal sense, he may write in a language with a shrinking readership: Erasmus and George Buchanan would still be literary names to conjure with if they had not happened to write in Latin, and Dafydd ap Gwilym, if his works were not in Welsh. But for very similar reasons writers in the great tradition of humanist learning of the Renaissance and the Enlightenment suffered from the rapid erosion of that tradition in the early nineteenth century. In the first half of the century, the population of England doubled, but the reading public was multiplied many times over, and the vast majority of these new readers knew as little of earlier cultures as they knew of Latin. The aristocracy and gentry, who had originally been art's patrons, were still its principal consumers until early in the nineteenth century. Already, by that period, social changes were beginning to have a discernible effect upon the English artist. Art was becoming a commodity, which the artist sold through mass outlets to a public he never got to know. Peacock and Shelley lived late enough to experience the alienation of the artist in the new commercial situation; but they were also early enough to inherit the language of a stabler, more aristocratic culture, and it was classical and humanist. It is precisely because they lived in a transitional age that they have been subject to such persistent misreading. Even Shelley, though almost immediately acknowledged as a major literary figure, could not then find readers to share the assumptions in his classicism, and he has not found them since.

In the new, impersonal conditions in which art-products were marketed, it became increasingly meaningless for those writing about literature to focus upon the recipient, or reader, and increasingly necessary to concentrate upon the producer, or writer. Doctrines began to emerge which emphasised the isolation of the artist, and glorified it. Soon, by the time of Coleridge and Hazlitt, the critic can be seen to identify himself for preference with the artist in the process of composition, rather than, like Samuel Johnson, accepting the role of reader. Among the various art-forms, those which appear to speak most personally for the artist advance in prestige. It is the period of exaltation of the lyric, which can be read as the poet speaking in soliloquy. From longer works, cult-heroes emerge, because they are felt to represent portraits, agonised or ideal, of the artist: Hamlet, Satan, Faust, Childe Harold, Prometheus.

A process begins of *characterising* the writer for public consumption, as a poet-hero. Shelley's widow Mary devotes her life to his fame, and, if Shelley is to be accepted, he has to be made acceptable. Her commentaries on the poems, in her editions of 1824 and 1839–40, are full of useful information, but they are also special pleading. Not wholly consciously, it seems clear, she selects details to record which support one side of Shelley – and, as her mind is more sentimental and more conventional than her husband's, she does justice only to the literary idealist, and drastically curtails the range of that strong and learned mind. In an age of increasing public piety, she stresses the 'Platonic' elements in Shelley's thought, and notes that they are translatable into Christian idiom. 'It requires a mind as subtle and penetrating as his own to understand the mystic meanings scattered through the poem', she says in her note on *Prometheus Unbound*; and she turns *Alastor* into a religious poem, the 'lonely musings' of a poet who had recently expected to die. Just as she herself became embourgeoised, insistently and oddly respectable for the daughter of Godwin and Mary Wollstonecraft and the wife of Shelley,[7] so she tailored and tamed the reputation of her husband, until he fitted the Victorian stereotype of the doomed lyric poet. Mary's activities are less easily seen for the distortions they are than the grosser attempts of her daughter-in-law Jane (Lady Shelley) to tamper with the biographical record in the 1850s.[8] But Mary's highbrow genteelisms stand between us and the whole Shelley, and it was she more than anyone else who turned him into Matthew Arnold's ineffectual angel.

Insistence on Shelley's personality (or one version of it) was inevitable in mid-nineteenth century conditions, but it did violence to a writer who saw a traditional role for the poet within a unified culture. The same process of reinterpretation converted Peacock from a satirist whose interests were mainstream and topical into a frivolous eccentric. As with Shelley, the first phase of commentary was biographical, and created a potent myth about the personality. Peacock was a less central literary figure, and many of the most telling distortions introduced into his portrait did not originate with the small band who studied him directly. It is a curious feature of his life that it touches intimately on the lives of two greater celebrities. As the friend and executor of Shelley, and the father-in-law of George Meredith, between 1858 and 1861 he fell foul of what were, in effect, two separate vested interests: the group covering up for Shelley, and Meredith, who like the Shelleyans edited private facts for public consumption. Peacock believed in accuracy, and cared deeply about his friends, even those who were long dead. Moreover, he was indifferent to, and even contemptuous of, the Victorian proprieties. But he did not make a parade of his intransigence, which accordingly came to be read as something very different.

The late 1850s saw the first attempts authorised by the Shelley family to tell the whole story of the poet's life. It was, at this period, a very delicate assignment. Shelley's self-confessed atheism was on record, though Mary had already done much to play it down. Even worse in relation to Victorian attitudes was Shelley's desertion of his first wife Harriet, when pregnant with his child, and his adultery with Mary Godwin, the mother of the current baronet, Sir Percy Shelley. Nothing that could be said about the facts could make the behaviour of Shelley and Mary respectable, but it was possible to hint at a moral justification for both of them. This was to suggest that Harriet Shelley was unfaithful to her husband before he to her. Hogg's version of the parting, in his *Life* of 1858, did not go far enough for family susceptibilities. According to Lady Shelley's *Shelley Memorials* of 1859, the couple were already estranged in 1813, and (the narrative deviously implies) Shelley took up with Mary in 1814 to console himself for Harriet's adultery.

Peacock, now in his seventies and in retirement, did not want to write yet another *Life* of Shelley. He detested the avid nineteenth-century curiosity into the private lives of public men. As far back as the 1820s, he was complaining in print at the fast-growing market for gossip about personalities. Byron, memorialised by Leigh Hunt and Tom Moore, seemed the portent, on a wholly new scale, of 'an individual living out of society, and much talked of in it, and haunted in his retirement by varieties of the small Boswell or eavesdropping genus.'[9] Peacock rigidly avoided such vulgarity himself. He made a practice, which must have been very frustrating to his acquaintance of later years, of retailing no gossip, and of putting nothing in his infrequent letters but essential information. Six months after complaining of the readiness of Byron's friends to rush into print, he made a wry joke about Jefferson's martyrdom to correspondents, whom he saw as intruders upon that statesman's privacy:[10]

> he seems, though free from most superstitions, to have been not free from that of thinking it necessary to answer letters; and as he received one thousand two hundred and sixty seven in a single year, we may see to what an extent he was a victim to his urbanity. He says he had rather be a cabbage than have to write so many letters. ... The majority of these were 'letters of inquiry, always of good will – sometimes from friends – oftener from persons unknown. ...' Barring this dreadful infliction, his submission to which is wonderful, his life in retirement seems to have been a happy one.

It is, therefore, ironic that Peacock eventually felt obliged to write Shelley's life himself. But his *Memoirs* are in origin anti-biography, an effort to correct the falsifications in the recent wave of Shelleyana, and they give away as little as Peacock can contrive:[11]

> My purpose in undertaking the article for *Fraser*, is: first, to protest against this system of biographical gossip: second: to present an outline, clear of all offence to the living: third: to correct errors, where they appear to me to occur in the narratives under review.

The principal 'error' in the third category was the claim that Harriet was responsible for the break-up of Shelley's first marriage. Peacock had already intervened once before, in the 1820s, to prevent Leigh Hunt, originally backed by Mary Shelley herself, from publishing the same version of the parting. On that occasion, applied to again, Mary had ended by supporting Peacock.[12] This time there was no-one else alive with first-hand knowledge of the events of 1813–14, except T. J. Hogg – who, even if found unsatisfactory in the event, had undertaken his own biography with the Shelley family's approval. In fact, Hogg knew important things that Peacock did not about the separation: he had seen letters, at the time and since, that showed how Shelley was tiring of Harriet, and of a home in which her sister Eliza was always present. Shelley was already emotionally disengaged before he met Mary. Peacock on the other hand was true to his knowledge of Harriet's character, and loyal to her memory. Yet the literal rightness or wrongness of his narrative in the Memoirs has not been the decisive question, as far as Peacock's reputation is concerned. His deliberately restrained and restricted intervention in the biographical dispute did not appeal to Shelleyans, even when this group no longer had the immediate family's special interest in the line he took. What went on being noticed was Peacock's reductive, debunking tone: he was somehow anti-Shelleyan. Peacock's critical account of Shelley's tendency to fantasise,[13] for example, has its logical part in his scheme: he wants to show that Shelley, when prompted by his deeper emotions, can believe melodramatic falsehoods about his father, and so, by inference, about Harriet too. But the usual reaction of modern readers of Peacock's Memoirs of Shelley (who would not be shocked by any of the versions of Shelley's marital behaviour) is that Peacock is too cold, narrow, unimaginative, or, unconsciously, too competitive to sympathise with a genuine poet. More than one modern commentator has suggested that Peacock measured himself against his friend, and envied Shelley his greater talents;[14] and the likeliest source for this suggestion, in the absence of other evidence, is the reticent, negative tone of the Memoirs.

At the same time as the airing of the Shelley issue, a domestic drama in Peacock's own circle created further difficulties for him with posterity. Much the dearest object of his later years was his eldest daughter, Mary Ellen. A beautiful girl, brought up by her father to be cultivated and independent, she had been widowed within three months of her first marriage in 1844 to a lieutenant in the Royal Navy, Edward Nicolls. Five years later she married the youthful George Meredith. The story of this marriage is in one sense familiar, since it is told by Meredith himself, brilliantly, in his poem-sequence *Modern Love*. The problem is that Meredith was anything but impartial, and that because of mid-nineteenth-century attitudes the Peacocks' view could not be given at all.

From the first, Peacock and his son-in-law did not get on. The reasons provided for this antipathy, on Peacock's side, are various. Peacock is said not to have liked the fashion for beards, and to have detested cigarette smoking, and Meredith was a bearded smoker. Peacock and Mary Ellen, on the other hand, did enjoy good food and drink, and Meredith appears to have been dyspeptic. More generally, the Peacocks were sophisticated, humorous, and emancipated. Their style of life was more polished, leisured and lighter than anything that Meredith, the tailor's son educated at a German Moravian school, had ever been used to. They were deeply unconventional, or perhaps eighteenth century, in their attitudes. It is hard to say quite what went wrong with the marriage. But the young couple's poverty was a hard burden for Mary Ellen – Meredith would not take the job her father could have got him at the India House – both young people were highly strung and hard to live with, and *Modern Love* suggests that, after a passionate beginning, the sexual side of their marriage did not go well. After about four years, according to Meredith's later account,[15] the strain was obvious, and Mary Ellen took to living for periods apart from her husband, although there seems to have been no determination on either side that the marriage had finally broken down. At this time both Merediths came to know the painter Henry Wallis. Meredith is said to have been Wallis's model for the *Death of Chatterton*, in 1855; he also painted Peacock, in January 1858 (the portrait now in the National Portrait Gallery), and made the sketch of Mary Ellen which so vividly shows her attraction. In 1858 Mary Ellen bore a child who could not, Meredith knew, be his. Whether Peacock also knew that Harry Felix was Wallis's son is not clear, but it seems on balance probable that he did. He referred to the baby genially in a letter to Claire Clairmont, and maintained excellent relations with Wallis, whom he evidently preferred to his legal son-in-law. In 1858 Mary Ellen and the baby went with Wallis to Capri. By now her marriage with Meredith was at an end, although she got in touch with her husband after her return to England in 1859. Perhaps she wanted their son, Arthur, back, or perhaps she wanted access to him, or perhaps she even wanted, as Meredith afterwards claimed, to be reconciled. Meredith, deeply hurt and humiliated by her affair with Wallis, would not deal with her, and was with difficulty persuaded to let Arthur visit his mother when, in August 1861, she collapsed with a kidney ailment and for two months lay dying.

A lesser but disagreeable element in Mary Ellen's story has appeared to be the behaviour of her father. She was not only the last survivor among his three daughters; his lifelong closeness to her is a matter of record. It is confirmed by his notes to her, which show how he counted on their shared intellectual interests; by their collaborative writing; and by his virtual adoption of her first child, Edith Nicolls. Her independence and unconventionality was the result of an education he determined, which resembled that of his heroine Anthelia Melincourt, and was influenced by his feminine ideal, Maid Marian. Yet, according to one of his most authoritative biographers, Peacock did not see Mary Ellen after she went to Capri with Wallis.[16] If true, the youthful advocate of free love had dwindled into a Victorian father. The selfish old sybarite, whom Meredith's readers have spotted in Dr Middleton of *The Egoist*, could not be drawn from his cellar and his books by the prospect of a personal catastrophe, even when the sufferer was the person he loved best.

But in fact Peacock did not alter in his treatment of Mary Ellen. In 1861 she found a cottage near him, and that summer was staying with him. After she collapsed he visited her daily, and wrote of his feelings to his friend Lord Broughton:[17]

Day after day, I have tried to [write to] you, but always in vain. It seemed as if I could not trace the letters for what I had to say. At the same time with your last kind letter, I received a message from my eldest, and only surviving daughter, that she was extremely ill, and earnestly wished to see me. ... I have never seen such a fearful change in so short a time. I have been with her every day. She seems to grow rapidly worse. But while there is life, there is hope.

Though he did not attend her funeral, his absence seems to have been due not to too little emotion but too much. By Christmas, he still felt unable to pay his annual visit to Lord Broughton. Indeed, he never seems to have recovered from the blow of Mary Ellen's death, and in his final years became virtually a recluse (but a much less genial figure − a more miserable, and, perhaps, more embittered one − than the indulged old man of biographical myth-making).

Mary Ellen Peacock became, like Harriet Westbrook, the guilty heroine of an improving Victorian melodrama. She was the fallen wife, whose slip led inevitably to her being cast off by her husband, her father, and finally her lover. Outside this fantasy, in reality, there is no evidence of any break between Mary Ellen and Wallis, who was given some of her possessions after her death; and Peacock certainly did not side with her wronged husband, or with society.[18] Society's expectations of the father in the case are nicely conveyed by the annotations made by Mr Vulliamy, Meredith's second father-in-law, when Meredith sent him an account of the first marriage:[19]

> After the Institution of Sir C. Creswell's Court in 1859, why did he [Meredith] not seek the Remedy which was now open to him? It seems very strange that he should suffer this woman to bear his name and unaccountable that she lived partly with her father. Was her mother still living? What is her father? and where does he reside?

Peacock's real behaviour amounted to condoning Mary Ellen's. No doubt his family, and those well-disposed towards him, and even towards Meredith, thought it better for all concerned if he were shown to posterity doing the proper thing. Equally, Mary Ellen's assertion of sexual freedom was represented as a single fatal step: an elopement seems much less of a challenge to the social mores than her preference, over several years, for living under her own roof rather than under her husband's. As a result, an old man who ended his life misanthropic, and inconsolable, is converted into a selfish if amusing elderly eccentric, too busy perhaps with his

Greek to recognise that he had been a witness to yet another of the nineteenth century's real-life tragic love-stories.

There was, in actual fact, no opposition between Peacock's interest in the Greeks and his belief in free love, which he maintained both in Shelley's day, and after Mary Ellen was dead.[20] It is not without cause that Diane Johnson calls Peacock a passionate man; and yet it is hard to find specific evidence for the warmth of someone so firmly bent on remaining elusive. Certainly Peacock was always deeply rooted in his own family life. His mother, a strong-minded and intelligent woman, to whom he was much attached, remained in his house after his marriage until her death in 1833 at about eighty. From about 1807 he was frequently in love – his cousin Harriet recalled his 'thousand and one loves' – and during the years he knew Shelley seemed often on the point of marrying a girl called Marianne de St Croix. At last, when in 1819 he could afford to marry, Marianne seems to have refused him, and his proposal instead to a Welsh girl he had been in love with eight years earlier struck Shelley as romantic and eccentric – 'it is altogether extremely like the *dénouement* of one of your own novels.'[21] His marriage to Jane Gryffydh appeared happy until, in 1826, on the death of their baby daughter Margaret, Jane suffered a breakdown from which she never recovered. Peacock was left to bring up the two surviving girls and a boy, with his wife a 'nervous invalid', as the Victorian euphemists put it. ('Quite mad' is the phrase used in a letter by Mary Shelley.)[22] In all this, as in Peacock's stricken reaction to the deaths of Jane in 1851 and Mary Ellen ten years later, there are signs of a man of deep and permanent affections. His losses left him like Orlando, in his favourite Pulci, 'standing alone by the fountain of Roncesvalles, with his dearest friends and his favourite horse lying dead at his feet ... he wishes to follow those that are gone.'[23] It is possible also to read a more than commonplace loneliness into his mood after Shelley left England for Italy, when he was 'as melancholy as a gib cat',[24] and on the point of resolving to give up his independent life for the service of the East India Company.

Yet, unquestionably, solitariness was also his choice and his style. Many people testified to his likeability, especially in later life. The impressions are alike – 'a warm-hearted, genial man'; 'a teller of "good stories"'. Wherever he went he kept his auditors in roars of laughter, and he was an immense favourite with all the directors.'[25] But this is the popularity of a man with many acquaintances and few close friends. In his youth, several members of the Shelley circle, including Mary, had found him cold. Even Shelley repeated the charge of coldness more than once around 1814. As Richard Holmes points out in his biography of Shelley, the two friends were temporarily estranged when Shelley went off with Mary, leaving Peacock as the champion of Harriet, and Shelley's cutting, angry expressions certainly do not reflect the warmth and depth of this friendship over time.[26] Even so, Shelley and Mary (who for some years kept up her resentment against Peacock) could not repeatedly have alluded to Peacock's coldness unless there was something in his manner, at least, that gave colour to the idea. It is very noticeable that even at the stage when Peacock had proved himself the most important intellectual contact of Shelley's life, Shelley could write to the more emotionally expressive Leigh Hunt as 'our best friend'.[27] Hunt meanwhile, having inherited Peacock as a friend from Shelley more or less involuntarily, was prepared to be mildly malicious about him:[28]

Peacock has been reasoned by some mathematician out of his love for the opera, and is to read Greek, they say, on Saturday nights – the Dithyrambic, of course – to begin at 7 precisely. What do you think of this debut of mine in scandal? But he glories in doing nothing except upon theory. He falls in love, as it were, upon a gravitating principle. His passion literally, as well as metaphorically, is quite problematical. Let B. be Miss Jenkins, etc.

Four months after this letter, Peacock wrote to propose to Jane Gryffydh in a style that bears out Hunt's exasperated description:[29]

It is more than eight years since I had the happiness of seeing you ... I long entertained the hope of returning to Merionethshire under better auspices than those under which I left it: but fortune always disappointed me, continually offering me prospects which receded as I approached them. Recently she has made me amends for her past unkindness, and has given me much present good, and much promise of progressive prosperity, which leaves me nothing to desire in worldly advantage but to participate it with you.

If Hunt was not in Peacock's confidence over his intended marriage, he proves that he knew his man. In addressing his friends, as well as in addressing his public, Peacock hid himself behind a mask, reserved, ironic and paradoxical.

The posture relates, as we shall see, to a conscious philosophy of life. But it is nevertheless also true that Peacock's childhood and youth were in some special senses alienating, and must have contributed to that impression recorded of him all his life, that, though gifted with exceptional good looks, charm and wit, he was unusually hard to know. Born in 1785, he was an only child whose father lived apart from him and his mother, and died when Thomas was eight or thereabouts. He was brought up by his mother, Sarah Peacock, née Love, who conveyed to him her own liberal deistical opinions, including a strong taste for the anti-clerical Gibbon. Between the ages of six and twelve he attended a private school kept by John Harris Wicks at Englefield Green. After that he taught himself, by private reading, notably in the classics. He became learned, and, like many auto-didacts, somewhat inflexible, not readily amenable to habits of thought other than his own. It was a training which helped to keep him on the fringes of the groups to which his sympathies and his friendships naturally took him.

In England, schools and universities have generally helped a man to define his social allegiances, and Peacock went to neither. His classicism was nothing like the inherited syllabus of sleepy, Tory Oxford, with its emphasis on linguistic prowess, grammar, and the rules of prosody. It was, or it became, an angular neo-classicism, sharp, urgent and topical. Peacock had taught himself the international intellectual medium of the Enlightenment, and at the time, during the French Revolutionary Wars, the connotations were not at all quietly and quaintly antiquarian, but pagan, republican and democratic. While England was at war with France — from the year Peacock was eight, to the year he was thirty — his opinions, which he apparently did not trouble to hide, must have tended to make him unpopular. In rural Wales, where he spent much time walking, he was a marked man, as Shelley found when he went there after him in 1812.[30]

'Ah!' said she 'there Mr. Peacock lived in a cottage near Tan y bwlch, associating with no one, & hiding his head like a

13

murderer, but', she added altering her voice to a tone of appropriate gravity, 'he was *worse than that*, he was an *Atheist*.'

Jane remembered this fearsome reputation for atheism, as her nervous reply to his proposal proves.[31] Several times during his long life, the orthodox were to express hostility to Peacock on this account. In 1826 the Rector of Shepperton, who no doubt already knew his parishioner's reputation, objected to the wording of his epitaph for the two-year-old Margaret, 'Long night succeeds thy little day', on the grounds that it denied the immortality of the soul.[32] Peacock in some measure got his revenge when in old age he encouraged the village children to celebrate May Day in pagan style.[33] Though his biographers afterwards treated such behaviour as amiable eccentricity, at the time the irreverence of the 'clever old man', as Meredith called him,[34] must have been alienating to most of his neighbours, rather as if Byron had lived on into Victorian times, and settled down on the outskirts of London.

The mask is seldom dropped even for the like-minded. Seen with hindsight, Peacock appears to have created, wilfully, a pattern of life that was unusually antisocial. During the war-time years of his youth, a small income enabled him to write poetry and follow his own inclinations. Apart from a short spell as a clerk after he left school, and another as captain's clerk on board HMS *Venerable* in 1808–9, he had no regular employment until he joined the East India Office in 1819 at the age of thirty-four. Living always in the Thames valley above London, he spent his formative years reading, walking, and versifying. Until he was twenty-seven he had few real friends, though there were at least two exceptions. One was the publisher Edward Hookham, and another was Thomas Forster, who seems to have been closer to Peacock than anyone until, some time in the second decade of the century, he left England to study abroad. In 1859, after Forster had unexpectedly come all the way from Bruges to pay Peacock a brief visit, Peacock described their youthful friendship to Lord Broughton:[35]

> We had the same tastes and pursuits, classical, metaphysical, and, under the spell of Horne Tooke, etymological. We never missed an opportunity of being together; and when separate, we corresponded almost continuously by returning posts, more frequently in Latin than in English. We called each other Tom,

and considered ourselves Pylades and Orestes. But some forty
years ago, he went to reside on the Continent, and from that
time we have had little intercourse. Once, there were many who
called me Tom. Of all these he alone remains.

Despite this important exception, Peacock had nothing resembling
a circle until he made the acquaintance of Shelley at the end of
1812. At that point the Shelley social ambience, based on
Bracknell, was itself made up of a heterogeneous collection of
outcasts. It was probably rather later – in that winter of 1816 at
Marlow which Hogg described as 'a mere Atticism' – or the year
1817–18, when the Shelleys were within even closer reach, that
Peacock experienced what most other established literary men took
for granted – easy and frequent conversation with intellectual
equals. After Shelley's departure for Italy in 1818 Peacock seems to
have reverted in his personal life to the pattern that was natural to
him. Before Jane's illness, he and she were not much seen as a
couple. At the India House, though liked, he was thought of as a
less gregarious figure than his colleague John Stuart Mill.[36] The
most congenial of his new colleagues, men like Edward Strachey
('a genially-abrupt man', said Carlyle, who scorned 'the general
humbug of the world'),[37] visited him at his cottage at Halliford, as
did T. J. Hogg. In London he is said to have dined once a week
with Jeremy Bentham, whose acquaintance he made through his
superior James Mill.[38] John Cam Hobhouse, Byron's friend, who
was created Baron Broughton in 1851, was one of the few friends
he would go away to visit. He liked best staying at home with his
family, including his cousin Harriet Love, his adopted daughter
Mary Rosewall, and his granddaughter Edith Nicolls, in the two
white houses beside the Thames. As he aged, it was a retirement on
the whole interrupted only by the young men who admired his
work, or perhaps wanted to hear about Shelley: Robert Buchanan,
Thomas L'Estrange, and Strachey's son, the future Sir Edward.
Long before grief turned him into a recluse, Peacock made a point
of his apartness. He wore a seal with a motto from Horace: '*Nec
tardum opperior nec praecedentibus insto*,' 'I neither follow in the rear,
nor pursue those who run before me.'[39]

There is some justification, then, for the received picture of

Peacock as a laughing bystander; but at the same time it is profoundly misleading. To some extent, the aristocratic attitude – cynical, reserved, exaggeratedly independent – is no more than the upper-class posture of the day. Taking it as special to Peacock saddles him with a coldness and emotional detachment which the facts contradict. Equally, the manner has been translated into intellectual indifference, and here there is much more evidence that Peacock's true attitudes were of quite another kind.

On one occasion, Peacock appears to give countenance to those who see him as intellectually frivolous, the caricaturist of anything amusing that catches his eye. He is describing the circle Shelley introduced him to at Bracknell, probably in 1813:[40]

> I was sometimes irreverent enough to laugh at the fervour with which opinions utterly unconducive to any practical result were battled for as matters of the highest importance to the well-being of mankind: Harriet Shelley was always ready to laugh with me.

There is, after all, a potentially significant phrase in this account – 'unconducive to any practical result'. Peacock could have meant – in fact, his writings will suggest he did mean – that the Bracknell circle was ridiculous not because it was enthusiastic but because it was impractical. But the passage has been cited in evidence, far beyond its intrinsic significance, and out of its context, to sustain an impression of Peacock as a universal scoffer, an inveterate sketcher of eccentricity in all its forms, and a man who laughed at people simply because they had opinions.

The same rather too memorable glimpse of life at Bracknell supports an even more pervasive conception, which is at the very heart of the image of frivolity and intellectual detachment. Peacock is taken for a caricaturist of people in real life whom he knew or had read about. Again, 'identifications' of characters in fiction were very much in keeping with the personality-mongering spirit of the age. Some guesses at Peacock's originals were soon believed in Peacock's own circle, and got back to the author himself.[41] But, surprising though this will seem, there is no sound evidence that Peacock drew what can fairly be called *portraits* of real-life individuals. In fact, the best testimony, Peacock's own, is directly to the contrary. In the Preface he wrote for *Melincourt* when it was reprinted in 1856 he specifically denies any attempt to represent anyone's 'private' character. 'Of the disputants whose opinions and public characters (for I never trespassed on private life) were shadowed in some of the persons of the story, almost all have passed from the diurnal scene.' Peacock's careful phrasing concedes that in some of his novels the name of a minor character is deliberately meant to bring a real-life thinker or public figure to mind. It will usually be a public figure, rather than someone Peacock knew personally. But it is important to realise that, even when a specific connection can be made, the individual concerned is not one man, not as it were himself, but a public persona, which is in turn the representative of a type. Even this practice, of using real-life exempla, is rarer than has been supposed, for with his major figures Peacock is careful to blend characteristics in such a way as to frustrate identification with real people.

The most celebrated instance of an apparent portrait is Scythrop Glowry in *Nightmare Abbey*, who has been universally taken to 'be' Shelley. The steady growth of this belief follows a typical enough pattern: its first known appearance in print was in the 1840s,[42] and after Peacock's death it was alluded to as a more or less established fact by Medwin and Buchanan.[43] And yet, when the references Shelley makes to Scythrop in his letters are checked, it will be found that Shelley nowhere states unequivocally that Peacock intended to portray him as Scythrop – while Peacock himself (who is seldom unequivocal) avoids a clear statement both about his own intention, and about what Shelley felt his intention to be – 'he took to himself the character of Scythrop'.[44]

At a period when he already saw that his comic kind was no longer liked or understood, Peacock defined that tradition as he saw it, a comedy of ideas rather than of character. He was reviewing a French comic writer of the 1830s, Paul de Kock, and finding him interestingly different from Pigault le Brun, a predecessor of the French Revolutionary period. Le Brun had belonged to an older, classic, tradition of French comic writing, one which 'embodied opinion in a very cogent and powerful form':

> Rabelais, one of the wisest and most learned, as well as wittiest of men, put on the robe of the all-licensed fool, that he might, like the court-jester, convey bitter truths under the semblance of simple buffoonery ... It would be, we think, an interesting and

amusing enquiry to trace the progress of French comic fiction, in its bearing on opinion, from the twelfth century to the Revolution; and to show how much this unpretending branch of literature has, by its universal diffusion through so many ages in France, contributed to directing the stream of opinion against the mass of delusions and abuses which it was the object of those who were honest in the cause of the Reformation, and in the causes of the several changes which have succeeded it to the present time, to dissipate and destroy.

Peacock concedes that the liberal causes for which such writers have worked have often been only partially successful:[45]

we shall find, nevertheless, in the first place, that every successive triumph, however perverted in its immediate consequences, has been a step permanently gained in advance of conscience and freedom of inquiry; and we shall find, in the second place ... that comic fiction has contributed largely to this result.

It was a comic tradition which was ultimately European rather than only French, for it embraced Aristophanes, Petronius, Cervantes, Swift, the Fielding of *Jonathan Wild*, as well as Rabelais and Voltaire. It aimed to intervene in affairs, a general aspiration which made it quite distinct from the less ambitious comedy of character. Though Peacock is too modest to say so, it is impossible to believe that this article does not contain a manifesto for his own purposes and methods as a writer of comedy.

But, if this is the case, there is a certain perversity in the favourite contribution of Peacock's critics, and above all his editors: the note, footnote or introductory essay identifying the originals of Panscope and Escot, Philomela Poppyseed and MacLaurel. This was a process begun, needless to say, in Victorian times, by Richard Garnett and Saintsbury among the editors, but it is a vein which has by no means run out. A good recent editor of Peacock, David Garnett, added considerably to the number of identifications in his edition of 1948. Eleanor L. Nicholes has provided a by now almost traditional list, in a passage which begins confidently, 'Peacock's novels are all in some measure *romans à clef*'.[46]

It is a scholarly guessing-game which cannot have contributed to Peacock's readability, or not at least as far as the general public is concerned. As time has gone on, rendering most of the supposed originals shadowy – who now knows Amelia Opie or J. F. Newton, or even Jeffrey and Gifford? – the slowly growing corpus of annotation has given the satire an increasingly antiquarian air. Readers of Peacock remain fixed in much the position of readers of Pope in the 1920s and 1930s. The clutter of obscure personalities is confusing and wearisome: a world peopled with cranks, not richly caricatured (as in Dickens) but thinly announced by a single governing attribute (as are most of the minor figures in the *Dunciad*).

The difference between his characterisation and that of the novelist Dickens is significant. Analysis of a speech uttered by one of Peacock's figures tends to reveal a rich texture: sentence by sentence, allusion to a specific text, a pre-existent *locus*; while the speech in its entirety, and still more the attitude of the speaker, call to mind in the most literal sense *opinion* – that is, a familiar contemporary controversy. Here, of course, is the centre of the problem concerning Peacock, the real reason why he became, and has remained, so profound a puzzle. While he is offering ideas, he appears to deal with character, and for this his modern readers have elaborate training, and expectations. Like the Victorians, we have a set of assumptions derived from novel-reading and, supported by the professional expertise of the psychiatrist, we have what is in a sense an even more developed interest in personality. By the standards of either the novelist or the psychiatrist, Peacock's characters are disappointing. In fact, his dislike of his period's taste for personality is maintained in his work, and he does not deal in character at all. Of all his unorthodoxies, his humorous gestures of intellectual sabotage, it has been perhaps the most uncomfortable, the hardest to forgive.

It is no new discovery that Peacock's writing is in one sense or another learned and traditional. He was prodigiously well read in Greek and Latin, French and Italian, as well as in English literature, and takes a special pleasure in confounding the reader by allusion to an esoteric favourite, such as the *Dionysiaca* of the fifth-century poet Nonnus.[47] His friend and fellow-Platonist Thomas

Taylor no doubt intended a compliment when he christened him Greeky-Peaky, but the attainment has been found largely rebarbative since. Shelley's lines about Peacock have proved apt and prophetic, except that (as in other spheres) the better times Shelley anticipated have not yet arrived:[48]

> ... his fine wit
> Makes such a wound, the knife is lost in it;
> A strain too learned for a shallow age,
> Too wise for selfish bigots; let his page
> Which charms the chosen spirits of the time,
> Fold itself up for the serener clime
> Of years to come, and find it['] s recompense
> In that just expectation.

And yet, it is not necessary to know as much Greek as Peacock did, or indeed any Greek at all, to understand in general terms what he took Greece to signify. Men have been known to lose themselves in a past era, or in its literature, out of some kind of nostalgia, or rejection of the present. Sentimental antiquarians of this type were at large in Peacock's day; in Folliott and Chainmail of *Crotchet Castle* he was to satirise some of them. But such an attitude to the past, far from being his own, was peculiarly alien to the Greek spirit as he understood it.

When Greek literature was revived in the Renaissance, it was initially a study to which arcane matter, the accretions of the Dark Ages, adhered. Plotinus was as much a name to conjure with as Plato: the neo-Platonism of the sixteenth century is a curious growth, divorced from a clear historical sense, reminiscent of the Near East and Alexandria as much as of Periclean Athens. The tradition lingers on in the eighteenth century. It is present, for example, in the work of Thomas Taylor, that 'pagan Methodist', as Southey called him, who, like Blake, was the denizen of a tradesman or artisan world of esoteric religious cults. In the 'Preliminary Dissertation' to his *Mystical Initiations: or, Hymns of Orpheus* (1787), Taylor undertook to interpret the Orphic religion, through the commentaries 'of the latter Platonists, as the only sources of genuine knowledge, on this sublime and obsolete enquiry'.[49] Coleridge, whom Lamb long afterwards recalled at Christ's Hospital in the later 1780s, mouthing 'the mysteries of

Jamblichus, or Plotinus (for even in those years thou waxedst not
pale at such philosophic draughts), or reciting Homer in his Greek,
or Pindar',[50] had probably come by his impressively arcane
knowledge via Taylor. But this is not Peacock's Greece, even
though Peacock liked Taylor for preferring the pagan pantheon to
Christianity. Nor was Peacock primarily interested in another
flourishing tradition of classical scholarship, that of the great
editors. Earlier in the century, the greatest of English scholars,
Richard Bentley, had led the modern movement towards
establishing sound texts. But, though Peacock all his life was
interested in questions of language, grammar and metre, he was
always more interested in content; and in this above all perhaps he
differed from the mere specialist in ancient literature or art or
antiquities. To be 'Greek', one need not become a pedant. One did
not even have to know the language. Keats did not, and as late as
1817 Shelley was happy to read difficult works in translation, or to
gather their meaning imperfectly, without using a dictionary.
When Peacock thought of running a school in 1813 or 1814, he
stated firmly in the prospectus that the Greek he meant to teach
was no more than the means to an end.[51]

His classicism developed notably original features, especially in
collaboration with Shelley, but it was also in origin part of a
movement of the second half of the eighteenth century. For the arts
as a whole the era has been called a period of 'sharp action and
innovation' (as opposed to the first half of the nineteenth century,
the period of 'response and reflection').[52] Typically, the
Enlightenment implied for the arts the democratisation of content,
and the drastic simplification of style. From mid-century, the
visual arts especially tend to reject the charming, the detailed, the
decorative – the rococo, a style for an aristocratic coterie – in
favour of something grander, graver and more universal. Art-
forms which flatteringly mirror an advanced society give way to
primitivism: to the ancient Rome of Piranesi, the Greece of
Winckelmann, or, in literature, the Celtic twilight of Ossian or
Gray. In simpler times, the feeling runs, Man was nearer to
Nature, and also freer to be himself. Architects pursue the essential,
by evoking the Roman or the Doric, or by the even more brutal
simplification of triangle, circle and cube. Painters turn away from
the finicky, and implicitly affectionate, representation of colour,

clothing, and texture; they prefer to represent the middle-class family in the course of common daily life, or a motionless nude figure, recalling the *Apollo Belvedere*, drawn in pure outline against a minimal background.

For post-Romantic art critics, and even more for literary critics, 'neo-classicism' has commonly been a pejorative term. Invented in the 1880s, it still reflects that period's lack of sympathy with the eighteenth century, and especially its belief that eighteenth-century art was academic and derivative. But the real impulse behind the 'true style' advocated during the Enlightenment was not antiquarian. For Winckelmann, Diderot, Reynolds, the idea of copying the ancients was anathema. The study of the ancients they proposed was meant to recover a primal simplicity, free from the accretions of a too elaborate modernity. So Gluck, in his dedicatory epistle to *Alceste* (1769), rejects the 'florid descriptions' of the libretti of Italian opera, for his own librettist's 'strong passions' in 'heartfelt language'; or Joseph Warton complains of Pope's cleverness and artifice. The movement back to Nature to which the early Rousseau gave an impetus is perfectly neo-classical, as are Burns' poetry of mice and ordinary men, Cowper's divine chit-chat, Blake's drawings and Wordsworth's *Lyrical Ballads*.

The art of the Enlightenment was radical in its rejection of previous styles, but not necessarily radical in its politics. Its confident individualism, its dignity and idealism, was perfectly echoed, for example, in the parliamentary oratory of the *anciens régimes*: it was the international language of the European aristocracy. The American and French Revolutions neither caused radicalism in art nor were created by it, but were further manifestations of underlying social pressures, a deeper pattern of change. However, political revolution, especially the French, had a profound effect upon attitudes to the arts: what had been natural and a-political before the fall of the French monarchy became charged with meaning. Cowper's *Task* was loved by readers of all shades of opinion. Even Burns' obvious egalitarianism, and impropriety, caused relatively little outrage. But the reputations of Cowper and Burns were established before the Terror. Wordsworth's *Lyrical Ballads*, poems professing to be for and about the people, appeared at the height of the French Republic's military success. They were censured for their political unsoundness even by the liberal Whig Francis Jeffrey (who in private admitted to being moved by them); even, in retrospect, by Wordsworth's friend and co-author, Samuel Taylor Coleridge.[53]

As neo-classicism in its broader, artistic sense had to change after the Revolution – to become more defensive, less bold in its assertions and less universal in its appeal – so too the vogue for the Greek. In the eighteenth century, both republican Rome and ancient Athens could be used, unselfconsciously and more or less interchangeably, as models of freedom. Aristocrats engaging in ideological warfare against a monarch were particularly prone to idealise this kind of republic, along with modern oligarchies like Venice and Switzerland. So Gibbon exalts the memory of the Roman Republic, in *The Decline and Fall of the Roman Empire*, or Thomson of Athens in his *Ode to Liberty*. Ancient art, though praised in the language of taste, is valued above all as an advertisement for personal freedom. 'Only liberty', declares Winckelmann in the 1760s, 'has elevated art to its perfection.' By the end of the century, this kind of sentiment had a very different ring.

The French Revolutionaries make the common motifs of late eighteenth-century polemic their own. Their painter, J. L. David, takes classical subjects like *The Oath of the Horatii*, and the simple, severe setting, the idealised human figures, the noble gestures become the expression of revolution. The cropped revolutionary haircut, the sudden simplification in the lines of women's dress, help to legitimise the new republicanism, by making it seem older and more prestigious than monarchy. English sympathisers with the French Revolution in the 1790s adopt the republican style, both of dress and of language, but this kind of classicism, naive and propagandist, does not outlast the decade. In France, by a grim historical irony, it gives way to the heavy institutional grandeur of Napoleon's Imperial style. In England, neo-classicism survives for another generation as the dominant mode, in painting, in architecture, in formal criticism, but after the turn of the century its assertions are far less bold and universal. Blake's glorious or tortured human figures, which dominate his prints up to 1795, are succeeded by his obscurer and more detailed illustrations to the Bible. Sir John Soane's powerful geometric Bank of England (1798) is followed by the Regency terrace. The *Lyrical Ballads*, also 1798, are one kind of neo-classical statement; *English Bards and Scotch Reviewers*, 1809, is another. What is lost in the Counter-Revolution is the confident public gesture.

The classicism of the wartime radical necessarily takes on a special tone. In the later eighteenth century, republican Rome had been more fashionable in England than Greece. Italy, especially Rome itself, was more accessible. British artists like Gavin Hamilton and Robert Adam studied at Rome. Fuseli, Swiss-born but Rome-trained, settled in London. Piranesi became a strong influence. After England had fully absorbed the shock-waves of the Revolution, from about 1800, it was the cultural influence of Greece which seemed to advance, and some of the explanation for this is surely psychological. With the Revolution compromised — by the Terror, by French expansion, and now by Bonaparte's dictatorship — the beleaguered English intellectual needed something other than David's republican Rome as a cultural model. Liberals like Godwin could not now pin their hopes on radical action, or parliamentary reform; the alternative was an inward process, freedom not in action but in thought. Here Athens had the advantage. The Roman republic was an inspiring example of civic co-operation and personal responsibility, but its citizens were not blessed with (in the eighteenth-century phrase) enlarged views, and they had left few texts to keep alive the flame of liberty. Athens was the home of the Academy, of Socrates, Plato, and Epicurus.

The Greek was, after all, an intellectual, and characteristically an isolated one, in a world always dominated by men of action. Even in Athens's heyday this was so. Plato, Socrates and Aristophanes appealed to Peacock because their times, he thought, like his own, called upon them to be critics.[54] The long Greek twilight, when Athenian arts were overtaken by Roman practicality and progress, threw up other congenial iconoclasts. One of Peacock's particular favourites was the prose satirist Lucian, who satirised established religion, in graceful, witty dialogues, in the second century AD. Among Latin writers he tended to prefer those who acknowledged a debt to the Greek tradition. He shared with Shelley a veneration for Lucretius, who had substituted for the state religion of Augustus Epicurus's bleak, necessitarian concept of a universe of speeding atoms. Virgil, whose *Aeneid* grandiloquently canvassed the official view, was by contrast the court-flatterer *par excellence*. Shelley preferred to the *Aeneid* Lucan's *Pharsalia*, an account of the inception of the Empire which was firmly republican in its sympathies.[55] But Peacock, typically, liked a comic, scurrilous variant, Petronius's *Satyricon*, in which the action apparently turns on an impudent inversion of the *Aeneid*: instead of a solemn hero of epic times whose life is complicated by his unintentional affront to Juno, we have a vulgar hero of modern times whose adventures are brought about by his accidental insult to Priapus. This cluster of works which clearly refer to public affairs, and also wittily to one another, evidently fascinated Shelley and Peacock. On the one hand, Virgil's epic, the great Latin poem according to the received view; on the other hand, more or less offensive counter-epics by a group who seem to constitute an intellectual resistance movement. In Peacock's *Melincourt* and Shelley's *Prometheus Unbound*, the structure and the exalted intention of genuine epic appears to co-exist with the critical spirit, the iconoclasm, of early imperial counter-epic. It is a tone, and above all an example, which has far more to do with a dialectical conception of classical literature than with the mock-heroic of the English Augustans.

Peacock shares the original principles of the neo-classicism of the Enlightenment: so, partly through Peacock, does Shelley. The basis of this classicism is liberal, intellectual and humanist. Certain kinds of art are appropriate vehicles for a belief in man and in a regenerated society. But altered circumstances have drastically affected which works best seem to represent Greece for the new age. Humanism, individualism, universality – the abstractions which the Enlightenment found epitomised in Greek statuary – are all politically suspect. Without faith in Man, the *Apollo Belvedere* is no longer a fit model. Instead of proclaiming a common ideology for an upper-class world in various phases of radicalism, the progressive artist now finds himself in a minority. His target is not the effete, exploded cultural habit of the previous age, but the dominant orthodoxy of his own. Hence the paradox, that Peacock preaches activism, but is obliged to adopt the stance of a wry onlooker; the popular cause, through a terminology that becomes increasingly esoteric. It is not personal eccentricity, but a representative experience for the English intellectual of his age-group and the next.

Chapter 2

Experiments with Form:
Headlong Hall

All philosophers, who find
Some favourite system to their mind,
In every point to make it fit,
Will force all nature to submit.
              Butler: *Hudibras*
        (Peacock's epigraph to *Headlong
                              Hall*)

Peacock did not find the form for which he is remembered, the prose satire, until at the end of 1815, when he was thirty, he produced *Headlong Hall*. In his twenties he seemed destined for a career as a decidedly minor poet; for his first efforts as a writer have none of the innovatory fire of the best English poetry of the Enlightenment. Antique, derivative and insincere, the three long early poems he published during the wartime years, while he was still in his twenties, are public poetry in the derogatory sense of the term: that is, poems written for nobody in particular. *Palmyra* (1806), *The Genius of the Thames* (1810) and *The Philosophy of Melancholy* (1812) are the kind of eighteenth-century didactic poems which are kindred to the period's historical painting. Generalising, out-of-time rather than genuinely historical, they are occasions for grave reflections on Necessity, on the brevity of human life and on the sacredness of virtue. The underlying assumption of such art was that it spoke for all humanity, to a large but somehow also homogeneous audience. One problem was that the audience was beginning to be more diverse, as new classes became sufficiently rich and leisured to enjoy the arts. Another was that counter-revolutionary pessimism had worked to undermine the grand and naive statement, however apparently bromide the topic. Some types of neo-classical poetry quickly became out of date at the end of the eighteenth century, and Peacock's type was one of them.

The versification is that of a stiff-jointed Thomson, or perhaps Gray, with individual lines picking up the cadences of the newly fashionable Scott.[1] The instability of style seems symptomatic; Peacock's poems do not reflect the author's own opinions, even at the time of writing. For example, in *The Genius of the Thames* Peacock invokes other rivers, and the Thames of days gone by, to point an unfavourable contrast with present-day England:[2]

Where peace, with freedom hand-in-hand,
Walks forth along the sparkling strand,
And cheerful toil, and glowing health,
Proclaim a patriot nation's wealth.

En route downstream past Windsor he takes the opportunity to pay a compliment to George III,[3] and his view of British trading activity in the Port of London is unashamedly chauvinistic:[4]

Throned in Augusta's ample port,
Imperial commerce holds her court,
    And Britain's power sublimes:
To her the breath of every breeze
Conveys the wealth of subject seas,
    And tributary climes ...
The treasures of the earth are thine:
For thee Golcondian diamonds shine:
For thee, amid the dreary mine,
    The patient sufferers toil:
Thy sailors roam, a dauntless host,
From northern seas to India's coast,
And bear the richest stores they boast
    To bless their native soil.

Shelley, shown the poems by the publisher they both shared,

Thomas Hookham, instantly pointed out that on this evidence Peacock was no fellow-radical.[5]

> Mr Peacock conceives that Commerce is prosperity; that the glory of the British Flag, is the happiness of the British People; that George III so far from having been a warrior & a Tyrant has been a Patriot. To me it appears otherwise.

Strangely enough, that part of Peacock's message which glorified commerce really appeared otherwise to Peacock as well, or had done when his family were putting pressure on him to make a career at sea:[6]

> England is the modern Carthage: the love of gold, 'the last corruption of man', pervades the whole state from the centre to the extremities. If anyone be placed in a situation, attended with immediate or consequent profit, it is sufficient for the multitude to pronounce him well employed, and to raise a most vehement argument against all who dare to dissent from them.

The problem was to find a form capable of expressing what were really more equivocal attitudes. Peacock caught a glimpse of what his might be, as he did local research for *The Genius of the Thames*, and perceived that the subject could be treated in a much less favourable light:

> The Thames is almost as good a subject for a satire as a panegyric. – A satirist might exclaim: The rapacity of Commerce, not content with the immense advantages derived from this river in a course of nearly 300 miles, erects a ponderous engine over the very place of its nativity, to suck up its unborn waters from the bosom of the earth, and pump them into a navigable canal! It were to be wished, after all, that the crime of *water-sucking* were the worst that could be laid to the charge of commercial navigation: but we have only to advert to the conduct of the Spanish Christians in South America, of the English Christians in the East Indies, and of the Christians of all nations on the coast of Africa, to discover the deeper die of its *blood-sucking* atrocities. –[7]
> A panegyrist, on the contrary, after expatiating on the benefits of commercial navigation, and of that great effort of human ingenuity, the Thames and Severn Canal, which ascends the

hills, sinks into the valleys, and penetrates the bosom of the earth, to unite the two noblest rivers of this most wealthy, prosperous, happy, generous, loyal, patriotic, &c, &c, &c, kingdom of England, might say: 'And yet this splendid undertaking would be incomplete, through the failure of water in the summer months, did not this noble river, this beautiful emblem, and powerful instrument of the commercial greatness of Britain, contribute to that greatness even at the instant of its birth, by supplying this magnificent chain of connection with the means of perpetual utility.[8]

Some months before he wrote this, he was already contemplating a comedy.[9] It is hardly surprising that when during the next few years he did complete two apprentice farces for the stage, *The Dilettanti* and *The Three Doctors*, they turned out satires in a radical vein, which resembled Thomas Holcroft's mildly jacobin comedies of the 1790s, and were thus more faithful to Peacock's real opinions than his solemn poetry had been.

Holcroft and Peacock both use for their plot the romantic imbroglio of a pair of young lovers of unequal fortune, who have to overcome the hostility of the parent of the richer one. Some such conflict between the generations is the universal comic situation of the eighteenth century, with a pedigree going back indeed to Roman new comedy. But like other dramatists of their revolutionary generation, for example like Mercier and Beaumarchais in France, Holcroft and Peacock make the traditional routines convey a radical point of view. Though the form hardly lends itself to extended realism, they make it suggest that the actual society of the present day is a grubby world ruled by snobbery and cash. The routine love-plot, even if tepidly executed, assumes the dialectical force of so much that is deliberately naive in the writing of the period. The idealism and naturalness of the young is posed as a challenge to their parents' generation, those with a vested interest in the present system.

But where Holcroft was content with rather generalised criticism of snobbery and hidebound class attitudes, Peacock was already developing the specific interest in opinion, or intellectual systems, which was to characterise his career. The satiric subject of both his plays supplies the title of one of them – the dilettanti. He assembles a representative group of artists and specialists at the home of a *nouveau-riche* patron. The topic is culture, those who make it and those who buy it. Thin though the comedies are, Peacock has found his first subject.

Holcroft, for all his ambitions as an intellectual, aspired to put nothing so serious on the stage. But Peacock looked elsewhere for his inspiration, and the real idea for *The Three Doctors* and, after it, for *Headlong Hall*, came not from any dramatist or imaginative writer, but from a prose controversialist. Already, at the time when he was meditating on the limitations of the panegyrist's approach to the Thames, and perceiving how differently a satirist might have dealt with the topic, he was following (in periodical journals and in books borrowed from Hookham's library) a full-blown controversy about man's treatment of the landscape. A satirist, or at least a moralist with distinct satiric gifts, had been before him, censuring man-made intrusions in the natural world, and comparing over-wrought modern civilisation with the harmonious life-style of the ancients.

The controversy which, as the letters show, absorbed Peacock in 1809–10 had begun in the 1790s, with an attack from the radical side on that most oligarchic of eighteenth-century art-forms, the landscape garden. The debate was all the more noted for being launched by a rich and cultivated gentleman. Richard Payne Knight, 1750–1824, of Downton in Herefordshire, was a collector of ancient bronzes and coins, an authority on both, and a member of the Society of Dilettanti. In 1794 he published a didactic poem, *The Landscape*, which is dedicated to his friend and neighbour Uvedale Price, and is a full-scale critique, from a broadly Rousseauistic viewpoint, of the sophisticated practice of doctoring the landscape. In preference to the landscaper's ideal of cultured harmony, Knight advances one of simplicity and naturalness. He admires Nature in the wild, and Man too. Ancient Greece constitutes for him a Golden Age, the only period when 'the advantages of savage joined to those of civilised life'.[10] There is also a marked distaste in the poem for conspicuous aristocratic display, for houses which dominate their landscape, or for such signs of idleness as pleasure-grounds and shrubberies. Utility is the second criterion, after naturalness; Knight prefers a farm to a park.

Clearly we might interpret such a discussion in purely aesthetic terms. In the visual arts as in literature, interest was shifting to extremes: on the one hand the grandest, wildest and largest phenomena of Nature, on the other the private inward experience of the solitary individual. The attempt of the neo-classical garden to make a synthesis, or, as the next generation might think, to force Nature into a human perspective, was fast becoming an anachronism. As it happened, Knight offered his original critique as a contribution not to aesthetics but to ideology.[11] He opposed the landscape garden on social grounds as the plaything of an idle aristocracy. For good measure he followed up *The Landscape* in 1796 with another didactic poem, *The Progress of Civil Society*, in which he set the whole issue in a vast historical perspective, in the favourite manner of the time. Presented in these terms the challenge was of course a great deal more provocative. Accordingly, the conservative satirist T. J. Mathias several times pilloried Knight in *The Pursuits of Literature*,[12] and did not confine his attack to the two poems. Knight had written a dissertation, 'The Worship of Priapus', which passed around privately among the Society of Dilettanti in 1786, and Mathias was able to represent him not merely as a social leveller, but as a man bent on subverting the morals of the nation. The hint was enough. Richard Payne Knight, primitivist and classicist, became one of the little band of radical intellectuals who were regarded by English opponents of the French Revolution as a potential fifth column. Along with Godwin, Southey and Erasmus Darwin, he became a favourite target for the ridicule of Canning, Frere and their friends, in their Tory satiric journal, the *Anti-Jacobin*.[13]

Knight was not of course the innocent victim of the drastic politicisation of literary debate during the 1790s. He openly provoked the conservatives when he represented landscape-gardening, polemically, as the toy of a degenerate and parasitic oligarchy. From his point of view the ancient villains of the piece were the great gardeners William Kent (1684–1748) and Capability Brown (1715–83), the latter attracting special odium as the most celebrated of them all.[14] But both were dead, and the current leader of the profession was Humphry Repton (1752–1818), whom, accordingly, Knight teased in an impudent footnote to *The Landscape*. According to Knight, when Repton was commissioned to improve Tatton Park, he devised many expedients for showing off the extent of the property, including that of engraving the family's arms on the neighbouring milestones.[15] Knight's attack on Repton was quickly taken up and enlarged by Uvedale Price in his *Essay on the Picturesque* (1794). Without much obvious zeal for the fray, Repton was obliged to defend himself.

He did so in the same year in his brief and rather deferential *Letter to Uvedale Price, Esq*. Repton's line, now and later, was that no large differences of principle existed between him and the two gentlemen who chose to attack him. It is indeed true that Repton's style was more natural than Brown's, and that he continued to modify it in order to keep abreast of fashion. But because his patrons were the very rich, Repton was also bound to resist Knight's more democratic sallies. In his *Observations on the Theory and Practice of Landscape Gardening* (1803), he rejects, albeit defensively, the proposition that parkland can and should be reconciled with farmland:[16]

> I am aware that in the prevailing rage for agriculture, it is unpopular to assert, that a farm and a park may not be united; but after various efforts to blend the two, without violation of good taste, I am convinced that they are, and must be distinct objects, and ought never to be brought together in the same point of view. ... The shape and colour of corn fields and the straight lines of fences, are so totally at variance with all ideas of picturesque beauty.

Readers of *Mansfield Park* will recall that Henry Crawford, an admirer of Repton, also takes it as axiomatic that Edmund Bertram will have to get rid of the farmyard at his parsonage at Thornton Lacey.

By the early years of the nineteenth century, it was Uvedale Price, rather than Knight, who was generally considered to be the leading polemicist against the improvers. A more elegant writer than Knight, and a less craggy personality, he had the further advantage of friendship with many leading Whigs. The grounds on which he opposed gardening were mixed, and often positively old-fashioned. He could be safely supported by moderates who had no truck with republicanism. In discussing Knight's new book, *An Analytical Enquiry into the Principles of Taste* (1805), the *Edinburgh*

Review carefully placed it in the context of Price's work, and on these terms gave it support:[17]

> Of Mr. Price's treatises it is not incumbent on us to give any general character. The bold attack, which they made upon the prevailing system of improvement in ornamental grounds, was supported with such taste and ability, that, though ... Mr. Repton defended himself with some ingenuity, it seems to be gaining ground with the public, and will probably, in a few years, put an end to the tyranny which Mr. Brown and his school have so long exercised over nature. In this practical part, Mr. Knight is so far from differing with his friend, that a great part of his work is dedicated to the same purpose; and they co-operate, like Theseus and Perithous, amicably and heroically, to clear the world of monsters.

It is interesting that as late as 1806 the *Edinburgh Review* still sees Knight and Price as two heroic controversialists, bent on tilting against Repton, the champion of the aristocracy and the latter-day representatives of the school of Brown. That dispute really belonged to the polemical 1790s, and Knight and Price had latterly been engaged in a much less explosive exchange of views on the definition of the picturesque and the beautiful. But all Price's publications on landscape, together with Repton's *Letter* to him, were collected in a three-volume edition in 1810. This book is of special interest here, because it is likely to be one of Peacock's immediate sources. At least, he must have consulted a fifteen-year-old work by Price, which was now reprinted – *A Letter to Humphry Repton, Esq.*, which originally followed up Price's 1794 *Essay on the Picturesque* – before he wrote *The Three Doctors*, and he surely took fresh inspiration from the same essay for *Headlong Hall*.

Price's argument in *A Letter to Humphry Repton* is that gentlemen should not employ professional improvers, because their text-book approach is likely to destroy the beauty and individuality of a particular place. In a comparison extending over several pages, he likens the improver to a quack doctor peddling a single patent medicine; and in Price's view no doctrinaire plan or medical remedy will suit every case, 'neither Brown's plan nor James's powder'.[18] The gentleman would do much better to leave the plan to nature, or to his own instinctive good taste. Price supplies an example of the likely difference in outcome from his own knowledge of an attempted improvement in Wales. It was at Powis Castle, where Lord Clive had inherited an ancient building on a magnificent site. Price describes the archway through which a fine view of the Welsh mountains could be obtained:[19]

> beyond the archway projects a rock, a sort of abrupt promontory, shooting forward from that on which the castle is built: on this is a terras [*sic*] surrounded by an old massive balustrade, such as the massiveness of the castle required: steps of the same character descend from it to the bottom of the rock, great part of which is mantled with ivy, some of whose luxuriant shoots twine round the balusters. The effect which this projecting terras has in throwing off the mountains, – the richness of the foreground made by its ivied balustrade, – its light and shadow, – the perfect union of its character with the mountains and the castle, – could hardly be conceived by those who have not seen it. The professor [i.e. the landscape gardener] proposed to blow up this rock and all its accompaniments with gunpowder, in order to make the whole ground smooth, and gently falling from the castle: in short, to place this ancient irregular fabrick, on a regular green slope. The noble owner, both from his own natural judgment and feeling, and from the advice of Mr. Knight, to whom he mentioned the proposal, not only rejected it, but has repaired all that was broken and defaced in this terras; and has preserved, in its true character, what would have been equally regretted by the painter, by the antiquary, and by every man of natural judgment and reflection.

When it equates its landscape gardener with three medical men, *The Three Doctors* is adapting Price's idea that an improver is nothing more nor less than a fashionable quack. In *Headlong Hall*, this idea is to be abandoned, and Mr Milestone the improver becomes one of a group of fashionable performers, such as writers and musicians, who resemble more closely the dilettanti of the earlier play. But elsewhere *Headlong Hall* continues to make new use of Price's essay, and the near-miss at Powis Castle provides the occasion for its funniest episode:[20]

> The squire and Mr. Milestone ... had set out immediately after breakfast to examine the capabilities of the scenery. The object

that most attracted Mr. Milestone's admiration was a ruined tower on a projecting point of rock, almost totally overgrown with ivy. This ivy, Mr. Milestone observed, required trimming and clearing in various parts: a little pointing and polishing was also necessary for the dilapidated walls: and the whole effect would be materially increased by a plantation of spruce fir, interspersed with cypress and juniper, the present rugged and broken ascent from the land side being first converted into a beautiful slope, which might be easily effected by blowing up a part of the rock with gunpowder, laying on a quantity of fine mould, and covering the whole with an elegant stratum of turf.

Though it is amusing and often instructive to see how Peacock makes use of such detail, his general response to an issue like the dispute between Knight, Price and Repton is even more interesting. Price furnishes excellent points against the landscapers, but no principles. In fact, the appeal he makes is not to the reader's radicalism, nor even, perhaps, to his intellect. Price does not want promontories blown up or lanes converted into gravel drives or copses replaced by a tidy clump of firs, because he values the individuality, the quiddity given a place by age and natural evolution; Price's improver vandalises by straightening, rationalising, even by cleaning. Thus Price's is really an emotive appeal to a conservative instinct; it is reminiscent of the arguments used in favour of the existing political order by Edmund Burke. If Henry Crawford in *Mansfield Park* sounds like a classic Repton man, the sentimental conservative Fanny Price uses the argument for continuity and naturalness best set out by her own namesake.

Knight, as we have seen, places the emphasis differently. Where Price defends an existing landscape against innovation (the landscaper), Knight sees the cultivated garden as the emblem of the existing civil order, to which he is radically opposed. And Peacock, though he utilises Price's detail, cleaves closer to Knight in his understanding of what principles are at stake. In both *The Three Doctors* and *Headlong Hall*, Mr Milestone is the representative figure of an advanced society. The alternative to him, which Peacock certainly sees as preferable, is a state of primitive simplicity – not, as Price would have it, the world as it is, made dear by custom and familiarity.

Moreover, there is potentially in Knight's more radical approach a profounder criticism than his rivals ever mean to offer, of the role of all the arts in the modern world. From the beginning, Knight sees beauty as related to function; later, in 1805, he makes his case in theoretical terms.[21] A social critic, which is what Knight is, cannot help observing at the end of the eighteenth century that, as wealth increases, the wealthy classes feel the need to display their superior riches: hence their concern with extravagant, and very visible, remoulding of the landscape, and their zeal to collect artefacts, usually for the monetary value that rarity brings. It is a society in which art tends to become more and more divorced from any concern with function. What is true of landscape gardening is equally true of a hired ensemble of musicians, or of a gallery of pictures. Once, the greatest music might have been part of religious observance; the greatest paintings were church frescoes or altarpieces, designed to function in a context and to speak meaningfully to the worshippers who viewed them. Taken from Italian churches or classical temples, displayed in a rich man's gallery, such artefacts became divorced from function and from their original direct meaning, and instead became (at most) objects of merely aesthetic pleasure. In fact, Knight does not spell out the case against current art – essentially art patronised by the wealthy classes – as fully as this, but some such social and ethical critique is implicit when his three books are considered together, and in the context of current controversies. His fundamentally ethical approach, classical in so serious and humanist a sense, makes him far more interesting to Peacock than a mere disputant about gardening could have been. In Peacock's formative years, Knight helped to shape his lifelong attitude to the arts – what they ought to represent and what they generally did represent; and his hostility to the hireling artist, or the specialist in the esoteric and useless.

In Knight's way of viewing the controversy, therefore – in which the garden becomes the emblem for an unwholesome relationship between modern man and his environment – Peacock first finds his subject. Though landscape itself is only the first issue of several, the disputes on which he later focuses share the same leading characteristics. Broadly, Peacock always confronts a very large question: what is contemporary society like? Trained no doubt by Gibbon, Volney and others in the Enlightenment's grandeur and universalism, he sets the question within a large historical framework. Explicitly and implicitly, his presentation of the modern age continues to involve comparison with much earlier, more primitive and natural times. But — and here again the issue of the landscape is already characteristic — he is also invariably explicit, topical, immediate. Peacock's satires are all centred on a recent controversy large in its ideological implications but also amusingly rich in personality and detail. For its full effect, the satire requires the reader to be in the know.

Already in 1810 Peacock seems to have sensed that he would find his matter in some contemporary issue which was being publicised in a widely-read journal. He refers several times in his letters to Knight and Price; and he asks impatiently after the latest copy of the *Edinburgh Review*, above all, or one or two others:[22]

> I should be much pleased if you could make it convenient to send
> me a small box, or parcel, *punctually every month*, with the
> *Critical Review, Graphic Illustrations* and what others you think
> proper: a certain and regular literary novelty of this description
> is a thing to which I look forward with inconceivable
> satisfaction: it is one of my hobby-horses.

Peacock approached the topic of the landscape not as an admitted disciple of Knight, though his sympathies lay in that quarter, nor as a parodist or critic of any of the individuals concerned, but as an intellectual observer who reacted with sharp interest to the general issue. He certainly read most of the books to which he alludes — their texts find their way into his text — but the journals remain a prime source, because it is controversy that interests him. He observes to Hookham that he thinks Knight misguided to retaliate aggressively in print whenever he is criticised.[23] But Knight's doughty battles, to which he continually alludes in his subsequent works,[24] even in reviews of other men's books, are nevertheless grist to Peacock's mill, a spectacle he enjoys, an example he notes, and a genuine inspiration behind his new form of satire.

Yet, around 1812, that form was still eluding him. It is tempting to foreshorten a complex process, which took three more years to produce *Headlong Hall*, by guessing that in the end it was the live debate with Shelley that brought home to Peacock the literary potential of disputation. Each was just what the other had so far lacked: a really intelligent companion, another writer of the same generation, someone to sympathise and argue with. Earlier in 1812, before the two met, Shelley's new acquaintance, William Godwin, had advised Shelley to study the classics, and Shelley had resisted. In December, shortly after meeting Peacock for the first time, he gave way, and from Wales ordered two lists of more than sixty books, nearly half of which were classical.[25] The greater number of titles on these lists may well be Godwin's nominations rather than Peacock's. Godwin, true to his generation, was still interested in republican Rome, and in the study of political history, and many titles reflect his tastes. But several esoteric Greek authors, and two or three of the modern names, sound much more typical of Peacock. If these are analysed, it turns out that Peacock's taste is quite unlike Godwin's, for sober and sonorous history. Instead it is for the disputatious critic who uses the perspective of the past, and the materials of learning, to comment radically on modern society.

Among the modern but in various ways classically-minded authors whom Peacock may have recommended were James Burnett, Lord Monboddo; Sir William Drummond; and John Horne Tooke. In his *Origins and Progress of Language*, 1775–92, which Shelley now ordered, and in his *Antient Metaphysics* (1779–99), Monboddo drew on Plato's idealism and humanism in order to attack mechanistic tendencies in modern philosophy and, above all, complacency about the progress of advanced society. For all the eccentricity of his detail, his approach − detached, civilised, humanistic − was exactly after Peacock's own heart. Drummond, whom Shelley initially ordered as an antiquarian, the author of 'An Essay on a Punic Inscription', was to influence both him and Peacock more via *Academical Questions* (1805), which was essentially a summary of various systems of philosophy for the intelligent layman. Though not now thought of by philosophers as original, Drummond had opinions, and some influence. His dismissive pages on Kant carried weight with Shelley for many years, and with Peacock for a lifetime. But Drummond, like Monboddo, counted himself an idealist, an opponent of eighteenth-century materialism. Moreover, he was for activity in thought, and clarity in expression, and he thought intellectual timidity and sloth the vices of the age. 'Philosophy, wisdom and liberty support each other; he who will not reason, is a bigot; he who cannot, is a fool; and he who dares not, is a slave.'[26]

Horne Tooke's discipleship of Plato is more lively, more vulgar, and in key respects closer still to Peacock's interests. His *Diversions of Purley* (1787 and 1805) is made up of two Socratic dialogues. Nominally the topic is philology, and in fact Tooke was making a genuine if also erratic contribution to the history of that subject. But the word-hunting also has an immediate practical application, and it is this that Peacock presumably finds congenial. As a radical, a survivor of the age of Wilkes,[27] Tooke sets out to challenge the easy assumptions which are masked by the words people use. A chief target of his satire is Samuel Johnson, not because he is a lexicographical rival, but because of the latter's emotive, unanalytical approach to received ideas, his tendency to invoke grand magical concepts by incantation. Tooke's conversationalists at one point begin to look up the word 'right' in Johnson's dictionary, but think better of it. 'Seek no further for intelligence in that quarter, where nothing but fraud, and cant, and folly is to be found – misleading, mischievous folly: because it has a sham appearance of labour, learning and piety.'[28] Johnson's notions of the Established Church, traditional and reverent, are everywhere challenged by Horne Tooke's impudent subversions:[29]

So *Church*, for instance (*dominicum*, aliquid) is an Adjective; and formerly a most wicked one; which misinterpretation caused more slaughter and pillage of mankind than all the other cheats together.

When Godwin first advised Shelley to return to the classics, part of Shelley's resistance lay in the fact that he had learnt, perhaps at Eton and Oxford, to associate classical learning with orthodoxy: 'Did Greek and Roman literature refine the soul of Johnson, does it extend the thousand narrow bigots educated in the very bosom of classicality [?]'[30] Horne Tooke's quite different understanding of what that tradition stood for at its best looks back to the iconoclasm of Socrates, condemned to death for his challenge to received ideas. The dialogue used in this Socratic sense has, after all, a good eighteenth-century pedigree, not least in the hands of the sceptic Hume. Tooke uses it very consciously to shake the orthodoxies of his conversational opponents, casting himself in the role Plato gave to his teacher Socrates. The philosopher figure remains the questioner, teasing, probing, picking away at the encrusted intellects of his fellow citizens.

Queen Mab may have been Shelley's demonstration to Peacock of what a modern classical poem should be like. The Socratic dialogue is surely Peacock's formal contribution to the exchange of ideas and forms that followed the meeting of the two writers. Shelley's most Tooke-like performance is his fine philosophical dialogue in the classic eighteenth-century vein, *The Refutation of Deism* (1814). With *Headlong Hall* Peacock was not far behind.

For, when its experimental form comes to be considered, *Headlong Hall* is nothing else but a Socratic dialogue too. Of course it is illustrated and enormously enlivened by the material made over from the plays: the satire on contemporary follies, *The Dilettanti*, together with its foil, the romantic love story. But these two elements are framed, given shape and point, by the discussion between the three philosophers, Escot, Jenkison and Foster, which in classic dialogue-manner addresses itself to a single subject: is the world getting better or worse?

Editors of Peacock, failing to identify the element of Socratic dialogue in *Headlong Hall*, have felt puzzled by the three philosophers. Whom do they represent? Is Shelley the optimistic Foster and Peacock the pessimistic Escot, with perhaps Thomas Jefferson Hogg as the indeterminate Jenkison? Or is Escot really based on Shelley's most colourful friend at Bracknell, F. J. Newton, the vegetarian and student of the Zodiac?

Even when such speculations confine themselves to the opinions of the real men, not their personalities, they are essentially wrong-headed. No doubt Peacock and Shelley had argued over some or all of the ground covered by the fictional philosophers. But whether the dialogue is used by Plato in the *Symposium*, Dryden in the *Essay of Dramatic Poesy*, or by Hume, Berkeley or Shelley, as a form it is impersonal. 'Characters' may be given names, and these may be the names of real people. This, too, is a rhetorical device to give shape and clarity to the argument: it does not lead us to expect distinct portraits of the people behind the voices. The dialogue requires not characters, but spokesmen. Foster and Escot represent between them a gallery of eighteenth-century intellectuals. Their debate is the grand debate of the Enlightenment on the nature of contemporary society, and whether or not it is conducive to the happiness of the individual.

The speeches of Escot and Foster do not derive from any single individual. On the contrary, each paraphrases the arguments of a series of philosophers who are on one or other side of the central issue. In the very broadest terms, Escot's arguments that society has deteriorated recall the early Rousseau: especially the *Discours sur les Arts et les Sciences* (1750), with its deeply provocative theme that as civilisation (knowledge of the arts and sciences) advances, so moral virtue necessarily declines; or its sequel, the *Discours sur l'origine et les fondements de l'inégalité parmi les Hommes* (1755), a critique of social and political institutions, and an exposé of the abuses of man's life in a society manipulated by the rich. At times Escot's speeches echo the model of universal history proffered by Monboddo, with its anthropological concern, its more genuine scientific curiosity about man's evolution from the very earliest stages to the present. Monboddo, like Rousseau and like other Scots philosophic historians, such as Adam Ferguson, registered profound disquiet about the pressures of advanced societies upon the lives of individuals.[31] It was Mandeville, in his *Fable of the Bees*, who originally used the man of war to illustrate the division of labour.[32] Most recent, and probably most familiar to Peacock's own readers, are the pessimistic prophecies of Thomas Malthus.

If the debate between Escot and Foster must be narrowed down to a real dialogue between two men, it is less useful to centre on the private conversations of Peacock and Shelley than on a public controversy still fresh in the consciousness of both, the debate enacted in the 1790s between William Godwin and Thomas Malthus. In *Political Justice* (1793) and *The Enquirer* (1797), Godwin (whom of course Shelley still venerated) had advanced a view of human nature as perfectible. It is true that from the first Godwin's optimism was hedged with scepticism and qualification, as befitted a genuinely sophisticated thinker. He had nevertheless allowed his reader a glimpse of a visionary future, in which man mastered both himself and his environment by exercise of his reason — and, after only one or two hours daily labour, spent his time communing with himself and his fellows in an idyllic rational leisure.

Ask anyone to imagine Utopia, and the result will be distinctive:

a large part of the population, promised Godwin's paradise, might not think it much to look forward to. And yet the idea that ordinary individual men and women may one day lead lives that are happy and fulfilled is politically essential to the revolutionary. Without such a promise, it is hard to see why the present generation should submit to the hardship, the danger and the horror that violent political upheaval brings immediately in its wake. The political desirability of holding out the prospect of such a future does not remove the logical difficulty in the way of believing in it. Most eighteenth-century radicals looked back to a less organised society as a golden time, while they viewed the present advanced civilisation as irremediably corrupt. It was not of course logically impossible that the Golden Age might some day be restored, and that society might revert to organising itself more simply, as the anarchist Godwin for one certainly hoped. Yet, if history was perceived as having had up to now a linear development, then it had to be admitted that present portents were against the notion of a pastoral future. A vision like Godwin's was a matter of faith and hope rather than of rational expectation.

It was to this weakness in the progressive position that Malthus addressed himself in 1798. It was a year for bitter polemic, to which Malthus was contributing, in the sense that *An Essay on the Principle of Population* was designed as an immediate reply to Godwin's work; but unlike virtually all other anti-Godwiniana, *An Essay* is a model of temperate intellectual discussion. Without heat, indeed with a plausible show of personal reluctance, Malthus outlines the practical difficulties in the way of the Godwinian vision of a happier future:[33]

> I have read some of the speculations on the perfectibility of man and of society with great pleasure. I have been warmed and delighted with the enchanting picture which they hold forth. I ardently wish for such happy improvements. But I see great, and, to my understanding, unconquerable difficulties in the way to them. ...
> I think I may fairly make two postulata.
> First, that food is necessary to the existence of man.
> Secondly, that the passion between the sexes is necessary and will remain nearly in its present state. ...
> Assuming then my postulata as granted, I say, that the power

of population is indefinitely greater than the power in the earth
to produce subsistence for man.

Population, when unchecked, increases in a geometrical ratio.
Subsistence increases only in an arithmetical ratio. A slight
acquaintance with numbers will show the immensity of the first
power in comparison of the second.

By that law of our nature which makes food necessary to the
life of man, the effects of these two unequal powers must be kept
equal. ...

The germs of existence contained in this spot of earth, with
ample food, and ample room to expand in, would fill millions of
worlds in the course of a few thousand years. Necessity, that
imperious all pervading law of nature, restrains them within the
prescribed bounds. The race of plants and the race of animals
shrink under this great restrictive law. And the race of man
cannot, by any efforts of reason, escape from it. Among plants
and animals its effects are waste of seed, sickness, and premature
death. Among mankind, misery and vice. ...

This natural inequality of the two powers of population and
of production in the earth, and that great law of our nature
which must constantly keep their effects equal, form the great
difficulty that to me appears insurmountable in the way to the
perfectibility of society. ... And it appears, therefore, to be
decisive against the possible existence of a society, all the
members of which should live in ease, happiness, and
comparative leisure; and feel no anxiety about providing the
means of subsistence for themselves and families.

Malthus's counter-proposition of a bleak future was sketched
with a force that was surely to haunt the imagination of Shelley
and Peacock alike. But Peacock must also have been struck by
Malthus's elegance and by the cool impartiality with which he
rebukes the un-selfcritical partisans of right and left:[34]

In this unamicable contest [about perfectibility] the cause of
truth cannot but suffer. The really good arguments on each side
of the question are not allowed to have their proper weight. Each
pursues his own theory, little solicitous to correct or improve it
by an attention to what is advanced by his opponents.

The friend of the present order of things condemns all

political speculations in the gross. He will not even condescend to examine the grounds from which the perfectibility of society is inferred. Much less will he give himself the trouble in a fair and candid manner to attempt an exposition of their fallacy.

The speculative philosopher equally offends against the cause of truth. With eyes fixed on a happier state of society, the blessings of which he paints in the most captivating colours, he allows himself to indulge in the most bitter invectives against every present establishment, without applying his talents to consider the best and safest means of removing abuses and without seeming to be aware of the tremendous obstacles that threaten, even in theory, to oppose the progress of man towards perfection.

A temperament like Peacock's was not given to personal discipleship. He never attached himself to an obvious leader, like Bentham, nor became an adherent of an intellectual system. But it is possible to sense in Peacock's work a serious, consistent admiration for the type of disinterested intellectual whom Malthus might at this date be taken to represent. Richard Payne Knight was another example of the species, though superficially quite different. Knight's primitivism, his learning, his jovial interest in Priapus, were all traits that Peacock would find congenial. But Malthus had an advantage as a critic of modernity, that his reservations about modern society were listened to with respect by the very people who were apt to be most sanguine about it.

At about the time *Headlong Hall* was being written, Malthus was in the news for his contributions to the corn law and bullion questions. Both were serious problems, seriously dividing the propertied classes, and Malthus's contributions pin-pointed the real conflict of interests. The *Edinburgh Review* reviewed him with great respect on this account. 'The well-earned reputation of Mr. Malthus – his total freedom from any interested bias – and, above all, the extreme candour with which his opinions are stated, entitle his publications to the patient attention of every impartial enquirer.'[35] The *Edinburgh Review* was not actually more impartial than anyone else, but elsewhere in liberal circles there is evidence that Malthus was considered disinterested. Maria Edgeworth, years later encountering two intellectuals of a younger generation, could pay them no higher compliment than to recall Malthus and his friend David Ricardo:[36]

Jones and Herschel are very fond of one another – capable of admiration pure from envy – often differing but always agreeing to differ like Malthus and Ricardo who hunted together delightfully in search of Truth and huzzaed when they found her on whichever side she was and without caring who found her first. Indeed I have seen them put both their able hands to the windlass to drag her up from the bottom of that well in which she so strangely loves to dwell.

It is as the type of the rigorous and independent intellectual critic that Malthus is paid a compliment in *Headlong Hall*. In the Socratic dialogue, the Malthusian and Rousseauistic Mr Escot takes the role Plato gave to Socrates himself. Escot is the convinced critic of the system, or, more accurately, of his contemporaries' complacency about the system. He plays the Socratic role of gadfly, and challenges both those who approve of things as they are, and those who blindly trust things to get better, to prove the reasonableness of their position. When he is not recognisably speaking in the tones of Rousseau or Monboddo, he often sounds very like Malthus:[37]

these improvements, as you call them, appear to me only so many links in the great chain of corruption, which will soon fetter the whole human race in irreparable slavery and incurable wretchedness: your improvements proceed in a simple ratio, while the factitious wants and unnatural appetites they engender proceed in a compound one; and thus one generation acquires fifty wants, and fifty means of supplying them are invented, which each in its turn engenders two new ones; so that the next generation has a hundred, the next two hundred, the next four hundred, till every human being becomes such a helpless compound of perverted inclinations, that he is altogether at the mercy of external circumstances, loses all independence and singleness of character, and degenerates so rapidly from the primitive dignity of his sylvan origin, that it is scarcely possible to indulge in any other expectation, than that the whole species must at length be exterminated by its own infinite imbecility and vileness.

But it is a clash of two intellectual positions, not of individual thinkers. Ideas from *Queen Mab* may be brought in on either side. When occasion suits Peacock, Mr Escot borrows as readily from

Godwin as Mr Foster has ever done.[38] Two points should be borne in mind about Peacock's strategy of freely anthologising the work of eighteenth-century thinkers. The first is that he is working very openly in the established tradition of 'learned wit'. The quotations he selects are all, purposely, familiar; they could hardly be missed by anyone who had ever picked up any of the authors concerned. The second is that *Headlong Hall*'s philosophic debates are evidently designed to leave the impression that the deteriorationist is winning the argument. This does not mean that the author himself believes the world to be getting worse. Still less need Peacock subscribe to some of the odder propositions Escot advances, such as the opinion of Monboddo's, logically extended to the point of absurdity, that since the human race is getting smaller, it must, some day, shrink to nothingness.[39] He is ready to laugh at Escot, but he also makes him eloquent – which need not mean that Peacock personally suffers from some inability to come to terms with modern life. It simply means that he has adopted the traditional satirist's strategy, at least as old as Socrates and Aristophanes, and older than Lucian, of challenging contemporary complacency by enquiring if sophisticated times are really better than primitive times.

As in so many dialogues, the presentation of the debate purports to be evenhanded, while in fact the author's thumb is in the scale. But the treatment of the rest of the cast is quite different. In fact, it is essential in reading *Headlong Hall* to keep the various types of character and their functions separate in the mind. The two main groups, the philosophers and the dilettanti, are contrasted with one another. The occupation of the philosophers, with their open spirit of enquiry, is the book's positive, while the confused activity of the dilettanti, and their obsessive clinging to a single system, is its negative. The framework is the Socratic dialogue resembling the controversy between Godwin and Malthus; within the frame are illustrations, sketches of advanced society as it actually is.

These distinctions are preserved and pointed with considerable elegance. *Headlong Hall* has fifteen chapters. The central one, the eighth, is 'The Tower': the abortive scheme of landscape gardening at Powis Castle becomes Peacock's central symbol for the tastelessness, pointlessness and extravagance of advanced society.[40] The house in its garden had long been such a symbol:

Jonson, Marvell, above all Pope in the fourth of his *Moral Essays*, exploit the visual possibilities of the subject, while their main concern is a moral commentary on the quality and the goals of civilised living. Peacock handles his version so lightly that the weight of literary tradition is hardly felt, and yet it would be rash to think him unconscious of it. In 'The Tower' Peacock makes a classic satirist's point, and uses a classic image to do it, and he handles both with aplomb. The scene has virtually no dialogue, and needs none. The action is sufficiently expressive of ingenious futility to confirm Escot's diagnosis.

> Mr. Milestone superintended the proceedings. The rock was excavated, the powder introduced, the apertures strongly blockaded with fragments of stone: a long train was laid to a spot which Mr. Milestone fixed on as sufficiently remote from the possibility of harm: the Squire seized the poker, and, after flourishing it in the air with a degree of dexterity which induced the rest of the party to leave him in solitary possession of an extensive circumference, applied the end of it to the train; and the rapidly communicated ignition ran hissing along the surface of the soil.

The explosion does not make a contribution to the landscape, because it is never followed up. Its only outcome is Mr Cranium's fall from the tower, an event described with such splendid particularity that it imprints itself on the mind as the acme of dilettanti activity:[41]

> [Mr. Cranium's] ascent being unluckily a little out of the perpendicular, he descended with a proportionate curve from the apex of his projection, and alighted, not on the wall of the tower, but in an ivy-bush by its side, which, giving way beneath him, transferred him to a tuft of hazel at its base, which, after upholding him an instant, consigned him to the boughs of an ash that had rooted itself in a fissure about halfway down the rock, which finally transmitted him to the waters below.

The attack upon the rock with gunpowder could not stand as an emblem of advanced society in all its silliness if its significance had not been carefully established. The dilettanti arrangements for the futile explosion occur at the same moment as the three philosophers are walking through the natural mountain landscape of North Wales. The philosophers' conversation provides an appropriate counterpoint, since it raises the underlying humanistic enquiry about modern science, the demand to know what it is *for*:[42]

> Profound researches, scientific inventions: to what end? To contract the sum of human wants? to teach the art of living on a little? to disseminate independence, liberty, and health? No; to multiply factitious desires, to stimulate depraved appetites, to invent unnatural wants, to heap up incense on the shrine of luxury, and accumulate expedients of selfish and ruinous profusion. Complicated machinery: behold its blessings. ... Where is the spinning-wheel now, and every simple and insulated occupation of the industrious cottager? Wherever this boasted machinery is established, the children of the poor are death-doomed from their cradles. Look for one moment at midnight into a cotton-mill, amidst the smell of oil, the smoke of lamps, the rattling of wheels, and dizzy and complicated motions of diabolical mechanism: contemplate the little human machines that keep play with the revolutions of the iron work, robbed at that hour of their natural rest, as of air and exercise by day.

Though Mr Milestone with his pointless improvements is to be the chief representative of the modern intellectual, he is supported by a typical cross-section of others. The central episode, Milestone's attempt on the tower, is flanked in the first half of the satire by a sketch of the current literary scene, headed by MacLaurel. The philosophers' conversation on their walk, and the use of explosive, prepare for a change of topic in the second half to contemporary science, and for Mr Cranium to play the representative part. Where 'The Tower' was a narrative chapter, its meaning conveyed graphically to the eye, the chapters which centre on MacLaurel and Cranium depend on dialogue. These two are spokesmen for formulated ideologies, and both briefly become the conversational adversaries of Escot. Their symmetrically placed exchanges are central to the satiric case Peacock is making in *Headlong Hall*.

The critic MacLaurel is a thinker of an advanced school, who believes that art responds to the laws of supply and demand:[43]

Ye mun alloo, sir, that poetry is a sort of ware or commodity,
that is brought into the public market wi' a' other descreptions
of merchandise, an' that a mon is pairfectly justified in getting
the best price he can for his article.

In general terms Peacock was a historical critic who shared the
fundamental aesthetic approach of such Enlightenment figures as
Hume and Voltaire – that is, he thought art a product of social
circumstances; as society changed, art changed with it.[44] But he
disliked the determinism often associated with the historicist
approach. He did not want to think that the pressure of historical
necessity entirely deprived the individual artist of free will, or
absolved him from responsibility for his productions, or made the
question of value in art meaningless. Peacock implies, through
Escot, that he finds MacLaurel's mechanistic utilitarian ethics
cynical and immoral. In fact, Escot throughout opposes all theories,
however up-to-date and apparently scientific, which minimise
volition: which, by providing a mechanical explanation for a
pattern of behaviour, effectively deprive the human being of moral
responsibility. Mr Cranium the phrenologist significantly agrees
with MacLaurel on this point: 'I perfectly agree with Mr.
MacLaurel in his definition of self-love and disinterestedness:
every man's actions are determined by his peculiar views, and
those views are determined by the organization of his skull.'[45]

Cranium's lecture, an exposition of the conformation of the
brain, proves to be an extreme example of the intellectual sin of
determinism, as, indeed, is his denial that he owes Escot anything
for saving his life. 'The motive ... adhibited in the person of a
drowning man, was as powerful on his material compages as the
force of gravitation on mine; and he could no more help jumping
into the water than I could help falling into it':[46]

I no more blame or praise a man for what is called vice or virtue,
than I tax a tuft of hemlock with malevolence, or discover great
philanthropy in a field of potatoes, seeing that the men and the
plants are equally incapacitated, by their original internal
organisation, and the combinations and modifications of
external circumstances, from being anything but what they are.

In flanking the primarily comic figure of Milestone with the more serious MacLaurel and Cranium, Peacock adds a large dimension to his study of contemporary intellectuals. A moralist might, from a number of viewpoints, condemn the frivolity, artifice and conspicuous waste involved in landscape gardening. It is a more particular commentator who singles out MacLaurel and Cranium as embodying the sins of the time. Evidently Peacock fears above all those tendencies in contemporary life which teach acceptance and negate individual effort. He condemns a reactionary like Gaster on the score of his quietism, but that kind of churchman is almost too easy a target. ' "It requires no proof," said Dr. Gaster: "it is a point of doctrine. It is written, therefore it is so." '[47] Escot's attacks on his fellow progressives reveal more that is distinctive about Peacock's position. Escot has a significant exchange with Mr Jenkison, for example, when the latter suggests that it is only *natural* for the poor to have to work to sustain the rich:[48]

MR. JENKISON.
That a man should pass the day in a furnace and the night in a cellar, is bad for the individual, but good for others who enjoy the benefit of his labour.

MR. ESCOT.
By what right do they do so?

MR. JENKISON.
By the right of all property and all possession: *le droit du plus fort.*

MR. ESCOT.
Do you justify that principle?

MR. JENKISON.
I neither justify nor condemn it. It is practically recognised in all societies; and, though it is certainly the source of enormous evil, I conceive it is also the source of abundant good, or it would not have so many supporters.

Foster meanwhile looks forward cheerfully to the state of enlightenment which is rapidly arriving − 'in process of time, moral science will be susceptible of mathematical demonstration'.[49] It is this all-pervading complacency that Peacock is attacking, but not because he takes seriously the scholastic dispute about whether the world is getting better or worse. The crux of the matter is whether modern society's very real evils are to be reformed. If they are, it will be by the progressive party. But a fashionable habit of mind stands in the way – that optimism which leads progressives to expect political change to come naturally, without the actual intervention of individuals on the political scene:[50]

> 'I am inclined to think ...' said Mr. Escot, 'that the deterioration of man is accelerated by his blindness – in many respects wilful blindness – to the truth of the fact itself, and to the causes which produce it; that there is no hope whatever of ameliorating his condition but in a total and radical change of the whole scheme of human life, and that the advocates of his indefinite perfectibility are in reality the greatest enemies to the practical possibility of their own system, by so strenuously labouring to impress on his attention that he is going on in a good way, when he is really in a deplorably bad one.'

It is a direct reference to Godwin, arch-exponent of revolutionary optimism, who was content to theorise about the perfectibility of man, and felt a dislike – stronger even than the intellectualist reason he gave – for the kind of practical engagement that was likely to bring reform about. 'Discussion, reading, inquiry, perpetual communication, these are my favourite methods for the improvement of mankind', Godwin wrote to Shelley, in the year the latter met Peacock, 'but associations, organized societies, I firmly condemn. ...'[51] Godwin had been through the 1790s, the decade of the treason trials and the 'Gagging' Acts, and it was understandable that he should stress the philosophic side of his calling rather than put himself forward as the kind of political leader who is calling for action. But in 1815 the danger had receded, the war with France was over, and reform was a live cause again. After exposure to the Godwin-worship which characterised Shelley during the first three years of their acquaintance, Peacock was ready to give weight to Escot's gibe against a school of politicial idealism so inert on the field of political action.

Headlong Hall is thus a discussion of modern intellectual life, an illustration and analysis of its weaknesses. It can claim so much because it specifically avoids two types of 'satire' infinitely commoner in its period – the blanket assault of one well-defined party upon another, or the lampoon directed against personalities. Works that have superficial points of resemblance with Peacock's – satirical *romans à clef* like D'Israeli's *Vaurien* (1797) or *Flim-flams* (1805), or Eaton Stannard Barrett's *Six Weeks at Long's* (1817); satirical verse like William Gifford's *Baviad* (1791) and *Mæviad* (1794), T. J. Mathias's *Pursuits of Literature* (1794–7), the poetry of the *Anti-Jacobin* (1797–8), Byron's *English Bards and Scotch Reviewers* (1809), and the Smith brothers' *Rejected Addresses* (1812), all testify to the period's rage for satire – but not satire that resembles Peacock's. Much of the difference lies in the rank personal offensiveness of the contemporary mode. Peacock may mean to remind us of the name of Mrs Opie when he calls a novelist Philomela Poppyseed. Rather more doubtfully, his polymath Panscope may be intended to suggest Coleridge. The fact that Peacock offers one novelist, one polymath, and so on, indicates that he is pointing not to the individual but to the species. The point is best made by the portrayal of Mr Milestone, who so frequently suggests Humphry Repton that critics and editors do not hesitate to say he *is* Repton. Yet the most striking thing that he does (blowing up the tower) is not Repton. At one moment, Peacock gives Milestone an idea that originated in an *Edinburgh Review* article on one of Knight's books; elsewhere, he slyly introduces the famous catch-phrase that gave Capability Brown his nickname.[52] The informed contemporary reader should have been able to tell the difference between static caricature, and a moving kaleidoscope of allusion.

The phrenologist Cranium affords a useful example of the process of accretion and generalisation that goes into the typical Peacockian figure. Though Shelley and Mary were discussing the new rage for phrenology in 1814,[53] Peacock's invention seems to have been stimulated, as so often, by reviews of a new book in the *Edinburgh Review* and the *Quarterly Review*. The work in question was by two German scientists, Gall and Spurzheim, who claimed physiological discoveries of great significance.[54] Beginning with the principle that the brain is the organ of the mind, they divided the mental powers of man into a definite number of independent faculties. These faculties were, they believed, innate, and they each had their seat in a different region of the surface of the brain. The size of each region on a particular head gives evidence of the development of the appropriate faculty in that individual; and the correspondence between the outer surface of the skull and the contour of the brain is close enough for an observer to draw conclusions about a subject's characteristics from an outward examination alone.

Though their studies were related to genuine discoveries about the nervous system and the brain, Gall and Spurzheim were trying to claim an exactitude which their evidence simply could not support – as John Gordon in the *Edinburgh Review* points out. He is a lively reviewer and it is hardly surprising that his sallies in particular seem to have caught Peacock's attention:[55]

> Our readers will here recognise ... the same man of skulls, whom we had occasion to take notice of, more than twelve years ago. Long before this time, we should have looked for his craniological death. But he ... has discovered the inestimable secret, that a man's reputation, as well as his health, may often be prolonged, by a little well-timed locomotion.

Gordon proceeds to describe the doctrines of 'these two modern peripatetics' as '*thorough quackery* from beginning to end', and laments that it is currently the fate of the British, above all nations, to be the 'dupes of empirics'. After extracting considerable entertainment from some of the examples the phrenologists give – for example, a cow with an unusual faculty for opening gates – he proceeds to a tongue-in-cheek exposition of their central doctrine, a passage which may well have been the one to set Peacock's imagination going:[56]

> When ... any uncommon bump of this sort presents itself on the head of an individual, it is only necessary to ascertain what faculty that person is remarkable for; and thus the particular part of the brain, which constitutes the *organ* of that faculty, is at once demonstrated. By a steady application of this method, to the skulls or busts of the celebrated dead, and to the heads of the living, unshaven as well as shaven, in all classes of society ... Drs. Gall and Spurzheim have had the merit of ascertaining the exact size of the thirty-three organs. ...

In the frontispiece to Spurzheim's book, a most extraordinary and engaging spectacle presents itself. The human head there appears in different aspects, cleanly shaven, and the whole of its upper surface divided into regions, like the maps of revolutionized France. The regions are of different sizes ... but by far the greater number, as it appears to our eye, like the scales of a salmon magnified. The facilities which these diagrams must afford, in the application of the intellectual topography to practice, must be very great. When we discover any unusual projection or depression, any remarkable specimen of hill and dale, on the head of a stranger, we have only to consult a copy of the frontispiece quietly; and without a moment's delay, we shall be enabled to decide, whether we ought to approach him as an honest man, or shun him as a knave.

Perhaps it was the word 'topography' which struck Peacock's attention and made him see in this form of quackery a further parallel to his quack of quacks, the landscape gardener. He certainly made a close mental cross-connection between the two 'sciences', for in *Headlong Hall* Mr Milestone boasts that gardening has given 'a new outline to the physiognomy of the universe!'[57] In the same passage by Gordon, Peacock could have found the idea of examining the skulls of the distinguished dead, and the allusion to the criminal, both used for Mr Cranium. The opening of the article had already implanted the comic possibilities of lecturing. But behind the review's tone of disapprobation there looms the larger ethical problem – quite unsatisfactorily dealt with, according to Gordon, in Gall and Spurzheim – of how far characteristics are pre-determined and so beyond the control of the individual's moral will.

It cannot really be said that Dr Cranium is one of the successes of *Headlong Hall*. In so far as he *is* a quack and a dilettante, he fits the book's scheme and supports its case. But Peacock cannot refrain from making a second use of him, and Mr Cranium's lecture belongs to a quite different tradition. It is a portrait gallery of 'heads' rather like Hogarth's famous caricature, or Pope's Moral Essay 'The Characters of Women': a satirical survey of the rich and great, which Peacock passes on with such evident relish that Cranium's lack of intellectual respectability as a phrenologist is somewhat overlaid. As a satirist, Peacock could not help succumbing to the opportunity offered by George Alexander

Stevens's popular monologue entertainment, 'A Lecture on Heads', first delivered in 1764 – though this creates problems for him, since Stevens's 'objective' satirical portraits of real-life targets cannot easily be reconciled with Cranium's phrenological guesswork.[58] Worse, Cranium has still a third part to play, as Cephalis' mercenary father, the obstacle in the young lovers' path to happiness.

It is all too much, and it means that the second half of *Headlong Hall*, where Cranium is the principal satiric target, necessarily lacks the incisiveness of the first. It may well be that Peacock saw the article in the *Edinburgh Review* when he was already advanced in thinking about or even in writing *Headlong Hall*,[59] and that, cleverly though he has incorporated the new character, some of the displacements entailed are bound to show. Mr Milestone's business, the improvements at Headlong Hall, surely ought not to drop out of account so completely, and one guesses that in an original scheme they did not. As the closing scenes now run, with their speedy arranging of four marriages, the resistance of Mr Cranium to Escot as a son-in-law is the major focus of interest. But Harry Headlong also gets married, though without feeling, or of course conveying to the reader, that there is anything significant in his choice of bride. But there is, by Uvedale Price's reckoning: he marries Miss Tenerosa, who is all for leaving his rocks and trees, his streams and his ivy, in the tumbled profusion in which Nature created them.

Yet, even if the character of Cranium is not executed with perfect consistency, it is admirable in its main conception, as is evident when we compare it with its principal source. Most of the points that strike Gordon as really funny – the cow and the peripatetics – are left out. Peacock does not hint that Cranium is a mountebank, as Gordon does of Gall and Spurzheim. Peacock's treatment actually manages to make Gordon look somewhat philistine in relation to scientific evidence, as well as unduly malicious in respect of the personalities. For Peacock clearly has no interest in making the real-life phrenologists look ridiculous. He wants to extrapolate a moralistic and wider deduction, that in physiological science, as in other branches of knowledge, a view is gaining ground that reduces drastically the scope left for man's own will, energy and rational intelligence.

Headlong Hall is imperfect, although, as one of its first critics remarked, it is anything but the work of a novice.[60] Its analysis of contemporary cultural life blends two distinct major themes: a sense of the undue passivity of modern intellectuals, and of their corrupt dependence upon wealthy patrons. Each is a symptom of decadence among the intelligentsia; its opposite is evoked by the philosophers, when they mime the vigorous debate about society which was conducted by the intellectuals of the eighteenth-century Enlightenment.

It should be clear that any approach to Peacock's characters by way of received ideas about characterisation will get nowhere. His figures are neither personalities from real life, nor the rounded characters of novels. Northrop Frye is far closer to the real tradition to which Peacock's approach belongs when he invokes the main stream of prose satire, going back to Peacock's admired Lucian, and to Lucian's mentor Menippus. Frye uses the term 'Anatomy' for this mode, which generally employs a loosely-jointed narrative, mainly prose though perhaps incidentally using verse. It may vary in tone from the entirely fantastic to the entirely moral. If short, it may be a dialogue; or it may expand into a symposium, or a country-house weekend, as in Peacock or Huxley. A common feature is the concentration not upon character, as in that other narrative form, the novel, but on intellectual attitudes and themes:[61]

> The Menippean satire deals less with people as such than with mental attitudes. Pedants, bigots, cranks, parvenus, virtuosi, enthusiasts, rapacious and incompetent professional men of all kinds, are handled in terms of their occupational approach to life as distinct from their social behaviour. The Menippean satire thus ... differs from the novel in its characterization, which is stylized rather than naturalistic, and presents people as mouthpieces of the ideas they represent. ... A constant theme in the tradition is the ridicule of the *philosophus gloriosus*. ... The novelist sees evil and folly as social diseases, but the Menippean satirist sees them as diseases of the intellect, as a kind of maddened pedantry which the *philosophus gloriosus* at once symbolizes and defines.

This is an excellent diagnosis of the spirit and intention of

Peacockian satire, invoking as it does the very writers to whom Peacock himself consistently pays tribute. However, in the light of the preceding discussion of *Headlong Hall*, it seems that Peacock is also an innovator. All his obvious models — Petronius, Lucian, Rabelais, Burton, Swift, Sterne — to a greater or lesser degree aim at a rambling effect, dialogue and perhaps song linked together in a loose narrative structure. But *Headlong Hall*, though containing precisely these elements, is more controlled. It is the essence of the book that the various parts — philosophical dialogue, symbolic central scene, romantic sub-plot, satiric 'anatomy' — are kept distinct from one another. It is equally essential that the lesser controversies — landscape gardening, the critics, craniology — are ultimately subsumed in the grand controversy: whether modern society is the best world for man to live in. The control is not perfect, any more than the intellectual connections are quite satisfactorily made. Yet for a first step into satire it is a virtuoso performance, a work all the more original for its intimate relationship with tradition.

Chapter 3

Satire and Romance: *Melincourt*

> And while you thrive by ranting, I'll try my luck at canting,
> And scribble verse and prose all so dry, dry, dry:
> And Mystic's patent smoke public intellect shall choke,
> And we'll all have a finger in the CHRISTMAS PIE.
> Mr Paperstamp in the glee at Mainchance Villa

1815, the year of *Headlong Hall*, marked the beginning of Peacock's real intimacy with Shelley, an intellectual friendship of crucial importance in deciding the future tone and quality of his work. It was also the year of Waterloo, a divide of great significance for Britain and for Europe. Both circumstances, the private and the public, helped to bring about a decisive change in Peacock's writing. *Headlong Hall* is obviously the work of an eighteenth-century iconoclast who disliked many features of an England dominated by a frivolous élite: perhaps it hints at reform, but, if so, only in the most general terms. *Melincourt*, written mostly in 1816, is, like the satires that follow it, much more specific and topical. Contact with politically minded writers supplied Peacock with the spur essential to the satirist, the glimpse of what began to be a sympathetic public, and beyond that, however notionally, the possibility that expressing a political point of view might be the first step towards action.

Literary works in a generalised way reflect a national mood, but they do so most decidedly in stirring times. The years of most fruitful literary activity in the era, the late 1790s and, especially,

1814–22, were precisely the years of English political crisis and hence of most open ideological tensions and polemic.

The later period began with apparent victory in Europe and Bonaparte's banishment to Elba, events celebrated in England with writing that at different levels gloried in the triumph over an enemy still thought of as republican and atheistic. Robert Southey, since 1813 the Poet-Laureate, marked the occasion with odes to sundry crowned heads.[1] With *The Excursion*, Wordsworth proclaimed himself the Establishment's poet at a much more august level, out-laureating and certainly out-poeting the Poet Laureate. From 1815 Coleridge made his contribution, in what must have been the most productive short period of his entire life. He began with *Zapolya* (1815), a re-working of *The Winter's Tale* intended as an allegory about the restoration of the European monarchs. In the *Lay Sermons* (1816–17) he went on to meditate upon the proper nature and role of the upper orders of society and, with the *Biographia Literaria* of 1817 as a further exemplification, he proposed to the educated gentleman a model way of life, Christian, traditionalist, and conservative.[2]

Much literature of the time had less obvious bearing on contemporary events than any of this, but would still have carried some sort of message to the nation, of a generally inspiriting kind. The religious revival of the decade, which itself had political implications, expressed itself in a vein of novel-writing in which young girls, especially, were exhorted to be pious, public-spirited and self-effacing, and thus to reproach the worldliness of some of their elders. Except for its quality, *Mansfield Park* is a fairly representative novel for 1814, and a kind of moral rearming – the renewed self-dedication of a secure governing class – is a central part of its meaning. Even the most successful novel of 1814, Scott's *Waverley*, which seems anything but typical, is applicable to the hour, with its theme of a hero who grows up in putting war behind him, and in settling down to a regenerative, post-war existence.

The moment of victory must, logically, be a good one for writers upholding Church and King, and for the time being they seemed to have the nation with them. It did not offer an obvious opening to the radical or the iconoclast. The parliamentary opposition, the Whigs, had fared badly during the war. It had divided them, cost them national popularity, and even lost them the support of the commercial interest, which was fully behind the government. Now, quite rapidly, in 1815, a series of developments seemed to promise the collapse of government popularity in the very period of victory. At a time of low wages and unemployment, the price of corn became a bitterly divisive issue. To import cheaper foreign corn would hit farmers and the landed gentry hard, but would also bring relief to the poor and above all to the growing industrial population in the towns. Parliament was still dominated by the landed interest, and in 1815 it passed a law to impose high duties on imported grain. Meanwhile other issues – like the high taxation which the war had brought, and the instability, in some respects the chaos, of the banking system – aroused political feeling from its wartime dormancy. But Whig hopes of benefiting from the government's difficulties were dashed by the severity of the crisis of 1816. Businesses failed, prices fell, and wages fell still further: the outcome, in the summer of 1816, was a series of popular disturbances, spreading gradually from the eastern counties to the outskirts of London. At first they were caused by agricultural labourers, who proclaimed their distresses by firing barns and breaking threshing machines. By mid-summer the agitation had spread to the manufacturing North and Midlands, and processions of unemployed weavers, hosiers and colliers paraded through the streets of towns and cities, demanding relief. In the autumn, strikes were reported in South Wales and in Scotland. Increasingly the protesters asked not for relief only, but for reform of the franchise; for, as their radical sympathisers urged them, while they were totally unrepresented in parliament they must expect their interests to give way to those of the landed and monied. Meanwhile, terror at the reports of violence and outrage coming in from all parts of the country produced a most unusual cohesion among the propertied classes. The Whig moment of 1815 was quite lost by 1816, for the upper and middle classes, landed and mercantile, believed England to be in serious danger of revolution.

The last years of the war and the first of the peace were thus both encouraging and frustrating for the liberal young. With the gradual waning and at last removal of the external threat from France, impatience began to develop with the provincialism and conformity of England's wartime intellectual atmosphere, which contrasted so sourly with the excitement of the early 1790s. During these years, indifference to religion and republicanism continued to manifest themselves, but in half-submerged, theoretical forms. A significant focus of direct intellectual opposition to the Tory government, and to oligarchy generally, was growing around the increasingly effective spokesmen for the middle-class interest, Jeremy Bentham and his interpreters Etienne Dumont and James Mill, together with the economists Malthus and Ricardo. The viewpoint of these groups was represented around 1816 in the principal organ of the Whig opposition, the *Edinburgh Review.* But the inhibiting effect of what was felt to be the danger of revolution from below was very apparent. Writers for the *Edinburgh Review* were in a difficult position, when they would have preferred to see a Tory government replaced by an equally aristocratic Whig alternative, but shrank from dealing any blow that would disturb the political system in its entirety.

The *Edinburgh Review*'s treatment of literary books with partisan implications reflected the underlying political problem for opposition writers. Hazlitt, a rising journalistic star, attacked the leading conservative poets, Southey, Wordsworth and Coleridge, with the greatest personal venom,[3] but refrained from theoretical analysis of their position, or from suggesting alternatives. Similarly, he poured out invective against the right-wing European despots (by now widely unpopular in England, after the euphoria of 1814), but failed to tackle the much more politically sensitive subject, reform at home.[4] Tom Moore, an established and favoured supporter of the Whigs, wrote an unsympathetic, politically inspired review of Coleridge's *Christabel,* and did not reveal on what principle, political or poetical, he was relying.[5]

However, the *Examiner,* the weekly journal run by John and Leigh Hunt, did advocate parliamentary reform in its political columns, and began in its reviews from 1816 to advance the claims of a new generation of liberal poets. It was because he was cast in this role by the *Examiner* that over the next years John Keats was reviled by the Tory *Quarterly,* and Blackwood's *Edinburgh Magazine,* and neglected in embarrassment by the *Edinburgh Review.* But both as a political and a literary journal, the *Examiner* now suffered from the unpopularity of radicalism with its potential readership, which was middle-class. Far more successful was William Cobbett's non-literary *Political Register,* because, unlike other newspaper proprietors, and most newspaper writers, Cobbett did not identify himself with the middle or governing classes. He was an independent farmer, who happened to own his own newspaper: he was free to represent himself as a spokesman for the yeomanry, a class oppressed by the present troubles, and with little to fear from change. Cobbett, in many respects an old-fashioned Tory despite his radicalism, particularly detested the 'fund-holders' and 'monied interest', what he considered to be the selfish conspiracy of wealth that maintained and manipulated the present 'System'. Unlike the Hunts, Cobbett no longer depended on finding liberal sentiment within an alarmed middle class. Instead, he addressed himself direct to the masses. From November 1816, his leading articles were reprinted as leaflets on the same day as the journal and, avoiding the stamp duty which made most newspapers too expensive for the poor, sold at twopence to a vast readership. They were couched in language suitable for the uneducated to understand, and very plainly meant to awaken the masses not merely to economic realities, but to a perception of their own strength:[6]

> Whatever the Pride of rank, or riches or of scholarship may have induced some men to believe, or to affect to believe, the real strength and all the resources of a country, ever have sprung and ever must spring, from the *labour* of its people. ...
> With this correct idea of your own worth in your minds, with what indignation must you hear yourselves called the Populace, the Rabble, the Mob, the Swinish multitude; and with what greater indignation, if possible, must you hear the projects of those cool and cruel and insolent men.

Cobbett's 'twopenny trash' overnight made him the most feared of the government's opponents, and a hero to those intellectuals whose sympathies remained radical, among whom were Peacock and Shelley.

Nevertheless, for artists, whose métier was directed at the élite, Cobbett's answer was hardly possible. While a strain of radical feeling became more pronounced, and potentially practical, among liberal writers between 1809 and 1819, its expression remained, on the whole, necessarily indirect, and even increasingly subtle. The government's powers of censorship were not negligible, especially after 1817, and were certainly sufficient to deter most publishers; but in any case authors had to consider the nervous susceptibilities of the educated reading public. While Cobbett sought a mass audience, and wrote with simplicity (which is another man's crudity), poets tried to find a liberal audience within the élite through devices that were necessarily allusive: the codes inherited from the Enlightenment, or new strategies, evolved in a prolonged and increasingly pointed ideological exchange with the writers who championed orthodoxy.

What made the liberal poets' position all the more frustrating around about 1816 was that there had been a false dawn for liberal sentiment in England, and for its expression in literature, in the latter years of the war. As Napoleon could more and more generally be seen as a tyrant – in his oppression, for example, of Spanish patriots – Englishmen of all shades of political opinion on home affairs united in championing the liberty of foreigners. Coleridge, who, like Wordsworth, published a pamphlet on behalf of the Spanish patriots in 1809, rejoiced that in doing so he returned to the style of his youth:[7]

> It was the noble efforts of Spanish patriotism, that first restored us, without distinction of party, to our characteristic enthusiasm for *liberty*; and presenting it in its genuine form, incapable of being confounded with its French counterfeit, enabled us once more to utter the names of our Hampdens, Sidneys, and Russels, without hazard of alarming the quiet subject, or of offending the zealous loyalist.

Equally, English Tories as well as Whigs became absorbed in the cult of Renaissance Italy, which acquired many aspects, but in its early stages seemed to promise a revival of the libertarian, individualistic phraseology of the Enlightenment. The veneration for Italy is hard to separate, in its intellectual roots, from the veneration for Athens. What Athens had represented at the very close of the eighteenth century, fourteenth-century republican Florence also represented from about 1805. The two city-states and their cultures were seen as markedly similar. They were indeed historically linked: for the rise of the Italian republics was felt to signalise the break-up of the hegemony of feudal monarchs and an obscurantist church, the long post-classical Dark Ages which Gibbon had depicted, sardonically, as 'the triumph of barbarism and religion'. The true achievement of Venice and especially Florence was liberty; the great art which they produced was the natural expression of a new and nearly ideal social organisation, the small republic of free citizens. Enlightened Florence had recovered ancient art, above all by re-creating the conditions which in classical times made great art possible.

It was, then, historians with a commitment to the liberal side who, in the new dark days of Napoleon's tyranny over Europe, revived the memory of the Italian republics as a living inspiration. William Roscoe had done something to prepare the English public with his *Life of Lorenzo de Medici* (1795), and *Life and Pontificate of Leo the Tenth* (1805). But the real leadership of the Italian movement in England went to the Swiss J. C. L. de Sismondi, for it was his *History of the Italian Republics, Being a View of the Origin, Progress, and Fall of Italian Freedom*, which brought home the symbolic meaning of Florence to the generation of the younger Romantics.

The impact Sismondi's great book made on the educated English public can be measured in the Reviews.[8] From both the *Edinburgh* and the *Quarterly* it received a more ecstatic welcome than that other important and comparable polemical history which emanated from the Continent at the same time, Mme de Stael's *De l'Allemagne*.[9] Mme de Stael and Sismondi were members of the same circle, a power-house of intellectual resistance to Napoleon. Mme de Stael's book represents one kind of challenge to the Emperor: she decries rationalism, clarity, faith in progress, the literary values and political ideals associated with the French Enlightenment. Sismondi's protest against French imperialism is launched from the opposite point of view. A trained political economist, and very recognisably a thinker of an eighteenth-century type, he celebrates as an ideal society the kind of small autonomous state Napoleon has swept away. His book is in a way a natural sequel to Gibbon's great valediction for the Roman republic, and as such it speaks to upper-class Englishmen educated in the Enlightenment habit of mind. The Tory *Quarterly* welcomes the history with extreme cordiality, because it sees in it an implicit compliment 'to our happy constitution', and an 'implied and covert censure on the principles and conduct of the Gallic emperor'. 'The quality which most forcibly characterizes his history, is the zeal which it displays in the cause of national independence, the abhorrence of tyranny and of the lust of dominion.'[10] The reviewer finds it hard to leave this vein, but here and there his phrasing indicates how the example of the Italian republics might have a more idealistic and imaginative resonance for modern Europeans:[11]

> The histories of ancient Greece, and of Italy during the middle ages, possess many points of analogy. ... In Florence we cannot hesitate for an instant to recognize the Athens of Italy, with the same genius and enthusiasm for arts and letters, the same popular levity and restlessness, the same ardent attachment to the very extreme of a democratic constitution. ... The history of Florence presents more objects of importance than that of almost any other nation – we mean, not the history of Florence under the Medici, still less under the sovereigns of the House of Lorraine, but the history of Florence during the ages of her *real* greatness, free, active, and independent, the protectress of Italian liberty, the maintainer of her political balance, the fostering inventress of art and science, the patroness of original genius. Those who have formed their opinions of political importance, on extent of conquest and possessions, on the magnificence of monarchy, or the apparent riches of an empire, will hardly conceive how a comparison between the present situation of our own country and that of an Italian city, the mistress of a dominion twenty or thirty leagues in extent, can reflect upon the former any motives for pride or self-congratulation. Yet this may be easily imagined by others who have, more philosophically, considered that in a small society every individual is of importance, whereas in an extensive one, we contemplate the operations of bodies of men, not of particular persons, and lose the nice discrimination of character, and impressions of a more general nature.

If Sismondi sounded a political chord in 1812, so equally did the young Byron. The poem with which Byron made his name, the first two cantos of *Childe Harold*, drew deeply on contemporary public interest in the politics of the Mediterranean countries where it was set. True, it alluded to the literature of the Renaissance period too: it was deliberately based on Ariosto's discursive epic manner, and the stanza form was that of the nearest English equivalent, Spenser. But *Childe Harold* did not seem a close imitation of any earlier mode. The thrust was offered by its themes: a fascinating exiled hero, certainly; but also the national contrast, in the first Canto, between the slavishness of the Portuguese and the hardy resistance offered to the French by the Spaniards; in the second Canto, the contrast between the tough modern Albanians and ancient Greeks on the one hand, and the slavish modern Greeks on the other. The first two Cantos of *Childe Harold* celebrated liberalism and liberty, and in 1812 seemed exactly right for the hour. Their publication was a characteristic coup by the great opportunist among major poets.[12]

Though the most ambitious poetic model employed by both Shelley and Peacock had until now been the long, formless eighteenth-century didactic poem, between 1813 and 1815 Peacock began a literary experiment of some significance.[13] His 'Ahrimanes' was to have been an epic poem in twelve books, like the *Faerie Queene*. It was written in Spenserian stanzas, and was clearly an attempt at a full-scale romantic epic. By the summer of 1816, when he took up *Melincourt*, Peacock had apparently dropped 'Ahrimanes' for good, and resigned his interest in it to Shelley, who next year, 1817, made use of its form and ideas for his twelve-book poem in Spenserian stanzas, *Laon and Cythna, or The Revolt of Islam*. Peacock's abandoned poem, and Shelley's completed one, have always been recognised as sharing a mode and a theme. Each is about a pair of young lovers, struggling to achieve love and some kind of absolute good in a world which is under the sway of evil. But Kenneth Neill Cameron, distinguishing between the two poems, makes what would certainly be the usual judgement of Peacock as a writer – that he is less political than Shelley, and more cynical:[14]

> Shelley presents a much more directly political message than does Peacock. ... The struggle he depicts is not only – as it is with Peacock – one between good and evil principles, but between progressive and reactionary social and political forces. Nor does Shelley share Peacock's cynical attitude towards the prevalence of evil in the world. For him there is ... a constant,

ever-present struggle between good and evil, progress and reaction, in which the not-too-distant triumph of the progressive forces is inevitable.

It is true that Peacock and Shelley always differed over the last point, since Peacock thought optimism unwarranted by the facts, and likely to breed complacency. As far as an air of urgency goes, 'Ahrimanes' is partly typical of its date, since 1813 to 1815 were years of less bitter political feeling then 1817. But it would be most unsafe to judge on this evidence that Peacock is generally less concerned with immediate politics than Shelley, or more cynically resigned to the continued existence of powers that be; absurd, in fact, since *Melincourt* is to pick up where 'Ahrimanes' leaves off.

It is in a sense arbitrary to single out one work or one author as dominant at a given time in Peacock's highly stocked literary consciousness. Just as he read the Greeks, so he read the Italians; he was reading them before he met Shelley, in 1809.[15] Among Italian writers his own favourite, rather surprisingly, may well have been Tasso. As a man Tasso fascinated both Shelley and Byron: he had led a deeply mournful life, since he was believed to have fallen in love with his patron's sister, the princess Leonora d'Este, and to have been incarcerated for seven years in a madhouse largely on that account. Both Byron and Shelley could identify themselves with such a poet, and they wrote movingly about his personal sufferings.

Tasso's great poem, the *Jerusalem Delivered*, makes a wholly different kind of appeal. It takes the action and many of the characters of Homer's *Iliad*, and turns the Greek heroes into a band of Catholic knights redeeming the Holy City from the infidel. If the ardent Christian didacticism would seem at first sight unpalatable to liberals in the age of the French Revolution, the manner of treatment might be equally alien. Tasso belongs to the elaborate High Renaissance. His is an intricately ordered poem. Its twenty books divide in half, with the first, unsuccessful assault on Jerusalem as a climactic central sequence. The two halves of the poem are designed to match one another, the characters entering and leaving at elegantly symmetric moments: Rinaldo, the Achilles-figure, the leading hero, departs in the fifth book, and the quest to release him from the enchantress Armida begins in the fifteenth book. During his absence, the central parts of the epic are taken up with the adventures of the secondary hero, Tancred, and his warrior-maid Clorinda.

The conscious literariness must have been the very quality that made the *Jerusalem Delivered* a favourite with the iconoclast Voltaire,[16] and with the equally irreligious Peacock. All Peacock's own work has the same elegance of shape, the same movement towards and away from a central pivotal scene. His narratives also have the awareness at complex levels of a received version, a text, that Tasso displays of the *Iliad.* Just as he admired Roman epic writers who knew they were also writing counter-epic, so he seems to have admired Tasso for his pervasive allusiveness, his exploitation and rejection of the pagan model. The taste for intricate irony of this type was to be something Peacock shared with Shelley, all of whose major poems are richly saturated with cross-references to literary archetypes.

Melincourt is not closely based on Tasso, yet it seems to take from the *Jerusalem Delivered* both symmetry and a sense of high idealism in the central characters. The action, moreover, is much more decidedly allegorical than it would be in Ariosto, or in any other writer of romance epic, except Spenser. Anthelia, whose favourite reading is in Tasso,[17] resembles his high-minded heroines more closely than the feminine characters of comparable literature. In fact, she is a heroine of romance herself. Besieged by lovers in her castle in the first volume, she sets them a task, to behave by the standards of chivalry. Much later, when she is imprisoned in another castle, she is followed and rescued by the one true knight and his companion. Forester, Sir Oran and Anthelia are not characters in a novel, but figures from romance. There is no attempt to give them the surface detail of novel characters; instead, they have the elusive depth of allegory. Equally, the adventure in which all three are involved, of quest and rescue, has the dream-like inconsequence of romance. *Melincourt* has been much censured both for its flat characters and its awkward plotting by critics used to a more naturalistic convention, but Forester's quest of Anthelia has the same kind of logic as a book of the *Faerie Queene*, and Peacock justifies his final achievement of her on the same grounds as Spenser would.

As the hero's companion, Sir Oran Haut-ton is so rich a conception that he needs separate consideration. Among other things, he has his roots in the narrative literature of the Renaissance. The name of the hero, Sylvan Forester, suggests that he stands for simplicity. No-one could be more agreeably simple than the orang-utan Forester is training to enter human society. The constant friendly presence of Sir Oran intensifies our awareness of the hero's leading moral characteristic, as well as lending him assistance in chivalrous adventures. Though the one has a savage exterior his true gentility reveals him to be the brother of the other: they are Valentine and Orson, as Sir Telegraph Paxarett remarks.[18]

The allusion to a fifteenth-century French romance is carefully planted. Elsewhere Sir Oran is compared with Hercules and Orlando Furioso, and with a figure adapted by Fletcher from Spenser.[19] Of these, the last is perhaps the most revealing. Spenser's Sir Satyrane, in Book 1 of the *Faerie Queene*, and Fletcher's Satyr, in the pastoral play *The Faithful Shepherdess*, are two rough but loyal creatures, who prove their native nobility by championing a woman and saving her from rape by a so-called civilised man. It is, of course, highly ironic that they should do this, since the satyr's partly bestial nature traditionally connoted lust.[20] But, as so often in pastoral, conventional values are inverted and received opinions upset; for the sake of the moral commentary, the satyr behaves like a gentleman, and the gentleman like a beast. In Renaissance romance the point was a generalised ethical one, and did not imply that a levelling spirit was abroad. The civilised men with lustful designs in *Melincourt* are a peer of the realm and a clergyman of the Church of England. The satire is a good deal more sharply pointed than it was in Spenser, and the quest has a very different goal in view.

A blend of satire and romance, of the aims of Voltaire grafted on to the mode of Spenser, seems at first sight a curious development, but Peacock's rationale lies in the increasing politicisation of literature in England after 1814. Of all intellectual apologists for the present order of things, to other writers, especially to the young and radical, one had easily the most significance: Wordsworth. *The Excursion* was announced by Wordsworth in 1814 as the central part of the *magnum opus* of his life, but it is also a public poem designed for its hour. Wordsworth calls upon the English nation to consolidate its military victory over revolutionary France. Europe has experienced turmoil – 'Long-reverenced titles cast away as weeds;/Laws overturned.'[21] Let England now morally show the way: let her keep herself 'entire and indivisible'; traditional in her customs and above all in her 'genuine piety'; strong in the performance of duty.[22] The admirable personal qualities derive from a Christian ethical tradition – prudence, caution, humility; the modern vices (well illustrated by intellectuals like Voltaire, and by Scottish utilitarians) are self-love and self-esteem.[23] Wordsworth sounds evangelical when he suggests that a healthy national life requires above all private individuals to put their religious lives in order:[24]

– The discipline of slavery is unknown
Among us; – hence the more do we require
The discipline of virtue.

But his central meaning is conveyed less by his exhortations than by the form he adopts. *The Excursion* is like a series of monologues – or the effective equivalent, a series of lives of individuals. The emphasis is on the separateness of each one of us; social relationships are of small value. The Solitary, who took part in the French Revolution, shows that a life dedicated to the brotherhood of man ends in bitter disillusionment. Through his sermonising Pedlar, whom he calls the Wanderer, Wordsworth preaches that the only true solace for human unhappiness is communion, through Nature, with God.

Shelley, on returning in 1814 from the Continent, whither he had eloped with Mary Wollstonecraft Godwin, eagerly picked up this cathedral of a poem, to which everything else Wordsworth had ever written was to be regarded as only 'little cells, oratories, or sepulchral recesses'.[25] The anger and sense of rejection with which he read the poem is recorded by Mary in her journal – 'much disappointed. He is a slave.'[26] Better, far better, was the example of Byron, who was following *Childe Harold* with a series of poems about active heroes. The Giaour, the Corsair and Lara were all rebel leaders of the Eastern Mediterranean, who could be seen (and by liberals were seen) as exemplifying the spirit of resistance to the Ottoman Empire, and indeed to tyranny in general. The proximity of the publication of *The Excursion* and *Lara*, both in the summer of

1814, offered two polarities between which aspiring poets could choose. The debate thus stimulated was the effective beginning of the literary relationship between Peacock and Shelley, and it was of formative importance in the careers of both.

The discussion prompted by *The Excursion* was essentially about the role of the poet. What should his relationship be with the world? Should he set himself apart, like a sage, or prophet, to preach to the rest of the community, or was this attitude pretentious, and socially useless? Shelley meditated the answer in his poem *Alastor*, a critique of the notion of the poet as a solitary idealist with which Peacock seems to have been concerned, since he proposed the title.[27] Then, during the summer of 1816, Shelley went with Mary to Switzerland, a country which conveyed to Englishmen a rich complex of associations. The Swiss republics had been the modern political organisation most admired by Gibbon, who had chosen to spend his later years there. Rousseau was a citizen of Geneva. Shelley in Switzerland was reminded of both, but of Rousseau in particular. He was also struck, like Byron viewing Greece in *Childe Harold*, by the degeneracy of the modern inhabitants of a place of such heroic tradition. No doubt he was familiar with the essentially religious response to the Alps of Gray in his letters, and of Coleridge in his 'Hymn before Sun-rise in the Vale of Chamouni'. But the real literary ghost of the Swiss tour was Wordsworth; it was Wordsworth whom the modern Englishman thought of as the poet of liberty, and associated with retirement alone into the mountains. Shelley's *Letters* sometimes allude to Wordsworth; his 'Verses Written on Receiving a Celandine' is both an imitation and a rebuke; but his poem 'Mont Blanc' is something more, a full-dress revocation of the Wordsworthian manner and matter. Like Lucan or Tasso, Shelley brings a great original to mind in order to revise him. Wordsworth's mountains, his Nature, are manifestations of a religious presence, but Shelley's aloof and destructive Mont Blanc is an impersonal, Necessitarian phenomenon, without comfort:

Power dwells apart in its tranquillity
Remote, serene and inaccessible:
And *this*, the naked countenance of earth
On which I gaze, even these primaeval mountains
Teach the adverting mind.

The sense of vacancy which the poet of *Alastor* finds at the end of his quest, and which Shelley records as a final response to Mont Blanc, is a revised version which throws doubt upon the enterprise of going into the mountains to seek great truths.

Meanwhile, during the same Swiss visit, Mary Shelley was beginning her most famous novel, *Frankenstein*. The Gothic is a form which invites introspective, often Freudian, explanations, and many have been offered for the remarkable power with which the author (in 1816, still nineteen) manages to invest her plot. Is Frankenstein, the Promethean inventor, really Shelley, the poet-inventor, and the plot thus Mary's dramatisation of her own desperate need for love? Such speculations are wonderfully tempting; but it is a type of reading which needs to be checked against the strikingly similar themes handled by Shelley and by Peacock between 1815 and 1817. Mary may indeed have experienced acute distress from her frequent pregnancies, the loss of her babies, and the alienation of her much-loved father; (if her character Frankenstein resembles anyone in her own life, it is surely Godwin rather than Shelley). But she was also the member of a circle reacting angrily to the posture of the greatest writer of the time, who was felt by liberals to be failing in moral leadership. *Frankenstein* is, like *Alastor*, a fable about a man who goes apart from his fellows in order to pursue an idealism – only to find it evil. The didactic message of the novel lies in the Monster's rebuke to Frankenstein, which is surely meant to strike the reader as fundamentally just: all created beings have a right to companionship, and need to be loved. The mountains, emblem by now of Wordsworthian solitariness, are associated in Mary's book with sterility and lovelessness. When her characters leave them for the Rhineland, they experience relief:[28]

> The mountains of Switzerland are more majestic and strange;
> but there is a charm in the banks of this divine river, that I never
> before saw equalled. Look at ... that group of labourers coming
> from among their vines; and that village half hid in the recess of
> the mountain. Oh, surely, the spirit that inhabits and guards this
> place has a soul more in harmony with man than those who pile
> the glacier, or retire to the inaccessible peaks of the mountains of
> our own country.

But much of this was still to be written – indeed, at the same time as *Melincourt* – and meanwhile Peacock was more familiar with Shelley's thinking. In poems and in his letters, Shelley recorded the comfortless grandeur of the mountains, and the servility of their inhabitants, the modern Swiss. While still at Geneva, he resolved to come back to live in the Thames valley, promising Peacock that he was reserving much talk about his travels 'for some future winter walk or summer expedition'.[29] One of his directions to Peacock, about the location of the house he should look out for, supplied the name of the hero of the new book Peacock was now beginning to write – 'Certainly the Forest engages my preference, because of the sylvan nature of the place.'[30] But the very notion of the Swiss journey gave Peacock yet more, since it gave him the central idea for his allegory – a young writer's search for idealism among the mountains of the English Lake District, and his disillusionment with them as a source of insight into the problems of the present day.

Those who know anything of Peacock's life are tempted to assume out of hand that Forester is a portrait of Shelley (though Byron, who had once owned a bear not unlike the hirsute Sir Oran, believed he was the young idealist Peacock had in mind).[31] In fact, the idealised intellectual, whose story is represented allegorically, now becomes Peacock's standard hero. In this respect, Forester is a prototype for Scythrop, Taliesin and Falconer. And yet, like Mr Escot in *Headlong Hall*, Forester is also something else again – a philosopher engaged in a discussion. As a debater, he recalls eighteenth-century thinkers: his discussions with Fax, like Escot's with Forester, re-enact the debate about civilisation in its various stages which was waged in real life by the cultural and philosophical historians, or anthropologists and sociologists, of the Enlightenment.

Like Escot in *Headlong Hall*, Forester is a pessimist. He believes that an advanced society is a worse environment for the individual than a primitive society, and much worse than classical Athens or republican Rome. As a scientific thinker, Mr Fax is committed to the idea of progress, but his optimism is tempered by his fear that the population is out-growing the means of feeding itself. Clearly, the general grounds of their discussions resemble those of the debates in *Headlong Hall*, but the philosophers in *Melincourt* are less fanciful and extreme than their predecessors. Their topics of debate are often those of the journals of the day. It is more difficult to make the error of assuming they are being satirised. In fact, the philosophers in *Melincourt*, especially Fax, have usually been censured for not being funny enough, which is an oblique way of recognising that their discussions are nothing other than a linked series of philosophical dialogues.

As in *Headlong Hall*, the philosophical element retains its serious intellectual quality. From two opposite poles of reputable progressive opinion, Forester and Fax consider the society which *Melincourt* as a whole depicts. The action would not seem typical, if they did not demonstrate it to be so; the issues raised could not be generalised, nor placed in their true historical context. The philosophers exist to deepen the comedy by relating it to the world of ideas. Because this is so, they are primarily types, and decidedly not to be identified with individuals. All the same, each does in a generalised sense remind the reader of a real-life prototype, and it is important to recognise whose system of thought is being brought to mind.

The identification of Fax with Malthus has never been in dispute. He is introduced in chapter vii, 'The Principle of Population', where he expounds at length the gloomy calculations for which Malthus is best remembered. He illustrates Malthusian forebodings when he tells the story of Desmond, who married and had children he could not support. He attempts without success to dissuade the rustic couple, Robin and Zukey, from further adding to the population. He also resembles Malthus in his dislike of the potato, that crop for sustaining a large population at the subsistence level.[32] Malthus had written of recent years on the bullion question, the issue whether or not the nation should return to the gold standard, and Fax's investigation of the failed bank (chapter xxx: 'The Paper-Mill') alludes to his mentor's analytical powers in this field. But compared with Mr Escot in *Headlong Hall*, Mr Fax is a narrowly conceived, less enthusiastic portrait of Malthus. He is sympathetic enough: despite his anxieties about the population, and his professional disapproval of charity, he *does* relieve the Desmonds,[33] and his motives for wishing to postpone the hour when Robin and Zukey procreate are depicted as genuinely benevolent (even if his earnest celibacy is comically out of key with the natural enthusiasm of those he is trying to advise).[34] Nevertheless, Peacock has shifted his point of view a little on Malthus. His old admiration is not quite so evident.[35] He no longer identifies himself with the Malthus-voice, since he allocates to Fax the general demeanour of an optimist, though a sceptical one. Peacock's own sympathies lie, as before and always, with the pessimist, the convinced critic of society, who in *Melincourt* is not the Malthus-figure, but the more literary idealist Forester.

Forester has proved less easy than Fax to pin to a single real-life thinker. As a theorist who holds that, in terms of his own happiness, man's conditions have deteriorated, he has a general resemblance to the Rousseau of the two *Discourses*. But there are much more frequent references to the work of James Burnett, Lord Monboddo, whose two books, *The Origin and Progress of Language* (1773–92) and *Antient Metaphysics* (1779–99), have considerable importance in the intellectual evolution of Peacock and Shelley. Monboddo belonged to the type of controversialist Peacock particularly liked. He was immensely learned, and in some of his beliefs cranky. He had also shown genuine brilliance in projecting his narrative of the evolution of society back into pre-history. Rousseau had guessed, purely hypothetically, about primitive man in a state of nature. The more empirical Scots tried to construct a scientific picture of the earliest stages of social development, before history proper began. Their anthropological model was obtained by comparing modern primitive peoples, and by arranging existing economies and societies into a plausible evolutionary sequence, which they projected into the remote past. Thus, for Monboddo, man was 'at first quadruped', and solitary; next he banded in herds, and afterwards took to hunting and fishing; later came agriculture and the invention of language, and finally the 'state of civility and arts' represented by ancient civilisations within historical times.

Monboddo's contributions to the nascent study of anthropology look potentially interesting, after the passage of two centuries; his discussion of man's affinity with the higher apes was vindicated even sooner. Peacock does not commit himself to a clear opinion on the validity or otherwise of his scientific theories. Most of the long footnotes gravely offered in *Melincourt* from Monboddo's work deal directly with the humanoid characteristics of the orang-utan, and are surely meant to seem engagingly dotty. However, Peacock is probably not thinking of Monboddo as primarily a scientist. He knows him as a student of Rousseau, particularly of the *Discourse on Inequality*: that is, as a critic of man, of his pretensions, and of the status of his so-called civilised arts.[36] When he discusses the orang-utan, Monboddo challenges the idea that the higher brute is fundamentally different from man. He is a moralist rather than a scientist when he demands to know whether our definitions of what is human are adequate. A tradition of religious thought rested on *a priori* notions about the soul, and about a divine plan which made man perfect and immediately capable of speech, like Adam in Genesis. Monboddo challenges this with his notion of historical evolution. On the other hand, a current, more scientific complacency rested its claims for man's superiority on the faculty of speech, which Monboddo declares to be a superficial acquired skill. Though the qualities he bestows on the orang-utan often sound comic – including, for example, the capacity to play musical instruments – Monboddo is not laughable when he suggests that courage, faithfulness and deep affection (all claimed as within the scope of the higher apes) are good tests for determining a man.

The portrait of Forester touches the real-life Monboddo at a number of points, leaving no doubt that Peacock admired him as a moralist and a social critic. Monboddo was a sufficiently celebrated character for material about his life to be readily available.[37] His friend and fellow-lawyer, Lord Woodhouselee, gave an affectionate and respectful portrait of his classicism, which Peacock too would have found admirable, as well as funny:[38]

> His notions of the origin of language, arts, and sciences are much akin to those of the Epicureans, of which Lucretius has given an ample detail in his fifth book 'De rerum Natura'.... Lord Monboddo carried his admiration of the ancients to such a pitch, as to maintain their superiority over the moderns, not only in philosophical attainments, recondite science, the arts of painting, sculpture, architecture, music, poetry, oratory, and all the various species of literary composition; but even in bodily strength, stature, and longevity; esteeming the present race of mortals a degenerate breed, both with respect to mental and corporeal endowments. Yet, with all these eccentricities of opinion, his writings display great erudition, an uncommon

acquaintance with Greek philosophy and literature, and a just and excellent spirit of criticism, both on the authors of antiquity, and on the English classical writers of the last and preceding ages.

Woodhouselee also remembered Monboddo's 'Attic banquets' as convivial and highly conversational evenings. Others recorded that he had refused a seat on the court of justiciary, the supreme criminal court, on the grounds that it would take him too much from his studies, and from his estate. There he liked to live, and to dress simply, like a plain farmer, in the manner of the ancients. He despised a carriage as an effete mode of locomotion, preferring to go on horseback, or to walk.[39] His attitude to his tenants, again modelled on the paternalism of the ancient world, made him a natural antagonist for Malthus:[40]

> His patrimonial estate was small, not affording a revenue of more than 300*l.* a year. Yet he would not raise the rents, would never dismiss a poor old tenant, for the sake of any augmentation of emolument offered by a richer stranger; and, indeed, shewed no particular solicitude to accomplish any improvement upon his lands, save that of having the number of persons who should reside upon them as tenants, and be there sustained by their produce, to be, if possible, superior to the population of any equal portion of the lands of his neighbours.

Whether or not Forester 'is' Monboddo, his opinions and behaviour are clearly modelled on Monboddo's to a very considerable degree. At the most abstract end of the scale, both share an altruistic notion of man's potential: Monboddo depicts him gradually elevating himself from an animal condition, in which his mind is immersed in matter, to a state in which mind operates independently of body.[41] At the most specific, and entertaining, both believe in the orang-utan, and argue his merits, as other eighteenth-century critics idealise the Noble Savage – for the purpose of making a case against the modern world.

It is hard to do justice to Sir Oran Haut-ton, who is probably the most memorable and amiable of Peacock's characters. Technically he is a fine specimen of Peacock's learned wit, since he is built almost entirely out of *The Origin and Progress of Language* and out of Buffon's *Histoire Naturelle*. As with other characters' ideas, so with the silent Sir Oran's actions: everything he does, from playing the flute and drinking to rooting up trees and falling in love, has its origin in a learned source. It is a comic *tour de force*, and yet the concept itself – man in a primitive state, and how he compares with man in an advanced state – is one that Peacock approaches with all the seriousness an eighteenth-century social theorist could ask for. Sir Oran has to perfection the simplicity of feeling and the dignity that go with the dream of Natural Man. From these attributes comes the charm with which Peacock endows him, conveyed throughout with a gravity matching Sir Oran's own:[42]

> The Reverend Mr. Portpipe, who was that day of the party,
> pronounced an eulogium on the wine ... Mr. Forester and Mr.
> Fax showed no disposition to destroy the unanimity of opinion
> on this interesting subject. Sir Oran Haut-ton maintained a
> grave and dignified silence, but demonstrated by his practice that
> his taste was orthodox.

In fact, Sir Oran is only within strict limits a *comic* figure at all. He has his role in the romance allegory, as a personification of native sincerity and true feeling. Though wordless, his role in the satiric structure is that of a third philosopher (and a great improvement too on Mr Jenkison of *Headlong Hall*). While the first and third volumes of *Melincourt* are primarily romance, and suggest a Renaissance genealogy, the middle one is satire, and there Peacock develops for Sir Oran a distinct and indeed a central role, in an eighteenth-century tradition.

Sir Oran goes on his travels to investigate the current state of England, as did other fictional Noble Savages – Voltaire's Huron, Goldsmith's Man in Black and Bage's Hermsprong. Though, unlike the others, he cannot report what he sees, his dignity and innocence nevertheless allow him to act as a touchstone or corrective to the vice all around him. As in the passages of *Melincourt* that owe more to romance, he stands for simple truth, and acts as a sound test of its presence or absence in others. Mrs Pinmoney, on hearing that he is rich, a baronet, and about to be an MP, declares him less ugly than she first thought, and allows him to take her in to dinner. He unmasks Lord Anophel and Mr Grovelgrub, literally and figuratively. When he stands for election he is, of course, unable to deliver an address, but his colleague and representative Mr Sarcastic delivers one on a novel system of total frankness:[43]

> Nothing, you well know, is so rare as the coincidence of theory and practice. A man who 'will go through fire and water to serve a friend' in words, will not give five guineas to save him from famine. A poet will write Odes to Independence, and become the obsequious parasite of any great man who will hire him. A burgess will hold up one hand for purity of election, while the price of his own vote is slily dropped into the other. . . . This then is my system. I ascertain the practice of those I talk to, and present it to them as from myself, in the shape of theory: the consequence of which is, that I am universally stigmatized as a promulgator of rascally doctrines.

Mr Sarcastic's 'system' is indeed so totally unheard of in political and polite society that he functions much like the totally naïve outsider of the Voltairean satiric method. Providing such a partner for Sir Oran on the hustings has the effect of giving him a voice in the one situation where the satiric necessity demands it.

As the complexity of Sir Oran's part illustrates, *Melincourt* is a most conscious literary production, a performance even more elegant and finished than *Headlong Hall*. It is also considerably more ambitious in scale. Perhaps driven by commercial considerations, also perhaps emboldened by favourable (though brief) reviews for *Headlong Hall*, Peacock now set to work to write a book that had all the outward appearance of a conventional, three-volume novel. Certainly the style of the opening leads the reader to suppose that a leisurely and perhaps routine novel is what he has to expect. 'Anthelia Melincourt, at the age of twenty-one, was mistress of herself and of ten thousand a year, and of a very ancient and venerable castle in one of the wildest valleys in Westmoreland.' As an opening sentence it strongly resembles one first heard half a year earlier: 'Emma Woodhouse, handsome, clever and rich, with a comfortable home and a happy disposition, seemed to unite some of the best blessings of existence, and had lived nearly twenty one years in the world with very little to distress or vex her.' Every reader knows that what follows must be a question of the rich young woman's marriage, but Anthelia's adventures to a husband are a great deal more unorthodox at their date than Emma's. In her education and in her independence, Anthelia recalls the views of Mary Wollstonecraft. Her preference for a wild and free life in the Lake District, rather than a London season, is ultimately Rousseauistic, but has precedents in more recent English novels, notably Godwin's *St. Leon* (1799) and *Fleetwood* (1805). Equally, the adventure which befalls her, of abduction and threatened rape, recalls the Richardsonian tradition in a general way, while actually reading more like Thomas Holcroft's jacobin *Anna St Ives* (1792). To the extent that it resembles novels at all, *Melincourt* reverts to the 1790s, the decade when some writers – including some poets still living – were radical and Rousseauistic.

But such reminders are incidental, and the more important point about *Melincourt* is that it does *not* resemble the novels the reader is most used to. Novels are factual, prosaic: mirrors of a mechanistic modern world and, in terms of the value-system they convey, a part of it. Written largely for women, and often by women, they tend to urge upon girls such virtues as obedience, service and prudence. The business of the heroine of the routine novel is to marry *well*; and the novel itself will spend much of its effort defining just what that 'well' means. Heroine after heroine in respectable fiction of the period is schooled to discipline her own first, spontaneous choice, in favour of a man who would seem to a middle-aged, establishment judgment more worthy. Jane Austen herself so clearly advocates the social, conservative type of marriage (as opposed to stressing personal preference and self-fulfilment) that Scott, in his review of *Emma*, takes the opportunity to demand whether the whole prudential reaction has not by now gone a little too far:[44]

> Before the authors of moral fiction couple Cupid indivisibly with calculating prudence, we would have them reflect, that they may sometimes lend their aids to substitute more mean ... motives of conduct, for the romantic feelings which their predecessors perhaps fanned into too powerful a flame.

If Scott is capable of good-tempered protest, Peacock is willing to go a good deal further. In *Melincourt* he gives a sharp sketch of one conventionally prudent young woman and her parental adviser – Danaretta and her mother, the Hon. Mrs Pinmoney, who comes into conflict with Anthelia on the matter of choosing a husband. If Mrs Pinmoney satirises the type of prudential elder, in fiction and in life, Anthelia, with her idealism and her exalted vocabulary, sounds a note like nothing in the contemporary novel. No character Jane Austen approves of speaks like this; no character she conceives of, unless it is Marianne Dashwood:[45]

THE HON. MRS. PINMONEY.

Tastes, feelings and character! Why my love, you really do seem to believe yourself in the age of chivalry, when those words certainly signified very essential differences. But now the matter is very happily simplified. Tastes: — they depend on the fashion. There is always a fashionable taste: a taste for driving the mail — a taste for acting Hamlet — a taste for philosophical lectures — a taste for the marvellous — a taste for the simple — a taste for the brilliant — a taste for the sombre — a taste for the tender — a taste for the grim — a taste for banditti — a taste for ghosts — a taste for the devil — a taste for French dancers and Italian singers, and German whiskers and tragedies — a taste for enjoying the country in November, and wintering in London till the end of the dog-days — a taste for making shoes — a taste for picturesque tours — a taste for taste itself, or for essays on taste: — but no gentleman would be so rash as to have a taste of his own, or his last winter's taste, or any taste, my love, but the fashionable taste.

ANTHELIA.

I am afraid I shall always be a very unfashionable creature; for I do not think I should have sympathized with any one of the tastes you have just enumerated.

THE HON. MRS. PINMONEY.

You are so contumacious, such a romantic heretic from the orthodox supremacy of fashion. Now, as for feelings, my dear, you know there are no such things in the fashionable world ...

ANTHELIA.

I am sorry for it.

THE HON. MRS. PINMONEY.

Sorry! — Feelings are very troublesome things, and always stand in the way of a person's own interests. Then, as to character – a gentleman's character is usually in the keeping of his banker, or his agent, or his steward, or his solicitor; and if they can certify and demonstrate that he has the means of keeping a handsome equipage, and a town and country house, and of giving routs and dinners, and of making a good settlement on the happy object of his choice – what more of any gentleman's character would you desire to know?

ANTHELIA.

A great deal more. I would require him to be free in all his thoughts, true in all his words, generous in all his actions – ardent in friendship, enthusiastic in love, disinterested in both ... the champion of the feeble, the firm opponent of the powerful oppressor – not to be enervated by luxury, nor corrupted by avarice, nor intimidated by tyranny, nor enthralled by superstition – more desirous to distribute wealth than to possess it, to disseminate liberty than to appropriate power, to cheer the heart of sorrow than to dazzle the eyes of folly.

THE HON. MRS. PINMONEY.

And do you really expect to find such a knight-errant? The age of chivalry is gone.

Here Mrs Pinmoney speaks one of the key sentences of *Melincourt*, and directs the reader to its proper kind. The age of chivalry certainly does not survive in the modern novel, for chivalry is the ideal of a lost age and form, namely of romance. Anthelia's adoption of the notion aligns her with Tasso's exalted heroines, in a different imaginative world entirely. Like so much of Peacock's complex, wry wit, it is a word which functions on two quite separate levels, as a positive ideal about which he is serious, and as a satiric tool which undercuts his enemies.

For the word 'chivalry' was naturally a part of the vocabulary of conservatives. It had been a word to conjure with ever since Burke employed it in his famous rhapsody over Marie Antoinette:[46]

Little did I dream that I should have lived to see such disasters fallen upon her in a nation of gallant men, in a nation of men of honour, and of cavaliers. I thought ten thousand swords must have leaped from their scabbards to avenge even a look that threatened her with insult. But the age of chivalry is gone. That of sophisters, economists and calculators has succeeded; and the glory of Europe is extinguished for ever.

Latterly the word has become even more of a conservative favourite, as nostalgia for feudalism and a romanticised Middle Ages gained ground. Liberals were accordingly liable to approach the term with scepticism, even ribaldry. In 1813, for example, Byron replied to some adverse comments on Childe Harold's unknightly behaviour:[47]

> The vows of chivalry were no better kept than any other vows whatsoever; and the songs of the Troubadours were not more decent, and certainly were much less refined, than those of Ovid ... If the story of the institution of the 'Garter' be not a fable, the knights of that order have for several centuries borne the badge of a Countess of Salisbury, of indifferent memory. So much for chivalry. Burke need not have regretted that its days are over, though Marie Antoinette was quite as chaste as most of those in whose honours lances were shivered, and knights unhorsed ... I fear a little investigation will teach us not to regret these monstrous mummeries of the Middle Ages.

Peacock's adoption of chivalry, as the ideal quality required in a man by a radical heroine, is characteristically sly and unexpected, and gives him much incidental amusement. His aristocrat, Lord Anophel, does not know what the term means, and has to ask his toadies for enlightenment:[48]

> Mr. Feathernest was taken by surprise. Since his profitable metamorphosis into an *ami du prince*, he had never dreamed of such a question. It burst upon him like the spectre of his youthful integrity, and he mumbled a half-intelligible reply, about truth and liberty − disinterested benevolence − self-oblivion − heroic devotion to love and honour − protection of the feeble, and subversion of tyranny.
>   'All the ingredients of a rank Jacobin, Feathernest, 'pon honour!' exclaimed his Lordship.

Renaissance romance and Voltairean satire, dialogue, anatomy, and yet also allegory: *Melincourt* is, it seems, everything that the naturalistic novel and Wordsworth's naturally-constructed, biographical long poem are not. Its ambitious elaboration has received short shrift from most critics. Everyone seems agreed that it is much too long. Brett-Smith, the most learned and reliable of its editors to date, is even convinced that Peacock could not have planned the book in the form in which we have it. He points out that *Melincourt* was advertised as being in the press in the second edition of *Headlong Hall*, which appeared in August 1816, and infers that an original, shorter version of *Melincourt*, perhaps ending with the Chess Dance (the end of volume 2) may actually have been in the printer's hands by July. Yet Shelley reported Peacock to be still working on *Melincourt* on 8 December 1816, and it was not in fact published until 9 March 1817. Parts of the third and last volume cannot have been written until after 11 February 1817.[49] It seems to Brett-Smith that the explanation which best fits the advertisement, the late material in the last volume, and his own boredom in reading it, is that Peacock added it at the publisher's request.[50]

The main objection to the theory is that it seems gratuitous. That kind of reliance cannot be placed on a publisher's advertisement: the same publisher, Hookham, anticipated *Nightmare Abbey* two years later in precisely the same way. The argument that there was a change of plan arises from Brett-Smith's subjective response, to the last part in particular, and from his failure to perceive that the book has a shapely design based on three volumes and not on two.

The structure can be outlined diagrammatically, as in Figure 1. It seems reasonable to suppose that Peacock thought of his forty-two chapters as dividing equally – that is, with fourteen chapters to each volume; although the printer, as so often in the period, blurred the intended effect to suit his own convenience.[51] The first edition is in fact bound up with thirteen chapters in the first volume and fifteen in the second. The diagram follows what would seem to be the author's design, according to which each volume is symmetrically laid out, but also formally linked with the other two. For example, the first volume introduces the topic of marriage, and its fourteen chapters are divided in a markedly regular fashion into four sections: three chapters with Anthelia at Melincourt, four with Forester at Redrose, and again three with Anthelia, four with Forester. Broadly, Anthelia's chapters,

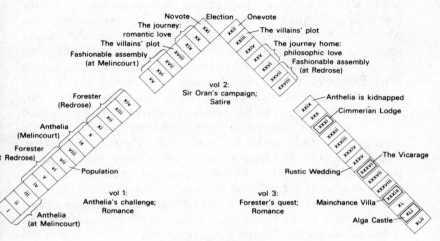

Figure 1 *Melincourt*

romantically set in her castle, establish her challenge to her suitors. Most of the space in these chapters is given to sketching the attitudes of those who are not worthy of her, as in 'Fashionable Arrivals' and 'The Philosophy of Ballads', but in 'The Torrent' she is rescued from danger, in the first occasion of three, by the hero's representative, Sir Oran. Meanwhile, in the Redrose chapters, the philosophers Forester and Fax extend the topic of marriage on to a more general and social plane.

The second volume again has four very distinct movements, and is arranged in an even more markedly symmetrical pattern. It should have opened at Melincourt with one large concourse of fashionable characters ('The Symposium', 'Music and Discord'); it does close at Redrose with another ('The Anti-Saccharine Fete', 'The Chess Dance'). Thus the Chess Dance, a scene adapted from Rabelais, is far from being, as Brett-Smith suggests, a fitting close to the romance: on the contrary, it is a stylised representation of the characters with whom Anthelia does not really wish to consort, a mime of the hard and rather meaningless elegance of fashionable life. Though the characteristic theme of the second volume really seems to be the public contemporary world, interposed between the fashionable sequences are more private chapters which advance the courtship of Anthelia and Forester. The expedition from Melincourt towards One vote shows the lovers lyrically coming together. The journey home towards Redrose establishes the identity of their attitudes at a more philosophical level: the visit to Miss Evergreen proves that Forester is as benevolent a rural landlord as Anthelia is shown to be in the first volume. However, the second volume has a fifth section, a centrepiece – and it is hard to believe that it was not designed from the beginning as the centrepiece to the entire book. Chapter xxi, 'The City of No vote' and chapter xxii, 'The Borough of One vote', give proper pride of place to Sir Oran's election campaign, that magnificent demonstration of the political system in action.[52]

The volume of which Brett-Smith was particularly suspicious was the third, which certainly is arithmetically less neat than the others are intended to be. But it is surely not fanciful to see here too the same pattern of four key locations – the 'houses' of what in Renaissance allegory would no doubt be evil magicians – Mr Mystic's Cimmerian Lodge, Mr Portpipe's Vicarage, Peter Paul Paperstamp's Mainchance Villa, and Lord Anophel Achthar's Alga Castle. The pattern seems more varied than before because, as a kind of fulfilment of Anthelia's challenge in the first volume, Forester is undertaking a chivalric quest on her behalf. His wanderings must be made to seem desultory, as in Renaissance romance. He does not know how to find her, and the note struck at the beginning and end of these chapters is one of unhurried, almost dreamlike travel in a strange and desolate winter landscape – the traditional, suggestive setting of allegory.[53] Yet, as in fact in the Books of the *Faerie Queene*, the adventures are carefully varied, major ones set off and relieved by minor. Forester's lesser adventures are mere encounters with townsfolk or peasantry, or in one case a trivial skirmish ('The Fracas'), while the major ones, the set-pieces in the allegorical houses, represent real intellectual temptations.

The minor episodes, like 'The Paper-Mill' and 'The Deserted Mansion', are useful ways of picking up public themes and handling them with more specificity than was appropriate even in the second volume. The instability of paper finance and country banks, and the ruin of the older breed of farmer, were two favourite campaigning topics of Cobbett. Giving a chapter to 'The Rustic Wedding' makes it possible for Peacock to define his attitude to Malthus, which he somehow manages to do without heat, and without either prudery or grossness. Though in itself well done, the chapter probably has its place (seventh in its volume) solely on account of Peacock's concern for overall symmetry: it matches chapter vii in the first volume, the more theoretical Malthusian discussion on 'The Principle of Population'. Presumably the two philosophers were kept waiting rather aimlessly in 'The Churchyard' for the previous chapter in order to bring this neat effect about. But, after these necessarily desultory adventures, the second half of the last volume becomes purposeful, and devotes itself without redundancy to the discussion and allegorical action which completes the satire.

The third volume seems structurally essential, but less smoothly executed than the other two. The simplest explanation would seem to be that, as Peacock was writing, two events occurred which could be accommodated within his original plan, but at a cost to its simplicity of outline. The allegorical plot was surely always provided for: Forester would prove himself worthy of Anthelia, and do so by displaying active, sociable qualities quite different from the withdrawn Wordsworthian altruism. Then, late in 1816, came two new conservative provocations: a strongly polemical book by Coleridge, the *Statesman's Manual*, and a Tory campaign against the liberty or licence of the press, which was joined by Southey.

Even the prior announcement of Coleridge's title was enough to provoke a clamour from Hazlitt that August in the *Examiner. The Statesman's Manual, or, The Bible the Best Guide to Political Skill and Foresight, A Lay Sermon, Addressed to the Higher Classes of Society* rather too clearly meant to preach the two allied conservative causes, religion and the present aristocratic order of things. Sure enough, the book, when it appeared in December, was a defence of the present constitution, which Coleridge perceived as divinely sanctioned, and arriving at its present form by a Burkean organic process, like a gigantic tree.[54] But the relevance to *Melincourt* was closer than this suggests. Coleridge evidently had a lively fear of revolution in England. He perceived that revolutions are brought about by a mysterious, newly definable phenomenon in advanced society – public opinion – and the opinion is formed and led, even if insensibly, by a nation's intellectuals.[55] Elaborately, discursively, the *Statesman's Manual* calls upon conservative intellectuals – whom Coleridge expects to find among the hereditary gentry and the clergy – and demands of them a kind of internal reformation, the moral rearmament once more, a return to the Bible and to essentially religious ways of thinking. 'The rank which you hold, the influence you possess, the powers you may be called to wield, give a special unfitness to this frivolous craving for novelty.'[56] On the negative side, he identifies the nation's *mis*leaders: that part of the educated class which is sceptical, modern-minded and ultimately 'French', though the habit of mind has been naturalised in Britain by Locke and Hume; the spirit of science and commerce which activates the 'stirring' middle class; the democratic appeal to the labouring class, from whom no more than a decent knowledge of religion and of their own crafts need properly be called for. 'So best *will they maintain the state of the world.*'[57]

Coleridge's book illustrates the inveterate practice of the period, of dividing intellectuals into sheep and goats along broadly political lines. Coleridge's positive creed is a learned but also highly emotional 'enthusiastic' Christianity; it does not closely resemble eighteenth-century Anglicanism, but is strongly influenced by European counter-revolutionary movements of feeling, the mystique of 'throne and altar' that grows up in reaction to French republicanism. It has very little in common with Methodism, which is for the vulgar, and rejects Unitarianism entirely, as too secular and rational. ('If fanaticism be as a fire in the flooring of the Church, the idolism of the unspiritualised understanding is the dry rot in its beams and timbers.')[58] It is a creed for the opinion-forming classes, in whom Coleridge flatteringly assumes a knowledge of Greek and Latin, the scriptures and the commentaries. The style accordingly makes no concessions: Dorothy Wordsworth comments that it is 'ten times more obscure than the darkest parts of the *Friend.*'[59] Implicitly, those to whom Coleridge addresses himself, his ideal readers, are also his intellectual champions: the clergy, 'as the conservators of the national faith, and the accredited representatives of learning in general among us,'[60] or individual right-minded philosophers, the ultimate opinion-leaders, with their 'visions of recluse genius'.[61]

On their travels in search of Anthelia, Forester and Fax meet a 'recluse genius' in the Coleridgean Mr Moley Mystic, and a clergyman who may also owe something to the *Lay Sermons*, the Rev. Mr Portpipe. The latter is a sybarite and obscurantist much along the lines of Mr Gaster in *Headlong Hall* but, after Coleridge's resounding claims for the erudition of the Anglican clergyman ('names that must needs be so dear and venerable to a minister of the Church in England, as those of Hooker, Whitaker, Field, Donne, Selden, Stillingfleet'),[62] Mr Portpipe's selective little library seems a pleasantly apposite touch:[63]

> Homer, Virgil, and Horace, for old acquaintance sake, and the credit of my cloth: Tillotson, Atterbury, and Jeremy Taylor, for materials of exhortation and ingredients of sound doctrine: and, for my own private amusement, in an occasional half hour between my dinner and my nap, a translation of Rabelais and the Tale of a Tub.

Meanwhile the type of intellectual whom Coleridge does mean to recommend is portrayed in the reclusive Mr Mystic of Cimmerian Lodge, who lives in a perpetual symbolic fog of his own manufacture. The speeches he is given are not primarily parodies of Coleridge's style, although the obscurity, the disconnectedness and the oracular mannerisms are well caught. They are a kind of anthology culled from the *Statesman's Manual*, and thus a literal presentation of Coleridge's own propositions:[64]

> The main point is to get rid of analytical reason, which is experimental and practical, and live only by faith, which is synthetical and oracular. The contradictory interests of ten millions may neutralize each other. But the spirit of Antichrist is abroad: – the people read! – nay, they think!! The people read and think!!! The public, the public in general, the swinish multitude, the many-headed monster, actually reads and thinks!!!! Horrible in thought, but in fact most horrible! Science classifies flowers. Can it make them bloom where it has placed them in its classification? No. Therefore flowers ought not to be classified. This is transcendental logic.

All the points, and most of the key words, can be traced to their original in Coleridge's first *Lay Sermon* or in one of its appendices. There has been a misconception that Peacock attempts to *characterise* Coleridge in Mr Mystic. It is true that the sage 'talked for three hours without intermission' — a much-publicised feature of Coleridge's real-life conversation. But otherwise Mystic is not endowed with the kind of characteristics that should suggest a portrait. Peacock does not even try to *type* Coleridge's literary persona through the whole body of his writing, as Hazlitt certainly does when he accuses him of having been consistently 'the advocate of servility',[65] or bitterly attributes to him large and unworthy aims — 'there is something worse than the occasional error — systematic imposture; something worse than the collision of different opinions — the suppression of all freedom of thought and independent love of truth.'[66] Peacock's is a more ideological and genial construct, a mythical conservative intellectual built out of materials supplied by Coleridge when he applies himself to the same task.

With the arrival at Mainchance Villa, the philosopher-heroes confront their last and severest allegorical 'temptation'. Of all the scenes in Peacock, this is perhaps the one which has been most disliked. Critics have felt protective towards the four principal targets, Canning the politician (Mr Anyside Antijack), Gifford the editor of the *Quarterly Review* (Mr Vamp of the *Legitimate Review*), Wordsworth (Mr Paperstamp), and Southey (Mr Feathernest). At least, they have felt protective towards the latter two, the literary figures, just as they have towards Coleridge; it seems that anything goes in strictly political abuse, but that great creative writers are sacrosanct. 'There is less excuse, however, for the acrid arraignment of Wordsworth as Peter Paul Paperstamp, Esq. ... Moley Mystic, Esq. of Cimmerian Lodge, plainly enough aims to be a portrait of Coleridge, but the caricature is a mere daub. ...'[67] Once again, however, a misconception has arisen, first because not enough weight is given to the allegory. When, after some difficulty, the travellers arrive at the Villa, they find a sinister atmosphere. Their host and his invited guests are in cabal, 'holding a consultation on the best means to be adopted for totally and finally extinguishing the light of the human understanding'.[68] The other neglected element in the scene is its precision of reference. The general allusion is to the topical controversy about the role of the press, and the balance of its duty, between preserving the safety of the constitution and enlightening the public. Once again, the dialogue is not invented, but selected from a single source. Peacock is neither arbitrarily abusing the group to which Wordsworth and Southey belong, nor caricaturing them, but quoting their actual words and sentiments.

In the autumn of 1816, while Peacock was writing *Melincourt*, the political situation worsened rapidly. The change, the sense of a real crisis, is felt above all in the chapter set at Mainchance Villa. As so often, Peacock's chief sources are articles in the leading journals, and this in itself gives the closing chapters of *Melincourt* a unique kind of topicality, since the journals and newspapers themselves now briefly became the location of action. Cobbett changed the complexion of national affairs, or appeared to supporters of the government to do so, when in November 1816 he gave mass circulation to the *Political Register* by selling it for twopence. The conservative press – *The Times*, the *Courier*, the *Sun*, the *Morning Post* – began to clamour that measures should be taken against him. If, in the present state of the law, the government could not put a stop to the nuisance, then it must introduce new gagging legislation. Meanwhile the Tory press played its own part in advancing the mood of near-panic. When on 2 December 1816 a London meeting was followed by a riot, the press represented the occasion as an attempted revolution.

Some members of the government concluded that the present crisis was, if not invented by the press, at least much exacerbated by it.[69] At the close of the year, and at the beginning of the new session in January 1817, the ministers still showed no signs of taking the measures demanded of them. Apart from the wartime acts of 1795–6 and 1799, there had been no such suspension of civil rights in England since 1688. For the moment, as Peacock wrote the closing chapters of *Melincourt*, the politicians were inert, while the writers staged a war with words.

Cobbett threw down the gauntlet directly to the pro-government writers in October, before the launching of the 'twopenny trash'. A sharply worded leader on the topic 'What *good* would reform do?' held up to ridicule an argument against reform much in vogue with adherents of the government: namely, that what reformists see as corruption – the buying of seats and the gift of places – is actually a beneficial element in the system, because it has the effect of allowing the new monied interest to share power with the old landed interest. In the course of his argument, Cobbett names individuals who receive public money, while at the same time exhorting the mass of the public to accept sacrifices:[70]

> If it be acknowledged, that *we have made sacrifices*, let us ask what sacrifices the Royal Family, the Judges, the Placemen, the Sinecure-men, the Pensioned ladies, the Police Justices, and others, have made. Their incomes have been *augmenting* during the whole of this long *season of sacrifices*! This is a most curious matter. Well might Canning and Gifford, in the Anti-Jacobin newspaper, call upon the people for sacrifices, while they themselves and GILLRAY the Caricature-man, were obtaining sinecures and pensions! It is now acknowledged, even by the very hirelings themselves, even by that most corrupt of prints, the *Times* newspaper, which was conceived in sin and brought forth in iniquity, and which has never belied its origin ... *that great and general distress prevails* ... will none of those who wallow in luxury, out of means derived from the public purse, *do anything in the way of making sacrifices?* Will Canning and Gifford still cling to their sinecures?

The article in the Tory *Quarterly* dated October 1816 looks very like a reply to this leader of Cobbett's. It repeats the conservative argument that reform is 'a silly question'.[71] In terms of *real-politik*, the monied interest has been steadily gaining ground through the natural pressure of market forces, 'and that purchase of seats, which is complained of as the most scandalous abuse in parliament, is one means whereby it effects this desirable object.'[72] As for pensions, 'if every office, sinecure, and pension, which the boldest reformer has yet ventured to proscribe, were abolished, the whole saving would scarcely be felt as a feather in the scale.'[73] The scene at Mainchance Villa ends with a glee in which the *Quarterly* group chorus – 'And we'll all have a finger in the CHRISTMAS pie.' Though often received as in poor taste, the glee is a satiric equivalent for the *Quarterly's* actual line of defence. Moreover, Peacock's riposte would have seemed apt at the time, once it

became known (as it almost immediately did)[74] that the author of
the *Quarterly*'s article was himself the holder of a sinecure – none
other than the Poet Laureate, Robert Southey.

In a sense, of course, Southey and the conservative faction were
right. Corruption *was* an essential element in the parliamentary
system throughout the eighteenth century, and government
business could not have been carried on without its bought
majority. This did not lessen the moral fervour with which the
opposition denounced it, from Swift and Pope onwards. Peacock in
Melincourt, like Cobbett, could be represented as having some right
to the high moral tone which all satirists adopted. Unlike the Tory
Augustans, he was not, apparently, operating on behalf of a
parliamentary opposition – who if 'in' would have behaved in
much the same way as the current administration – but on behalf
of those campaigning to replace the System altogether.

This, at any rate, would be the implication of openly proclaiming sympathy with Cobbett early in 1817. As a whole it cannot
be said that *Melincourt* is a pro-Cobbett tract. With his much
more cultivated manner, Peacock is not one to share Cobbett's
reactions to 'Parson' Malthus, a blend of genuinely humane indignation with prudery. He also disassociates himself, with much
more emphasis, from Cobbett's indifference to the issue of slavery,
which, to do Cobbett justice, seems to have originated not in simple
chauvinism, but in suspicion of Wilberforce's activities in England,
and in a belief that Evangelicals put religion to work as an opiate
for the people. While sharing the more general suspicion of the
working of religion in the body politic, Peacock introduces into
Melincourt the topic of boycotting sugar, as the product of the
West Indian slave plantations. Forester declares his belief in the boy-
cott, in speeches which are an indication of Peacock's own view,
and a light rebuke to Cobbett's hearty narrowness of vision.[75]

Yet, by and large, the political goals of *Melincourt* are identifiably
Cobbett's goals, and his presence is felt powerfully in the last
volume, which Peacock was finishing just as Cobbett's dispute
with the government press came to a head. Forester in effect
answers Coleridge's élitist argument in the *Statesman's Manual* by
citing Cobbett's popular campaign in the *Political Register*:[76]

> The people read and think; their eyes are opened; they know
> that all their grievances arise from the pressure of taxation far

beyond their means, from the fictitious circulation of paper-money, and from the corrupt and venal state of popular representation.

Above all, Peacock shows his hand by himself attacking, with what is for him unusual feeling and directness, the leaders of the current outcry against Cobbett. Though he takes up Cobbett's smear, that the government writers have been hired, Peacock is much more deeply stirred by the peroration to Southey's article. Here Southey, reacting in a tone of hysteria to the dangers of the current situation – 'God is in the populace as he is in the hurricane, and the volcano, and the earthquake'[77] – builds up to the call that the law should be used to censor the radical press:[78]

> Of all the engines of mischief which were ever yet employed for the destruction of mankind, the press is the most formidable, when perverted in its uses, as it was by the Revolutionists in France, and is at this time by the Revolutionists in England. ... Why is it that this convicted incendiary, and others of the same stamp, are permitted week after week to sow the seeds of rebellion, insulting the government, and defying the laws of the country? The press may combat the press in ordinary times and upon ordinary topics. ... But in seasons of great agitation, or on those momentous subjects in which the peace and security of society, nay the very existence of social order itself is involved, it is absurd to suppose that the healing will come from the same weapon as the wound. ... We have laws to prevent the exposure of unwholesome meat in our markets, and the mixture of deleterious drugs in beer. – We have laws also against poisoning the minds of the people, by exciting discontent and disaffection; – why are not these laws rendered effectual, and enforced as well as the former?

Peacock reacts to this outburst in kind, that is with indignant emotion on behalf of free speech and radicalism. In the philosophers' discussions which precede and follow the scene at Mainchance Villa, on 'The Mountains' and 'The Hopes of the World', he deals in declamatory style with the association between the Lake poets and liberty:

MR. FAX.

What have the mountains done for freedom and mankind?
When have the mountains, to speak in the cant of the new
school of poetry, 'sent forth a voice of power' to awe the
oppressors of the world? Mountaineers are for the most part a
stupid and ignorant race,[79] and where there are stupidity and
ignorance, there will be superstition; and where there is
superstition, there will be slavery.

MR. FORESTER.

To a certain extent I cannot but agree with you. The names of
Hampden and Milton are associated with the level plains and flat
pastures of Buckinghamshire; but I cannot now remember what
names of true greatness and unshaken devotion to general liberty
are associated with these heathy rocks and cloud-capped
mountains of Cumberland. We have seen a little horde of poets,
who brought hither from the vales of the south, the harps which
they had consecrated to Truth and Liberty, to acquire new
energy in the mountain winds: and now those harps are attuned
to the praise of luxurious power, to the strains of courtly
sycophancy, and to the hymns of exploded superstition. But let
not the innocent mountains bear the burden of their
transgressions.

MR. FAX.

All I mean to say is, that there is nothing in the nature of
mountain scenery either to make men free or to keep them so.
The only source of freedom is intellectual light. The ignorant are
always slaves, though they dwell among the Andes. The wise
are always free, though they cultivate a savannah.[80]

Forester agrees with Fax's utilitarian proposition, that art must
contribute to the well-being of mankind: 'In many cases, science is
both morally and politically neutral, and its speculations have no
connexion whatever with the business of life.'[81] But scientists are
not justified in withdrawal into entirely abstract fields of enquiry. It
is equally a fallacy to think that a private life out of the world is *per
se* a life of virtue. As Fax puts it, 'that retirement must be
consecrated to philosophical labour, or, however delightful to the
individuals, it will be treason to the public cause.'[82] Those who are

not against the System are with it. The retirement of the Lake poets is another aspect of their *trahison des clercs.* That this view is not only that of Mr Fax, but of Peacock, is indicated by the simple-minded little speech he afterwards puts into the Lakists' mouths in his essay *The Four Ages*, supposedly accounting for their decision to retire into the mountains:[83]

> Society is artificial, therefore we will live out of society. The mountains are natural therefore we will live in the mountains. There we shall be shining models of purity and virtue, passing the whole day in the innocent and amiable occupation of going up and down hill, receiving poetical impressions, and communicating them in immortal verse to admiring generations.

Peacock denies the altruism of Wordsworth's Wanderer and Coleridge's recluse genius, and suggests that, as far as the community is concerned, poets might as well be venal, for the effect is the same:[84]

MR. FORESTER.

Insatiable accumulators, overgrown capitalists, fatteners on public spoil, I cannot but consider as excrescences on the body politic, typical of disease and prophetic of decay: yet it is to these and such as these, that the poet tunes his harp, and the man of science consecrates his labours: it is for them that an enormous portion of the population is condemned to unhealthy manufactories, not less deadly but more lingering than the pestilence: it is for them that the world rings with lamentations, if the most trivial accident, the most transient sickness, the most frivolous disappointment befal them: but when the prisons swarm, when the workhouses overflow, when whole parishes declare themselves bankrupt, when thousands perish by famine in the wintry streets, where then is the poet, where is the man of science, where is the *elegant* philosopher? The poet is singing hymns to the great ones of the world, the man of science is making discoveries for the adornment of their dwellings or the enhancement of their culinary luxuries, and the *elegant* philosopher is much too refined a personage to allow such vulgar subjects as the sufferings of the poor to interfere with his sublime speculations. *They are married, and cannot come!*

The dialogues of *Melincourt* have been trying to thrash out the question – originally Coleridge's question – of what kind of part intellectuals should play in contemporary England. The last chapters, where barbed assaults on individual conservative writers alternate with general moral propositions from Monboddo and other idealists, show Peacock's allegorical framework stretched to the limit, to accommodate very diverse kinds of material. It can, logically, be made to do so, even if the effect is unfortunately heavy. Forester has always championed the two ideal courses, of active intervention (against Sir Telegraph),[85] and of truth-telling (against Mr Feathernest).[86] So, of course, has his surrogate Sir Oran, with, where necessary, the verbal assistance of Mr Sarcastic. Anthelia too has stood for activity and truth-telling, as is shown by comparing her with Danaretta, a romantic only in words. Though in some respects Forester and Fax oppose each other, with Peacock allowing Forester the victory, on the key issue of how a philosopher should live they prove in accord. Activity, efficacy, the utilitarian's criteria, are goals of the ancient philosopher too.[87]

In short, there *is* a single, coherent ideal of human behaviour in Peacock's mind. His sympathies are not divided, as is so often claimed, neutrally between a range of available viewpoints. Forester stands for an ideal, but one amplified by a number of other characters represented as virtuous. As befits so philosophic a book, what he stands for emerges both from allegorical action, and from discussion. The contemporary evils he faces are largely the attitudes of conservative writers, and his challenges to the worldly in debate are the intellectual equivalents of the battles of romance.

It has been agreed, virtually without a dissenting voice, that *Melincourt* is Peacock's failure. It was of course a political failure, a fact which to Peacock would have mattered a good deal. On the first day of March 1817, the month in which it appeared, the Habeas Corpus Suspension Act passed through the Commons. It was followed before the end of March by three other extraordinary measures, the last of which was designed severely to restrict the right of public meeting. There was little opposition to the rapid progress of the bills, in Parliament or in the press; Cobbett, who did oppose them, during the month fled to America. There was not even much overt resentment by the masses. The Tory press was

inclined to put the public quiet down to the strong measures –
'Once more we feel that we possess a Government', crowed the
Courier – though later historians are more likely to diagnose an
upturn in the economy. What is certain is that the radical
intellectual, like Peacock and Shelley, now felt himself
unpleasantly coerced by the law. Moreover, and as at few other
times, such people were blatantly out of line with public opinion.
Their views were anathema to the great majority of those who
would normally read polite literature; they were too intellectual
and even too jacobinical – that is, free-thinking or atheistic – to
appeal to the masses with whom, politically, they sympathised. It
was the outset of the splendid brief literary golden age, the era of
the 'younger Romantics' – Byron, Shelley, Keats – and *Melincourt*
is in essential ways a typical product of that movement. Its striking
untimeliness in relation to most educated public opinion – a prose
epic about intellectual freedom, in the month when the suspension
of Habeas Corpus proved so easy – is an expressive comment on the
uncomfortable relationship between those poets and their public.

But most critics of later days have been interested in the book as
an aesthetic achievement, and here its failure has seemed to them as
complete as it undeniably was in politics. It is, we are told, too
long; and though on the one hand it can be described – like the rest
of Peacock's work – as unmeaning, it is also condemned on the
other as too didactic. To claim *Melincourt* now as an unqualified
success would be perverse. Its aesthetic integrity is always
threatened by a technical awkwardness, that the essentially prosaic,
epigrammatic spirit of the philosophic dialogue does not merge
easily into a tradition of romance which requires both extension
and mystery. But if *Melincourt* is a flawed book, it is also Peacock's
largest, his most ambitious. It models itself, after all, upon romance
epic. There is a consciously grand conception – an attempt to
represent current politics in the perspective of human history. Such
ambitiousness of scale in fact proves uncharacteristic of Peacock;
the theme does not. In *Melincourt* Peacock develops for the first time
his most typical and important idea: the satiric portrait of
contemporary intellectuals as a complete class, measured against a
single idealised figure, the type of the poet. To some extent the
theme was prefigured in *Headlong Hall*, in the implicit admiration
conveyed by the drawing of Escot for the role played in real

intellectual life by Malthus. The difference in *Melincourt* is that literary devices are employed, analogies evoked – Lucretius and Milton, Homer and Spenser – to give imaginative presence and beauty to what in *Headlong Hall* was a still unrealised ideal.

The handful of critics who reviewed *Melincourt* in the journals saw perhaps as far as they were likely to see. The liberal *Monthly Magazine* applauded 'a wit ... a philosopher, a patriot, and a man of taste'[88]; the Tory *British Critic* recognised 'the cloven hoof of infidelity'.[89] The best and most responsive reader *Melincourt* has ever had was Shelley. Peacock's book had evolved out of what was now a joint enterprise, 'Ahrimanes', and it had received a decisive impetus from Shelley's reactions to the mountains of Switzerland, with their reminders of Rousseau and of Wordsworth. It is clear that Shelley followed the progress of *Melincourt* as it was being written – 'He is not writing "Melincourt" in the same style, but, as I judge, far superior to Headlong Hall.'[90] When it was complete, Shelley did not waver in his good opinion. He ranked *Melincourt* also above the only other satire Peacock concluded in his lifetime, *Nightmare Abbey*:[91]

> May you start into life some day, and give us another 'Melincourt'. Your 'Melincourt' is exceedingly admired, and I think much more so than any of your other writings. In this respect the world judges rightly. There is more of the true spirit, and an object less indefinite, than in either 'Headlong Hall' or Scythrop.

It seems that Shelley conveyed his own admiration of *Melincourt* to Byron[92]; and, after all, it would not be surprising if the future author of *Beppo* and *Don Juan* did find food for thought in a satire on the English present, steeped in the literature of the European past.

The impression made on Shelley remains probably the more profound and interesting. It is surely significant that with *Melincourt* Shelley's doubts about Peacock seem to cease. Especially at the time when Peacock befriended Harriet, in 1814, Shelley expressed reservations about him as a friend – 'expensive inconsiderate & cold'[93] – as a radical – 'his enthusiasm is not very ardent, nor his views very comprehensive'[94] – and as a literary influence upon himself – 'Perhaps in truth Peacock had infected me; my disquisitions were cold, my subtleties unmeaningly refined.'[95] Remarks of this type are not recorded after *Melincourt*. 'He is an amiable man of great learning, considerable taste, an enemy to every shape of tyranny and superstitious imposture.'[96]

It has always been assumed that Shelley liked *Melincourt* simply because he liked the political lesson it preached. This is an inference which does a real injustice to Shelley's critical powers. His favourite works of the past, in literature as in philosophy, were the most imaginative; he detested overt didacticism. It is a great pity that like other critics of his day Shelley did not stoop to technical analysis. Why did he think so well of *Melincourt*? 'It has more of the true spirit, and an object less indefinite ...' Surely 'an object less indefinite' is not just the campaign for the reform of parliamentary representation? 'The true spirit' is likely in Shelley's usage to allude to the idealist positives, Mind and Intellectual Beauty. Without more explicit information one has to guess, but it would seem reasonable from what we know of Shelley to guess that he liked *Melincourt* not because it was more solemn than *Headlong Hall*, but because it was more imaginative.

Whatever the reason, there is much to be said for Shelley's preference. In *Melincourt* Peacock creates a work which is simultaneously a satire – a contemporary commentary on England – and an allegorical romance which claims affinity with the great literature of the past. In the winter of 1816–17, when Shelley saw it evolve, his own longest poems to date were *Queen Mab* and *Alastor*. Within another year, he would have written *The Revolt of Islam*; a year beyond that, and *Prometheus* was begun. The style towards which he was moving was superficially a narrative one, but the story would be essentially allegorical, and would often deliberately invoke as parallels familiar literary models, variant versions of a myth found in Spenser, Milton, Dante, Aeschylus, or the Book of Genesis. At the same time Shelley's sense of the political present was to become far sharper than in his earlier work; *Queen Mab* can be prosily political, but its definition of the immediate *now* is less consciously contemporary than it is in Act 1 of *Prometheus Unbound*. It was Peacock who first used the technique later brilliantly adapted by Shelley, of writing almost with literalness about a foreground of contemporary events, while through allegory and allusion evoking a background of limitless dimension:

philosophic history, the imagined worlds of literature, a shifting pattern of ideal interior landscapes.

Much the finest compliment ever paid to *Melincourt* is implicit, in the quickening refinement of Shelley's narrative art.

Chapter 4

The Critique of Romanticism:
Nightmare Abbey

There is a fever of the spirit,
    The brand of Cain's unresting doom,
Which in the lone dark souls that bear it
    Glows like the lamp in Tullia's tomb.
        Mr Cypress's Song in chapter xi

Though it received little notice on its first appearance,[1] *Nightmare Abbey* is now perhaps Peacock's *Pride and Prejudice*, his most generally liked and frequently read book. There are a variety of possible reasons. One is the continuing fame of some of the real-life figures featured – Shelley, Coleridge, and Byron. But *Nightmare Abbey* surely owes its popularity above all to the fact that, of all Peacock's books, it is the one that most resembles an ordinary novel. It has more story than the others. Its setting, a mouldering Gothic pile equipped with owls and lugubrious servants, is imaginatively realisable, as well as funny. Its hero, Scythrop Glowry, is (unusually for Peacock) a figure to grow fond of rather than to laugh at, not essentially different from a Catherine Morland or a Waverley. Scythrop's excesses, both his indiscriminate falling in love, and his extravagant, gloomy reaction to love's setbacks, read like a familiar tale, the staple of many a novel about the trials of youth.

In appearing, however superficially, like a novel, *Nightmare Abbey* differs from Peacock's earlier satires. Other details are equally untypical. It is the only one to have a single location; most of Peacock's stories involve travelling, and even in *Gryll Grange*, the next most static, the action moves between two houses. The clarity and tightness of the arrangement is matched by an apparently restricted theme. Instead of the national political scene, as in *Melincourt*, or even the diverse cultural world of *Headlong Hall*, the book focusses on literary men, and on literary problems. Nothing in Peacock is ever quite simple, but at face value *Nightmare Abbey* is a tale satirising a writer, who strongly resembles Shelley, and a literary movement, the Gothic.

If this is the case, *Nightmare Abbey* appears to represent a drastic change of direction which, because of the date and circumstances of its writing, could be read as a literary retreat. In March 1817, the very month when the repressive legislation passed through the Commons and Cobbett left for America, Shelley and Mary moved to Marlow in the Thames valley. Peacock was then living a few minutes' walk away. From 6 April to 25 June Leigh Hunt and his family stayed with Shelley. Godwin intermittently visited them; the classically-minded T. J. Hogg came from time to time, generally staying with Peacock. The circle which established itself at Marlow in the summer of 1817 was coherent and even tight-knit, and the distinctive literary manner it evolved became virtually a school, a dominant force in English poetry in the next few, rich years. Its influence can be seen proliferating. When the Shelleys went to Italy a year later, in 1818, Shelley remained in contact with Peacock and Hunt at home, as well as with Byron in Italy. Meanwhile, in England, what is demonstrably the same group, with its distinctive interests, became associated with Hampstead, where Hunt lived, and, nearby, Hunt's friend John Keats.

After the political excitements of March, when Peacock published *Melincourt* and Shelley his *Proposal for Putting Reform to the Vote*, the activities of that summer of 1817 look absorbedly literary. Shelley was busy with *Laon and Cythna*, which he finished on 23 September 1817. Though this epic was certainly a political allegory, it was also a work which had been generating for years, alongside *Melincourt*; and in any case its abstruse manner of treatment seems to lift it above the hurly-burly of real-life politics, which are so sharply etched in *Melincourt*. The newer enterprises of that summer appear even less topical. As usual when Shelley and Peacock were together, much of their reading was in the classics. It was probably at this time, and through Peacock, that Shelley became enthusiastic about a series of poems that were afterwards central to his understanding of classical literature and thought: the Homeric 'Hymns' to the various pagan deities.[2] Peacock translated part of the 'Hymn to Dionysus' in *Rhododaphne* (Canto 5, ll.159–202); Shelley over three years translated seven others, including the Hymns to the Sun, the Moon, the Earth and Mercury.

The significance of the Homeric 'Hymns' for both friends seems to have been that they captured the essence of the Greek spirit, what Andrew Lang called 'the delight in life, and love, and nature; the pious domesticities of the sacred Hearth'.[3] During this summer, Peacock and Shelley developed an interest in the ancient religion which these poems typified, that went beyond the merely literary. Their absorption with love as an ideal, especially as it had been represented in the ancient world, probably arose from the fact that love is supreme among the social virtues. Ever since he had read *The Excursion*, as *Alastor* indicates, Shelley had associated Christian idealism with asceticism, an inward spirituality that appeared to exclude the social virtues and love. The positive interest in love, which became almost a cult from the summer of 1817, was thus associated, like so much else, with rejection of the example of Wordsworth.

In May 1817 Shelley was reading Apuleius' *Golden Ass*, and was delighted with it, especially with the episode of Cupid and Psyche. Peacock, he reported, was equally enchanted.[4] So too was Mary, who translated about half the story between 24 October and 16 November 1817.[5] That summer, Shelley also read *The Symposium*, which contains Plato's extended treatment of love; and Lucretius, whose discussion of love in the fourth book of *De Rerum Natura* he professes – rather surprisingly, in view of its cynical tone – to find profound and congenial.[6] By the autumn Shelley had also begun 'Prince Athanase', a poetic fragment, intensely classical in atmosphere, which deals with love in various aspects. His writing and some at least of his reading was being done 'in a study adorned with casts, as large as life, of the Vatican Apollo and the celestial Venus.'[7] It is no wonder that Hunt, in his sentimental way, equated the Marlow circle with paganism, and took its divinity to be the god Pan:[8]

I hope you paid your devotions as usual to the Religio Loci, and hung up an evergreen. If you all go on so ... a voice will be heard along the water saying 'The great God Pan is alive again', – upon which the villagers will leave off starving, and singing profane hymns, and fall to dancing again.

So far, each of Peacock's satires had been born out of a period of intense and fruitful interchange with Shelley. Dialectical themselves in form, they bear the marks of mutual reading and debate. In the autumn of 1817, it is not clear if Peacock was planning another satire. If he was, it may have been the fragment 'Sir Calidore'. Hitherto, most scholars have assigned this abandoned story, and a much shorter version of it, 'Sir Satyrane', to 1816; but there is no obvious time in 1816 when Peacock was free to work on it, and the autumn of 1817, or March 1818, seem more plausible dates.[9] The plot of 'Sir Calidore' describes how, after his defeat by Mordred, Arthur and his court are transported by means of Merlin's magic to a South Sea island, where they await still the end of the reign of evil in England and in the civilised world.[10] They have settled down amicably there with a further group of exiles, the gods and goddesses of Greece, prominent among whom are Bacchus and Pan. A generation before the action proper opens, a missionary ship, the Puff, is wrecked near the island, casting ashore a single survivor, a long-faced Bible-wielding Puritan. After a month spent on Arthur's instructions with a beautiful nymph, the missionary returns, dressed like a Bacchanal and, by general agreement, much improved. ' "Such is the difference," said Bacchus, "between cheerful and gloomy creeds. Cheerfulness is the great source and fountain of beauty: but the ugliest object in nature is a human visage distorted by a fanatical faith." '[11]

It looks as though the satiric, 'anatomising' part of 'Sir Calidore' was to have followed the hero (the son of the missionary and the nymph) on an embassy to England, where his instructions from Arthur were to find a wife for himself and a representative philosopher for the islanders to examine.[12] But the other thread of the story – the island itself, with its joyous Greek civilisation – was to have been the book's positive. Sex and its taboos were clearly to have played a leading part in 'Sir Calidore'. Once more Peacock was setting up an opposition between Ancients and Moderns, especially, it seems, in relation to religion, and love. The natural religion of the Greeks was to have been compared, wholly advantageously, with a sour, repressive Christianity, a satiric representation of the religion of contemporary England.

For whatever reason, 'Sir Calidore' was discontinued, and Peacock's next serious publication after *Melincourt* was the poem *Rhododaphne*, which appeared in February 1818. Again, in *Rhododaphne*, though this time not in satirical terms, Peacock resumes the topic of ancient natural religion: more specifically, he considers what sexual morality would be, in a religious system which placed man harmoniously within the world of nature. The direct contrast with contemporary Christianity and its taboos is not spelt out, as in 'Sir Calidore'. Because the poem lacks both the sharp contemporaneity of the satires, and the dialectical technique, it appears to be a simple story, virtually in the Leigh Hunt manner, of long ago and far away. In fact, Peacock had learnt from his satires how to handle the techniques of irony, allusion, and significant use of structure, and *Rhododaphne* is a much less bland work than it is commonly taken for.

Its story is freely based on Apuleius' beautiful treatment in *The Golden Ass* of the Cupid and Psyche myth. In Apuleius, Cupid falls in love with the mortal, Psyche, but because he does not wish to be known he builds her an enchanted palace and comes to her each night under cover of darkness. The idyll is destroyed by her envious sisters, a fine comic pair of respectable killjoys who, warning Psyche that her dealings are too unconventional, persuade her to light the lamp and so, fatally, to reveal the god. In Peacock's fable, too, what could have been a beautiful pagan love-idyll, in all essentials innocent, is destroyed by arbitrary man-made fears and taboos.

Anthemion, a Greek shepherd boy, goes to the shrine of Love – a three-fold divinity, Creative, Heavenly and Earthly – in order to pray for the recovery of the girl Calliroe. Before the altar he meets a beautiful enchantress, Rhododaphne, who falls in love with him; but Anthemion is persuaded by an elderly sage (the prototype, presumably, for Keats's Apollonius in *Lamia*) that Rhododaphne and her love are evil. What follows, with characteristic Peacockian elegance and stylisation, is the death successively of each maiden. In the first half of the poem, the real girl, Calliroe, appears to die, magically poisoned by Anthemion's kiss. In the second half, the enchantress Rhododaphne really dies, because Anthemion's guilt brings upon her the vengeance of a repressive Jove through his agent, Uranian or Heavenly Love.

> It was not Love's own shaft, the giver
> Of life and joy and tender flame.

The death-dealing blight is a concept of love, an intellectualisation which appears to originate in Anthemion's conscience or superego: for it is he who thinks that love must be restricted to one object, while the nymph holds it to be indivisible. Because Anthemion believes that Rhododaphne's love is illicit, and purely sensual, it does indeed incur the vengeance of the excluded, affronted spiritual aspect of love. The point of Peacock's poem, far more discreet (and indeed to most readers obscure) than 'Sir Calidore' could have been, is the glorification of natural religion and the assertion of the essential beauty and innocence of sexuality.

Rhododaphne has been taken to be antiquarian and nostalgic, and little else. Certainly it breathes nostalgia —[13]

> great Pan is dead:
> The life, the intellectual soul
> Of vale, and grove, and stream, has fled
> For ever with the creed sublime
> That nursed the Muse of earlier time.

But this is, after all, nostalgia to some purpose. Shelley wrote a review, intended for Hunt to publish, in which he was guarded, and yet ready with clues. 'It is a Greek and Pagan poem. ... There is here, as in the songs of ancient times, ... the luxury of voluptuous delight.'[14] Hunt meanwhile obviously equated the Pan-worshippers at Marlow with something more pointed than a little mild antiquarianism: he still associated them with an interest in starving villagers, which implies the active social reformism of a year earlier.[15] While 1817–18 was an inauspicious period for open calls to political action, an assault on Christian sexual ethics – if the poem was recognised as such – was hardly, in the context of the hour, a neutral gesture. Peacock's intention in *Rhododaphne* was to charge dualistic moral systems, like Christianity, with negativism, and to suggest that sexual taboos have a deadly effect upon man's relations with his body, with his fellow-man and woman, and with his environment.

Leigh Hunt, who did not care much personally for Peacock, did not publish Shelley's review of *Rhododaphne*, nor publicise the poem in any other way. Yet in 1818 he too was enthusiastically imagining a revival of the cult of the nymph in England,[16] and his protégé Keats had already begun to develop similar themes. While Peacock was writing *Rhododaphne*, Keats was writing *Endymion*, and in December 1817, when he was introduced to Wordsworth, he chose to recite its invocation to Pan. Haydon records Wordsworth's sharply unfavourable comment, but he concentrates on the hurt Keats must have felt, without noticing that Wordsworth evidently felt provoked by the choice of subject – 'A very pretty piece of paganism'.[17]

The question is why, in 1817 and 1818, paganism, perceived as the adversary of Christianity, suddenly seemed to Shelley, Peacock, Hunt and Keats so meaningful and topical a subject; and why, too, it readily gave offence to those who differed from them politically. With the passage of time, their elaborate Greekishness looks like the cult of intellectuals constructing an alternative ideal world, having been disappointed of reform in this. There is inevitably a flavour of coterie art in the rage for evoking a colourful, sensuous late-Greek civilisation, as there is in the very similar vogue for the Italian Renaissance, now entering its heyday. Art which alluded to the classics, whether visual or literary, always needed its audience to be in some degree familiar with the original, and to share the artist's assumptions about what that original ultimately stood for. This was as true of Blake's inherited language of gesture in his prints, as it was of Pope's pervasive references to the *Aeneid* in the *Dunciad*. For liberals, the origins of the appeal of Athens and Florence had for some time lain in republicanism, as a social system and as a fosterer of the best art. Now, as the religious revival swelled and flourished, and as church institutions all over Europe were closely identified with restored monarchies and the new, traditionalist status quo, another enemy appeared in addition to secular tyranny – established, orthodox religion. Hence the growing insistence, in all the young English writers, on the repressiveness of Christianity, symptomatically in the sphere in which the church's teaching is familiarly felt by the young: its ruling that sexuality is guilty. As the revolt against the personal restraint imposed by Christianity becomes a leading theme in the work of Byron, Shelley, Keats and Peacock, so does the more positive conception, the beauty of a free and humanistic paganism. The rationalism of the eighteenth century no longer seemed an effective weapon against the church: the appeal of the one religion could be matched only by the appeal to another. Not that the new warmth and intensity of tone in the manner of the young English poets can have been a matter of calculation. While Europe was in the grip of an irrationalist and nostalgic religious revival, opponents of its political implications could not resist its imaginative pull, but responded with an alternative that was itself religious too.

Well before the post-war period, when the young English writers took up their new combative stance in relation to religion, Continental writers had christianised literature in a political cause. Already, in the Germany of the late 1790s, Friedrich Schlegel's circle, the first group to coin for itself the epithet 'Romantic', declared its interest in the subjective and irrational, and turned its back on the social and political goals of the Enlightenment. In the first decade of the nineteenth century, as Napoleon established his dictatorship over Europe, intellectual feeling, especially in Germany, more aggressively rejected the ideals of the French revolutionary era – its rationalism, its political liberalism, and its optimism for the future – in favour of a mystical Catholicism and idealisation of a 'Germanic' past: the early Middle Ages, when the Northern tribes had asserted themselves over the degenerate civilisation of the Mediterranean south. Worship of religion and of the Christian Middle Ages was by no means peculiar to the Germans. The cult was represented in France itself, for example, by Chateaubriand, beginning with *Le Génie du Christianisme* (1802), and by Mme de Stael. But, as a complex of ideas, ardent Christianity, medievalism, and political conservatism received their strongest impetus from Germany, and continued to be fed alike by German nationalism, and by a sophisticated philosophic subjectivity, adapted from Kant. A. W. Schlegel did not actually become a Catholic; his brother Friedrich was converted in 1808, a fact which, as Wellek remarks, 'on the whole limited the appeal of his later work to the definitely conservative and Catholic world of the Restoration [i.e. post-Napoleonic] period'.[18]

General histories of English Romanticism have tended to seem dazzled by the brilliance of the theoreticians of that movement, all of whom were German or (as in the case of Mme de Stael and Coleridge) acknowledged popularisers of the Germans. They have taken it as a symptom of English parochialism that the younger group of English 'Romantic' poets did not respond more positively to the thought of their German contemporaries. 'In England none of the romantic poets recognized himself as a romanticist or recognized the relevance of the Continental debate to his own time and country.'[19] But this is a misconception, since the debate of Classic v. Romantic, Pagan v. Christian, liberal v. conservative, *was* waged in England, and crucially, between 1817 and 1822. And the work of German critics had its bearing on the course of the discussion, though so far it was only very partially available, or refracted by Mme de Stael and Coleridge. If it was not received as a whole, and if its terminology was not accepted, this was partly due to the bitterly polemical habit of the Germans themselves, to their overt proselytising and to their exclusive spirit. The German critics appeared in England at just the wrong time, either too early or too late. In the late 1790s, when in fact Coleridge was first attracted by German thinking, England was also in the grip of counter-revolution and anti-French hysteria. By the late 1820s, a christianised intelligentsia was ready to receive and to be further exalted by the Germanism of Carlyle. But Byron's England, immediately after the Napoleonic Wars, with its long-ruling, oligarchic, and by now rather negative Tory government, was not an environment where youthful intellectuals were disposed to welcome a Continental group associated with religion and political reaction.

The first popular source of knowledge about the new German ideas was Mme de Stael's *De l'Allemagne*, translated into English in 1813. As the friend of a new generation of German intellectuals, and a focus of resistance to Napoleon, she was no longer in sympathy with the liberalism and rationalism that helped to bring about the French Revolution. Her book was sufficiently clear in its counter-revolutionary alignment to have been banned in France on its appearance in 1810. It contrasts German literature with

French, to the detriment of the latter. Two cultural traditions are defined, one of which, the 'Latin', is polytheistic, and copied from the ancients, while the other, the literature of the Northern nations, has a chivalrous basis, and a spiritual religion. The eighteenth-century French literary idiom, which derives from the Latin, sinks in the scale beside a German tradition which is made to seem as culturally exciting and imaginative as it is religiously mystical and politically backward-looking.

Though Madame de Stael's book was welcomed in England because it was hostile to Napoleon, her line appeared to appeal rather less immediately and universally than had the more eighteenth-century and secular work of Sismondi. She was received more coolly in the Whig journal than Sismondi had been in the Tory *Quarterly*.[20] The widely admired spokesman for Whig opinion, James Mackintosh, reviewing *De l'Allemagne* for the Edinburgh, correctly identifies Mme de Stael's link with the modern German criticism and regrets its bias:[21]

> The general tendency of the literary system of these critics, is towards the manners, poetry and religion of the middle age. They have reached the extreme point towards which the general sentiment of Europe has been impelled by the calamities of a philosophical revolution, and the various fortunes of a twenty years universal war. They are peculiarly adverse to French literature.... Their system is exaggerated and exclusive.... Nothing is less natural than a modern antique.

He accuses Mme de Stael of failing to understand what is now the intellectual base of the English liberal, the doctrine of utility. She confounds utility with selfishness, while Mackintosh argues that it is disinterested, by way of a significantly classical intellectual genealogy. 'The loftiest visions of Plato, and the sternest precepts of Zeno, may be justified by, and even deduced from, the elements of the theory of Epicurus';[22] and for Mackintosh, as for Peacock, the hedonist Epicurus, sceptical, practical, natural, hostile to system and to theory, is ultimately the father of all thinkers of the utilitarian type. In modern times the penal reforms proposed by Jeremy Bentham, at this moment a favourite cause of English Whigs, are disinterested, and based on utility.[23] Mackintosh too identifies a polarity: he sees on the one hand a liberal programme of economic progress and the gradual amelioration of political institutions, and on the other political reaction, with behind it the blind panic of religious bigots. He remarks that the concern to uphold religion is a major motive impelling German philosophers of Kant's school. 'The system of *Kant* was one of the efforts of philosophy to expel the poison of scepticism which Hume had infused into it.'[24]

Mackintosh's assumption in 1813 that bigotry was obnoxious to all rational men would have been harder to make in the much more heated atmosphere of 1817. By then, religion was naturalised in England as a subject for literary controversy. Its champion was Coleridge, whose *Lay Sermons* of 1816 and 1817 were an attempt, increasingly polemical in tone,[25] to christianise the English upper classes.

In the second of his *Lay Sermons*, Coleridge explained that he had a new book ready for the press, which would illustrate more fully what a true philosophy, and a truly 'learned and philosophical public', might be like.[26] The book he was referring to, the *Biographia Literaria*, appeared in the same year, 1817, and it is indeed a version of his own life which stands representatively for that of the Christian intellectual. The first half of his book describes his discovery of the true, that is the religious, German philosophy. It leads up to Coleridge's celebrated account in chapters ix–xiii of the new German tradition, which, as has often been observed, has the peculiarity of turning Kant into an apologist for Christianity. There was not much in Coleridge of that disinterestedness which Peacock admired in his favourite eighteenth-century thinkers. Like Fichte before him and Carlyle after him, Coleridge was not concerned with exegesis of Kant's system, but used it as a weapon in an ideological battle against eighteenth-century materialism and scepticism:[27]

> he fell into a mere philosophy of faith. Light was in his heart, but as soon as he carried it into the intellect, it began to flicker in twilight and dusk. Coleridge stands again where most of the Kantians of his time landed. Like Hamilton he preaches 'learned ignorance'. Like Carlyle he preaches divine faith. And though he is more speculative than either, he became as they did, a

defender of orthodoxy, of resignation, a prophet of the end and failure of Reason.

No-one has more responsibility than Coleridge for the deep suspicion in which German philosophy was held by most of the English educated élite in the period, nor indeed for the fact that among the younger poets, only the exceptionally open-minded and linguistically able Shelley still felt the urge to approach the Germans for himself.

The second half of the *Biographia Literaria*, which is concerned with culture in a more literary sense, proceeds in large measure negatively. Coleridge has an ideal, philosophic, Christian poetry in mind, and among modern poets Wordsworth, in his loftiest vein, has sometimes written it. But he finds it easiest to isolate the true by identifying various manifestations of the false. English eighteenth-century poetry, in the over-cerebral and worldly tradition of Pope, is a false light. So is Francis Jeffrey, hailed universally as the period's greatest critic, with his 'French', that is, Enlightenment, techniques (ch. xxi). Most false of all, because it purports to be German, is the melodramatic, Gothic style of the 1790s, practised then by 'Monk' Lewis and more recently by C. R. Maturin, in his play *Bertram*: a subversive, irreligious and jacobinical mode (ch. xxiii).[28] But by far the most interesting of the false lights is the enterprise which Wordsworth rashly essayed in his youth, with which Coleridge himself was associated: the over-democratic *Lyrical Ballads*, aberrations because, with their simple style and themes from common life, they depart from the principle that great literature is necessarily conceived at the loftiest level, for an intellectual and social élite. Having demonstrated, in his rambling style, the wrongness of so much, Coleridge has produced for the current English cultural scene a polarity resembling that of the Schlegel brothers for Germany and for Europe. The 'true style' — that term once used by Enlightenment critics for a universal manner best exemplified in the classics — is now, in his terminology, Christian and Germanic, intense, introverted, difficult, and recluse.

Nightmare Abbey has two faces, negative and positive. Its negative, or satiric, face is the anatomy of a current intellectual scene swept by a craze for the Germanic. Seen from this angle, Peacock's satire re-examines the question of what German literature stands for, using Coleridge's own statements as the prime piece of evidence. *Nightmare Abbey* is indeed largely cast as a reply to Coleridge's opposition to the French tradition in his *Lay Sermons*, and his praise of the Germans in the *Biographia Literaria*.

As in *Melincourt*, some of the fun is at the expense of a style, and comes near to parody. Coleridge's praise of Kant, and his observation that he finds him *clear*, is unfortunately written in Coleridge's obscurest, most Germanic manner, and overloaded with his personal system of emphasis, which makes free use of italics and capitalisation:[29]

> The few passages that remained obscure to me after due efforts of thought, (as the chapter on *original apperception*), and the apparent contradictions which occur, I soon found were hints and insinuations referring to ideas which KANT either did not think it prudent to avow, or which he considered as consistently *left behind* in a pure analysis, not of human nature *in toto*, but of the speculative intellect alone. Here therefore he was constrained to commence at the point of *reflection*, or natural consciousness: while in his *moral* system he was permitted to assume a higher ground (the autonomy of the will) as a POSTULATE deducible from the unconditional command, or (in the technical language of his school) the categorical imperative, of the conscience.

Peacock sends this up nicely in the remarks of his Coleridgean sage, Mr Flosky, to Marionetta:[30]

> Subtleties! my dear Miss O'Carroll. I am sorry to find you participating in the vulgar error of the *reading public*, to whom an unusual collocation of words, involving a juxtaposition of antiperistatical ideas, immediately suggests the notion of hyperoxysophistical paradoxology.

But the more serious business in hand is Coleridge's analysis of contemporary intellectuals as falling into two camps, the sceptics and the believers. Mr Flosky sums up the arguments of the two *Lay Sermons*, catching, in a sardonic undertone, the pervasive élitism of their appeal:[31]

Sir, the great evil is, that there is too much commonplace light
in our moral and political literature; and light is a great enemy
to mystery, and mystery is a great friend to enthusiasm. Now
the enthusiasm for abstract truth is an exceedingly fine thing, as
long as the truth, which is the object of the enthusiasm, is so
completely abstract as to be altogether out of the reach of the
human faculties; and, in that sense, I have myself an enthusiasm
for truth, but in no other. ... Analytical reasoning is a base and
mechanical process, which takes to pieces and examines, bit by
bit, the rude material of knowledge, and extracts therefrom a few
hard and obstinate things called facts, every thing in the shape of
which I cordially hate. But synthetical reasoning, setting up as
its goal some unattainable abstraction, like an imaginary
quantity in algebra, and commencing its course with taking for
granted some two assertions which cannot be proved, from the
union of these two assumed truths produces a third assumption,
and so on in infinite series, to the unspeakable benefit of the
human intellect. The beauty of this process is, that at every step
it strikes out into two branches, in a compound ratio of
ramification; so that you are perfectly sure of losing your way,
and keeping your mind in perfect health, by the perpetual
exercise of an interminable quest; and for these reasons I have
christened my eldest son Emanuel Kant Flosky.

It is a beautifully executed passage, located in the actual text of
the *Lay Sermons*, echoing the ramifications of the Coleridgean
sentence, and at the same time placing the ideology. Peacock
allows Mr Flosky intellectual distinction, while noting his enmity
to the scientific spirit of free enquiry which is characteristic of the
Enlightenment. A Coleridgean might justly complain that it is a
misrepresentation to make Mr Flosky an obscurantist, like those
other idle and bigoted clerics, Dr Gaster of *Headlong Hall* and Mr
Portpipe of *Melincourt*. 'Think is not synonymous with believe –
for belief, in many most important particulars, results from the
total absence, the absolute negation of thought, and is thereby the
sane and orthodox condition of mind.'[32] But it does not belie the
Coleridge of the *Lay Sermons* to observe that in practical matters he
will be supine – as Mr Flosky is when Marionetta asks him for help
with Scythrop. 'I do not take any interest in any person or thing on

the face of the earth.'[33] Coleridge's intellectual alignment implies quietism, even more deliberately than Wordsworth's decision to retire to the Lakes.

In an influential article, Humphry House gives credit to Peacock for dealing in ideas rather than in personalities, and even claims that his main topic is one that sounds deeply interesting — 'the critique of Romanticism'. But House also feels that this critique must stand or fall by its handling of Coleridge, and that, with Coleridge, Peacock 'mis-hit completely. ... The joke is so monotonously directed against Coleridge's transcendental obscurity that we are forced to the conclusion that Peacock had never really tried to understand one of his works; he was writing too plainly from hearsay.'[34] In reality, the specific, textual fidelity of Peacock's method can be measured by the difference between Mr Flosky of *Nightmare Abbey* and Mr Mystic of *Melincourt*. In Mr Mystic Coleridge's specifically political stance was satirised, the reservations about free speech and the fear of the reading public that he expressed in the *Statesman's Manual*. In Mr Flosky it is Coleridge's recent reflections on culture, both philosophy and literature, that are examined, with the *Biographia Literaria* as the principal source. For example, chapter vi, where Mr Flosky is at his most eloquent, exploits Coleridge's actual diatribe against jacobin Germanists like Maturin, so slyly that Flosky ends up implying that one kind of German irrationalism is not, after all, so very different from another.[35] This time, where it is appropriate, Peacock also draws upon some other Coleridge texts: *The Friend*, and newspaper reports of his latest lectures,[36] as well as the *Lay Sermons* again. But the selection of detail is done discriminately. There is nothing in the Flosky portrait that does not have a bearing on the immediate cultural situation which is Peacock's subject, and on the use already being made by Coleridge for polemical purposes of an emotive complex of ideas surrounding the name of Germany. *Nightmare Abbey* is a satire, in the first place, on Coleridge's ideology, as Coleridge himself defined it in specific passages in two books; and in the second place, as we are about to see, on Coleridge's influence.

It follows, then, that Peacock has no intention of assailing Coleridge as a poet. Immediately after *Nightmare Abbey*, in the unfinished 'Essay on Fashionable Literature', Peacock began a defence of the newly-published *Christabel* which shows that he read

Coleridge's poetry with care and sympathy. When Peacock attacks Coleridge's obscurantism, he is referring to his current system, and certainly not libelling his versification. The stale jibe that Coleridge's poetry was unintelligible was directed against *Christabel* by (probably) Moore in the *Edinburgh Review*, and Peacock alludes to this attack with contempt. 'The poet's meaning is clear, and the critic who proclaims his own inability to comprehend it, comes forward like Dogberry, and gravely intreats to be written down an ass.'[37]

In its sense of intellectual relevance and its avoidance of personality the portrait of Flosky is a very rare conception in the polemical warfare of its day. It quite lacks the cutting personal innuendo of, say, Hazlitt in 'On my first acquaintance with Poets', or De Quincey in his *Reminiscences of the English Lake Poets*. But both these portraits belong to somewhat later years, and it is probably more salutary to contrast Peacock's approach to Coleridge in *Nightmare Abbey* with the liberal Hazlitt's during the period of Coleridge's most resounding engagement in political controversy. Hazlitt reviews Coleridge several times for the *Edinburgh*, the *Examiner* and the *Yellow Dwarf*, and each time lets his animus against the man and his views take precedence over other qualities in the work. His review of *Christabel* for the *Examiner* is a little less offensive than the *Edinburgh*'s, but not much less philistine.[38] On the *Lay Sermons* and the *Biographia Literaria*, Hazlitt brings up the charge of plagiarism.[39] In three successive numbers of the *Examiner* he ridicules Coleridge's backward-looking occlivity, under the title, 'Sketches of the History of the Good Old Times'.[40] His most vitriolic treatment probably appeared under the title 'Mr. Coleridge's Lectures' in the radical *Yellow Dwarf*. Coleridge had issued a prospectus for his course on Shakespeare, in which he had promised that topics of conversation would be furnished on all subjects except politics and religion. But an adulatory paragraph about the first lecture had appeared in the conservative paper, the *Courier*, which declared that Coleridge had spoken of Caliban 'as an original and caricature of Jacobinism, so fully illustrated at Paris during the French Revolution'. Hazlitt admitted that he had not attended any of Coleridge's lectures, but he was sufficiently provoked by the *Courier*'s short review to offer some general reflections on the lecturer and on his political career as an apostate jacobin:[41]

He says that Jacobins are envious people, – and that envious people, not being able to praise themselves openly, take an indirect method of doing this, by depreciating and secretly slandering others. Was it upon this principle that the reformed Jacobin, Mr. Coleridge ... took such pains, two years ago, to praise himself by depreciating and canting profound German mysticism against Mr. Maturin's successful tragedy of *Bertram*, which he proved, being himself in the secret, to be ultra-Jacobinism, and quite different in its philosophical and poetical tendency from his own sweet injured *Zapolya*, – the harbinger of Legitimacy and the Bourbons.

Hazlitt's charge of meanness and deviousness can be set against Peacock's less personal, more theoretical, and of course funnier account of the career of Mr Flosky:[42]

He had been in his youth an enthusiast for liberty, and had hailed the dawn of the French Revolution as the promise of a day that was to banish war and slavery, and every form of vice and misery, from the face of the earth. Because all this was not done, he deduced that nothing was done; and from this deduction, according to his system of logic, he drew a conclusion that worse than nothing was done; that the overthrow of the feudal fortresses of tyranny and superstition was the greatest calamity that had ever befallen mankind; and that their only hope now was to rake the rubbish together, and rebuild it without any of those loopholes by which the light had originally crept in. To qualify himself for a coadjutor in this laudable task, he plunged into the central opacity of Kantian metaphysics, and lay *perdu* several years in transcendental darkness, till the common daylight of common sense became intolerable to his eyes. He called the sun an *ignis fatuus*; and exhorted all who would listen to his friendly voice, which were about as many as called 'God save King Richard', to shelter themselves from its delusive radiance in the obscure haunt of Old Philosophy. This word Old had great charms for him. The good old times were always on his lips; meaning the days when polemic theology was in its prime, and rival prelates beat the drum ecclesiastic with Herculean vigour, till the one wound up his series of syllogisms with the very orthodox conclusion of roasting the other.

Peacock ridicules the creed, conservatism, while Hazlitt sneers at Coleridge the man.

If *Nightmare Abbey*'s assessment of Coleridge as the leader of a trend towards the subjective and emotional had been made later – as Mill's was, in his celebrated essays on Bentham and Coleridge, where he describes them as 'the two great seminal minds of England in their age'[43] – Peacock's perspicuity in noting Coleridge's centrality might be less impressive. Within the next generation, the trend he discerns manifests itself in national life for all to see – the Oxford Movement in the church, the Young England movement in the Tory party, the prose ardours of Carlyle and the poetic ardours of Tennyson. There was nothing specially observant between 1816 and 1818 in noticing the literary rage for indulging gloom and misanthropy: those who were not attacking it were generally busy imitating it.[44] It was much more usual at that time, however, to blame Byron, and especially the spectacular misanthropy of Canto III of *Childe Harold* (1816). But Byron was a portent: the most obvious feature of the literary scene, rather than a thinker, and still less a religious or reactionary one. Peacock, with his historical, generalizing tendency, is less interested in the symptom than in the cause, and his satire concerns itself with the wider movement, for which Coleridge is the spokesman. The first wave of German Romanticism exalts a deliberately formalistic religion, and is associated politically with counter-revolution. What is superficially a question of literary fashion is also, and more importantly, a matter of ideology.

The omnipresence of Flosky, and its significance, has been missed by commentators on *Nightmare Abbey*. Peacock carefully associates him, as a mentor or as an intellectual ally, with a varied group of other writers (and readers), many of them supposed radicals, but all influenced by the German style. Flosky is made Scythrop's best friend.[45] He helps to interpret and to generalize the views of *Nightmare Abbey*'s representative fashionable reader, Mr Listless, in chapter vi,[46] and of its most representative writer, Mr Cypress (a Byron-figure) in chapter xi. With Byron, as with Coleridge, *Nightmare Abbey* is selective, and topical. At the outset of his career, with the first two Cantos of *Childe Harold* in 1812, Byron was certainly thought of as a liberal poet, the campaigner for Spanish and Greek independence. Latterly, however, his poems had become more solipsistic. It was possible to take *The Giaour* or *The Corsair* as idealising the man of action in a corrupt Mediterranean world, and thus still having something to do with independence movements. But there could be no mistaking Byron's growing tendency to dwell on the inner intensities of these heroes: hence Peacock's side-glance at *The Corsair* ('Paul Jones, an amiable enthusiast – disappointed in his affections – turns pirate from ennui and magnanimity – cuts various masculine throats, wins various feminine hearts – is hanged at the yard-arm'),[47] and his sustained mimicry of the cosmic glooms of the fourth Canto of *Childe Harold*.[48] Other reviewers, such as Scott, had rebuked Byron for the emotional self-indulgence of Cantos III and IV, without giving Peacock's political objection to it. Byron, as a peer, with a seat in the House of Lords, has potential influence in his country's affairs. Instead he chooses to go abroad, to absorb himself in private miseries, and to tell the world about very little else. 'Sir, I have quarrelled with my wife, and a man who has quarrelled with his wife is absolved from all duty to his country.'[49] It is a way of behaving that delights Flosky, who knows very well which political cause it is likely to benefit. Indeed, Flosky, conservatism's theorist, is gratified to see how on every side fashion is playing into his hands:[50]

> let society only give fair play at one and the same time, as I
> flatter myself it is inclined to do, to your [Cypress's] system of
> morals, and my system of metaphysics, and Scythrop's system
> of politics, and Mr. Listless's system of manners, and Mr.
> Toobad's system of religion, and the result will be as fine a
> mental chaos as even the immortal Kant himself could ever have
> hoped to see; in the prospect of which I rejoice.

If at first sight it is surprising to see the outstanding radical literary men of their generation, Byron and Shelley, thus linked with Coleridge, it is even more unexpected to find his fictional equivalent cordially associating himself with William Godwin, the leading English radical philosopher of the revolutionary era. There is much more about Godwin in *Nightmare Abbey* than first meets the eye: it is hard, in fact, to resist the thought that, though Coleridge's ideas are intellectually the chief target, Peacock may actually have picked up his pen under the influence of an irritation nearer home. Godwin's new novel *Mandeville* (the *Devilman* of *Nightmare Abbey*)[51] arrived in the Shelley household, where Peacock was a daily visitor, on 1 December 1817.[52] *Nightmare Abbey* was written between April and June 1818. It surely owes to the immediate example of *Mandeville* its novelistic qualities, the narrative line and concentration which seem so distinct from the technique of Peacock's other satires. The opening of *Nightmare Abbey* comes close to actual burlesque of *Mandeville*, for Godwin had chosen a setting for his misanthropic hero that was obviously too much for Peacock's sense of humour. Mandeville's uncle and guardian had (like Scythrop's father, Mr Glowry) been disappointed in a woman in his youth, with the result that – though a wealthy man, with no fewer than five other mansions – he chose to live in the most gloomy spot available to him:[53]

> The sound of the dashing waters was eternal, and seemed calculated to inspire sobriety, and almost gloom, in the soul of everyone who dwelt within the reach of its influence. ... Indeed it was one wing only that was not tenanted, and that imperfectly: the central and the other wing had long been resigned to the owls and the bitterns.

Immediately outside was an overgrown courtyard, a vast expanse of marshland, and on three sides the sea. The house was connected with the rest of the world only by 'a rough, sandy and incommodious road'. All these details are duly enlisted in the description of Nightmare Abbey. Since Godwin does nothing by halves, he adds that 'a tree was hardly to be found for miles' and that the nearest market town was fully seventeen miles away.[54] As if all this were not enough, Godwin fleetingly contemplates the possibility that there might be something comic in the desolation he describes – only to dismiss the idea, and obligingly leave it to Peacock:[55]

> The entire household, as always happens to a certain degree in the mansion of an opulent country-gentleman, were moulded after the fashion of their master. ... To an observer of a satirical and biting vein, which was not my case, it would have appeared a ludicrous spectacle to see how every one, from the steward down to the scullion, seemed to ape the manners of the master.

They had all and severally a solemn countenance, and a slow
and measured step.

Peacock's Mr Glowry chooses his servants for a long face or a
dismal name, though in the case of Diggory Deathshead the two
criteria turn out to be disastrously at odds. But Peacock's concern
with Godwin is also more serious than parody. Perhaps he never
admired him much, even as the uncompromised anarchist of the
period of *Political Justice*: one is led to suspect some reservations by
Headlong Hall, and *Nightmare Abbey* appears to contain at least one
unflattering allusion to *Caleb Williams*.[56] More fundamental than
any of this, Peacock evidently deplores the contemporary Godwin,
and the philosophy emanating from *Mandeville*. For that novel can
certainly be read as conveying the most rigid determinism, almost
amounting to fatalism, an insistence – which *Political Justice* at least
tries to qualify – that environment determines character to an
irremediable degree.[57] The reader is led to believe that Mandeville
simply cannot help becoming envious, malignant and solitary,
crazily possessive of his sister, and vindictively jealous of the man
she loves. He is just such a glorified bad man as both Peacock and,
in reality, Coleridge deprecate. The book as a whole expresses the
negativism, the hopeless withdrawal, not only from the public
scene, but from command of oneself, which was how Peacock
thought contemporary quietism manifested itself in characterisation in the drama and the novel.

Unlike Wordsworth and Coleridge, Godwin could not be
charged with apostasy. His courage in sticking to unpopular
opinions, and as a result enduring semi-ostracism, was commented
upon in his lifetime.[58] But, though he did not join the *Quarterly*
group, neither did Godwin cleave to the dour anarchism of *Political
Justice*. Many of his amendments to his earlier statements are
philosophical, and easy to justify; others reflect, no doubt often
unconsciously, the terrible pressure society puts on its intellectual
nay-sayers. Godwin was courageous, but he was also suggestible.
He never recanted, and his first novel after the revolutionary
decade, *Fleetwood* (1805), still contains some social criticism; but it
is far more introspective than his earlier work, and its visions of
happiness are domestic, not social. Godwin becomes plagued,
understandably in view of his experiences, with a near-neurotic
sense of personal isolation. He seems to have communicated it

(unless her rather loveless upbringing is wholly to blame) to his daughter Mary. But Mary had also, together with Shelley and Peacock, developed the intellectual case against solipsism, which all three saw as the central moral tendency of the literary school to which they were opposed. She conveys disapproval when a character like Frankenstein voluntarily chooses a way of life that is neither affectionate nor useful;[59] Godwin appears merely resigned when his hero does the same. A novelist who in *Caleb Williams* had been outer-directed was now inner-directed. In practical terms, the influence Godwin once wielded in favour of political change was over. It is a sign that Peacock's preferences are still for activism, that he includes *Mandeville* in the targets of his satire, and suggests that its manner links it with intentionally conservative literature. Flosky certainly looks upon the appearance of the novel called *Devilman* with special satisfaction. 'Modern literature is a north-east wind — a blight of the human soul. I take credit to myself for having helped to make it so.'[60]

So much, then, for *Nightmare Abbey*'s negative satire, its anatomy of a contemporary rage for literary introspection and misanthropy, which it traces back to a conservative religious ideology. As in *Melincourt*, the satiric survey of contemporary intellectuals is countered by an allegorised story which advances, however notionally, the ideal solution. The 'story' in *Nightmare Abbey* is tighter than before, a fact which marks Peacock's steady advance in technique since he began with *Headlong Hall*. Then, the book's three elements — dialogue, anatomy, still residual romantic plot — were kept severely distinct. In *Melincourt* all three remain discernible, but the romance of Anthelia's challenge and Forester's quest overlies and begins to blur the clear-cut distinctions. *Rhododaphne*, intervening, is an organic narrative without extraneous comment, in which meanings are conveyed by the sequence of choices offered to the characters. Similarly, in *Nightmare Abbey*, the plot, Scythrop's story, fills up the framework of the book. Peacock has taken a decisive step towards making his action coherent, his narrative the vehicle of his meaning. The dialogues now no longer stand outside the action, as either the dominant medium (*Headlong Hall*) or a choric commentary (*Melincourt*). They are naturalised, conversations that seem to arise between the characters as they might in a novel, or in life.

As in *Rhododaphne*, everything turns on the decisions to be taken by the hero. In resembling Anthemion, and seeming a fallible human being rather than a notional idealist or champion of a philosophical attitude, Scythrop departs from the precedents of Escot and Forester. The character he most resembles is perhaps the hero of Shelley's *Alastor*, another young writer at the outset of his career, and in the grip of a wrong idea of how to be a poet. But where Shelley's hero in 1815 is implicitly misled by the example and teaching of Wordsworth, Peacock's Scythrop is unmistakably a Coleridgean. He is a thorough-going Germanist – though Peacock teases Coleridge by making him also a radical incendiary, and an addict, indiscriminately, of the German writing Coleridge actually approved, and of the earlier, jacobin vein he now denounced. Scythrop's obsession with secret tribunals and bands of Illuminati conspiring to bring about revolution probably goes back to Marquis Grosse's *Genius*, translated into English in 1796 as *Horrid Mysteries*, though allusions to secret societies are too common for one source to be picked out with certainty. The 'venerable eleutherarchs' who disturb his dreams originate in the romance of his friend T. J. Hogg, the *Memoirs of Prince Alexy Haimatoff*.[61] His mystical deductions about the seven readers who buy his book – 'they shall be the seven golden candlesticks with which I will illuminate the world'[62] – echo the first chapter of the Book of Revelations, that favourite reading-matter of Mr Toobad and of the German Higher Critics. Scythrop's proposal of the method by which he and Marionetta should plight their troth is another borrowing from *Horrid Mysteries* – 'Let us each open a vein in the other's arm, mix our blood in a bowl, and drink it as a sacrament of love.'[63] Celinda, the dark lady who mysteriously appears at the castle, is the double of Geraldine in *Christabel*. The name she adopts comes from Goethe's play, *Stella*, the sliding panel behind which she hides perhaps from Schiller's *Ghost-Seer*. The climax of the plot, Scythrop's proposed suicide, certainly recalls one of the earliest and still one of the most famous examples of German sentimental individualism, Goethe's *Sorrows of Young Werther*. In short, Scythrop's career is an ingenious anthology of German literature, and hence a humorous counter-proposition, in narrative form, to Coleridge's solemn account in the *Biographia Literaria*.

Scythrop is always viewed as a caricature of Shelley, which has led to the hypothesis — surely deeply mistaken — that the two girls he loves are Shelley's successive wives, Harriet Westbrook and Mary Godwin. The reader used to novels is also tempted to take his amorous adventures more or less at face value, as a story. But the book is far more ironic and allusive than either of these premises allows, and its meaning is not conveyed so simply through Scythrop's experience as its novelettish form at first suggests. As always in Peacock's work, the structure is classically disciplined and expressive. Both in length and in shape, *Nightmare Abbey* resembles *Headlong Hall* rather than *Melincourt*. Like the first of the satires, it has fifteen chapters, so that the middle one, the eighth, has a special, central significance. In this case, it marks the arrival at Nightmare Abbey of the second heroine, Celinda or Stella, and thus heralds a second movement distinct from, though often echoing, the first.

While Marionetta is Scythrop's beloved in the first half, she is succeeded by Stella in the second. Each heroine dominates her own half of the book, and is supported by an appropriate set of characters and topics of conversation. Apart from Marionetta herself, the most representative character in the first half is the fashionable, trivial reader Mr Listless, whose mindless pursuit of dismal reading merely because it is *à la mode* is ably interpreted by the ubiquitous Mr Flosky.[64] The chapters in which Mr Listless has the limelight, the fifth and part of the sixth, are balanced in the second half by the eleventh, in which the other representative character, Mr Cypress the poet, expounds his misanthropy, to be annotated, once more, by Mr Flosky. These are thus key chapters, in which the meaning of the apparently confined burlesque is enlarged to take in the general reading public, and its favourite writers.

The symmetry of the two parts encourages a second look at the two heroines, whose roles are thus thrown into relief. Though they have always been connected with Shelley's two wives, more sensitive critics have expressed some uneasiness at the attribution.[65] It seems intolerably vulgar of Peacock, and out of character for so private a man, if he really thought Marionetta might be taken for Shelley's first wife Harriet, who had drowned herself less than two years earlier. In fact, Scythrop's indecision between the girls is probably meant for something much more in keeping, a further literary allusion.

Who, or what, is Marionetta? A literary idea, surely: not a person, but a personification. Her first name, signifying puppet, alludes to Mary Wollstonecraft's description of fashionable women as mere dolls; her surname alludes to her favourite art-form, the song. 'Her conversation was sprightly, but always on subjects light in their nature and limited in their interest: for moral sympathies, in any general sense, had no place in her mind.'[66] Marionetta represents light literature, the literature of pure amusement, that keeps the man of fashion awake during a long evening in the country, or helps him to do battle with Time in the mornings in town.[67] Moore's songs, and perhaps Leigh Hunt's, all favour and prettiness, are recaptured in her manner, and archly parodied in her own 'Why are thy looks so blank, grey friar?' As the perennial favourite of those who really do not want to think, she ends up, appropriately, married to Mr Listless.

Stella, who is eventually to be well matched with Mr Flosky, represents the other prevailing style, which to superficial appearances is so much more weighty and altruistic – though Peacock thinks it ultimately as meretricious, as servile and evasive, as the simple literature of entertainment. Stella's half of the book is much more densely packed with literary allusion and burlesque, as befits the more intellectual and pretentious of the two girls. For Marionetta is in a sense any pleasing pastime, a temptation to which the whole public (as is evidenced by Mr Listless) is equally exposed. Stella, the highbrow, the enthusiast, touches Scythrop's special weakness.

The elegance of the structure and the degree of stylisation point to a literary allusion that will not seem far-fetched to those who know *Melincourt*. At first sight, Scythrop's hesitation between the two girls seems designed for nothing beyond a send-up of the familiar Romantic triangle, as it occurs for example in *La Nouvelle Héloise, Werther, Stella,* and *Bertram*. But behind this is a more serious frame of reference. Just as he clinches his case in *Melincourt* by alluding to Milton, Peacock does so here. Scythrop is the young writer on the threshold of his career, pausing between two courses, *L'Allegro* and *Il Penseroso*.[68] But in the early nineteenth century, the poet's situation is a very different one from Milton's. The comparison works with a touch of savagery that greatly deepens *Nightmare Abbey*'s significance. For Milton, either path is a possible one, worthy of a great poet. For Scythrop, either would be pandering to the public, or leaving Mr Flosky to have it all his own way. It hardly matters that Scythrop loses both girls, since the choice between them is not really a choice at all.

The satire does not deal in biographical terms with Shelley, still less with the Shelley household, but the key to its significance lies in Peacock's intellectual relationship with his friend. Shelley first heard of the planned 'Night Mare Abbey' in a letter that reached Milan on 20 April 1818, but from the first he clearly recognised the full potential of the theme.[69] The gestation period had been the year when they were seeing each other almost daily, and intellectually had been most closely in accord. In the coach in which he crossed France, Shelley took with him to read A. W. Schlegel's *Dramatic Art and Literature*, which represents the polarity between the literature of the South and the North, classical and romantic, in terms which Shelley would perhaps not much have dissented from.

> The mental culture of the Greeks was a finished education in the school of Nature. ... The whole of their art and poetry is the expression of a consciousness of this harmony of all their faculties. They invented the poetry of joy. Their religion was the deification of the powers of nature and of the earthly life.

It was a social, extrovert religion, compared with the intense inwardness of the post-classical and Christian North: 'The stern nature of the North drives man back within himself; and what is lost in the free sportive development of the senses, must, in noble dispositions, be compensated by earnestness of mind.'[70] But Shelley disagreed with Schlegel, and agreed with Peacock, in preferring, on these terms, the literature of the South. In his preface to *Laon and Cythna* of the previous autumn, he had condemned the exaggerated pessimism that followed 'the first reverses of hope in the progress of French liberty':

> Hence gloom and misanthropy have become the characteristics of the age in which we live, the solace of a disappointment that unconsciously finds relief only in the wilful exaggeration of its own despair. This influence has tainted the literature of the age

with the hopelessness of the minds from which it flows.
Metaphysics, and enquiries into moral and political science,
have become little else than vain attempts to revive exploded
superstitions, or sophisms like those of Mr. Malthus, calculated
to lull the oppressors of mankind into a security of everlasting
triumph. Our works of fiction and poetry have been
overshadowed by the same infectious gloom.

In the December of 1817 Shelley received from his father-in-
law William Godwin the copy of *Mandeville*, and though he was
naturally obliged to write politely to the author, it is interesting
that the passage he singles out for praise − Henrietta's speech − is
actually an argument against the misanthropy of the hero, her
brother, in favour of love.[71] When not addressing the author,
Shelley placed *Mandeville* firmly in the category *Nightmare Abbey*
was to satirise: to Byron he writes of it as 'a Satanic likeness of
Childe Harold the first'.[72] And *that* would not be meant or taken
for a compliment, since Shelley had already written to Byron to
complain of the tone of his *Manfred*.[73] Perhaps the remonstrance
was effective: Byron not only turned to comedy, with *Beppo* and
Don Juan, but apparently made a personal gesture which sounds
like a humorous surrender to Shelley's denunciations of gloom.
Shelley had in effect been guardian of Byron's baby daughter by
Claire Clairmont, hitherto known as Alba and, in the same letter
that described *Mandeville*, he asked Byron if he had any preference
how his daughter should be christened. Since the baby was given a
different name in the new year, there is a presumption that it was
Byron's choice, and that it conveys his verdict on the dispute
concerning the two cultures: Allegra.

Shelley obviously looked forward to the book that evolved
during the summer into *Nightmare Abbey*. From Italy he supplied
Peacock with a useful epigraph, from Ben Jonson, and with
encouragement − 'I hope you have given the enemy no quarter.
Remember, it is a sacred war.'[74] But when he eventually got the
book to read, it seems to have taken him by surprise. Perhaps he
had been expecting a hero like Forester, a champion on the side of
light. Scythrop has attributes which amplify his character in a
different direction. He is, of course, tainted with literary corruption
(in ways which touch, very lightly and amusingly, on Shelley's
own early penchant for the Gothic). He has equally extravagant

political tastes, for conspiracy and revolutionary action for its own
sake, no matter how impractical, or even potentially mischievous.
Shelley, who in his youth had planned a secret society of like-
minded liberals,[75] rebuked his friend goodnaturedly:[76]

> I suppose the moral is contained in what Falstaff says *'For Gods
> sake talk like a man of this world'* and yet looking deeper into it, is
> not the misdirected enthusiasm of Scythrop what J[esus] C[hrist]
> calls the salt of the earth?

Not the least of *Nightmare Abbey*'s fascinations is the sense it
conveys of a real-life dialogue between two liberal writers, wittily
modulated into art. Peacock has, as usual, a text on which to
ground his character's ideas and, in this case, behaviour. Scythrop's
dominant characteristic, his 'passion for reforming the world', is
the subject of a chapter in Robert Forsyth's *Principles of Moral
Science* (1805), a book which Peacock first read in 1809. Though
Forsyth is liberal in his politics, and even potentially practical,[77] the
aspect of his discussion which evidently appeals to Peacock is that
he is firmly opposed to revolutionary extremism.

Revolution itself is, according to Forsyth's broad historical
account, natural and inevitable. Men act out of self-interest, so
that 'disorders accumulate to an alarming extent, and the moral
order of the world is totally deranged';[78] until, by a natural process
of reaction, a passion for change builds up in the best and deepest-
thinking men. This is an interesting account of a natural cycle
which incorporates the revolutionary and destructive, those
elements which Burke had tried to depict as profoundly *un*natural.
But Forsyth acknowledges a danger. Experience (especially painful,
recent experience) seems to show that Nature's swings of the
pendulum are sometimes over-violent; and that the would-be
reformer may become his own worst enemy, or the enemy of the
oppressed masses he wants to help, or an obstacle in the path of his
own reforms:[79]

> The degree in which it [the passion for reforming the world] at
> last fills the whole memory and thoughts, and the vehemence to
> which it gradually rises, prevent his perceiving that any means
> are extravagant or irrational which have the appearance of
> tending to promote its success. ... The danger is rather increased
> than diminished by the circumstance, that the most intelligent,

accomplished, and energetic minds, are most apt to be seized by
this passion. It is even apt to increase in retirement and amidst
the pursuits of science; because temporary solitude and reflection
are favourable to the strong discernment of what exalts and
degrades our nature. ...

In times of public contention or alarm, when this passion is
most apt to be excited, it is the duty of a virtuous man to
recollect often, that human affairs are ... so contrived, that their
amelioration is slow and progressive, and that great good is
never suddenly or violently accomplished. It is also his duty to
render the passion we have now described unnecessary in his
own mind, by acquiring that self-command which, on every
occasion, may enable him to do his duty to society, without
suffering himself either to be so much inflamed by opposition, or
so much blinded by attachment to particular projects or notions,
as to forget that force is not reason, that the edge of the sword
introduces no light into the human mind, and that the certain
and immediate commission of sanguinary actions can seldom be
balanced by the doubtful prospect of future good.

Scythrop *is* one of the salt of the earth, then, but he also exhibits the
dangers of a radical type. Altruism, and solitariness, have made
him impractical, and led him to adopt extravagant means. He is
flirting with violence, which is almost always counter-productive.
It is Forsyth's chapter, not the actual man Shelley, which supplies
the mould for Scythrop, but this does not lead to impersonality in
Nightmare Abbey, nor divorce it from the real world of Shelley and
Peacock's friendly disputation. There evidently was a difference of
temper between them, which made Peacock advocate common
sense and gradual, reformist methods, while Shelley, who could
when he wished talk like a man of this world,[80] also acknowledged
a temperamental preference for the revolutionary's imaginative
gesture. When Shelley 'took to himself the character of Scythrop',[81]
he did so not because he sportingly recognised his own absurdities,
least of all his habit of falling in love with new women, but because
he did basically identify with Scythrop's extremism. His
reservations about *Nightmare Abbey*, compared with *Melincourt*,
surely relate to his inability, this time, fully to approve of Peacock's
position. Goodhumouredly, but also defensively, he accepted in the
preface to *Prometheus Unbound* (written autumn 1819) that his

notion of being a radical differed from either Forsyth's or Peacock's:

> Let this opportunity be conceded to me of acknowledging that I have, what a Scotch philosopher characteristically terms, 'a passion for reforming the world': what passion incited him to write and publish his book, he omits to explain. For my part, I had rather be damned with Plato and Lord Bacon, than go to heaven with Paley and Malthus. But it is a mistake to suppose that I dedicate my poetical compositions solely to the direct enforcement of reform, or that I consider them in any degree as containing a reasoned system on the theory of human life. Didactic poetry is my abhorrence.

The challenge apparently directed at Forsyth, what passion incited *him* to publish, seems in truth meant for Peacock. Again, though it is not clear that he is addressing a friend (like Peacock, Shelley observes reticence in print when personal relationships are touched on), the observations on didacticism seem to develop a point implicit in *Nightmare Abbey*. When all their exchanges, including the critical essays, are taken into account, it seems likely that Shelley felt Peacock was asking him to be too crudely and simply political, 'like a man of this world'. Shelley would not sympathise with Peacock's regard for moderation merely because it was likely to be practically effective, nor with so firm a premium put on the ability to communicate with a politically significant number of readers. In his Preface, he goes on to promise that 'the advocates of injustice and superstition' *will* find him a revolutionary; but his methods will remain deliberately indirect and imaginative, until he is ready to attempt the 'reasoned system' which Peacock demands of him. Peacock is thus wrong to have read his poems so literally, as political statements; they are designed to convey a revolutionary meaning only allusively, to 'the highly refined imagination of the more select classes of poetical readers'.

The tendency of good art to be difficult was, of course, an intractable problem for the radical side. Severely though they criticised Coleridge for advocating élitism, earnestly though they censured one another for not appealing to the masses, cultural and social conditions were in reality driving both writers into a subtlety which relatively few of the population could be expected to penetrate. If Peacock whole-heartedly meant what he said about clarity, he would not have been so complicated in *Nightmare Abbey* about his own positive beliefs. To be sure, he correctly goes through the motions of putting the classical and utilitarian case. In the first half of the satire, Mr Listless, who is pleased by the lightest kind of literature (Marionetta's), but by anything else fashionable too, finds himself opposed by the intellectual who does not stand for literature at all, the scientist Mr Asturias. Asturias's quest for a mermaid is as extravagant a foible as any in Peacock's satire;[82] but his way of life, his belief in truth and in its efficacy for the public at large, is a positive intellectual ideal:[83]

> a morbid, withering, deadly, antisocial sirocco, loaded with moral and political despair, breathes through all the groves and valleys of the modern Parnassus; while science moves on in the calm dignity of its course, affording to youth delights equally pure and vivid – to maturity, calm and grateful occupation – to old age, the most pleasing recollections and inexhaustible materials of agreeable and salutary reflection; and, while its votary enjoys the disinterested pleasure of enlarging the intellect and increasing the comforts of society, he is himself independent of the caprices of human intercourse and the accidents of human fortune.

Though there is every reason to suppose that Peacock approves of this type of Epicureanism, he does not further tip the scales to lend support of an overt didactic kind to this particular character. Here, Mr Asturias is seconded by Mr Hilary. Later in the book, their respective roles are reversed: it is Mr Hilary, as the advocate of Greek wholeness, sweetness and light, who opposes the self-absorption and misanthropy of modern literature,[84] Mr Asturias who plays a secondary role, that of usefully fishing Mr Toobad out of the moat.

However, Peacock is clearly aware that these two stilted characters are inadequate to convey his positives. He has the unfunny Mr Hilary helped out by Mr Toobad, who gives a much more memorable account of the degeneracy of modern times:[85]

> Where is the manifestation of our light? ... What do we see by it which our ancestors saw not, and which at the same time is

worth seeing? We see a hundred men hanged, where they saw one. We see five hundred transported, where they saw one. We see five thousand in the workhouse, where they saw one. We see scores of Bible Societies, where they saw none. We see paper, where they saw gold. We see men in stays, where they saw men in armour. We see painted faces, where they saw healthy ones. We see children perishing in manufactories, where they saw them flourishing in the fields. We see prisons, where they saw castles. We see masters, where they saw representatives. In short, they saw true men, where we see false knaves. They saw Milton, and we see Mr. Sackbut.

It seems, on the face of it, odd that Mr Hilary is not more persuasive in his arguments in favour of Greece. Moreover, Marionetta's kind of cheerful literature seems to cast some doubt on the general truth of some of his principles. But, as in Shelley's case, so in Peacock's: what is lost in polemical clarity is gained in artistic refinement. Peacock is not really giving away his position, but choosing a subtler vehicle for it. He has other resources, and relies neither upon the empathetic character, nor upon the crude spokesman for the side of light, to carry his point with the reader. A neat and unexpected turn in the plot gives a new, ultimately decisive extension to the debate: no longer the Germanists' more familiar formulations, South v. North, or Classic v. Romantic, but a version dear to Peacock's own heart, and freshly a topic of dispute with Shelley, the merit of Comedy as opposed to Tragedy.

After their agreement on the matter of classicism, and after Shelley's public and private denunciations of gloom, Peacock obviously thought that Shelley's position on this question was amusingly compromised. Peacock, having got him with some difficulty to the theatre at all, had quite failed to give him a taste for comedy:[86]

[Shelley] had a prejudice against theatres which I took some pains to overcome. I induced him one evening to accompany me to a representation of *The School for Scandal*. When, after the scenes which exhibited Charles Surface in his jollity, the scene returned, in the fourth act, to Joseph's library, Shelley said to me − 'I see the purpose of this comedy. It is to associate virtue with bottles and glasses, and villany with books.' I had great difficulty to make him stay to the end. He often talked of 'the withering and perverting spirit of comedy'. I do not think he ever went to another. ...

In the season of 1817, I persuaded him to accompany me to the opera. The performance was *Don Giovanni*. Before it commenced he asked me if the opera was comic or tragic. I said it was composite, – more comedy than tragedy. ...

From this time till he finally left England he was an assiduous frequenter of the Italian Opera. He delighted in the music of Mozart, and especially in the *Nozze di Figaro*, which was performed several times in the early part of 1818.

With the exception of *Fazio*, I do not remember his having been pleased with any performance at an English theatre. Indeed I do not remember his having been present at any but the two above mentioned. I tried in vain to reconcile him to comedy.

It was in fact worse than this. After Shelley went with Peacock in February 1818 to see H. H. Milman's *Fazio*, a recent pastiche in the most blood-boltered jacobean manner, he was actually fired to write a tragedy himself. It was in preparation for this task that he was studying the book from, as it were, the enemy's heartland – Schlegel on the Drama. Peacock had so far quite failed in life to persuade his friend to adopt what he saw as, in present circumstances, the more essentially classical form, that of comedy. But at least he had the inspiration which enabled comedy to triumph on the page.

Within the world of *Nightmare Abbey*, which is meant to sketch the contemporary English cultural scene, the prevailing taste of most characters is for tragedy, and no sprightliness of Marionetta's, or argument by Mr Hilary, does much to change anyone's mind. However, with the exposure of the ghost as a sleep-walking servant, and the accidental ducking of Mr Toobad, it begins to seem as though real life, as opposed to the characters' prepossessions, is taking an irresistibly comic turn. In this way Peacock prepares the way for his adroit coup, the set-piece dénouement in the classic stage manner which decisively signals the victory of comedy.

The discovery of Stella in Scythrop's tower not only entangles all the plot's threads in the time-honoured manner, it is even constructed according to the best stage principles. It begins with Mr

Glowry eavesdropping outside the door on the two lovers, develops into a sequence in which it is Stella who overhears the father and son, builds up into a fine dramatic confusion as the entire cast crowds on to the stage, and eventually leaves Scythrop in soliloquy, proclaiming total despair. So aware is Peacock of the theatrical potential that at one stage he is conducting two dramas simultaneously. Scythrop desperately improvises a play in the high-flown sentimental Germanic style, while he and his father are actually involved in a comedy of a homelier kind.

The immediate allusion is presumably to the very play Peacock and Shelley attended together, Sheridan's *School for Scandal*, and indeed to the very scene in Joseph's library which made Shelley so indignant, where Lady Teazle is discovered behind the screen. But Peacock's dénouement is equally in the spirit of the comic artist whom even Shelley venerated — Mozart. Shelley's favourite, *The Marriage of Figaro*, has the fast-moving light and lively complications of *The School for Scandal*; based as it is on Beaumarchais's radical play, it has a serious substratum of meaning; above all, its mode of expression is Mozart's music, dazzling, polished, complete. Peacock used a very significant argument when, taking a speech of Fletcher's as an example, he tried once more to reconcile Shelley to comedy — 'You must admit the fineness of the expression.'[87] Mozart's operas epitomize Peacock's view of what art should be, and it is fine.

One critic has made large claims for Peacock's self-alignment, as an artist, with Mozart. Paulina June Salz proposes that, at its most thorough-going, Peacock's technique is an attempt 'to express, through the behavior of his characters, a musical ensemble'.[88] 'He uses musical forms in the structures of his plots and applies tone and rhythm both internally and externally in the verbal style.'[89]

Earlier critics noticed some aspects of Peacock's pervasive musicality. Edmund Wilson, for example, detected an atmosphere, a harmony of style, which he equated, specifically, with the music of Mozart. 'It all makes a delicious music, at the same time sober and gay, in which words fall like notes from a flute.'[90] A. H. Able had a further useful insight when he saw how consistently in Peacock the part is subordinated to the whole:[91]

As the line of argument passes from one to the other of them, ...

their contradictory points of view are shown to be
complementary, for each is a segment of truth made
contributory to a rounded whole. Truth is discovered on all
sides, although the wranglers themselves are unaware of it; all
parties are justified, while none is accredited. ... The characters
themselves are really the threads of an argument, logical
partitions of a subject, the pros and cons of debate.

Miss Salz synthesises the positions of these two earlier critics,
and describes a form wholly governed by a musical principle:[92]

What Able missed and Wilson perceived was that Peacock was
aiming not merely to create a whole idea but also to create an
audi[b]le texture in the prose itself. It is in this purpose that the
influence of operatic practice is evident. Each character
maintains his thread of argument, speaking his piece and
allowing the others to speak without his thread's being changed.
The separate strands of all the characters, woven together, create
a true whole. Similarly, in a vocal ensemble, particularly in
contrapuntal music, each voice sings its own melody, the less
important melodies are subordinated to the more important
ones, but each is complete in itself. One may be in dissonance
with another but the weaving together of these separate melodies
... creates a harmonious whole. And the factor of dissonance is
imperative; if the melodies were in constantly harmonious
relation with each other the effect would soon become cloying
and boring. Dissonance is needed to create interest and provide
contrast; whenever dissonance resolves into harmony there is
created a feeling of relaxation and rightness.

Now this version, expressed in quite these terms, must be an
exaggeration. A comedy which aspires quite so severely to the
condition of music is not (as Peacock's surely is) the radical comedy
of opinion. Meaning, in this description, seems hardly allowed for
at all. Nor is developing technique between one satire and another.
In fact, Peacock's first two satires do not seem greatly indebted to
music, and there is no reason why they should be: they precede the
vogue for Italian opera in which, after 1817, Peacock becomes
absorbed. It is the 'prose' device of the philosophic dialogue – rather
than the duet, quartet or ensemble – which dominates the first two
satires, controlling their form and conveying much of their

meaning. The last two satires, *Crotchet Castle* and *Gryll Grange*, will also employ dissonance in entirely distinctive ways, according to the satirical point Peacock wants.[93] But *Nightmare Abbey* really does make use of Mozartian opera, texturally as well as formally: 'dissonance' is woven into harmony. And the technical discovery of music, working on both these levels, is of great importance in Peacock's art, for it determines the way he is henceforth to go — away from the naturalistic effects sought by the novelist, always in the direction of stylisation and an abstracted harmony.

At first sight Peacock's conversion of his satire on the Christian literature of gloom and self-absorption into a witty Mozartian structure may look like a narrowing of his meaning, a turn into a private joke between himself and Shelley. It seems a smaller debating base than the religious idealism of *Rhododaphne*, with its sense of man not driven in upon himself, but at ease with his natural world. If his concerns were merely those of a critic assailing the school of Coleridge, he would certainly be giving away too much. But it is eventually by its form that *Nightmare Abbey* refutes the other party's point of view. None of the Germanic dénouements Scythrop has prepared for himself — not cohabitation with two women, as in *Stella*, nor suicide, as in *Werther*, nor misanthropy, as in *Mandeville* — prevails against the comic outcome his creator has in store for him. Peacock begins with the concerns of a controversialist, but he proceeds like an artist. At one level or another he never ceases to make out his case, against Coleridge and, more lightly and genially, against Shelley, in favour of the rationality of the Enlightenment, the practicality and humour of the Greeks. It may be advisable to have a character such as Hilary, to invoke Greek literature by name, and so give the cultural perspective its required historical depth and explicitness. But the point is essentially achieved by other means, that is by fitting all the densely-packed references to modish gloom into an elegant comic framework. For the first time he achieves a real effect of formal harmony, and sustains it through his writing, with its balance, its precision of phrase, its cogency and sharpness. Shelley is as acute and ultimately as generous a critic of Peacock as Peacock is of him — 'I know not how to praise sufficiently the lightness, chastity & strength of the language of the whole.'[94]

Is it great criticism? Is it great satire? Peacock would have wanted his case against the 'German' taste in contemporary English literature to be considered on its intellectual merits. We need not agree with all his preferences, any more than we need agree with Swift's case against, say, the Royal Society, to see, in both cases, the underlying historical acumen. Peacock was right to discern major shifts in taste, and to link them with the changing nature and way of life of the reading public. Where in the eighteenth century some of the best literature had tended to be intellectualist, and a medium of opinion on controversial matters, in the nineteenth century literature bid fair to become irrational and subjective, and unconcerned with public affairs. Peacock could not help being carried along in some degree with the new aestheticism. Nor, in the age when writers were so profoundly aware of the growth in literacy, could he in reality evade the charge of élitism. All artists were affected by a change which made their potential public so much larger than their real public; artists have not escaped the problem since. But he could, and did, note what would be lost with the eighteenth-century tradition of satire and engagement. If he can be described as after all writing a critique of Romanticism, the critique amounts to this, that the spirit of German Romanticism is intense and inward to a degree that may be in complex ways socially irresponsible. A large element in the impressiveness of Swift in *Gulliver's Travels*, and Pope in *The Dunciad*, is their historical range, their prophetic insight. Though there was so much 'Augustan' verse satire in the Romantic period, it is hard to think of anyone except Peacock who attempts a similar comprehensiveness, or even begins to join it with such precision of reference. The accuracy of *Nightmare Abbey*, its 'prose' qualities of dissecting a historical change as it takes place, genuinely belong to a high order of literary creation. The presence of such qualities refutes the charge commonly made against *Nightmare Abbey*, that it is inaccurate and superficial as a comment upon Coleridge, but it does not give a full idea of the book. A great satire is more than great criticism. It is an art-object on its own, which in form and manner supersedes the system of life or thought that it assails. *Nightmare Abbey*, in which Peacock no more tells Scythrop what he should do next than Swift tells Gulliver, nevertheless implies its answers by creating a world of high comedy. The book is as dialectical as the earlier satires, but its opposing elements are so fused that its form best says what it has to say.

When he claimed that art could be criticised only by art, Friedrich Schlegel certainly set too high a standard. It is hard to think of much English Romantic criticism that reaches it, outside Peacock:[95]

> Poetry can only be criticised by poetry. A judgment on art which is not itself a work of art, either in its matter ... or in its beautiful form and a liberal tone in the spirit of old Roman satire, has no citizens' rights in the realm of art.

Chapter 5

The Good Old Times:
Maid Marian and
The Misfortunes of Elphin

Three things that will always swallow, and never be satisfied:
the sea; a burial-ground; and a king.

> Triads of Wisdom: epigraph to chapter ix,
> *The Misfortunes of Elphin*

Maid Marian

Peacock began *Maid Marian* even before he published *Nightmare Abbey*, in the same disputatious times and the same mood of opposition. In the summer of 1818 he briefly kept a diary, which shows that he was writing *Maid Marian* busily that August, and confirms that the book must have been largely completed before he joined the East India Company in January 1819.[1] He meant it for a satire on the current emotional Continental brand of conservatism, with its nostalgia for the feudal, Catholic Middle Ages, and its mystique of monarchy, expressively summed up in the collective name for the various restored monarchies — the Holy Alliance. Where in *Nightmare Abbey* the satiric target was the literary aspect of the Continental medieval revival — its expression in the new Romantic movement — in *Maid Marian* it is the political face of the same tendency, the cult of Legitimacy. Peacock wrote cheerfully of his new book to Shelley, confident of his friend's general approval. 'I am writing a comic Romance of the Twelfth Century, which I shall make the vehicle of much oblique satire on all the oppressions that are done under the sun.'[2]

As usual, Peacock needed texts on which to ground his satire; in this case, partisan accounts of the English Middle Ages. The two classic documents of the legitimist controversy in English both dated from the 1790s: Burke's *Reflections on the Revolution in France* and Paine's *Rights of Man*. The quality of Burke's writing and especially the power of his irrationalism make the *Reflections* one of the essential documents of the early, conservative wave of Romanticism. Its governing image, of a society with a mysterious, organic, plant-like life, quickly had a profound influence on counter-revolutionary thought, perhaps even more in Germany, where it was early translated and popularised, than in England. Even so, the restoration of the old régimes all over Europe helped to bring the book freshly to the fore, and Burke's ideas and rhythms continued to be heard in English conservative rhetoric throughout the Tory post-war years. But the spirit of resistance also revived the memory of Burke's original opposition. Richard Carlile reprinted Paine's *Rights of Man* in 1817, and *Common Sense* in 1819, and both books had lessons for the times. 'A French bastard landing with an armed banditti and establishing himself King of England, against the consent of the natives, is, in plain terms, a very paltry, rascally original. It certainly has no divinity in it.'[3] *Common Sense*, which was originally written in the period of the American revolution, now became timely once more, since it proclaimed the superiority of a republic to the rule of 'crowned ruffians'. The even more celebrated *Rights of Man*, of the period of the French Revolution, might now seem excessively optimistic in some of its prophecies. Yet it also spoke to the post-war generation, and especially to the working-class radical, when it assailed Burke's central proposition, the argument from historical precedent: 'Hereditary right derives from bastardy, property from theft, the state is founded by conquest, the constitution evolves by military violence.'[4] Paine's robust tone, and his contempt for the historical myth so elaborately articulated by Burke, made a refreshing brutality for a new generation of readers in the age of the Holy Alliance.

Since Burke, formal history-writing had moved on, and in the main moved in his direction. Where the great historians of the

Enlightenment, such as Montesquieu and Gibbon, had also surveyed the growth and decline of institutions over a vast time-span, and drawn lessons for contemporary politics, they had done so with an air of detachment and irony. They viewed the steps in the social–evolutionary chain as in a literal way historical: that is, completed. Romantic historians were much more inclined to emphasise not the identity but the continuity of the present with the past. Implicitly or explicitly, they depicted an organic, a Burkean, culture, its origins in a Dark Age so hard to recover that a nation emerged from forest and swamp already a mystical entity – a race, or a folk. The people existed, the individual did not. Even priests and kings, who appeared to emerge from the anonymity of the masses, did so by virtue of their office, and were sacred because they represented the whole.[5] At an exalted level of perception, Hegel's, individual and national experience became one. It was, as Burke implied at the outset, a concept too vast for the modern rationalistic reformer to tamper with.

The tradition of Enlightenment history also survived, in England very influentially, and, though histories were usually interpreted as either Whig or Tory, the best of them were not invalidated by their party attachment.[6] Even so, a new habit of mind was gradually gaining ground, which valued the past in a way that the Enlightenment did not, partly because it found there the seeds of the present. Even Shelley, who in 1812 seemed to ignore Godwin's advice to study history, became gradually more historicist in a new, imaginative sense, so that his later prose was touched by organicist insights.

Peacock remains much less sympathetic to the new style. His *Four Ages of Poetry* is ironic and in effect anti-historical. It uses the concept of a historical cycle without allowing it real validity, where Shelley's reply, *The Defence of Poetry*, sees the present in genuinely historical terms, as part of a continuing process.[7] And Peacock nowhere seems more Voltairean, more a figure of the Enlightenment, than in his sardonic approach to the feudal past in *Maid Marian*. The notions he is debunking are not so much those of serious current historical writing (since the great Romantic histories of Niebuhr, Carlyle and Guizot were yet to be written), but of the pseudo-histories issued as propaganda by régimes struggling to re-establish themselves. In order to undercut legitimists' romanticising of the Middle Ages and the monarchy, he adopts a no-nonsense posture which implies that man is always the same. Like Fielding's lawyer in *Joseph Andrews*, Peacock's clergy, barons and kings — all of them greedy, violent, cynical and self-interested — have been alive these two thousand years. There is no hint of the mystique of their respective crafts, nor of their claim to represent the spirit of a united people.

Peacock's most important documentary source for such an attitude was a work by one of Burke's original opponents. Because Burke romanticised royalty and chivalry, those replying to him were sturdily populist; because he was fanciful, they tended to argue from a posture of commonsense, and from facts. One effective polemicist of the 1790s on the jacobin side was the crotchety collector of popular ballads, Joseph Ritson. Though not the most important of his books for the literary historian, Ritson's most popular work in his day was his *Robin Hood* (1795), a two-volume collection of largely comic ballads given a spicy topicality by Ritson's jacobinical introduction and notes. Burke had written sonorously if imprecisely of chivalry, of the clergy, of nobility and of kings. Ritson, using all the paraphernalia of scholarship, countered with the authentic words of the common people.

Another man might have assembled a collection of medieval ballads about Robin Hood without depicting William the Conqueror's successors as a race of brigands, and the church as an imposition, but Ritson's book is as much topical as antiquarian. His notes continually compare Robin with King Richard I, the point being that since all power resides in force, the one has no more claim to legality than the other. Thus Robin could not rightly be charged with rebellion, because he owed no allegiance, and the forests were his territories. 'What better title King Richard could pretend to the territory and people of England than Robin Hood had to the dominion of Barnsdale or Sherwood is a question humbly submitted to the consideration of the political philosopher.'[8] Like other radicals of the late-eighteenth and early-nineteenth centuries, Ritson saw the Norman kings as tyrants, usurpers and robber barons, while Robin, though certainly a robber too, took away the rich man's goods, and so could be viewed, like the Scotsman William Wallace, as 'the champion and deliverer of his country'.[9] There are, according to Ritson, two distinct versions of history – one official, and passed on largely by monks, the other popular, and transmitted typically by ballads. Robin is a hero in the latter tradition,[10]

> a man who, in a barbarous age and under a complicated tyranny, displayed a spirit of freedom and independence, which has endeared him to the common people, whose cause he maintained (for all opposition to tyranny is the cause of the people), and in spite of the malicious endeavours of pitiful monks, by whom history was consecrated to the crimes and follies of titled ruffians and sainted idiots, to suppress all record of his patriotic exertions and virtuous arts, will render his name immortal.

If Peacock wanted a medieval story that was anti-medievalist, he could hardly do better than adapt Ritson's version of *Robin Hood*. It needed only a little up-dating and pointing, such as sly deployment of that word fashionable in the Restoration period – legitimacy – and a scattering of references to the Holy Alliance. Otherwise Ritson gives him everything he needed in the way of source material. He not only provides, in individual ballads, the material for the adventures which fill out the action; his notes anticipate the underlying dialectical structure, the polarities of barons *versus* people, King Richard *versus* King Robin. In most of *Maid Marian*'s scenes, actual duels are fought between representatives of a militaristic régime, and freedom-loving individualists like Robin, Marian and Friar Tuck. The plot re-enacts the same opposition for, like Peacock's other satires, it divides into symmetrical and also contrasted halves. A first movement, which is a study of a venal church, greedy barons and a tyrannical crown – the Norman 'banditti' – is balanced by a second depicting the actual bandits – Robin's followers – in the greenwood.

As elsewhere in Peacock, the structure is an expressive vehicle for the author's meaning. In the first half, chapters i–ix, Matilda (Marian) is still mistress of Arlingford Castle and so a denizen, however reluctant, of the Norman world. The commonest motif is of a moment of joy and union – Marian's marriage with Robin, the Merry England festivities at Gamwell – interrupted by armed men who have come to separate the celebrants. The emissary of Prince

John, Sir Ralph Montfaucon, who would like to marry Marian, appears most often among these representatives of coercive authority. Sometimes, however, the pattern is inverted. Robin succeeds in putting a stop to a scene of intended violence when he rescues young Gamwell as he is about to be executed. Again, it is a kindly intervention in favour of true love when in the second half he prevents the forced marriage of the bride of Allen a Dale.

Though the unpleasant nature of government is thus implicitly conveyed from the beginning, it is best symbolised in a characteristic set piece, John's siege to Arlingford Castle, which has as its object the rape of Marian. The ninth chapter, which introduces the usurper's assault, is introduced by a broad survey of the estates of the realm; this gives the sequence a wider, symbolic significance, while also tying it to its analogies in modern times. The usual practice of the clergy (though not of the future Friar Tuck) is described as to give penance[11]

> with or without cause, for the sake of pious discipline, and what was in those days called social order, namely, the preservation of the privileges of the few who happened to have any, at the expense of the swinish multitude who happened to have none, except that of working and being shot at for the benefit of their betters, which is obviously not the meaning of social order in our more enlightened times: let us therefore be grateful to Providence, and sing *Te Deum laudamus* in chorus with the Holy Alliance.

Prince John's exploits are made possible by the Palestinian campaign of his brother Richard I – a Holy War which is in reality waged for profit; just as 'that most legitimate and most Christian king, Richard the First of England' is[12]

> the arch-crusader and anti-jacobin by excellence, – the very type, flower, cream, pink, symbol, and mirror of all the Holy Alliances that have ever existed on earth, excepting that he seasoned his superstition and love of conquest with a certain condiment of romantic generosity and chivalrous self-devotion, with which his imitators in all other points have found it convenient to dispense.

After the clergy, barons and king, the portrait of the court is completed by the poet Harpiton, who like his modern counterpart Southey is ready to do any kind of dirty business for those in power.

The battle which follows between the tyrant and the lovers at the beginning of chapter x, the novel's actual mid-point, thus has a climactic quality, a truly central significance. Marian, breaking out of Arlingford Castle, joins forces with her lover Robin against the usurper John. Here is Peacock's favourite structure, two symmetrical halves linked by a central set piece, and the fact that — as in *Melincourt* — the action turns upon a *battle* again brings to mind the example of a neo-classical epic. The central sequences of Tasso's *Jerusalem Delivered* and of Milton's *Paradise Lost* are both battle-pieces. Tasso's is even a siege, and set in the very period of *Maid Marian.*[13]

The obvious antithetical relationship of the pastoral second half to the worldly first half enforces the intended comparison between the two styles of life. The key passages in establishing the intellectual significance of the greenwood are chapter xi and the last, chapter xviii; the most significant speech is one in the grand manner by Friar Tuck, which draws out the contrast between Westminster and Sherwood, 'in the high Court of Nature, and in the midst of her own nobility':[14]

> This goodly grove is our palace: the oak and the beech are its colonnade and its canopy: the sun and the moon and the stars are its everlasting lamps: the grass, and the daisy, and the primrose, and the violet, are its many-coloured floor of green, white, yellow, and blue: the may-flower, and the woodbine, and the eglantine, and the ivy, are its decorations, its curtains, and its tapestry: the lark, and the thrush, and the linnet, and the nightingale, are its unhired minstrels and musicians.

So much is pastoral scene-setting in the ornate Renaissance manner, echoing the older tradition of Sidney, Shakespeare, Fletcher and Milton. But the speech goes on to pick up the language of contemporary polemic, the Nurture—Nature debate in the form practised by Burke and Paine. The passage is rich in echoes of the original controversy, for example of Burke's refutation of Dr Price's claim that the people had a right to choose their kings.[15] It wittily compares Burke's notorious phrase for the people, the 'swinish multitude', with Jacques's more kindly flight of fancy about the deer in *As You Like It.* Gradually the speech slides into a parody of conservative rhetoric in favour of the *status quo*, with its claim that those entitled to vote are the 'virtual representatives' of the rest, and its ultimate, Coleridgean, recourse to the Old Testament:[16]

> Robin Hood is king of the forest both by dignity of birth and by virtue of his standing army: to say nothing of the free choice of his people, which he has indeed, but I pass it by as an illegitimate basis of power. He holds his dominion over the forest, and its horned multitude of citizen-deer, and its swinish multitude or peasantry of wild boars, by right of conquest and force of arms. He levies contributions among them by the free consent of his archers, their virtual representatives. If they should find a voice to complain that we are 'tyrants and usurpers to kill and cook them up in their assigned and native dwelling-place', we should most convincingly admonish them, with point of arrow, that they have nothing to do with our laws but to obey them. Is it not written that the fat ribs of the herd shall be fed upon by the mighty in the land? And have not they withal my blessing? my orthodox, canonical, and archiepiscopal blessing? Do I not give thanks for them when they are well roasted and smoking under my nose?

Unlike Ritson, Peacock does not glamorise Robin as a popular hero, the taxer of the rich, but instead stresses that he is a robber and a bandit. Herein precisely lies the parallel between him and the Norman kings. 'William raised contributions. So does Robin. ... Why did any pay them ...? For the same reason to both: because they could not or cannot help it.'[17] This is a significantly different point, which requires further consideration, but at least Robin's greater honesty, as a professed robber, allows Peacock (or Brother Michael) to arrive at the proper radical conclusion, that the outlaw is the better hero, and Nature's the more agreeable court:[18]

> What need we then to constitute a court, except a fool and a laureate? For the fool, his only use is to make false knaves merry by art, and we are true men and are merry by nature. For the laureate, his only office is to find virtues in those who have none,

and to drink sack for his pains. We have quite virtue enough to need him not, and can drink our sack for ourselves.

With its range of reference to a generation of polemical writing about the Constitution – on the conservative side, to Burke, Coleridge, Canning, and Southey; on the liberal, to Price, Paine, and Ritson – the speech pulls together in one dense ironic texture the political rhetoric of the revolutionary era.

But this is essentially only one speech and, though it is in Peacock's best and most characteristic vein, it does not make a whole satire. The fact is that, taken as a whole, *Maid Marian* is the weakest of his books, for a number of possible reasons. To begin with, the Holy Alliance and its dogma of Legitimacy seems, given Peacock's particular method, an inadequate topic. The European despots were generally unpopular in England, and the Tory Foreign Secretary, Castlereagh, managed to avoid committing Britain to the doctrinaire policy of the Alliance, which was to intervene jointly to crush popular outbreaks wherever they occurred. Peacock, with his customary accuracy, evidently appreciated that Castlereagh was not the bogey painted by the opposition press: instead of lampooning him fiercely, as both Shelley and Byron were to do, he never mentioned him at all.

A different kind of partisan writer might have made active political capital out of the embarrassment of English conservatives (including Wordsworth and Coleridge)[19] at the Alliance England had got herself into. This was nowhere more acute than in the case of Ferdinand of Spain, currently the oppressor of those Spanish liberals who had been England's allies at the time of the Peninsular War. It was particularly painful that Ferdinand had been restored to the throne of his ancestors along with an institution hideous in English popular mythology: the Catholic church, together with its Inquisition. Foreseeably, Hazlitt, writing as a journalist, makes some shrewd opportunist hits, and is at his most trenchant on the subject of Ferdinand, whom he readily adopts as[20]

> our favourite King. 'Men should be what they seem;' and Kings should seem what they are. He is a model in his kind. In him is seen the copy of the good old times – what his predecessors were before him, and what they will be after him; what Kings were

and will be and ought to be. He is a King every inch of him; he has nothing human about him. He is not affected with the taint of modern philosophy, nor has he in his heart or on his lips any false, spurious, Ultra-Jacobinical notions of liberty, humanity, and justice. He is above all that. He is an honest King. He is a tyrant both by profession and practice. He has but one idea in his head, like the Editor of the *Times*, that a King can do no wrong, and he acts up to it, as the Doctor raves up to it, or as Mr. Coleridge cants up to it, or as Mr. Southey rhymes up to it, or as Mr. Wordsworth muses up to it.

But Peacock is a much more serious intellectual critic than Hazlitt, and his writing depends on a genuine substratum of intellectual conflict, to which, with his method of literal textual quotation, he can continually allude. Apart from Brother Michael's speech, which on the whole goes back to Burke's period, he finds no such texts. Accordingly *Maid Marian* has very few arguments, or characters who seem capable of intellectual discussion, though it has plenty of knock-about set-tos with staves. Ultimately the reason for its blandness is that, unlike all Peacock's other books, it has not detected any genuine movement of ideas in England which has currently found expression in one or more controversial documents. Nor, therefore, can Peacock achieve satiric precision on the occasion when he does have the words of real dialecticians in mind.

Peacock has to rely on Ritson, and he probably finds him simplistic, but in his general ideological position sympathetic: a circumstance which puts so ironic a writer into a serious difficulty. He seems unable to help turning Ritson's sturdy champion of popular liberty into a mildly dubious freebooter; it is the necessary consequence of Peacock's temperament, and also of the more cynical attitudes of his post-revolutionary times. Ritson's Robin can be likened to William Wallace; Peacock's cannot. Instead of seeing in Robin, as Ritson does, a symbol of heroic resistance to oppression, Peacock deploys Brother Michael to point with Godwinian rigour to the relativism in our respectable notions of law, morality, and heroic virtue – even, it is hinted, when the heroism is exercised on the popular side:[21]

Marry, your hero guts an exchequer, while your thief

disembowels a portmanteau; your hero sacks a city, while your thief sacks a cellar: your hero marauds on a larger scale, and that is all the difference, for the principle and the virtue are one: but two of a trade cannot agree: therefore your hero makes laws to get rid of your thief, and gives him an ill name that he may hang him: for might is right, and the strong make laws for the weak, and they that make laws to serve their own turn do also make morals to give colour to their laws.

Certainly the people have no God-given access to truth. Peacock makes that point formally, in effect, by subsuming the folk-material which was the very object and rationale of Ritson's collection, and placing it almost ironically within his framework. In the first half, in chapters vi and vii, Peacock anthologises three adventures based on Ritson's traditional ballads; at a comparable position in the second half, chapters xiii–xiv and xvi, he gives three more. These 'popular' sequences retain some of the charm and simplicity of their origin in ballad, but the effect of placing them so symmetrically within the structure is to bring them under the control of a sophisticated art.

In the satiric vacuum, what comes across is something resembling a private idyll. All Peacock's books, however disputatious, evoke pleasant worlds. In *Maid Marian* the paradox is even more striking than elsewhere, because it seems at first sight that the reader's first impulse, to escape into a remote feudal past, a romanticised Merry England, is firmly held in check by the large number of pointed allusions to the nineteenth century. And yet, even if it is not a medieval haven into which the reader escapes, it is nevertheless the greenwood, with something of the refuge-quality of the real countryside, and something of an artificial correlative of this, the fantasy-world behind the footlights of a theatre.

Peacock had already borrowed a climax from stage comedy in *Nightmare Abbey,* and his technique had even become clearly and consciously Mozartian. *Maid Marian* goes considerably further in evoking the new Italian romantic opera of Rossini, Bellini and Donizetti, which had just in 1818 arrived in London. There are moments when Peacock actually seems to think of himself as a librettist: an exchange such as the one in chapter iv between

Matilda, her father, Brother Michael and Sir Ralph was surely conceived as an operatic quartet, the heroine's first scene and an appropriately rousing finale to Act 1. Elsewhere he does not have immediate translation to the stage in mind. Though there are set pieces which would easily convert into scenes, there are other episodes which run on shapelessly, or oblige characters to change location without the help of an easy curtain. But it is no surprise that *Maid Marian* was at once, in 1822, adapted for the stage as an operetta, and successfully performed at intervals throughout the nineteenth century. A satiric element which is so muted, and moreover appears to cut both ways, with a-political even-handedness, could easily be made to serve the needs of entertainment. Almost inevitably, *Maid Marian* must with time have reached a larger and more heterogeneous audience than anything else Peacock wrote.

The countryside, and opera, were two of his favourite pursuits, and it is hardly surprising that the book conveys a frank enjoyment that has absolutely nothing to do with shaking European monarchs on their thrones. But the air of privacy also derives from an element that in the end takes over from the satire: the central character, Marian, who was no part of Ritson's polemical presentation, but in Peacock's version outweighs Robin in importance.

At face value and on first meeting, Marian is merely one in the series of Peacock's attractive, animate heroines. As an emancipated woman in Mary Wollstonecraft's feminist tradition, she resembles Anthelia, though at the same time her literary ancestry seems older than this: like so many heroines of romantic comedy, she appears to represent a healthy norm of independent judgment and warm human feeling in a hierarchical and egotistical masculine world.

Marian, Robin, Brother Michael and some of the lesser characters have two different names in the two parts of the romance. She is Matilda while at Arlingford Castle, and is translated into Marian when she begins her life in the greenwood. It is Matilda who resembles the sprightly true-hearted heroine of comic tradition. But, even more than most others of her literary type, she is especially associated with the impulse towards liberty, with impatience of the yoke of authority, whether it is vested in her temporal or her spiritual father. Shakespeare's Rosalind and

Fielding's Sophia, like Millamant and Elizabeth Bennet, think like free women, and their function is clearly to correct the stale values of those in supposed authority around them. But not one of them *acts* as unconventionally as Matilda — who declines to obey her father and looses an arrow at a priest (as Marian she will fight a duel with the king). She is introduced dressed in green, as for hunting, and in the first half the connotation is not much more than that of a nature-loving, emancipated girl. Yet already there are hints that Matilda's 'sylvan' characteristics do not belong primarily to a naturalistic tradition. Brother Michael describes how she and Robin 'reciprocally fashioned each other to the love of the fern and the foxglove':[22]

> Had either been less sylvan, the other might have been more saintly; but they will now never hear matins but those of the lark, nor reverence vaulted aisle but that of the greenwood canopy. They are twin plants of the forest, and are identified with its growth.

> For the slender beech and the sapling oak,
>   That grow by the shadowy rill,
> You may cut down both at a single stroke,
>   You may cut down which you will.

> But this you must know, that as long as they grow,
>   Whatever change may be,
> You can never teach either oak or beech,
>   To be aught but a greenwood tree.

It is as though even Matilda has an aura of the forest-world about her, is a personification rather than a person. When she becomes Marian, the process of abstraction is much more evident. Peacock adopts the old popular tradition that Robin's Marian remained a Maid, a notion which (together with her new name) links her with the Virgin Mary. Not wanting an embarrassingly Christian frame of reference, Peacock introduces a further comparison with pagan divinity: 'The hunter is Hippolytus, and the huntress is Dian.'[23] Where the Catholic Virgin Mary is mentioned, for history's sake, it is in a context of natural religion, of pagan wonder, that clearly owes more to ancient Greece than to medieval Rome. 'The matins of the lark' and 'the vespers of the

nightingale'[24] are very evidently not church services; Robin's
Virgin-worship is oddly merged in his feeling for his virgin-bride
– and juxtaposed, moreover, with the Dionysian rituals of the
Friar. Sherwood begins to resemble the pagan world of
Rhododaphne, instinct with separate divinities. Its gods are
abstractions, yet associated with ordinary daily activities:
indifferent, unsentimental, and yet pleasantly familiar.[25]

> Robin was very devout, though there was great unity in his
> religion: it was exclusively given to our Lady the Virgin, and he
> never set forth in a morning till he had said three prayers, and
> had heard the sweet voice of his Marian singing a hymn to their
> mutual patroness. Each of his men had, as usual, a patron saint
> according to his name or taste. The friar chose a saint for
> himself, and fixed on Saint Botolph, whom he euphonised into
> Saint Bottle, and maintained that he was that very Panomphic
> Pantagruelian saint, well known in France as a female divinity,
> by the name of La Dive Bouteille, whose oracular monosyllable
> 'Trincq', is celebrated and understood by all nations.

Peacock is not the man to grow solemn over a cult, especially
one borrowed from Rabelais. But he makes his outlaws religious
men, even if their religion is pagan and natural, and we are clearly
meant to give serious attention to the Friar's observation, 'Our life
is a craft, an art and a mystery. How much of it, think you, could
be learned at court?'[26]

The idealism is suggestive, though it is very lightly hinted at. It is
associated with what seems to have been a genuine religious feeling
in Peacock, reflected in his work as late as *Gryll Grange*,[27] and
alluded to by acquaintances at various points of his long life. There
was, for example, that strange little scene on his painful deathbed,
when his grand-daughter heard him 'calling upon the immortal
gods with reproaches because they persisted in tormenting one who
had served them for a lifetime and never wavered in the service'.[28]
One may guess, using not only *Maid Marian* but all the works, that
for Peacock true religion implied no pre-existent hierarchy, no
church, because official religion was compromised, coercive, and
(the more serious *Rhododaphne* suggests) life-denying and even
deadly. Instead true religion was the creation of a personal system
of worship, which each individual devised according to his own

needs, strengths, and idealisms: it was thus man- rather than god-centred, not extrinsic but innate. The late classical post-Olympian world, with its little local shrines, suggested something like this, as did the homelier face of medieval Catholicism. Such a creed would compare quite well with Shelley's thinking about religion at the same time.[29] The problem is thus not to fathom what Peacock meant by the passages about religion in *Maid Marian*, but to determine how much of it he meant his readers to understand, or how far he meant the subject to seem germane to the rest of his story.

Potentially the aura of paganism and of a personal religion that surrounds Marian is entirely relevant to Peacock's critique of the Church, which he portrays as a mere instrument for upholding the feudal order. Nevertheless, in *Maid Marian* Peacock's heroine can hardly be said to function primarily in a satiric way. The religion she represents is too profoundly idiosyncratic, and too mysterious; even her charm, though made real for the reader, carries with it the feeling of a personal reminiscence. Marian was, after all, the name of the girl Peacock still expected to marry in 1818. There is no record of what Marianne de St Croix looked like, but it was a tradition in Peacock's family that Susannah in *Crotchet Castle* resembled Jane Gryffydh, to whom Peacock proposed in 1819; and Marian, with her sweet singing voice, her healthy colour and dark hair, and her enthusiasm for the outdoors, strongly resembles Susannah. Finally, the fictional Marian afterwards seemed to merge with the real-life Mary Ellen, born in 1821. This was the book of his that Peacock gave his daughter to read. Herself, according to Holman Hunt, a 'dashing horsewoman', and emancipated, Mary Ellen might have been Marian's reincarnation. Her husband George Meredith seems to have thought so, for he was apt to use the name Marian when creating characters who touched a chord connected with his first wife.[30] Though much of this is after-history, it is symptomatic of a character evidently felt by Peacock from the first to have a deep private significance for him.

The book certainly cannot be said to lose grace and charm by Marian's presence, but it does lose a sense of urgency, or point of contact with the real world. Measured by his intentions, Peacock had not become more escapist, effete and Tory in the few months since Shelley left England. But the meaning of a book is as complex and multifarious as the combination of its words, its tone, its scene and its setting. No matter how robust and matter-of-fact the treatment of medievalism, a pastoral set in the Merry England of long ago is not the obvious dose for curing the public of nostalgia. Like *Rhododaphne*, *Maid Marian* has the savour of the charmed circle in which it evolved, the literary leafiness of Leigh Hunt and Keats. Even when it appears most critical of its own idyll, it has, like so many of Keats's poems, something of the air of a celebration.

The Misfortunes of Elphin

If *Maid Marian* is blander and more homogeneous than the satires, so at first sight is *The Misfortunes of Elphin*. The latter has the strongest, most continuous story of any of Peacock's books; and the sustained interest of the narrative plays its part in keeping the reader in sixth-century Britain.

In *Maid Marian*, Peacock is so anxious not to romanticise feudal times that he comes near to denying their distinctness. Human nature and society have always been fundamentally the same, and are not to be venerated: hence the continual interruption of the medieval atmosphere with references to the present, and the host of deliberate mistakes and anachronisms – the casual interchangeability of priests, monks and friars, and the easy modernity of manners.[31] *Maid Marian* virtually says that history is bunk.

At face value, *The Misfortunes of Elphin* has more to do with a remote world, and less with the conflicts of early nineteenth-century England, than anything else Peacock wrote. Nor can it be taken for a satire on sentimental historicism, since it is frankly antiquarian in taste and spirit. Edith Nicolls declared that it 'was written to introduce translations of Welsh triads and poems of the sixth century', while Sir Edward Strachey thought Peacock 'was proud of the fact that Welsh archaeologists treated his book as a serious and valuable addition to Welsh history'.[32] Brett-Smith is surely right to express scepticism, for Peacock's handling of Welsh legend is playful, and he can clearly be seen to have collated recent scholarship rather than to have undertaken fresh research of his own. It is nevertheless true that the elaborate narrative of *The Misfortunes of Elphin* is woven together from a considerable number of lyrics, fragments and triads, and three distinct stories. Thus far it could almost be taken as itself a part of the medieval revival, which began to have an irresistible influence on the arts in the 1820s.

Though Peacock introduces details which help to link his three main narrative elements together, they can still be perceived as distinct and as each occupying a different phase of his book. They are the legends of Seithenyn; of the birth of Taliesin; and of Arthur, Gwenyvar and Melvas. All of them are to be found in the learned books of the Celtic revival, which made prodigious headway especially in the early years of the nineteenth century. Since his marriage to the Welsh-speaking Jane Gryffydh, Peacock had been pursuing his reading in Welsh language and literature. He owned, for example, the three volumes of *The Cambro-Briton*, published in 1821-2, an anthology-like magazine which is certainly one of his principal sources; and he must have had access (if only at the British Museum) to a number of other recent scholarly works which could have supplied material. For example, the first volume of *The Myvyrian Archaiology of Wales* (1801) is a very large collection of (untranslated) Welsh poems, including those for which Peacock gives an English version in chapter xv, 'the Circle of the Bards'. 'The Song of Gwythno Garanhir, On the Inundation of the Sea over the Plain of Gwaelod', which Peacock gives in Chapter iv, and 'The Consolation of Elphin' of chapter v, both appear, and are also rather woodenly translated, in Samuel Rush Meyrick's *The History and Antiquities of the County of Cardigan* (London, 1808, pp. 51-4). But one of these in particular, 'The Consolations of Elphin', is a favourite which Peacock could easily have seen elsewhere, for example in the third volume of *The Cambro-Briton*. Attempts to pinpoint some of Peacock's Welsh sources have been made by Herbert Wright and David Garnett.[33] The general picture is clear enough, that Peacock was here doing what he did nowhere else – re-creating a setting that was by expert standards pretty well authentic.

Peacock certainly had no slavish attitude towards his sources. He left out what did not suit him – for example, the miracles and mumbo-jumbo surrounding Taliesin – and focussed on the version of a story which did, such as the legend that the inundation of Gwaelod was caused by the drunkenness of the watchman Seithenyn. The three legends and the genuine Welsh poetry are more or less tailored, as we shall see, to fit the immediate purposes of Peacock's narrative. An impressive artistic confidence in handling much diverse material is indeed the chief feature of *The Misfortunes of Elphin*. Antiquarian matter which might have been hopelessly unwieldy in fact helps to support a genuinely autonomous fictive world.

Yet, despite the difference in its attitude to history, in many respects *The Misfortunes of Elphin* is clearly a companion work to *Maid Marian*. Both are sorties into a picturesque and jovial past. Both are more restricted and specialised in subject than the five contemporary satires. But they do each have a subject in the nineteenth-century world, and it is strikingly similar. In fact, both are studies of the ideological attitudes of the current governing party, which in both 1818 and 1828 was perceived by liberals – not necessarily with full justification – as peculiarly reactionary.

The dates of composition of the two historical romances may be more significant than the dates of publication. We know *Maid Marian* was written in 1818 – the year after the suspension of Habeas Corpus, and *Melincourt*. There is less documentary evidence about the writing of *The Misfortunes of Elphin*. It was announced as in the press in February 1829, and first reviewed on 7 March 1829; but there is nothing decisive to date the point at which Peacock began to write. The references to Welsh material, for example, could all have been in Peacock's hands for some years. But, though there is no proof, there is some reason to think that Peacock wrote *The Misfortunes of Elphin* largely in 1828, beginning perhaps late in 1827 in response to some strong contemporary promptings.

One goad may well have been Thomas Moore's most unhistorical historical novel *The Epicurean*, which Peacock discussed in the *Westminster Review* of October 1827. Peacock may well have thought he could do better than this meretricious popular production, 'in the best style of M. de Chateaubriand', with its 'piety, very profound; and philosophy, sufficiently shallow'.[34] But presumably he needed to be triggered off by a contemporary topic for satire – and there are in *The Misfortunes of Elphin* two strong structural ideas which point to what this may have been. The first and shorter part is about an ill-kept embankment overwhelmed by a storm of the sea; the second, longer part is about a violent, anarchic governing élite, threatened by the invasion of human enemies. Both are surely analogies for a real-life innovation which was always imminent during the later 1820s, the ultimately irresistible groundswell of reform.

On the face of it, the events of 1825, 1826 and early 1827 would not seem especially likely to drive a satirist to take up his pen on the subject of reform. 1820 and 1822 were years when the campaign to rectify the inequalities of the franchise was much more urgently reflected in parliament. Then, after a series of defeats, the impetus to get reform on to the statute-book seemed to die back. It was Catholic emancipation which was the more live parliamentary issue in 1827 and 1828. And yet there is real reason to believe, as shrewd contemporaries did, that outside parliament the cause of reform imperceptibly continued to strengthen. Peel in 1820 noticed the underlying trend of public opinion – 'do not you think that the tone of England ... is more liberal – to use an odious but intelligible phrase – than the policy of the government?' A decade later, when Whig ministers did begin to press for reform in parliament, they wrote of a pressure for reform in the country, before which the government must bend or risk breaking. 'My information', wrote Grey to Palmerston in 1831, 'leads me to believe that the middle classes, who form the real and efficient mass of public opinion, and without whom the power of the gentry is nothing, are almost unanimous on this question.'[35]

In the spring of 1827, Canning, a lifelong opponent of reform, at last took office as Prime Minister. Canning was of Irish extraction and no bigot; he was the one man, moreover, who had the personal standing with the English public to carry through Catholic relief. Canning's mixed administration accordingly received a cautious welcome from liberal organs such as the *Edinburgh Review* and the *Examiner*. But Canning died in August 1827, after only four months as Prime Minister, to be eventually succeeded early in 1828 by what looked like a government of hard-liners. Wellington became Prime Minister, and his Cabinet excited much hostile comment by including an unusually large number of military men – 'a Government concocted out of the Army List', complained one critic, while another 'likened their minds to cartridge paper'.[36] In May 1828 a number of moderate ministers resigned, producing a more emphatically Tory administration. With soldiers, Tories and

Protestant ultras apparently dominating the government, either object of reform looked for the time being remote again, so shortly after Canning's ministry had aroused the expectation of cautious change.

There is evidence throughout 1828 of liberal and pro-Catholic despondency, while the 'Protestant' party felt joyously in the ascendant. On 30 May the Pitt Club assembled in the City of London Tavern, as they did every year, to revere the memory of the dead Tory leader, and the *Times* report of the 1828 meeting conveys the relief of honest Tories now that the danger represented by Canning's collaboration with the Whigs had passed over. In the course of what reads distinctly like a Peacockian convivial evening, the faithful drank the health of the King, the Navy and the Army, the Protestant Ascendancy, and the memory of the late Rt. Hon. William Pitt (three times three). The Chairman, Lord Skelmersdale, rejoiced that the government possessed the confidence of the inhabitants of the country:

> When I see at its head the noble Duke who led the armies of England victoriously over the great part of the Continent, where they met and overcame some of the most highly-disciplined troops in the world, how can I doubt that they possess that confidence?

Lord Harewood equally had no doubt that the Constitution was in safe hands, now that, following the equivocations of Canning, the 'principles of Pitt' again 'animate the counsels of Great Britain'. A high point of the evening was Mr Charles Taylor's stirring performance of Canning's song in praise of Pitt, the leader who had resisted the jacobin tide in the 1790s – 'The Pilot who weathered the storm'.

Those who wanted either emancipation or reform protested that a government of die-hards was not merely objectionable in principle; it was dangerous in practice. The young Macaulay pointedly warned against a policy of political inflexibility: the country as a whole might have cause to regret the present blind trust in the strength of 'a military government' and the 'power of the sword'.[37] This may be an allusion to his own major article, 'The Present Administration', which had appeared the previous year in the same journal, when he had suggested that the moderate

Canning, with his policy of relieving the Catholics, might be the last chance of the classes in power to accede gradually to the pressure for change. A policy of repression and reaction might lead to revolution, as it had in France when Louis XVI failed to heed the moderate counsels of Turgot.[38]

Wellington's strength and his intransigence were alike illusory. O'Connell's campaigns were fast rendering Ireland ungovernable, and the Prime Minister had privately resolved to yield to the claims of the Catholics. The proposal to emancipate them was made in the Speech from the Throne of the 5 February 1829; having passed through all its stages, the Emancipation Bill received the Royal Assent on 13 April, and thus became law. It was a concession which took the country, and organs of opinion, by surprise; and, like all such swift moves, made political comment instantly out of date. As a general satire on conservative government, which gained greatly from the present example of Wellington's supposedly die-hard administration, *The Misfortunes of Elphin* was in conception Peacock's most political and topical book since *Melincourt*. But already, by the time of its appearance at the beginning of March 1829, one major measure of reform was going through. Its satiric vision of an impenetrable governing class was being falsified by events.

Such a political volte-face may have affected the book's fame,[39] but does not detract from its aesthetic success. *The Misfortunes of Elphin* made an immediate point which lasted less well than that of *Melincourt*, but it is more inwardly coherent, more sustained and entire. And this manner of presentation, for all its specificity – its references both to Welsh historical sources, and to the political present – eventually alludes not to political events but to political theory, and is thus not tied to specific measures.

Peacock was always a great reader of the *Edinburgh Review*, and it is hard to resist the impression that he may have found the theme of *The Misfortunes of Elphin* in Macaulay's striking article of June 1827 on the administration of Canning. The peroration of this article eloquently compares the behaviour of recent British governments, standing out against popular pressure for reform, with the fatal delays of French governments before the Revolution:

There is one hope, and one hope only for our country; and that hope is in a liberal Administration ... which, by promptitude to redress practical grievances, will enable itself to oppose with authority and effect, the propositions of turbulent theorists. ...

The state of England, at the present moment, bears a close resemblance to that of France at the time when Turgot was called to the head of affairs. ... The philosophical Minister attempted to secure the ancient institutions, by amending them. The mild reforms which he projected, had they been carried into execution, would have conciliated the people, and saved from the most tremendous of all commotions the Church, the Aristocracy, and the Throne. But a crowd of narrow-minded nobles, ignorant of their own interest, though solicitous for nothing else, the Newcastles and the Salisburys of France, began to tremble for their oppressive franchises. ...

The Ministers stammered out feeble and inconsistent counsels. But all other voices were soon drowned in one, which every moment waxed louder and more terrible, – in the fierce and tumultuous roar of a great people, conscious of irresistible strength, maddened by intolerable wrongs, and sick of deferred hopes! That cry, so long stifled, now rose from every corner of France, made itself heard in the presence-chamber of her King, in the saloons of her nobles, and in the refectories of her luxurious priesthood.

In the French case the reforms had been granted too late. Macaulay described the paroxysm that followed, and then the aftermath – the restoration of the Bourbons – in terms which must surely have struck a chord in Peacock's memory:[40]

The exiles have returned. But they have returned as the few survivors of the deluge returned to a world in which they could recognise nothing; in which the valleys had been raised, and the mountains depressed, and the courses of the rivers changed, – in which sand and sea-weed had covered the cultivated fields and the walls of imperial cities. They have returned to seek in vain, amidst the mouldering relics of a former system, and the fermenting elements of a new creation, the traces of any remembered object. ... The Bastille is fallen, and can never more rise from its ruins. ...

Is this a romance? Or is it a faithful picture of what has lately been in a neighbouring land – of what may shortly be, within the borders of our own? Has the warning been given in vain? Have our Mannerses and Clintons so soon forgotten the fate of houses as wealthy and noble as their own? ... God grant that they may never remember it with unavailing self-accusation, when desolation shall have visited wealthier cities and fairer gardens; – when Manchester shall be as Lyons, and Stowe as Chantilly; – when he who now, in the pride of rank and opulence, sneers at what we have written in the bitter sincerity of our hearts, shall be thankful for a porringer of broth at the door of some Spanish convent, or shall implore some Italian money-lender to advance another pistole on his George!

It is a passage which evidently grew fascinatingly in Peacock's imagination. Macaulay likened the French Revolution to a devastating flood; from his Welsh researches, Peacock knew of such a disaster – one which was moreover allowed to happen, like the French Revolution, through folly and neglect. The inundation of Gwaelod takes up only the first four chapters of the satire's sixteen, but this is much the most striking episode, the poetic and dominant image. At a first reading one might assume that the breaking of the embankment alludes to any violent constitutional change, or even, as most critics have had it, to the campaign for the Reform Bill. In fact Peacock is surely following Macaulay, and has the history of France in 1789 in mind. Perhaps his honest Teithrin, who does his best to save the monarchy, is an equivalent of Turgot. Surely the detailed picture given of the unaccustomed hardships endured after the flood by Gwythno and his court reflects Macaulay's description of the woes of the French nobility (and it is a much longer passage than the extract given here). Above all Peacock clearly refers to the French Revolution in the pivotal third chapter, 'The Oppression of Gwenhidwy', when the sea breaks into Seithenyn's watchtower. For, though he had plenty of warrant in Welsh legend for a sea-flood, and for Seithenyn's drunkenness, he did not find in his sources any mention of a tower. 'The tower, which had its foot in the sea, had long been sapped by the waves. ...'[41] Its destruction inevitably brings to mind the Fall of the Bastille.

Seithenyn's disaster is, or could have been, an unforgettable object-lesson for the ruling classes who succeed him. If it does not work like this in Peacock's fable, it is for the reasons Macaulay hints at: the aristocracy, French and English, have learnt nothing. Seithenyn himself, the Lord High Commissioner of Royal Embankment, is the very representative of his class under the *ancien régime*, as Macaulay describes them – 'narrow-minded nobles, ignorant of their own interest, though solicitous for nothing else'. Entrusted with the care of the Embankment, which stands for the Constitution, Seithenyn does indeed regard it with affection, but entirely for motives of his own. 'It does its business well: it works well: it keeps out the water from the land, and it lets in the wine upon the High Commission of Embankment.'[42] His success in surviving after the inundation is apparently an engaging characteristic, but it is also heartless. Seithenyn is a colder character than Falstaff, with whom he is often compared. Established in his new life as Melvas's butler, he claims to have thought occasionally of his old royal master and his daughter.'I should be very glad to see them all; but I am afraid King Elphin, as you call him, (what he is king of, you shall tell me at leisure,) would do me a mischief.'[43] It is a sublime aside, but not precisely engaging; it nails beautifully one prevalent kind of Tory loyalism.

Like all Peacock's best satiric figures, Seithenyn is generalised: his experiences in the first part suggest France, but his speeches vividly evoke English parliamentary occasions. In a sense Seithenyn's rhetoric spans the entire forty-year revolutionary era, since it derives ultimately from Burke. But these are ideas and rhythms also employed by the greatest of recent parliamentary orators, George Canning. When on 25 April 1822, Lord John Russell moved 'that the present state of the representation of the people in Parliament requires the most serious consideration of the house', it is recorded that 'several members rose to speak at the same time, but the call for Mr. Canning was so loud and prevalent that they gave way'. Canning's argument on this celebrated occasion was that of his mentor Burke, that the Constitution is an organic thing, the work of ages, and best not tampered with:[44]

> I contend for a House of Commons, the spirit of which,
> whatever be its frame, has, without any forcible alteration,
> gradually, but faithfully, accommodated itself to the progressive
> spirit of the country. .... I value the system of Parliamentary

Representation, for that very want of uniformity which is complained of in the petition.

Canning saw the present function of the House of Commons as checking and balancing the powers of the other branches of the legislature, the Crown and the House of Lords, and he feared that reform would strengthen it unduly in relation to the other two. It was this possibility that made him reluctant 'to exchange that equality and co-ordination of powers among the three branches of our present Constitution, in which its beauty, its strength, its stability, and the happiness of those who live under it, consist'.[45] He was ready to admit that the system had always admitted influence:[46]

> While we dam up one source of influence, a dozen others will open. .... Whether the House of Commons, in its present shape, does not practically though silently accommodate itself to such changes, with a pliancy almost as faithful as the nicest artifice could contrive, is, in my opinion, I must confess, a much more important consideration, than whether the component parts of the House might be arranged with neater symmetry, or distributed in more scientific proportions.

Canning's collected speeches were published in 1828, the year when Peacock was probably writing *The Misfortunes of Elphin.* They surely inspired the language of Peacock's caricatured conservatives,[47] and this, the most celebrated of them, above all: for Canning's sentiments emerge unmistakably from the mouth of Seithenyn, even if the latter's drunkenness gives them a comically different ring:[48]

> 'Decay', said Seithenyn, 'is one thing, and danger is another. Every thing that is old must decay. That the embankment is old, I am free to confess; that it is somewhat rotten in parts, I will not altogether deny; that it is any the worse for that, I do most sturdily gainsay. .... Our ancestors were wiser than we: they built it in their wisdom; and, if we should be so rash as to try to mend it, we should only mar it.'
> 'The stonework,' said Teithrin, 'is sapped and mined: the piles are rotten, broken and dislocated: the floodgates and sluices are leaky and creaky.'

'That is the beauty of it,' said Seithenyn. 'Some parts of it are rotten, and some parts of it are sound.'

'It is well,' said Elphin, 'that some parts are sound: it were better that all were so.'

'So I have heard some people say before,' said Seithenyn; 'perverse people, blind to venerable antiquity: that very unamiable sort of people, who are in the habit of indulging their reason. But I say, the parts that are rotten give elasticity to those that are sound: they give them elasticity, elasticity, elasticity. If it were all sound, it would break by its own obstinate stiffness: the soundness is checked by the rottenness, and the stiffness is balanced by the elasticity. There is nothing so dangerous as innovation. See the waves in the equinoctial storms, dashing and clashing, roaring and pouring, spattering and battering, rattling and battling against it. I would not be so presumptuous as to say, I could build any thing that would stand against them half an hour; and here this immortal old work, which God forbid the finger of modern mason should bring into jeopardy, this immortal work has stood for centuries, and will stand for centuries more, if we let it alone. It is well: it works well: let well alone. Cupbearer, fill. It was half rotten when I was born, and that is a conclusive reason why it should be three parts rotten when I die.'

The whole body of the High Commission roared approbation.

This is not to say that Seithenyn is a portrait of Canning, Burke or any other identifiable Tory leader. The rhetoric may mimic theirs, but the character is universal – that of the place-holder who shelters behind the existing Constitution, and at the same time by his incompetence and folly contributes to its ruin. 'The pilot who weathered the storm' was the cant phrase for Pitt; Seithenyn is his antithesis, the officer who did not weather it. The Tories had coined another phrase for the current electoral system – 'virtual representation'.[49] In one of his best jokes, Peacock adopts it for Seithenyn's non-performance of his stewardship – 'virtual superintendence'.[50]

If the breaking of the embankment refers specifically to the French Revolution, the fact that Peacock allows a generation to elapse before continuing his narrative has additional significance. By analogy, Taliesin and Elphin are Peacock's own contemporaries, who have grown up with the sad and cautionary knowledge of revolution. The fictional political leaders of their generation are representations of the real-life politicians of the post-revolutionary era which followed the Bourbon restoration. The second part is no anti-climax, but the essential completion of the satiric subject – a study of opportunism and moral banditry, which is Peacock's judgment of the ruling class of his day. Just as Swift's Lilliput is also England under Queen Anne and Sir Robert Harley, so Peacock's sixth-century Britain is also England under George IV and the Duke of Wellington. Britain is really under a weak government, though the individuals seem strong. They are a band of military adventurers, out for what they can seize and hold, and they prove ultimately as stupidly blind to their own real interests as their predecessor Seithenyn.

The first of these leaders of the younger generation is Maelgon Gwynedd, who is compared with Nimrod, the mighty hunter of the Old Testament, and the traditional type of the tyrant.[51] When not hunting or feasting, Maelgon is employed in 'fighting with any of the neighbouring kings, who had any thing which he wanted, and which he thought himself strong enough to take from them'.[52] Maelgon commits the definitive act of the latter part of the book when he kidnaps Elphin, for henceforth Taliesin, the hero, is in quest of justice for his master. Maelgon's son Rhun, who is as brutal and tyrannical as his father, sets out to rape Elphin's queen, Angharad, and for this is likened to Tarquin, last of the kings of Rome.[53] The dynasty of Gwynedd is, then, an allegorical representation of monarchical government by brute force, a phenomenon certainly witnessed since the restoration of the Bourbons, though perhaps more familiar on the Continent than in England. It is the stupid, brutal, militant face of Toryism – and the new English Prime Minister, Wellington, the victor of Waterloo, is associated with it ideologically, and by virtue of his profession, though there is no suggestion that Maelgon is a portrait of Wellington.

The leading precept of these moral bandits, that might is right, is shared by Melvas, the last of Peacock's trio of conservative types. He is, after all, another kidnapper – of Queen Gwenyvar – and our first introduction to his name is at Dinas Vawr, which he has captured in a coup more bloody and profitable than any of Maelgon's. But Melvas is smoother and wilier than Maelgon, and seems an intellectual by comparison. In fact his speeches, like Seithenyn's, echo those of the most articulate of recent Tory politicians. Canning, a brilliantly opportunist Foreign Secretary, had withstood the pressures of England's Continental allies in the Holy Alliance, and had given *de facto* recognition to the South American republics, with which England stood to do profitable trade. Canning's rejection of monarchical (and liberal) sentiment in favour of *real-politik* is nicely caught in Melvas. 'His manners were, for the most part, pleasant. He did much mischief, not for mischief's sake, nor yet for the sake of excitement, but for the sake of something tangible.[54]

Melvas also illustrates the ruthlessness of Tory foreign policy. Canning had been prepared to threaten force when necessary, and at times his instructions took the country to the brink of war. A celebrated recent instance was the Battle of Navarino, at which the English and French fleet had fired on and virtually destroyed the Turkish navy, an act which ensured the liberation of Greece but also dangerously altered the balance of power in the Eastern Mediterranean. Though the battle took place on 20 October 1827, some two and a half months after Canning's death, it was a consequence of the policy he had initiated. Like so many of Canning's actions, it received a mixed reception at home, privately and publicly, as an operation that was both effective and indefensible. Melvas's activities seem strikingly similar:[55]

Have not you and I a right to this good wine, which seems to trip very merrily over your ghostly palate? I got it by seizing a good ship, and throwing the crew overboard, just to remove them out of the way, because they were troublesome. They disputed my right, but I taught them better. I taught them a great moral lesson, though they had not much time to profit by it. If they had had the might to throw me overboard, I should not have troubled myself about their right, any more, or, at any rate, any longer, than they did about mine.

But, though the echo is apt enough, it would be as much out of keeping with Peacock's practice to make Melvas identical with the politician Canning as it would to link Maelgon personally with the soldier Wellington. The point, as ever, is that each character is a type, and Peacock is surely relying more on a theoretical text than on real men or actual events. His picture of aristocratic government in *The Misfortunes of Elphin* must be indebted to a recent classic critique of it: James Mill's essay on 'The Law of Nations', originally written as an article for the *Encyclopaedia Britannica*, but privately published as a book in or before 1828.[56] This essay is very relevant to Peacock's theme, for it considers what ethical code (if any) binds an oligarchy. Mill's bleak answer must have reminded politically conscious readers of certain post-war régimes, and of recent dealings between the European powers:[57]

> To punish implies superiority of strength. For the strong, therefore, the law of nations may perhaps have a sanction, as against the weak. But what can it have as against the strong? Is it the strong, however, or is it the weak, by whom it is most liable to be violated? The answer is obvious and undeniable. – As against those from whom almost solely any violation of the laws of nations need be apprehended, there appears, therefore, to be no sanction at all.

Mill concludes that in a world where virtually all states are oligarchies, to employ ethical terms at all is misleading; for, as he observes with ironical understatement, 'an aristocratical code of morality ... is exceedingly different from that more enlarged and all-comprehensive code, on which the happiness of the greatest number depends, and to which alone the epithet moral in propriety belongs.'[58] Without positively committing himself on the last point, Peacock adheres faithfully to Mill's notion of aristocracy, by drawing a world in which only Might is Right.

As always, Peacock establishes his important satiric points through his structure. The portraits of the three complementary Tory types – the incompetent Seithenyn, the tyrannical Maelgon, the politic Melvas – are separated and yet also related by interlude chapters; and these urbane general essays on the historical organisation of the sixth-century Welsh are so worded that the parallels with modern Britain are inescapable. Chapter vi, 'The Education of Taliesin', is primarily a chapter about religion, and about the absence of real moral improvement, or even change, since the nation was converted to Christianity. Lest he should appear to be scoring points off the Catholics (he favoured Emancipation, as two contemporary verse squibs show),[59] Peacock is careful to hint that ultra-Protestantism is equally unattractive:[60]

> The British clergy were, however, very contumacious towards the see of Rome, and would only acknowledge the spiritual authority of the archbishopric of Caer Lleon, which was, during many centuries, the primacy of Britain. St. Augustin, when he came over, at a period not long subsequent to that of the present authentic history, to preach Christianity to the Saxons, who had for the most part held fast to their Odinism, had also the secondary purpose of making them instruments for teaching the British clergy submission to Rome: as a means to which end, the newly-converted Saxons set upon the monastery of Bangor Iscoed, and put its twelve hundred monks to the sword. This was the first overt act in which the Saxons set forth their new sense of a religion of peace. It is alleged, indeed, that these twelve hundred monks supported themselves by the labour of their own hands. If they did so, it was, no doubt, a gross heresy; but whether it deserved the castigation it received from St. Augustin's proselytes, may be a question in polemics.
>
> As the people did not read the Bible, and had no religious tracts, their religion, it may be assumed, was not very pure. ...
>
> The Druids were the sacred class of the bardic order. Before the change of religion, it was by far the most numerous class; for the very simple reason, that there was most to be got by it: all ages and nations having been sufficiently enlightened to make the trade of priest more profitable than that of poet.

Peacock felt that the satirist's mission was to assail complacency wherever he found it, and his contemporaries were much given to patronising any era of the past which did not subscribe to the Christian religion. He had recently handled such a book, in Moore's *Epicurean*.[61] No doubt he had also read *The Mythology and Rites of the Ancient Druids* (1809), by the Rev. Edward Davies, Rector of Bishopston, Glamorgan, which drew a moral Peacock would certainly have thought unacceptably lenient to the modern church:[62]

> A candid exposé of that mass of error under which they groaned,
> may inspire us with more lively gratitude for the knowledge of
> the true religion, and, perhaps, suggest a seasonable caution of
> the indulgence of vain speculation upon sacred subjects – a
> weakness to which the human mind is prone in every age.

In Peacock's view, one religious man – whether Druid or Celtic
Christian, Catholic or Protestant – proves much like another, and
the only religion of which he is remotely in favour is Taliesin's
worship of Nature.[63] In a similarly general chapter on Arthur's
court, symmetrically placed between the sequences on Maelgon
and on Melvas, Peacock again establishes his general satiric
position: that no-one can be confident of progress, for if the
modern Britain differs from Arthur's, it is rather for the worse.
Some of these touches, especially if they are taken out of context,
may be interpreted as a satire on modernity, and hence even of
progressivism. But when the structure of the book is considered as a
whole, its architecture suggests that the main object Peacock had in
view was not on this occasion either religious zeal or contemporary
complacency, though both were topics on which he could not resist
diverting himself. The essay-chapters may be seen as variations
upon the main theme, or as devices intended to link it more firmly
with the present. What they do not do is to modify the bold outline
of the portrait of contemporary Toryism.

A diagrammatic presentation of *The Misfortunes of Elphin*, Figure
2, shows how it is built around its three types of Tory politician. As
always with Peacock's books, the elegance pleases for its own sake,
not least when Peacock can be found adopting a clever device to
sustain it. It will be noticed, for example, that though chapters vi
and xii, the book's two general cultural essays, are exact
counterparts, chapters v and xi are not. For chapter v, Peacock
needs to introduce his real hero, Taliesin, and the short narrative is
thus taken up with the story of his miraculous birth, elaborated by
a translation of a genuine poem from the Welsh. For chapter xi
there is no such requirement; from the structural point of view, all
that is needed is to fill the space. Peacock does so by having Taliesin
visit the castle of Dinas Vawr while he is on his way to Arthur's
court. There can be no particular Welsh song for the occasion: the
needs of symmetry are met by a pastiche invented by Peacock.
'The War Song of Dinas Vawr' is Peacock's best-known poem,

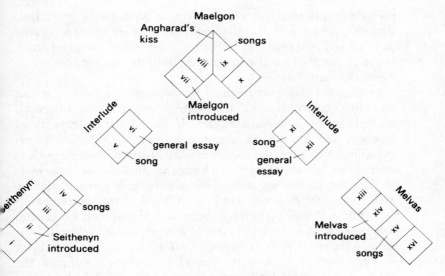

Figure 2   The Misfortunes of Elphin

and one of his best, but it is also cleverly designed to perform a function. As 'the quintessence of all the war-songs that ever were written, and the sum and substance of all the appetencies, tendencies and consequences of military glory', it links the stupid tyrant Maelgon with the cleverer adventurer Melvas – since both are variants of the militant Tory. Yet it is also the occasion for the re-introduction of that other opportunist, Seithenyn. The creed is that of all three:[64]

> The mountain sheep are sweeter,
> But the valley sheep are fatter;
> We therefore deem it meeter
> To carry off the latter.
> We made an expedition;
> We met a host, and quelled it;
> We forced a strong position,
> And killed the men who held it ...

Peacock is never a major poet, but the songs in his satires can be highly effective. By now he appears to have picked up a new mentor, Byron, from whom he takes fire and nervous energy, a pulse-beat that was noticeably absent in his earlier poetry. But, above all, the songs in *The Misfortunes of Elphin* are effective because they are skilfully deployed in their context. They are structurally essential, and they are also inseparable from the supposed creator of them, the bard Taliesin.

Perhaps the daring with which Peacock presents Taliesin as that rare character in his work, the positive hero, is partly an artist's solution to an inherent difficulty. If indeed the military types Maelgon and Melvas are meant to suggest the existing British government of 1828 and the immediate situation, then Peacock is structurally in the difficulty of Dryden in *Absalom and Achitophel*: he does not know how in real life his action is going to resolve itself, whether in some kind of political compromise, or in catastrophe. Peacock had faced a similar problem with the equally contemporaneous political satire, *Melincourt*, and had provided the same solution, which is stylised and ideal. Taliesin resembles Forester, but he is an even more abstracted and resonant figure: the very epitome of his kind, the seer-poet of classic Welsh literary tradition.

There is an additional force and point in the characterisation, compared with Forester, Escot, or any other Peacockian intellectual. For Peacock in 1828 was writing in a new cultural situation, in which poets were under attack as they had not been ten years earlier. On the whole he shared the moral and political attitudes of the utilitarians, whose leaders were now his colleagues and even his friends. James Mill was his superior at the India House; he dined weekly with the movement's sage, Jeremy Bentham. But Bentham himself was doubtful about the utility of art; and from the very first issue of their organ, the *Westminster Review*, his followers had become associated with a stance of outright hostility to poetry in particular. By mid-1824 all three of the leading younger Romantic poets, Byron, Shelley and Keats, were dead, and utilitarian reviewers tended to aim their fire at the most prolific and successful of writers who remained, Scott and Thomas Moore. In the first issue of the *Westminster Review*, for example, the lawyer Peregrine Bingham in one article wrote of the irrationality and childish nostalgia of poets of Moore's type; in another, of their tendency to encourage 'depression of spirits, discouragement, despair'.[65] Peacock was equally critical of Moore, and had moreover made these very points against fashionable literature, in his essay *The Four Ages of Poetry* and in his satire *Nightmare Abbey*. In principle Peacock was unquestionably himself a utilitarian critic. He agreed with Bingham and with the Mills, father and son, that what was known as 'polite' literature had fallen into the hands of their political opponents, an aristocracy resolved to hold on to power.[66] As James Mill argued in his famous article in the *Westminster Review* upon the *Edinburgh*, the literature produced for such a class was trivial and mostly derivative; it lacked intellectual content, purpose and utility. 'Polite literature, and what are called the fine arts' became 'a substitute ... for useful enquiry'; a conservative aristocracy wanted in its reading 'nothing that can excite controversy, nothing that can occasion dissatisfaction, all pensive, gentlemanly and subdued, all trifling and acquiescent as a drawing room conversation.'[67] But such points, reiterated, unfortunately gave the impression that all those associated with the *Westminster Review* were hostile to the arts as a whole. By 1829 Hazlitt was declaring that Peacock's position as a *Westminster* reviewer could not be reconciled with his passion for opera – or with his wit. Hazlitt finds a bleak philistine coincidence of view in the sermons of the Rev. Edward Irving, and in many reviews in the *Westminster*. In Irving he objects to

> privations made of the most trifling and innocent amusements, which, for no other reason than because you like them, the votaries of spiritual pride and presumption resent and denounce as incurring the loss of heaven and the vengeance of the Most High.

But the utilitarians[68]

> are seized with the same *hydrophobia* of music, painting, and poetry, as their pious predecessors. ... Will Mr. Irving let you go to Covent-garden or Drury-lane? No more will the *Westminster*, unless Mrs. Chatterley should act, 'who in herself sums all delight, so absolute she seems' to Mr. P[eacock]. Will Mr. Irving send you to the opera to hear sounds from Madame Pasta 'that might create a soul under the ribs of death?' No more will the *Westminster*! P[eacock], poor fellow! dare no more show his face there than his own Sir Ourang Outang!

The incompatibility perceived by Hazlitt was felt by Peacock too. He did not immediately dissociate himself from the *Westminster* when the Mills broke away, in 1828. Indeed, he wrote three articles in 1830 for the *Westminster* under Bowring, the editor with whom the Mills had quarrelled. But by late 1830, when he wrote *Crotchet Castle*, Peacock was satirising the more blinkered or over-sanguine utilitarian attitudes, and by the mid-1830s he had been recruited by John Stuart Mill to write for a new journal with more liberal utilitarian policies, the *London Review*. However, for the time being, in 1828, the very year of the breakup among the utilitarians, he was content to put forward, in *The Misfortunes of Elphin*, a counter-proposition — virtually a Shelleyan proposition — that the true poet *has* a utilitarian function, because he is for thought, and against tyranny: he is, in Shelley's phrase, the unacknowledged legislator of mankind.[69]

In terms of its satiric targets the book is (appropriately) triadic, though cunningly cross-referenced with motifs that re-emerge: the threat of flood in the first part, the threat of invasion in the third; Seithenyn in the first and third parts; a kidnapping, in the second and third. But viewed from another aspect, that of its central character Taliesin, the story seems a single unit. Taliesin is the real opponent of the Tory brigand-politician, for he is the public's true servant, bent on establishing truth and justice. In the first part, which takes place before he is born, his role is foreshadowed by the honest servant Teithrin. Teithrin reminds us not only of Turgot, but also of the type of man Peacock must have known at the India House, and indeed must often have felt himself to be — a man in a position of responsibility, who is just too junior for his efficiency and integrity to save the situation when others will not listen. 'Teithrin kept his portion of the embankment in exemplary condition, and paced with daily care the limits of his charge; but one day, by some accident, he strayed beyond them, and observed symptoms of neglect that filled him with dismay.'[70] He carefully explores the sea-wall along its whole length, discovers the extent of the neglect into which it has fallen, and sets off to warn the court. Though he succeeds in bringing prince Elphin to Seithenyn's tower on the ramparts, it is still Teithrin, as the man of action, who hurries out to establish that the storm is upon them, and who afterwards lights the warning beacon. But this of course is

Teithrin's limitation, which is not his personal defect but the consequence of his subordinate role. Though always efficient, and totally loyal to his masters in good times and bad, he has no power to do anything but issue warnings. Moreover, because he has no effective means of conveying his message, his warnings sound too faint and too late. The most effective act in his power during the crisis of the action is lighting the fire which marks that the wall has already fallen.

Taliesin's superiority to Teithrin resides in his office as bard. Peacock pokes some characteristic fun at certain aspects of Welsh bardolatry, at the mystification accompanying it, and at the failure of the great majority of bards to live up to their principles. One of the cleverest examples of his deployment of Welsh material is his adaptation of a poem known as 'The Indignation of the Bards', which Peacock slyly translates as 'The Indignation of Taliesin with the Bards of Maelgon Gwynedd':[71]

> False bards the sacred fire pervert,
> Whose songs are won without desert;
> Who falsehoods weave in specious lays,
> To gild the base with virtue's praise.
>
> From court to court, from tower to tower,
> In warrior's tent, in lady's bower,
> For gold, for wine, for food, for fire,
> They tune their throats at all men's hire.
>
> Their harps re-echo wide and far
> With sensual love, and bloody war,
> And drunkenness, and flattering lies:
> Truth's light may shine for other eyes.
>
> In palaces they still are found,
> At feasts, promoting senseless sound:
> He is their demigod at least,
> Whose only virtue is his feast.
>
> They love to talk; they hate to think;
> All day they sing; all night they drink:
> No useful toils their hands employ;
> In boisterous throngs is all their joy.

> The bird will fly, the fish will swim,
> The bee the honied flowers will skim;
> The food by toil each creature brings,
> Except false bards and worthless kings.
>
> Learning and wisdom claim to find
> Homage and succour from mankind;
> But learning's right, and wisdom's due,
> Are falsely claimed by slaves like you.
>
> True bards know truth, and truth will show;
> Ye know it not, nor care to know:
> Your king's weak mind false judgment warps;
> Rebuke his wrong, or break your harps.
>
> I know the mountain and the plain;
> I know where right and justice reign;
> I from the tower will Elphin free;
> Your king shall learn his doom from me.

Though it has reference to the genuine poem of the real-life Taliesin, this version is very much a poem of 1828. Peacock gives the case of the utilitarians against fashionable literature, and at the same time points out the positive role as Shelley argued it, for the true, disinterested artist. By issuing a challenge at this half-way point in the book to false, sycophantic poets, Taliesin establishes himself as the hero. He alone is consistently to live up to the Bardic motto – the Truth against the World.[72] As a bard he has two great moments – here at Maelgon's court in chapter ix, and afterwards in chapter xv at Arthur's court, where he again establishes his pre-eminence in a bardic competition. It has never been noticed, indeed, how completely the poems given to the bardic characters in *The Misfortunes of Elphin* subserve the main allegorical theme of the narrative. During the bardic competition before Arthur, famous bards of Welsh tradition recite a series of poems of widely differing kinds – Llywarch's descriptive nature-poem, Merlin's obscure and mystical prophecy, Aneurin's battle saga. It is not evident why Taliesin's contribution, as an individual poem, should win the contest, except that it is not so much an individual poem as a declaration of faith in poetry, providing it is serious, and engaged in affairs on the side of justice:[73]

And I am he: and well I know
Ceridwen's power protects me still;
And hence o'er hill and vale I go,
And sing, unharmed, whate'er I will.
She has for me Time's veil withdrawn:
The images of things long gone,
The shadows of the coming days,
Are present to my visioned gaze.

And I have heard the words of power,
By Ceirion's solitary lake,
That bid, at midnight's thrilling hour,
Eryri's hundred echoes wake.
I to Diganwy's towers have sped,
And now Caer Lleon's halls I tread,
Demanding justice, now, as then,
From Maelgon, most unjust of men.

If Taliesin's part is seen as a whole, then, it supports by
allegorical means, in action, the Peacockian view that the artist is
(or should be) an intellectual leader in society, and a moral agent.
At the book's half-way point, the close of chapter viii, Taliesin
kisses Elphin's daughter Melanghel, and so dedicates himself to her
service. Thereafter, he, like Forester, is consecrated to a quest. His
aim is to release the two hostages, Elphin and Gwenyvar, who are
held by the bandit-kings. It is tempting to allegorise the roles of the
captives too: to see them as representatives of the helpless populace
under the domination of the powerful and ruthless. Taliesin's task
of obtaining their release is acted out on an idealised level. The
abbot, who actually persuades Melvas to give up Gwenyvar,
resembles the mediating, trimming politician of real life; Taliesin
has a more than everyday power to out-manoeuvre him, by virtue
of his articulacy, and his insight into the truth. Peacock avails
himself only of subtle hints of Taliesin's remarkable powers, as
given in the Welsh. In one of his celebrated poems, the original
Taliesin speaks as a shape-shifter who 'had been with the cherubim
at the fall of Lucifer, in Paradise at the fall of man, and with
Alexander at the fall of Babylon'.[74] The insights Peacock bestows
upon him are more commonplace and more explicable in everyday

terms, as well as more useful. Peacock describes Taliesin's celebrated prophecy that the Britons would end by being dispossessed of all the land of Britain except Wales as 'a result which political sagacity might have apprehended from their disunion'.[75]

The resolution, with Arthur dispensing god-like justice, is necessarily notional, and has no counterpart in the real-life situation of 1828. The bard's moral victory belongs to the world of art. It makes a point entirely in keeping with Peacock's views of the artist's role as expressed elsewhere – notably in *Melincourt* and *Nightmare Abbey* – but does so with a force and positiveness of which critics have thought Peacock incapable. As a political satire, *The Misfortunes of Elphin* is, by Peacock's standards, unusually direct. George Saintsbury, a late-nineteenth-century editor of firm Tory convictions, professed to find political ambivalence in the book's theme and presentation, as much of an attack on insurgency as on the interests opposed to it – 'the invading ocean is quite as susceptible of being taken as a text as the rotten embankment'.[76] It is true that Peacock does not write as the advocate of violent revolution, for both the inundation and its moral equivalent, the Anglo-Saxon invasion, are presented as evils. Equally, the embankment, correlative for the existing constitution, is or should be a force for stability, and hence good:[77]

> Elphin gazed earnestly on the peopled plain, reposing in the calm of evening between the mountains and the sea, and thought, with deep feelings of secret pain, how much of life and human happiness was intrusted to the ruinous mound on which he stood.

It is an image which would be used only by a constitutionalist; a man who, as Saintsbury suggests, fears revolution. But, equally clearly, the author believes that revolution is more likely to be brought about by a government of Tory backwoodsmen than by gradual reformers like himself. What has misled Saintsbury and many modern readers is the blurring of party alignment in clever men in the 1820s. Interventionist solutions, whether through the state or through private agencies, attracted adherents of all shades of opinion, men hitherto as far opposed as Southey and Cobbett,

Coleridge and Robert Owen. Now they might be expressed as nostalgia for the monasticism and feudal social cohesion of the Middle Ages; now as incipient socialism. Meanwhile, although the Tories had been in power for so long – almost throughout the Napoleonic Wars, and since – Toryism as a real political force, and as an ideology which could rival an increasingly vigorous liberalism, was in fact collapsing. Genuine liberals like the youthful J. S. Mill, worried at the symptoms that progressive ideas were hardening into orthodoxies, toyed with what seem 'Tory' attitudes, such as nostalgia for the co-operation and religious idealism of the Middle Ages.[78] Similarly, Peacock in his two essay chapters writes in praise of Merry England.[79] And yet Peacock is much less an admirer of the past, than a sceptic about the supposed superiority of the present. He resembles John Mill, who uses the virtues of the past as a means to challenge modern society, rather than Coleridge, with his nostalgia for an imagined state in which temporal and spiritual authority were one, or Macaulay, who sees history as a series of inferior stages in preparation for the present day.

The Misfortunes of Elphin is in conception a satire on Toryism, but it specifically avoids adopting the solution implicitly favoured in James Mill's *Essays:* government by a progressive, commercial middle class. Peacock uses the opportunity of comparison with a past civilisation to challenge such modern middle-class benefits as steam, a paper currency, and evangelical Christianity. At the same time he avoids sentimentalising the feudal past, with its characteristic institutions – monasticism, the hereditary aristocracy, and the squirearchy. Like the Tory organicist, he sees a continuity between past and present – but for Peacock it is a continuing tale of self-interest and exploitation:[80]

They had no steam-engines ... wherein the squalid many, from infancy to age, might be turned into component portions of machinery for the benefit of the purple-faced few. ...
They were lost in the grossness of beef and ale. They had no pamphleteering societies to demonstrate that reading and writing are better than meat and drink; and they were utterly destitute of the blessings of those 'schools for all', the house of correction, and the treadmill, wherein the autochthonal justice of our agrestic kakistocracy now castigates the heinous sins

which were then committed with impunity, of treading on old footpaths, picking up dead wood, and moving on the face of the earth within sound of the whirr of a partridge.

In satirising the ruling class of the present day, his strategy is to imply that ruling classes have always been much of a muchness: a very different picture from the clerical and chivalric sentiment of Coleridge, whose *Constitution of Church and State* of 1830 was to imply the historical disinterestedness of the élite.

As satires, *Maid Marian* and *The Misfortunes of Elphin* are a genre on their own. Their historical setting separates them from the rest of Peacock's books, even though the point of departure is always the world as it is. Their approach to the present is necessarily more abstract and generalised, less densely cross-referenced, than in the conversation novels. But, if this difference appears a weakness in *Maid Marian*, it does not do so in *The Misfortunes of Elphin*.

Two factors, perhaps, do more than anything else to ensure the success of the later book after the relative failure of the earlier. One is a matter of content. The satire on European monarchies in *Maid Marian* is, deliberately, a topic somewhat removed from the field of immediate political controversy. It is also a topic on which Peacock has no immediate knowledge, nor a great deal that is pertinent to say. Consequently, *Maid Marian* seems unfocussed, its idealised characters left, somewhat ineffectually, in the never-never world of the greenwood. There is too little clash of ideas; too little useful tension between past and present. *The Misfortunes of Elphin* is a far more meaningful commentary on specific political events. Though apparently more antiquarian, it is also more dense in allusion to contemporary controversial literature, especially to Macaulay's criticism of one particular Tory administration, and to James Mill's philosophical strictures on Tory government in general. In bringing to mind the French Revolution, and in relating it to a currently unstable situation at home, Peacock in *The Misfortunes of Elphin* writes very immediately as a man of his time. Macaulay and J. S. Mill were writing, or thinking of writing, histories of the great revolution of 1789 during the very year in which *Elphin* appeared, though it was to be Carlyle, encouraged by Mill, who completed the task. As Carlyle mused:[81]

> To me it often seems as if the right *History* (that impossible thing
> I mean by History) of the French Revolution were the grand
> poem of our time; as if the man who *could* write the *truth* of that,
> were worth all the other writers and singers.

Like *Crotchet Castle* two years later, *The Misfortunes of Elphin* is
intimately caught up in the current of intellectual ideas at the
political centre of things. Where before he had been the friend of
Shelley, and an onlooker, a satirist without first-hand access to
politics, Peacock wrote now as an Indian administrator, the friend
of Bentham and the Mills, and a shrewd judge of political realities.

In addition, *The Misfortunes of Elphin* finds a new resource in its
plot. From the beginning, from *Headlong Hall* on, there is
autonomy in the worlds evoked by Peacock's satires. The titles
emphasise the location: each book set in modern times is named
after a large and civilised country house, situated in a beautiful
landscape. It is, in a literal sense, a world apart. It may not be an
accident that Peacock abandoned his one story set in London;[82] by
1818, such an idea may have become uncongenial. The interest in a
continuous narrative shown by members of Peacock's own poetic
circle, by Byron, Hunt and Keats in particular, is part of a growing
contemporary instinct for creating a sufficient art-world. Scott
anticipates them all, the first major novelist to expend his art on
sustaining a continuous web of illusion. Despite his belief in the
classical doctrine that art subserves life, Peacock could hardly help
responding to so irresistible a tide of taste. His growing passion for
music after 1817, especially romantic opera, inevitably influenced
his aesthetic ideas, for music, unlike literature, must operate apart
under its own aesthetic rules, and has nothing immediate to do
with manners, morals and ideas. The increasing perfection of the
worlds he creates, after the mid-point of his career, gives his last
three books, *The Misfortunes of Elphin*, *Crotchet Castle*, and *Gryll
Grange*, a special beauty, but also a piquancy, since the reality with
which they deal is increasingly complex, and prosy. With *The
Misfortunes of Elphin*, Peacock solves the paradox by introducing a
simple allegorical plot, of an intellectual knight-errant abroad in a
world of power-politics. Through allegory, he manages to avoid
personality, but to capture a subject which recurs in other societies
and times, the mentality of a conservative governing class on the

eve of a deluge. By comparison, *Melincourt* is too clogged with detail, *Maid Marian* not clogged enough. In *The Misfortunes of Elphin* he achieves one of his best books, and, moreover, his very best strictly political book — and that is to place it high among political satires in English.

Chapter 6

The March of Mind:
Crochet Castle

> Love is bought and sold.
> Lady Clarinda's Song at Chainmail Hall

Nostalgia may explain the affection of many of Peacock's readers for *Crotchet Castle*: it is a quintessential book, with something in it of all the others. In returning to a contemporary setting, initially a country house, it goes back to the pattern first established in *Headlong Hall*. The resemblance to the first three satires rather than to the two historical romances is confirmed by its title, simply the house in which most of the conversation takes place. At the same time the memory of the romances lingers. The second half of *Crotchet Castle* has the pastoral setting and the lyricism of *Maid Marian*; the way in which the songs are deployed in the last chapter is reminiscent of the bardic competition of *The Misfortunes of Elphin*. Even so, the relationship with *The Misfortunes of Elphin* is deliberately complementary rather than parallel. Where *The Misfortunes of Elphin* was primarily a satire on Toryism, *Crotchet Castle* is a satire on a world in which liberalism has become orthodoxy. Where *The Misfortunes of Ephin* was limited to one theme, politics, *Crotchet Castle* broadly and even amorphously directs itself to the subject of culture. Artistically the effect is of contrast rather than repetition. The earlier book is a relatively tight-knit narrative, the later a dispersed panorama – the book of Peacock's which best fits the term 'anatomy'.

The comparison with *Headlong Hall* also serves to confirm a breadth in *Crotchet Castle* not present in all Peacockian satire. Superficially we seem to be back in a world remarkably like that of the first book, with the action dividing itself between dinner-parties of disputatious guests, and walks in the Welsh mountains. Even the two hosts have something in common: in fashionable terms parvenus (in spite of Harry Headlong's Welsh genealogy), each with a taste for up-to-the-minute culture. But the resemblances do not go much beyond this point. The crowd of characters, the representative intellectuals of each book, are significantly different. The topics raised in conversation at Crotchet Castle touch upon areas of wider controversy than the disputes of their opposite numbers at Headlong Hall. But it is also true that in the earlier book the comic types could be broadly categorised into performers, aestheticians, and scientists: as such, linked with the current cultural situation, and (on fairly lucid grounds) condemned. The intellectuals in *Crotchet Castle* seem more genuinely heterogeneous. Apart from their narrow obsessiveness (which is also a characteristic of their counterparts in *Headlong Hall*), they have relatively little in common with one another. And they are individuals in a further sense. More than is generally the case with Peacock, they point to real-life originals. Mr Eavesdrop, who publishes gossip about his friends, evokes a common enough type, but would certainly have been identified by Peacock's contemporaries as one or other of the two friends of Byron who had recently published their reminiscences of him: Leigh Hunt and Thomas Moore.[1] It would take only a little more knowledge of London intellectual life to connect the lethal Mr Henbane with the surgeon, anatomist and toxicologist Benjamin Collins Brodie, who actually did poison a cat and bring it to life again: the cat lived on as the pet of the dramatist Joanna Baillie and clearly became something of a talking-point.[2] Another semi-public figure, Samuel Rush Meyrick, shared the leading characteristics of Mr Chainmail when first introduced, his penchant for arms and armour and his special interest in Welsh castles.[3]

In reality, Mr Chainmail is a different case from the others, with more significant functions in the story to fulfil. He soon becomes a more generalised figure — a lover of the past, a critic of the present. It is at this stage — the abstraction and typification common elsewhere to Peacock's minor characters — that the crowd of specialists in *Crotchet Castle* do not seem to arrive. The learned crank is a traditional target of satire, and another satirist might have been content with the slight point, that modern society often spawns such types. Peacock is generally far stricter than this in his selection, and in all the earlier satires the special folly of each of his learned butts is tied with some precision to the general theme. Only the guests at Mr Crotchet's dinner-table fail to illustrate the particular aspect of society's intellectual life which is the topic in hand. Though most of them are, certainly, scientists, the fancifulness of their schemes prevents the reader from linking them with those favourite subjects of the March of Mind – mechanics, chemistry and hydrostatics. They have nothing to do with the enlightenment of the masses. In reality, the impression of social chaos is a calculated effect in *Crotchet Castle*, the fruit of serious analysis.[4] But it looks for all the world as though the specialists are being ridiculed simply for having an intellectual passion; and such ridicule, while it has pleased some savourers of human oddity, has increasingly tended to give Peacock a bad name. A case in point is Mr Firedamp, with his proposal to rid the world of malaria by draining the swamps. Scientifically his case is a good one. He is by no means analogous with Mr Eavesdrop; he is not even so obviously grotesque in the method he uses as Mr Henbane. If Peacock was laughing at him, or at scientists like him, it looks as though the Firedamps have had the last laugh. It is because the group is heterogeneous, yet presented evenhandedly, that *Crotchet Castle* has been read as a philistine book, the surest proof that Peacock had no head for serious ideas. 'He makes his cranks representative of the men who shape destiny, as cosy reactionaries nearly always do. ... *Crotchet Castle* is altogether the harshest and least pleasing of Peacock's novels.'[5]

But, when all is said, the frivolous treatment of the scientists in *Crotchet Castle* is a very marginal affair; they have more influence on our sense of the book's structural coherence than on our reading of its theme. After all, these characters are minor, and (apart from Mr Chainmail) much less important to Peacock's central concerns than has ever been allowed. They have walk-on, or, more accurately, sitting-down, parts. Most of them barely speak. They exist to people Mr Crotchet's dinner-table, to provide a subject for Lady Clarinda's wit, to convey a sense, however imprecise, that what we are seeing is a representative cross-section of scientists in the age of the March of Mind. It is Peacock's attitude to that phenomenon which is significant. Only while the whole quality of his satire is being trivialised can the bit-players be seen as providing the key to it.

As always in Peacock's books, the real issue emerges in the form of a debate between the 'ancients' and the 'moderns'. And, as in every other case, the 'ancient' party is allowed to prevail; but that does not mean that here, any more than elsewhere, Peacock accepts the sentimental fallacies of those in love with a non-existent past. Instead he adopts the classic stance of the satirist, from Aristophanes to Swift, of seizing upon those weapons, however unlikely, that puncture complacency about the present. Dr Folliott *is* unlikely, and Peacock's relationship in *Crotchet Castle* to his champion of the ancients is a uniquely complex one. Nevertheless, the satire's ideological battlefield is laid out here, in the disputes between Folliott (occasionally supported by Mr Chainmail and Mr Trillo) and his two principal antagonists, Mr MacQuedy and Mr Crotchet.

It is an opposition between two fundamental kinds of cultural value. Peacock, himself broadly a utilitarian, and the friend or acquaintance of all the leading philosophical radicals, was well placed at the India House to see the strengths and weaknesses of the movement. Since his earlier satires, the group's role in national affairs had been transformed, and what at the close of the Napoleonic Wars had been a small intellectual élite, critical and radical, was now an amorphous general influence, a force upholding commerce and, in effect, a new orthodoxy. The need to simplify in order to speak to a mass public had driven some of the leading proponents of utilitarianism into crudities and catchphrases that were anathema to a man of Peacock's intellectual fastidiousness. Much has been made by some commentators of his personal dislike of James Mill, his immediate superior at the India House. One story of a confrontation between them dates back (if true) to 1832:[6]

> Mr. Peacock talked to me today at much length about Jeremy Bentham, with whom he had been extremely intimate – dining with him *tête à tête*, once a week for years together. He

mentioned, amongst other things, that when experiments were being made with Mr. Bentham's body after his death, Mr. James Mill had come into his [Mr. Peacock's] room at the India House and told him that there exuded from Mr. Bentham's head a kind of oil, which was almost unfreezable, and which he conceived might be useful for the oiling of chronometers which were going into high latitudes. 'The less you say about that, Mill', said Peacock, 'the better it will be for *you*; because if the fact once becomes known, just as we see now in the newspapers advertisements to the effect that a fine bear is to be killed for his grease, we shall be having advertisements to the effect that a fine philosopher is to be killed for his oil.'

Since Peacock himself is the source of this anecdote, it appears to tell us how he remembered James Mill. As Mill was an even closer friend of Bentham's than was Peacock, and much more indebted to him, it is (on this occasion) hardly in an amiable light. However, in his correspondence with Lord Broughton long afterwards Peacock remembered another side of James Mill, the man of educated taste who could delight in Spenser and Horace; by then Peacock could refer to him as 'our old friend James Mill'.[7] It may be that after all Peacock felt no inveterate personal dislike, at least not one that survived the years, but at the time he certainly had intellectual reservations. The elder Mill, in the 1820s the most dedicated and effective of propagandists for utilitarian goals, had the cast of mind of a religious dogmatist, a type which Peacock was always prone to suspect.

There must always be an uneasy relationship between a popular political movement, however ideological, and its intellectuals, however activist, since in some degree the intellectual also has to serve the truth. Such tensions had been evident among the utilitarians for many years. The period from 1808 and especially from 1815 had seen the movement's ideas disseminated until they had become the working creed of industrialisation, an inalienable part of the middle-class mind. Yet in the very same years its best intellectuals had developed what was essentially a critique of the workings of the capitalist system. As Halévy observes, from 1808 there were two kinds of utilitarian, the optimists and the pessimists.[8] The hopeful note was sounded for the public, in organs like the *Westminster Review*, the gloomy when utilitarians wrote for the élite and for each other. First Malthus and then Ricardo noted reasons why progress, and the increasing happiness of the greatest number, were not, after all, inevitable. Ricardo, for example, despite his superficial optimism, also saw that the interests of the landed aristocracy were tending to diverge from those of the manufacturers and the people. The strain, the delays, the potential suffering threatened by such a forecast made a poor programme for the hustings, and Ricardo's reservations did not find their way into the writings of the more popular James Mill and J. R. McCulloch.

Propagandists for sophisticated political theories of course face a difficulty when they come to translate a system into terms that are intelligible and, above all, attractive. Peacock's position with regard to the dogmatists and resolute optimists of his own party is curiously like Orwell's relationship with the orthodox left – even though no two writers could be less alike in tone and method. Though there is little direct biographical evidence about Peacock's uneasy relations with the two flanks of utilitarianism between 1828 and 1831[9] – the more sanguine, dogmatic group that continued to write for Bowring's *Westminster*, and the intellectual dissidents – his reservations about the former are deducible from *Crotchet Castle*. The book itself is self-explanatory, provided that the reader is attuned to Peacock's working method and, in this most topical and densely-packed of the satires, familiar with his sources.

His targets prove much broader than one party, still less one wing of a party. Dogmatism itself is a central subject, but it is not found only on one side. The more satiric passages dramatise the clash of opinion, especially on the divisive topics of popular education and the arts, as these debates are conducted in three of the leading journals of the day – the *Westminster*, the *Edinburgh*, and the *Quarterly* reviews. If Peacock had meant to single out particularly the utilitarians for ridicule, he would probably have made more use than he did of the *Westminster*, which was founded in 1824 as the group's campaigning journal. The *Westminster* is free with comment on the controversies of the day, and often delivers a brash message in a provocative tone:[10]

> From these same ancestors we received the distaff, the horsemill and the coracle. These we have converted into the cotton-engine, the steam-engine, and the three-decker. ... We have despised our ancestors, and we have proved their wisdom folly.

And, as we have despised them, we have risen and flourished.

Peacock would not have found passages like this congenial. He never accepted the materialist argument, that the wealth-producing industrial process, served by the new technology, was a basis for pride in things modern; and of course he detested the rosy belief that all was well. Strictly speaking, though, the classic boasts about materialism and modernity were not in the pages of the *Westminster*, even though individuals associated with it were the authors of some of them. James Mill's *Essay on Government* was one such document, and echoes of it are heard in *Crotchet Castle*, not in the form of direct quotation from Mill himself, but in allusions to one of the most celebrated performances in any journal of the 1820s, Macaulay's review of Mill's *Essay* for the *Edinburgh* in March 1829.

Macaulay's complaints against Mill are directed against a method, first as it is expressed in Mill's style: 'His arguments are stated with the utmost affectation of precision; his divisions are awfully formal; and his style is generally as dry as that of Euclid's Elements'.[11] Macaulay goes on to deride the scholastic systematizing, the intolerable abstraction of the kind of reasoning Mill employs:[12]

> We have here an elaborate treatise on Government, from which, but for two or three passing allusions, it would not appear that the author was aware that any governments actually existed among men. Certain propensities of human nature are assumed; and from these premises the whole science of politics is synthetically deduced!

Macaulay's objection to Mill's *Essay* is that of a sceptic and a pragmatist against a theoretician. 'We believe that it is utterly impossible to deduce the science of government from the principles of human nature.'[13] Peacock surely avails himself of Macaulay's arguments, especially in the speech he gives to Dr Folliott which begins, 'You have given the name of a science to what is yet an imperfect inquiry.'[14]

The *Edinburgh Review* is in fact Peacock's most fruitful source. When writing on Mill, Macaulay is assailing complacency, and thereby provides usefully hostile detail for the portrait of the utilitarian ideologue, MacQuedy. Elsewhere it might be Macaulay

himself who proves susceptible to the very charge he flings at Mill.
Reviewing Southey's *Colloquies*, for example, which are an attempt
at a critique of progress, Macaulay sneers at 'rants ... about
picturesque cottages and temples of Mammon', and declares that
statistics of longevity prove that man is better off than he has ever
been.[15] Peacock weaves observations about cottages and temples of
Mammon into Lady Clarinda's conversation, in terms which
indicate that his sympathies are rather with Southey in the
matter.[16] In fact, the *Edinburgh* is generally quite as guilty as the
Westminster when it comes to over-simplification and over-
confidence in the present order of things. Apart from the
commonly sanguine Macaulay, it has writing for it the arch-
reforming Whig, Brougham, and the busiest of middle-brow
popularising Scottish economists, John Ramsay McCulloch.[17]
Clearly Peacock's MacQuedy on the whole reflects McCulloch,
not the individual man (though Peacock had met him), but the
ineffably complacent *persona* emanating from the pages of the
Edinburgh.

The very best contributors to the early *Westminster Review* were
not complacent men. They certainly did not believe that the
progress they desired would come without intellectual effort, or
without ceaseless re-examination of their own premises. John
Stuart Mill's *Autobiography*, with its descriptions of the searching
discussions he had in this decade with his friends, is testimony to
the arduous, disinterested concern for the truth which Maria
Edgeworth also identified in Ricardo when she wrote of his
'perpetual life of mind'.[18] The passion for discussion which is the
leading characteristic of Mr Crotchet represents the admirable face
of utilitarianism:[19]

> The sentimental against the rational, the intuitive against the
> inductive, the ornamental against the useful, the intense against
> the tranquil, the romantic against the classical; these are great
> and interesting controversies, which I should like, before I die, to
> see satisfactorily settled.

In real life Peacock might joke about the dinner party of James
Mill's at which one guest, an economist, committed the barbaric
act of pulling out a discussion paper. He also knew of John Stuart
Mill's 'disquisition-meetings', or Utilitarian Debating Society, of

the 1820s, and introduced John Roebuck to them, which is in itself a sign of approval.[20] In his satire, it is not so much Mr Crotchet's penchant for discussion that he appears to laugh at, as his naive confidence that the issues can be settled: the heresy, again, of followers of the movement, and not of its leaders.

The true utilitarian believed, equally strongly, in the encouragement of mental activity in others. Perhaps the most important of the group's campaigns in the 1820s, more central even than reform of the law and political institutions, was the campaign for mass education. Here again, the progressive case, and the opposition it provoked, is conveyed in the three reviews.

Because they believed in an identity of interest between manufacturers and workers — the middle and the lower orders — liberals and radicals wished to extend the franchise; but many also feared democratisation unless it was accompanied or preceded by the education of the masses. Conversely, a Tory and High Church party, which felt it had much to lose by the extension of the franchise, was suspicious of schemes of mass education. The churches produced keen educators, like the Hackney phalanx and the Clapham sect, and in a period of sectarian expansion Protestant individualism unquestionably must have operated in a generalised way as a spur to self-betterment and intellectual self-reliance. Certain churchmen nevertheless resisted the powerful liberal tide of the 1820s, and put the ideological case against the promiscuous spread of enlightenment. For this reason, the Established Church was often a stalking-horse of the educators, notably those of a utilitarian cast of mind. For a decade from 1818, Bentham's favourite target was the Christian religion, which he assailed with the vigour and irresponsibility of a man born in the age of Voltaire. The atheist publisher Richard Carlile, who had reissued Paine's works in 1817–19, and spent the six years from 1819 in prison, was defended in Parliament by Ricardo and in letters to the *Morning Chronicle* by John Stuart Mill. James Mill pointed out roundly (what Peacock had always shown satirically), that the church had a perpetual interest in stifling free discussion. Certainly some Christian writers on education, Coleridge among them, lacked all enthusiasm for feeding the populace with ideas, and tended to fail to see the point of teaching them science. On the other hand, a population in a state of brute ignorance was a rabble, a mob: perhaps a riot or a revolution. Few, accordingly, advocated no education at all, but for one Tory and Church party the Bible, 'morals', and in a general sense one's duty were the proper goals of knowledge for the great majority, which included the lower orders, and women.

Churchmen were not standing on the sidelines when they commented on this issue. They had a powerful and in some spheres decisive influence on national education. Very many of the new schools, those which taught the poor their letters by the monitoring system of Joseph Bell, were built by the Churches, and remained in Church hands. Another source of the same very basic information, and often the only one available to working children, were the Sunday schools run by one or other religious sect. The country's oldest and most prestigious educational institutions, Oxford and Cambridge and the great public schools, were also religious foundations. Thus the real-life educational controversy of the 1820s, which is the very heart of the cultural controversy, polarises between the agnostic, scientific and liberal 'moderns' on the one hand, and the clerical 'ancients' on the other.

The *Westminster Review* was naturally in the forefront of the controversy on the radical side. Its columns gave ample coverage to the utilitarian goals achieved in the 1820s, including the setting up of Mechanics Institutes and, as a direct challenge to orthodoxy's Oxford and Cambridge, the new, non-sectarian and scientific University College, London. In addition, Brougham's Society for the Diffusion of Useful Knowledge produced a stream of pamphlets containing basic scientific information for all classes, the reviewing of which provided frequent occasion for the discussion of education.

From the beginning, the *Westminster* had been given to assailing the central position of classics in the English school and university syllabus. Latin and Greek, declared Southwood Smith in the first number, 'have nothing in common with the business of the world as it is transacted now'.[21] Throughout the later 1820s it returned to this topic whenever suitable occasion arose:[22]

> All this waste and neglect, with this consequent ignorance, are
> the results, primarily, of ancient fashions, descended from those
> days of darkness, in which Latin and Greek were the only
> knowledge, and therefore the only learning; though learning

now no longer. And while thus originating, this vicious and useless system is fostered by our venerable institutions, as they are called; venerable, however, for their age alone, as other aged, decrepid and useless things often command veneration equally blind. ... The universities and schools despise, as is common in mankind, or affect to despise, what they do not understand. And it is policy also to suppress or deny the utility or necessity of this knowledge, because they who are ignorant, would be compelled to learn themselves, before they could become teachers, as they who now repose in monastic indolence, would be forced to exert themselves. ... A man of science [is] ... looked on with a sort of contempt, as of a tradesman-like nature ...; while worship and respect are reserved for him, the Gentleman, who has gained the prize in Greek verses, or taken a high degree in Homer and Aeschylus. This is all very ingenious; and well has it served the purpose of those whose pecuniary interests depend on it: yet this is what must be broken through, before education shall really become what it ought to be, and utility succeed to the place of nonsense verses and longs and shorts.... The actions ... the business ... of our country ... depend on knowledge or on science, using that term as contradistinguished from classical knowledge, and even very widely on science in its most rigid and received sense. And that it does not, in any one point or manner, depend on classical knowledge, is equally too plain to require proof. It is not the England which it was under the Saxon Heptarchy, and Europe is no longer the Europe which it was even three centuries ago.

The subject is of such topical interest that the *Westminster* returns to it in a second article, which considers whether each learned profession would not benefit from a knowledge of science. The comments become particularly pointed when the writer arrives at the clergy:[23]

If the pursuit of general knowledge and of the sciences possesses that power in enlarging and strengthening the mental faculties which we have elsewhere demonstrated, and which is never the result of literary pursuits, far less of languages, the same reasons which apply to all classes, apply equally to the clergy; while, if it is further true that the narrowness of views, and the prejudices

193

which are the produce of an education and of habits, with them peculiarly monastic, are, with them also increased by their peculiar profession, and by a long-descended train of prejudices more ancient, there are additional reasons why we should use this, or any expedient, to correct this evil.

If the *Westminster* thus earnestly set about depicting the clergy as bigoted, narrow and self-interested, the *Edinburgh* made the same point with rather more style. So many barbs were hurled at clerical attitudes on education — and back again — that one must hesitate to claim a particular source for the sallies of Dr Folliott and his antagonists. Nevertheless, there is one article which, though written some years before *Crotchet Castle*,[24] nicely matches Dr Folliott's favourite obsessions. The occasion was the publication of an indignant pamphlet by the Rev. E. W. Grinfield,[25] entitled *A Reply to Mr. Brougham's Practical Observations upon the Education of the People, Addressed to the Working Classes and their Employers* (London, 1825). With less than perfect propriety, the editor of the *Edinburgh Review* seems to have allowed Brougham himself to review this attack upon his own pet projects. Brougham took advantage of the opportunity to reply to critics of earlier schemes of his as well, again with the editor's connivance, to judge by his running title, 'High Church Opinions on Popular Education'. Brougham roundly declared that there could scarcely be a good argument against the spread of knowledge:[26]

> We live in times, however, when the improbability of any act of folly being committed by persons engaged in controversy, especially on subjects capable of being allied with religious feelings, or rather with the zeal of churchmen for their establishment, is anything rather than a reason against expecting to see it done, and that too with abundant earnestness and exemplary ostentation.

It is the tactic of the experienced politician, slyly to transfer all the emotionalism and self-interest to the other side. Brougham as anonymous reviewer finds his opponents particularly absurd when they make some of the same accusations against Brougham as public benefactor. 'A carpenter or a ploughman', he declares, 'is not much more likely to follow Whig principles, because he

understands the doctrine of mechanics and vegetation.'[27] He recalls
that Brougham had been accused of self aggrandisement, even to a
wish to set himself up as dictator, as long ago as 1818, when the
project in hand was the setting up of the Charity Commission:[28]

> They would by no manner of means suffer Mr. Brougham to
> search into the abuses of charities, because he meant in fact to
> assume a dictatorial power over the whole property in the
> country! and they warned the legislature against becoming his
> accomplices or his dupes, by passing any act enlarging in any
> one of the particulars which he recommended, the powers of the
> commissioners. ... Painful as it may prove to the objectors, great
> progress has been made in remedying abuses, and restoring
> charitable funds to their original destination; and much
> discomfiture has everywhere attended those sincere friends of
> Church and State, those *disinterested* supporters of the established
> order of things, those *candid* and *honest* alarmists, who had
> quietly and regularly, and with true clerical and aristocratic
> dignity, appropriated to their own use the property of the poor.

Here in one article are gathered together Dr Folliott's principal
grievances against Brougham — his plans to bestow a scientific
education on the poor, which Tories see as either comically
irrelevant or subversive, and his so-called 'job', the Charity
Commission. When Brougham turns more specifically to consider
the Rev. Mr Grinfield's arguments, the actual character of Dr
Folliott seems to take shape. Brougham quotes Grinfield on the idea
of extending knowledge to the poor, a scheme ' "calculated, so
far as it can be accomplished, to ALARM all sober and prudent
persons among the middle and UPPER orders of society, and to
render the labouring classes, UNEASY, UNHAPPY and
DISSATISFIED." '[29] The notion of a scientific syllabus is
obnoxious to the 'reverent champion of ignorance and things as
they are' — ' "Let them [the common people] become conversant
with Morals and History and Biography, before we introduce them
to Chemistry, Hydrostatics or Astronomy." '[30] Grinfield is even
more frightened of the direct incitement to subversion offered by
the London [Mechanics] Institute, by organised meetings for
discussion, and by the most dangerous subject of all, political
economy. The educational institutions he does approve of are the

National Schools run on Bell's system, which aim to instil 'religion and morals':[31]

> Their system accords with the *order of society existing among us.*
> ... We inculcate a strong attachment to the constitution, *such as it now is*; we teach them to love and revere our establishments in Church and State, even *with all their real or supposed imperfections*; and we are far more anxious to make them good and contented citizens, than to fit them for noisy patriots, who would perhaps destroy the constitution whilst pretending to correct it.

Mr Grinfield is less classical, and more specifically religious, than Dr Folliott. Otherwise it is not hard to see in this review the underlying polarities of the educational debate which Peacock re-stages in *Crotchet Castle*. This particular article illustrates how the *Edinburgh Review* supplies Folliott with his unseen antagonist, Brougham, just as it gives him his sparring-partner MacQuedy. Moreover, further details which fill out Folliott's case against progressivism can be traced, with more or less probability, to the columns of the same journal. In 1828 it reviews a sermon on popular education by Dr Shuttleworth, the Warden of New College, Oxford: he claims it gives 'an undue preponderance to the interests of our carnal nature over our spiritual'. The same cleric suspects the Athenians, on account of their interest in 'corporeal objects'.[32] Peacock may have been stimulated by this hint to bestow prudery on Dr Folliott, and on Mr Crotchet an otherwise rather surprising enthusiasm for female nudity.[33] Other ideas and phrases for Folliott are gathered from conservative writing over a number of years. The derogatory expression for Brougham's project, the Steam Intellect Society, sounds strangely like Coleridge's description of the popular teaching-scheme he *did* approve of, Dr Bell's:[34]

> I cannot but denounce the so called Lancasterian schools as pernicious beyond all power of compensation by the new acquirement of reading and writing. But take even Dr. Bell's original and unsophisticated plan, which I myself regard as an especial gift of Providence to the human race; and suppose this incomparable machine, this vast moral steam-engine, to have been adopted and in free motion throughout the Empire; it

would yet appear to me a most dangerous delusion to rely on it as if this of itself formed an efficient national education.

At the end of *Crotchet Castle* Dr Folliott decides that the twelfth century is, after all, too dangerous and egalitarian for him – 'Give me an unsophisticated bowl of punch, which belongs to that blissful middle period, after the Jacquerie was down, and before the march of mind was up.'[35] He seems to be echoing Southey in his *Colloquies*, or perhaps Macaulay's ironic comment in his review in the *Edinburgh*:[36]

> The helotry of Mammon are not, in our day, so easily enforced to content themselves as the peasantry of that happy period, as Mr. Southey considers it, which elapsed between the fall of the feudal and the rise of the commercial tyranny.

Folliott is thus conceived as a representative high churchman. He is the embodiment of all Brougham's enemies of the 1820s, as these were represented in the columns of the reviews.[37]

> Such had been the terror and aversion that his name had inspired among the Tory country gentlemen and the clergy, declared one of his friends, that, had the appointment [as Lord Chancellor, in November 1830] been made a few years earlier, it would have been regarded as the precursor of a revolution.

Chapter ii, the first in which we see Folliott in dispute, establishes him taking up the classic Tory points one by one. He enters protesting volubly against the modern syllabus, the education of the lower orders, and above all Brougham:[38]

> I am out of all patience with this march of mind. Here has my house been nearly burned down, by my cook taking it into her head to study hydrostatics, in a sixpenny tract, published by the Steam Intellect Society, and written by a learned friend who is for doing all the world's business as well as his own, and is equally well qualified to handle every branch of human knowledge. I have a great abomination of this learned friend.

A second speech indicates Folliott's positive tastes – for food and drink, and for the classics. Of the nature of the latter learning we are soon to have evidence, for after Mr MacQuedy has alluded to the political scientists of Edinburgh as the modern Athenians, Folliott ripostes with his definition of what an Athenian is:[39]

> Athenians, indeed! where is your theatre? who among you has written a comedy? where is your attic salt? which of you can tell who was Jupiter's great grandfather? or what metres will successively remain, if you take off the three first syllables, one by one, from a pure antispastic acatalectic tetrameter? Now, sir, there are three questions for you; theatrical, mythological, and metrical; to every one of which an Athenian would give an answer that would lay me prostrate in my own nothingness.

It is a thoroughly pedantic answer – impossibly so, for the author of *Melincourt* – and the unfavourable impression is confirmed later in the book when the topic of the theatre is brought up a second time:[40]

> THE REV. DR. FOLLIOTT.
> I further propose that the Athenian theatre being resuscitated, the admission shall be free to all who can expound the Greek choruses, constructively, mythologically, and metrically, and to none others. So shall all the world learn Greek: Greek, the Alpha and Omega of all knowledge. At him who sits not in the theatre, shall be pointed the finger of scorn: he shall be called in the highway of the city, 'a fellow without Greek'.

> MR. TRILLO.
> But the ladies, sir, the ladies.

> THE REV. DR. FOLLIOTT.
> Every man may take in a lady: and she who can construe and metricise a chorus, shall, if she so please, pass in by herself.

> MR. TRILLO.
> But, sir, you will shut me out of my own theatre. Let there at least be a double passport, Greek and Italian.

> THE REV. DR. FOLLIOTT.
> No, sir; I am inexorable. No Greek, no theatre.

The man may be entertaining, but his notion of classicism is arid, and intended to be suspect. Folliott clearly wishes to keep culture in the hands of a very small élite. He opposes the emancipation of women – Mrs Folliott's place is in his kitchen. Though he is prepared to make a risqué joke, it is in the safety of a learned language, so that neither the ladies nor the footman can understand him.[41] He is very shocked at the notion that the same ladies might sit naked to a sculptor, or the same footman have ideas put into his head by the posture of the Sleeping Venus. Mr Crotchet's exemplary use of the classics to remove his prejudices cuts no ice with him at all:[42]

MR. CROTCHET.
Sir, the naked figure is the Pandemian Venus, and the half-draped figure is the Uranian Venus; and I say, sir, that figure realises the finest imaginings of Plato, and is the personification of the most refined and exalted feeling of which the human mind is susceptible; the love of pure, ideal, intellectual beauty. ...

THE REV. DR. FOLLIOTT.
... to any one ... who can be supposed to have read Plato, or indeed be ever likely to do so, I would very willingly show these figures; because to such they would, I grant you, be the outward and visible signs of poetical and philosophical ideas: but to the multitude, the gross carnal multitude, they are but two beautiful women, one half undressed, and the other quite so. ...

MR. CROTCHET.
Sir, ancient sculpture is the true school of modesty. But where the Greeks had modesty, we have cant; where they had poetry, we have cant; where they had patriotism, we have cant; where they had anything that exalts, delights, or adorns humanity, we have nothing but cant, cant, cant. And, sir, to show my contempt for cant in all its shapes, I have adorned my house with the Greek Venus, in all her shapes, and I am ready to fight her battle against all the societies that ever were instituted for the suppression of truth and beauty.

Dr Folliott is both a prude, and terrified of ideas, two features of his character which limit pretty decisively the level of his classical attainments, as Peacock would understand them. For Peacock Greece implied, as we have seen, a natural religion in which the sexual taboos of early nineteenth-century Christianity did not operate. Alternatively it meant 'the noblest philosophy of antiquity', that of Epicurus.[43] The name of Athens was linked with its Academy, with Plato and with Socrates. It signified the most intellectual and challenging of cultures, not the amiable torpor of Dr Folliott.

The assumption of nearly all critics, that Folliott either speaks for Peacock, or comes closest in the novel to expressing his point of view, cannot in fact survive a close reading. It is true that according to Sir Henry Cole Peacock 'used to say that this character was intended by him to make the *amende honorable* to the clergy for his satires of them in the Rev Dr Gaster, the Rev Dr Portpipe, and others in previous tales.'[44] But those who met Peacock in old age habitually put a rather sentimental construction on his words. If one looks sufficiently closely at *Crotchet Castle*, it seems likely that his meaning on this occasion was precise but restricted. Certainly Folliott produces some strong arguments, with which his creator must have sympathised, against MacQuedy's assumption that enlightenment can be promoted by a quasi-mechanical process. Certainly he is allowed to demonstrate that the activities of the Charity Commission may be less than useful. In order to point up a new appearance of impartiality in his treatment of the contemporary clash of opinion, Peacock makes Folliott personally more amiable than his earlier clergymen and, as Lady Clarinda reports, 'fonder of books than the majority of his cloth'.[45] Yet it would be wrong to overlook that this last observation is qualified in the course of the satire, and that Dr Folliott proves his lineal descent from Mr Portpipe by observing how 'there is nothing more fit to be looked at than the outside of a book. ... To enjoy your bottle in the present, and your book in the indefinite future, is a delightful condition of human existence.'[46]

If Dr Folliott's part were only to defend ancient learning against MacQuedy's overweening confidence in modern learning, Peacock might reasonably be supposed to sympathise with him – provided, of course, he had the same notion of what ancient learning really was. But Folliott is also the recurrent antagonist of Mr Crotchet, who delights, however naively, in discussion; and Folliott proves over and again the enemy of discussion – among the common people, it goes without saying, but among his peers too. Most critics have recognised that he is worsted by Mr Crotchet in the passage, quoted above, about the Sleeping Venus; they have tended to find the episode frankly puzzling. But they seem equally convinced that in Peacock's eyes he is invariably too much for Mr MacQuedy. In actual fact, Peacock seems bent on dramatising a whole debate, which means that he allocates, almost dispassionately, good points and bad to both sides. On education Folliott advances all kinds of opinions which there is no reason to think that Peacock held:[47]

> I hold that there is every variety of natural capacity from the idiot to Newton and Shakspeare; the mass of mankind, midway between these extremes, being blockheads of different degrees; education leaving them pretty nearly as it found them, with this single difference, that it gives a fixed direction to their stupidity, a sort of incurable wry neck to the thing they call their understanding.

It is hard to see why this negative view of human intellectual endeavour should be taken for a point scored — or, equally, why Folliott should be considered to have won an exchange like the following:[48]

> MR. MACQUEDY.
> Then, sir, I presume you set no value on the right principles of rent, profit, wages, and currency?
>
> THE REV. DR. FOLLIOTT.
> My principles, sir, in these things are, to take as much as I can get, and to pay no more than I can help. These are every man's principles, whether they be the right principles or no. There, sir, is political economy in a nutshell.
>
> MR. MACQUEDY.
> The principles, sir, which regulate production and consumption, are independent of the will of any individual as to giving or taking, and do not lie in a nutshell by any means.
>
> THE REV. DR. FOLLIOTT.
> Sir, I will thank you for a leg of that capon.

Evidence that Peacock's views were of a wholly different kind from Folliott's, not merely in all the earlier satires but in the very year of writing, is available on the written record. His critical remarks upon recent books on Byron incidentally contain unmistakable evidence of his own liberal attitudes on sexual freedom, politics, and religion, and of a contempt for the ancient universities stronger (and more specifically political) than Dr Folliott's.[49] Another article by Peacock published in the year in which *Crotchet Castle* was written, on Jefferson's *Memoirs,* conveys Peacock's zeal for both free speech and popular education. He expresses his intense admiration for the American democrat's character and opinions. The latter, to be sure, are not specifically utilitarian. Jefferson's wish to devolve power, to keep the central government weak in order to give the maximum liberty to the individual in his state, is characteristic of many types of early nineteenth-century progressive, but not of the Benthamite when he contemplated legal institutions.[50] There were two very distinct impulses in progressive thinking, and one was to suspect the small local community of being in the wrong hands – those of the aristocracy and the church; the solution to this problem would be to strengthen power at the centre, so that the radical could get hold of it in the interests of the many. The fact that Peacock admires Jefferson in 1830 does not, therefore, mark him out as specifically utilitarian at all, but it does imply his continuing adherence to certain progressive aspirations. He quotes with evident approval some remarks of Jefferson, dating from before the French Revolution, which put a very high valuation on the freedom of the press:[51]

> I am persuaded myself, that the good sense of the people will always be found to be the best army. They may be led astray for a moment, but will soon correct themselves. The people are the only censors of their governors; and even their errors will tend to keep these to the true principles of their institution. To punish these errors too severely would be to suppress the only safeguard of the public liberty. The way to prevent these irregular interpositions of the people, is to give them full information of their affairs through the channel of the public papers, and to contrive that those papers should penetrate the whole mass of the people. The basis of our government being the opinion of the people, the very first object should be to keep that right; and were it left to me to decide whether we should have a government without newspapers, or newspapers without a government, I should not hesitate a moment to prefer the latter.

But I should mean that every man should receive those papers, and be capable of reading them.

For the state to function according to Jefferson's principles, the masses must be literate; the problem hitherto in Europe has been that for historical reasons the masses have been a rabble. Jefferson recognises the fears that following the French Revolution attend all ideas of democracy, but he nevertheless holds firmly to the liberal solution:[52]

But even in Europe a change has sensibly taken place in the mind of man. Science had liberated the ideas of those who read and reflect, and the American example had kindled feelings of right in the people. An insurrection has consequently begun, of science, talents, and courage, against rank and birth which have fallen into contempt. It has failed in its first effort, because the mobs of the cities, the instruments used for its accomplishment, debased by ignorance, poverty, and vice, could not be restrained to rational action. But the world will recover from the panic of this first catastrophe. Science is progressive, and talents and enterprise on the alert. Resort may be had to the people of the country, a more governable power from their principles and subordination; and rank and birth and tinsel-aristocracy will finally shrink into insignificance, even there. This, however, we have no right to meddle with. It suffices for us, if the moral and physical condition of our own citizens qualifies them to select the able and good for the direction of their government, with a recurrence of elections at such short periods as will enable them to displace an unfaithful servant before the mischief he meditates be irremediable.

It is hard to see how the same man in the same year could praise Jefferson's opinions as 'confirming rational hopes of the progress of knowledge and liberty',[53] and intend his readers to admire the notions of Dr Folliott.

The doughty antagonist of the intolerably complacent MacQuedy must be an invaluable satiric tool. Folliott on occasion can score points. If only because of the vigour and comic invention of his speeches, we frequently come away with the impression that the less imaginative, more rigid economic theorist is temporarily floored. This is of course in keeping with Peacock's habitual satirist's preference for the spokesman for the 'ancients': the critic of the present is naturally more to his purpose than its blind partisan. The fact remains that Folliott, far from being a mouthpiece for his author, is the most 'placed' and distanced of his pessimistic dialecticians. He is quite unlike Escot and Forester, in being specifically denied insight. At times he wins an engagement, but it is a Pyrrhic victory. He is himself as obstinate and one-sided as his antagonists, and in the act of ridiculing their pretensions to the whole truth, he completely exposes his own.

It is for this reason that *Crotchet Castle*, apparently always like one or other of the books, also proves disconcertingly different. We are accustomed from the earliest of the satires to a clear distinction between the various elements – of discussion, satiric anatomy, and romance. Folliott looks for all the world like one of the 'philosophers' who debate the progress of the world in *Headlong Hall* and *Melincourt*, but the discussions in which he participates tend (largely because of his own limitations) not to be conducted at the same level of seriousness. They are, as a solitary critic has observed, 'mock Socratic dialogues without a guiding Socrates'.[54] A chapter like the sixth, 'Theories', makes no distinction between philosophers and comic targets, the representative figures of an 'Anatomy'. When young Mr Crotchet asks the company how each would spend a large sum of money to regenerate society, Dr Folliott weighs in alongside the rest with a particular scheme (for resuscitating the Athenian theatre), and with support for the general one – the deliberative dinner. 'The schemes for the world's regeneration evaporated in a tumult of voices',[55] and the seeming philosopher's is one of them. The effect is calculated: Peacock's portrait of social life in *Crotchet Castle* is in keeping with J. S. Mill's current Comtean analysis, that the age suffers from a diversity of uninformed opinions on matters that require specialist knowledge, and from the diffusion of superficial knowledge, which has left society as a whole without positive convictions.[56] But the reproduction of such a world at Crotchet Castle makes it harder than ever for the reader to divine Peacock's view – if he has one.

There is a remaining element, romance, which is far more elaborately developed in *Crotchet Castle* than in *Headlong Hall*. It has two pairs of lovers, both equally important. In the first half, set in Crotchet Castle, Lady Clarinda has enlisted among the worldly, and the course of true love – her earlier understanding with Captain Fitzchrome – is frustrated. In the second half, set in wild Wales, romantic values prevail. Susannah Touchandgo heals the heart wounded when she was jilted on account of her poverty by young Mr Crotchet; cures Mr Chainmail of his excessive veneration for rank; perhaps, through the Welsh ambience of which she is the guiding spirit, has an insensible effect in softening Lady Clarinda's heart. This romantic interest, this action, is very far from being cursory. It has the clarity of outline and expressiveness that the disputations in *Crotchet Castle* lack. Though at first the conversations seem fuller, more life-like and more brilliant than ever before, it is plain that compared with the debates in *Headlong Hall* and *Melincourt* they have lost their centrality. Peacock's means of conveying his message has long since ceased to be the 'prose' method of the analytic dialogue; he relegates it to the background, and instead employs the perhaps more operatic mode of action. As in *The Misfortunes of Elphin*, an apparently conventional story tells far more than appears at first sight.

It is part of a fundamental change, that the familiar two-part structure supports a contrast between two romantic plots; in *Headlong Hall*, the division into two parts served to distinguish between two kinds of satiric target.[57] In atmosphere the two halves of *Crotchet Castle* are as distinct as those of *Maid Marian*. The first half is worldly in tone and setting: Mr Crotchet's villa, which is pretentiously known as Crotchet Castle. The second half, in Wales, is much concerned with ruins of actual castles, beloved of Mr Chainmail, and finally ends in an imitation of a twelfth-century castle, Chainmail Hall. Thus far the change of scene resembles the transition from Arlingford Castle to Sherwood Forest. But there is also a significant difference. The set-piece linking the two, the book's literal centre, is 'The Voyage';[58] and this points to a very strong sense in *Crotchet Castle* of a movement, a progress. The journey, or quest, is the most familiar of allegorical plots, necessarily carrying with it overtones of wide significance. The general plan of the book, the movement of its action from Crotchet Castle to Chainmail Hall, and above all the voyage at its centre, between them ensure that it is to symbolic event rather than to endlessly incomplete conversation that the reader looks for a positive meaning.

At first sight, the journey of the house-party up-stream by boat seems not so much allegorical as hauntingly evocative, less to do with Peacock's present artistic purpose than with memories of his youth. He had himself twice systematically explored the length of the river: alone in 1809, when he did his research for *The Genius of the Thames*, and in a celebrated party in late August and September 1815, when he took Shelley and Mary and Charles Clairmont by boat past Oxford and Lechlade to the mouth of the Thames–Severn canal. All his life Peacock chose to live in the Thames valley. As he told Shelley, on receiving the latter's reports of his Italian travels, he was 'rooted like a tree on the banks of one bright river'.[59] For a while, between 1815 and 1817, he successfully communicated to Shelley his own feeling for the Windsor and Marlow area. Moreover, the image of the journey by boat enters Shelley's poetry in *Alastor*, written immediately after their trip up-river, and afterwards often recurs. Shelley was so enthused by the Thames voyage that he wanted to go on into Wales and, still using rivers and canals, to the Lakes and the Falls of Clyde – an inland water-journey, there and back, of two thousand miles. The following year he thought it might be feasible to tour the classic places of Europe by the same means, as Byron has Childe Harold do in his third Canto. For there was a unique imaginative appeal in such a journey by water. 'Rivers are not like roads, the work of the hands of man; they imitate mind, which wanders at will over pathless deserts, and flows through nature's loveliest recesses, which are inaccessible to anything besides.'[60]

The two chapters in *Crotchet Castle*, 'The Voyage' and 'The Voyage Continued', seem a kind of test case in the reading of Peacock. Superficially they are simply an elegant variation of scene, prompting some pleasant writing about pleasant places, and giving Peacock an opportunity, largely via Dr Folliott, to exercise his wit on the subject of Oxford University. Shelley-lovers take pleasure in picking up the allusion to the real-life journey, and to the poems it helped to inspire. But 'The Voyage' can suggest more, once its central position is noted, and the implications thoroughly felt. It takes the moderns of Crotchet Castle back in time, to medieval Oxford, and then to Wales, which stands notionally for the infancy of society. Like all allegorical journeys, it also has an inward point of reference. To one of the principal characters at least, it implies progress not on a physical but a spiritual plane. If we are to think of the actions rather than the words, Lady Clarinda has been the most important character of the first half of the book. She has been truly of Crotchet Castle. She quotes its governing spirit, Mr MacQuedy, as the mentor who guides her actions. 'He has satisfied me that I am a commodity in the market, and that I ought to sell myself at a high price.'[61] She is about to marry young Mr Crotchet, and so will eventually be mistress of Crotchet Castle, succeeding Miss Crotchet, who also 'thinks Mr. MacQuedy an oracle'.[62] But The Voyage begins to work a change in Lady Clarinda. 'The morning after they had anchored under the hills of the Dee', she speaks to Captain Fitzchrome in a more serious tone than her usual badinage, whereupon he goes off into the mountains, and she misses him more than she had anticipated.[63] In these mountains, at first appearing and disappearing like some spirit, is the other girl who has been engaged to young Mr Crotchet, Susannah Touchandgo, the book's alternative heroine, who is all heart where Clarinda is all head.

Peacock is incapable of simplifying, and even his idylls, such as Sherwood, are complicated by irony. Susannah's rustic paradise is not a bit like the usual late-eighteenth-century literary version of the simple life: Bernardin St Pierre's, for example, in *Paul et Virginie*, or Godwin's in *St Leon* or *Fleetwood*, or any other of a host of second-rate imitations of Rousseau. The Ap-Llymrys are hearty and evidently rather substantial, and their diet includes much more strong ale than one recalls in the wholesome, frugal fare of their literary ancestors. Miss Touchandgo's rustic swain, Harry Ap-Heather, is a typically many-sided Peacockian conception. His attempt to fight Mr Chainmail introduces a note of knockabout comedy in Smollett's manner, at a point where the romantic atmosphere is in danger of becoming insipid. When he blubbers into the stream, the only possible literary echo (and it is dangerous, in view of *Maid Marian*, to dismiss it as accidental) is of Jacques' deer in *As You Like It*. Shakespeare's pastoral also had its broad and earthy aspects. The allusion is a reminder that comedy may strengthen an idyll, and need not undercut it.

While Susannah finds one refuge in Wales, her father and his clerk find another in America, and their letters further disturb received views about what a primitive community might be like. Republican America, as an alternative society to monarchical Europe, was much argued over in England at this period, and with the usual bitter partisanship. The Tory Mrs Frances Trollope was about to make a great popular impression with her descriptions of American boorishness, vulgarity and (on the issue of slavery) hypocrisy.[64] A decade later an even more brilliant reporter, Dickens, successfully tapped the same market in *Martin Chuzzlewit*, and exploited the same deep fund of British snobbery. The criticisms of both are anticipated by Peacock who, with Jefferson's *Memoirs* in his hands, was currently very aware of America. A sentimental man, and a one-sided propagandist for the simple life, might have had Mr Touchandgo build a log cabin in the wilds and, perhaps after an encounter with an Indian savant, adopt a religion of Nature. Peacock gets his unrepentant financier to set up in the manufacture of paper currency in the same old way. As another society built upon the worship of capital, and ready to copy English banking practice, America bids fair to becoming as bad as the home country.[65] Culturally, as Mrs Trollope makes so very plain, America wants much that England has. And yet morally it still has the advantage. 'Mr. Touchandgo', reports his clerk Roderick Robthetill, 'is in a thriving way, but he is not happy here: he longs for parties and concerts, and a seat in congress. He thinks it very hard that he cannot buy one with his own coinage, as he used to do in England.'[66] Though certainly no idyll, Peacock's America is at worst a society which merely reflects back England's vices. At best, it has not advanced so far in the institutions of Old Corruption:[67]

> *Au reste*, here are no rents, no taxes, no poor-rates, no tithes, no church-establishment, no routs, no clubs, no rotten boroughs, no operas, no concerts, no theatres, no beggars, no thieves, no king, no lords, no ladies, and only one gentleman, videlicet, your loving father,
>
> TIMOTHY TOUCHANDGO

With the emergence of Susannah as the heroine of the second part, Mr Chainmail becomes more important. He is, as we shall see, a complex character, whose cult of the past combines a number of current idealisms. Among these, his desire for a simple life, rich in beef and ale, and his belief in fighting for his own, sound much like the New World as Touchandgo and Robthetill describe it. Peacock follows Macaulay in noting that morally such a concept is open to serious criticism: a simple society devoted to things is as materialistic, as bound up with property, and potentially as dangerous and inhumane, as an advanced society devoted to money.[68] The leading real-life worshipper of the social structures of the past whom Peacock had in mind – John Stuart Mill – currently believed in a limited kind of socialism, but also believed, like Mr Chainmail, in free enterprise and in property.[69] Peacock's satirical picture of American greed for possessions, and violence in defending them, is a wry reminder that it is hard to build an Eden on the acquisitive principle.

In spite of these ironic caveats, Peacock's positives in *Crotchet Castle* are not far to seek. On the whole, the simpler the social structure, the more promising the society. At least some aspects of Mr Chainmail's ideal, its simplicity and its sense of fellowship, are presented as reminders of values neglected in modern Britain. Susannah sings about the desirable discoveries she has made in the Welsh mountains, of 'kindly hearts and social glee'. Detached from London society and newly schooled in simplicity, she concludes that the morality and friendship of Londoners are both variables, which alter as fortune alters:[70]

> I am sure, when I recollect, at leisure, everything I have seen and heard among them, I cannot make out what they do that is so virtuous as to set them up for judges of morals. And I am sure they never speak the truth about any thing, and there is no sincerity in either their love or their friendship.

Crotchet Castle is perhaps Peacock's nearest to a novel without a hero: its young men matter much less than its young women. The reason is probably topical once more. In the same article which is all along one of Peacock's main points of reference, Macaulay draws attention to an illiberal feature in James Mill's observations about the right to vote – his exclusion of women:[71]

> 'One thing', says he, 'is pretty clear, that all those individuals whose interests are involved in those of other individuals, may be struck off without inconvenience. ... In this light women

may be regarded, the interest of almost all of whom is involved either in that of their fathers, or in that of their husbands.'

'If we were to content ourselves with saying, in answer to all the arguments in Mr. Mill's essay, that the interest of a king is involved in that of the community, we should be accused, and justly, of talking nonsense. Yet such an assertion would not, as far as we can perceive, be more unreasonable than that which Mr. Mill has here ventured to make. Without adducing one fact, without taking the trouble to perplex the question by one sophism, he placidly dogmatizes away the interest of one half of the human race. If there be a word of truth in history, women have always been, and still are, over the greater part of the globe, humble companions, playthings, captives, menials, beasts of burden. Except in a few happy and highly civilized communities, they are strictly in a state of personal slavery. Even in those countries where they are best treated, the laws are generally unfavourable to them, with respect to almost all the points in which they are most deeply interested.'

This passage provoked uneasy replies from the *Westminster* and implicit agreement from John Stuart Mill, who was to be a lifelong champion of women. Peacock similarly seems to respond to it by creating two girls who, though wholly distinct in their styles of speaking, are alike in their resolve to resist exploitation, and in their capacity to perceive a distinct feminine interest. Lady Clarinda, with her charm, wit, and apparent wrongheadedness, is especially successful, the Elizabeth Bennet among Peacock's heroines. In refusing Capt. Fitzchrome for so much of the action, and appearing ready to accept the book's villain, the swindler young Crotchet, she declines to fit the received idea of a heroine, and acts like all the acquisitive males around her. Her ironic truth-telling deals so steadily with the book's proper targets that she becomes its most effective satiric voice. Folliott's blinkered reactionary attitudes are perpetually shown balanced by the mechanistic views of MacQuedy. Their contest is a see-saw, which the reader can only watch with detachment. By contrast Clarinda is a genuine focus of intelligence.

Her feelings are in abeyance, rather than absent. Though the trueness of her emotions is formally revealed only at the end, the reader is never in doubt about them. She shares Susannah's

fundamental quality of warmth – just as Susannah under her
acquired naivety also has Clarinda's cultivated intelligence. Dr
Folliott thinks Susannah better read than a woman need be – 'she
reads moral philosophy, Mr MacQuedy, which indeed she might as
well let alone.'[72] Nevertheless, Clarinda's cleverness is emphasised,
and this is important, because it is the attractive side of
utilitarianism. She is a feminist who loves discussion. '... I like to
hear them dispute. So you see I am in training for a philosopher
myself.'[73] Her trick on Capt. Fitzchrome, to tell several of the
leading bores that he is of their party, is played in order to test his
ingenuity, and to stimulate conversation. Unlike Folliott, Lady
Clarinda is no opponent of the March of Mind, terrified of all its
manifestations. Indeed, she is one of its products, and it is
ultimately for better rather than for worse. With her acuteness, and
her inside position, she is well placed to penetrate to contemporary
society's moral weakness, which is not, for Peacock, modernism,
or liberalism, or science. Instead it is a gross and mechanistic way
of thinking, and above everything else the reduction of all topics to
the law of the market-place:[74]

LADY CLARINDA.
What, because I have made up my mind not to give away my
heart when I can sell it? I will introduce you to my new
acquaintance, Mr. MacQuedy: he will talk to you by the hour
about exchangeable value, and show you that no rational being
will part with anything, except to the highest bidder.

CAPTAIN FITZCHROME.
Now, I am sure you are not in earnest. You cannot adopt such
sentiments in their naked deformity.

LADY CLARINDA.
Naked deformity: why Mr. MacQuedy will prove to you that
they are the cream of the most refined philosophy.

Thus Dr Folliott is something of a sham as a critic of the
utilitarians, since his suspect viewpoint is always undercut by the
author's irony; Lady Clarinda, half a utilitarian herself, is a much
more devastating critic. The complexity of satiric effect which
results from this deceptive arrangement is maintained right to the

end. Most interpreters of *Crotchet Castle*, having felt confident that Peacock shares Dr Folliott's view of the March of Mind, have concluded that the rout of the hungry mob at Chainmail Hall, the principal subject of the last chapter, expresses in emblematic form Peacock's own view of the proper treatment of the masses. And yet the chapter begins with an epigraph from Rabelais against ignorance, which may be either the ignorance of the learned or of the common people:[75]

> Vous autres dictes que ignorance est mere de tous maulx, et dictes vray: mais toutesfoys vous ne la bannissez mye de vos entendemens, et vivez en elle, avecques elle, et par elle. C'est pourquoy tant de maulx vous meshaignent de jour en jour.

It is clear that there is more in all this than meets the eye. What follows will be an attempt to unravel its complexity, speculative because the chapter itself is dense in allusion, too brief, and thus more obscure than anything else of comparable importance in Peacock.

Like the last chapter of *Melincourt*, the final chapter of *Crotchet Castle* is peculiarly up-to-date. The second half, which offers a resolution to the story of Clarinda and Fitzchrome, must always have been envisaged in some form or other; the first half is based on specific events of November and December 1830, only two months before the book was published. One such event is Brougham's acceptance of office as Lord Chancellor in Grey's new Administration on 19 November 1830, an act widely interpreted as the selling-out of the Great Reformer.

Earlier in the book Folliott's jibes against Brougham, though no doubt often enjoyed by Peacock, were nevertheless the rueful complaints of a Tory, against a man who (possibly for self-interested motives) was bent on educating the masses. The complaint in the last chapter is for the first time from the opposite point of view – against the politician who has defected from the liberal camp – and it is unmistakably Peacock's own. Crotchet attributes to Folliott his usual Tory point of view: he supposes that Folliott must be afraid for his vested interests, with a great reformer in office. On the contrary, replies Folliott, 'my vested interests are very safe from all such reformers as the learned friend.'[76] In March 1831 Peacock even wrote a satirical poem expressing his disgust at

Brougham's taking office. It was published in the *Examiner* of 14 August 1831, and reprinted as a footnote to Dr Folliott's remarks for the first time in the Collected Edition of 1837. The poem is of interest because, although it confirms that Peacock is as suspicious of Brougham as his creation Dr Folliott, it also reveals a political attitude diametrically opposed to that of a Tory cleric:[77]

> Lo! in Corruption's lumber-room,
> The remnants of a wondrous broom;
> That walking, talking, oft was seen,
> Making stout promises to sweep clean;
> But evermore, at every push,
> Proved but a stump without a brush.
> Upon its handle-top, a sconce,
> Like Brahma's, looked four ways at once,
> Pouring on king, lords, church, and rabble,
> Long floods of favour-currying gabble;
> From four-fold mouth-piece always spinning
> Projects of plausible beginning,
> Whereof said sconce did ne'er intend
> That any one should have an end ...

The purpose of the remarks about Brougham in chapter xviii, even Dr Folliott's jibes, which stand unsupported in the first edition, is to convey a sense of anxiety that Reform may have been bought and sold.

But Brougham is always a side-issue in *Crotchet Castle*, something of a joke, and both the action of the last chapter, and the real core of the discussion, are concerned with the assault of the mob on Chainmail Hall. The rioters call themselves 'Captain Swing', which is the name of the mythical leader of the popular unrest in Kent in December 1830. Christmas at Chainmail Hall is, then, the actual Christmas that the first readers of the book had just experienced. But, though the event itself thus seems near enough home, another recent popular rising had also conditioned the minds of English intellectuals, certainly of Peacock and his friends. July 1830 had seen the barricades successfully manned once more in the streets of Paris. A second French Revolution, though on a much more limited scale than the first, had apparently undone the ultra-conservative settlement that followed the Napoleonic Wars, and given back to the French the liberal atmosphere and policies first promised in the late 1780s. A conservative French King, Charles X, was driven out and a constitutional monarch, Louis Philippe, brought in, by a disciplined and almost bloodless popular action. It was a promise that gave hope to English intellectuals that, after all, there could be reform without violent revolution, the extension of power without anarchy. France, and its entire history since 1780, seemed an extraordinarily timely topic in England.[78] Peacock was reacting to the same interest when in the *Westminster Review* of October 1830 he quoted at such length the reactions of the American democrat, Jefferson, to the events he actually witnessed in the France of the 1780s. July 1830 was a confirmation that the coming to power of the European masses had only been delayed, and that, with or without bloodshed, it would now continue.

John Stuart Mill hurried to Paris immediately after the July Revolution, to study events there at first hand. He wrote enthusiastic letters home to his father and, on his return, covered French events for the *Examiner*, which was now under the congenial editorship of a campaigning radical, Albany Fonblanque. Mill, that inveterate debater, must have talked about France among his English friends: at the India House,[79] to his wider circle, surely in one place or another to an audience which included Peacock. He and Peacock were not intimate, it is true. The absence of recorded comment by one on the other is curious. But, even if the personal relationship lacked warmth, all the evidence suggests that at this period their thoughts were moving along identical, or parallel, lines. Such evidence derives from their published writings at the time, from John Stuart Mill's later *Autobiography*, and from the groups or organs of opinion with which they chose to be associated between 1830 and 1835. Both had written for and been broadly in agreement with the original Benthamite *Westminster Review* of 1824, though they regretted its narrowness, especially on art.[80] Both had at first taken James Mill's *Essay on Government* as broadly a testament of faith, at least in so far as it argued against aristocratic government, and for an extension of real power to other classes of society. Both were evidently shaken by Macaulay's assault, though neither liked Macaulay's Whiggishness, nor his complacency, nor the blandness of his tone.[81] After Peacock's last articles for the old *Westminster Review*, in October 1830, he was associated during the next half-decade with the very journals with which John Stuart Mill was closely connected: Fonblanque's *Examiner* early in the decade, and afterwards Mill's own *London Review*.[82] Moreover, as we shall see, either Mill or the general atmosphere of the time induced Peacock to take up the study of French politics. An article published in the *London Review* in 1836 reveals an interest in French current affairs that goes back to the July Revolution.[83]

Essentially John Stuart Mill must have been a most congenial figure to Peacock at this time, as a flexible thinker and an admirer of both the American and the new brand of French democracy. Even more attractive was his passionate, radical opposition to hereditary distinction and privilege (he defended the new French régime's abolition of the hereditary peerage), and his willingness to denounce what he now saw as the dominant English characteristic, the 'disposition to sacrifice everything to accumulation'.[84] (Peacock had actually written a series of poems in 1825–6 satirising this instinct for acquisitiveness – *The Paper Money Lyrics* – which circulated privately at the India House; he did not publish them until 1837, when James Mill was dead.) But John Stuart Mill's doubts about his father's too neat system, and about the capacity for disinterestedness of the moneyed classes, had latterly taken him into strange company. It was an aspect of his spiritual crisis or near nervous breakdown of 1826–8, that he took up the alternative, literary tradition that his father had neglected, represented for example by the poetry of Wordsworth. After 1830 he also read attentively Coleridge's *On the Constitution of Church and State*, with its nostalgic vision of a feudal social cohesion, and its dream of an educated élite, or clerisy, to provide leadership in the current intellectual anarchy. He was far more ready than his father to be interested in the rapturous articles of Carlyle, with their strong infusion of German influence. More unexpected than any of these, he came into contact in 1828 with the ideas of a group of French visionaries, the Saint-Simonians, half feudalists, half socialists, and between 1829 and 1831 was deeply interested in a system which proposed a co-operative solution to replace competitive self-interest. In March 1831, immediately after the publication of *Crotchet Castle*, John Stuart Mill could refer to himself, only half jokingly, as the leading disseminator of Saint-Simonian ideas in England. 'I have been the means of making it known to some

persons, at their request: and in short, although I am not a St
Simonist nor at all likely to become one, *je tiens bureau de St
Simonisme chez moi.*'[85]

Mill disliked cults and he disliked despotism. Saint-Simonianism
degenerated into both, and became ludicrous to Mill when, in
1832, a band of bearded fanatics in monkish costume retired to
Ménilmontant to practise monasticism and mysteries under the
autocratic leadership of Barthélemy Prosper Enfantin. Yet it is
possible to see why, from 1829 to 1831, its blend of idealism and
radicalism should appeal to him as a comprehensive challenge to
the moneyed oligarchy. Saint-Simon himself had died in 1825. His
followers, having borrowed distinctive features from the historical
philosophy of the youthful materialist, August Comte, were
teaching that history was an alternation of 'critical' periods,
warlike, selfish and sceptical, and 'organic' periods of co-operation
and religious sentiment. The 'critical' phase, which had lasted since
the Reformation, was about to evolve into an organic, Saint-
Simonian age of progress. There would be an ideal communism, in
which private property would be abolished, and everyone would be
rewarded according to merit. This was no egalitarian prospect, in
that Saint-Simonians envisioned a hierarchy, based on the idea of
the medieval Catholic Church, but reflecting the spiritual, mental
and physical capacities of individual men. Because the feminine
nature was essentially spiritual, women would be not merely the
free equals of men, but naturally of the priestly caste.

Mill afterwards in his *Autobiography* probably rather exaggerated
the extent of his agreement with the Saint-Simonians about
property – he came nearer to socialism after the French revolution
of 1848 than he was in 1830 – but his retrospective account singles
out the extent to which the dogma usefully challenged the
competitive utilitarian orthodoxy, and offered in its stead a doctrine
of co-operation based upon brotherly, or rather family, love:[86]

> Their criticisms on the common doctrines of Liberalism seemed
> to me full of important truth; and it was partly by their writings
> that my eyes were opened to the very limited and temporary
> value of the old political economy, which assumes private
> property and inheritance as indefeasible facts, and freedom of
> production and exchange as the *dernier mot* of social
> improvement. The scheme gradually unfolded by the St.

Simonians, under which the labour and capital of society would be managed for the general account of the community, every individual being required to take a share of labour, either as thinker, teacher, artist, or producer, all being classed according to their capacity, and remunerated according to their work, appeared to me a far superior description of Socialism to Owen's. Their aim seemed to me desirable and rational, however their means might be inefficacious; and though I neither believed in the practicability, nor in the beneficial operation of their social machinery, I felt that the proclamation of such an ideal of human society could not but tend to give a beneficial direction to the efforts of others to bring society, as at present constituted, nearer to some ideal standard. I honoured them most of all for what they have been most cried down for – the boldness and freedom from prejudice with which they treated the subject of the family, the most important of any, and needing more fundamental alterations than remain to be made in any other great social institution, but on which scarcely any reformer has the courage to touch. In proclaiming the perfect equality of men and women, and an entirely new order of things in regard to their relations with one another, the St. Simonians, in common with Owen and Fourier, have entitled themselves to the grateful remembrance of future generations.

Mill was prepared to publish at the time his conviction that the 'present age of loud disputes but generally weak convictions' was a transitional period, which would give way to an organic period in which 'convictions as to what is right and wrong [would be] deeply engraved on the feelings by early education and general unanimity of sentiment'.[87] In a series of articles he wrote for the *Examiner* between 9 January and 29 May 1831, called 'The Spirit of the Age', he tried to apply the Comtean historical vision to present circumstances in England. He represented the present disputes, the crisis of opinion which was to enforce reform, as characteristic of a dying critical age, and suggested that the ideal solution for the future would be an enlightened despotism by an élite, which would inaugurate peace, plenty and the religion of humanity. This did not sound like, and indeed was not, liberalism as most Englishmen understood it. But it was radical, in the degree and kind of social change Mill appeared to be calling for. 'There must be a moral and social revolution, which shall, indeed, take away no men's lives or property, but which shall leave no man one fraction of unearned distinction or unearned importance.'[88]

In private he was willing to declare to his Saint-Simonian correspondent 'that your social organisation, under some modification or other ... is likely to be the final and permanent condition of the human race.'[89] He even faced tranquilly the possibility that in England a violent revolution might be necessary before such a social transformation could come about. If a holocaust should happen, he would be content to see most of the existing upper classes go to the wall, including practical Tories. 'Practical Toryism simply means, being *in*, and availing yourself of your comfortable position *inside* the vehicle without minding the poor devils who are freezing *outside*.' But, in his present very flexible frame of mind, and in his impatience with liberal dogma, he would save the speculative Tories:[90]

> for it is an ideal Toryism, an ideal King, Lords, & Commons, that they venerate; it is old England as opposed to the new, but it is old England as she might be, not as she is. It seems to me that the Toryism of Wordsworth, of Coleridge (if he can be called a Tory) of Southey even, & of many others whom I could mention, is *tout bonnement* a reverence for *government* in the abstract: it means, that they are duly sensible that it is good for man to be ruled; to submit both his body & mind to the guidance of a higher intelligence & virtue. It is therefore the direct antithesis of liberalism, which is for making every man his own guide and sovereign master.... It is difficult to conceive a more thorough ignorance of man's nature ... than this system implies. But I cannot help regretting that the men who are best capable of struggling against these narrow views and mischievous heresies should chain themselves ... to the inanimate corpses of dead political & religious systems, never more to be revived. The same ends require altered means; we have no new principles, but we want new machines constructed on the old principles; those we had before are worn out.

Mill was often inclined to write with exaggerated approval of doctrines with which, as fundamentally a liberal, he might be expected to disagree. During the 1830s he was, for example, to write one celebrated essay apparently praising Coleridge at the expense of Bentham; in the 1840s he was to suggest that at a certain epoch in history the Catholic Church had been a progressive institution.[91] He was being deliberately provocative when he wrote to his friends about his theoretical Toryism, and for the public about the desirability of change, even of communism. He accounted for this impulse afterwards by saying that he wanted to liberalise the wealthy oligarchy, and ultimately to contribute to the enlightenment of the masses:[92]

> I was as much as ever a Radical and Democrat for Europe, and especially for England. I thought the predominance of the aristocratic classes, the noble and the rich, in the English constitution, an evil worth any struggle to get rid of; not on account of taxes, or any such comparatively small inconvenience, but as the great demoralizing agency in the country. Demoralizing, first, because it made the conduct of the Government an example of gross public immorality, through the predominance of private over public interests in the State, and the abuse of the powers of legislation for the advantage of classes. Secondly, and in a still greater degree, because the respect of the multitude always attaching itself principally to that which, in the existing state of society, is the chief passport to power; and under English institutions, riches, hereditary or acquired, being the almost exclusive source of political importance; riches, and the signs of riches, were almost the only things really respected, and the life of the people was mainly devoted to the pursuit of them. I thought, that while the higher and richer classes held the power of government, the instruction and improvement of the mass of the people were contrary to the self-interest of those classes, because tending to render the people more powerful for throwing off the yoke: but if the democracy obtained a large, and perhaps the principal share, in the governing power, it would become the interest of the opulent classes to promote their education, in order to ward off really mischievous errors, and especially those which would lead to unjust violations of property. On these grounds I was not only as ardent as ever for democratic institutions, but earnestly hoped that Owenite, St. Simonian, and all other anti-property doctrines might spread widely among the poorer classes; not

that I thought those doctrines true, or desired that they should be acted on, but in order that the higher classes might be made to see that they had more to fear from the poor when uneducated, than when educated.

In this frame of mind the French Revolution of July found me.

Mill's diagnosis of England immediately before the Reform Bill, a society in which 'riches, and the signs of riches, were almost the only things really respected', is that of Lady Clarinda and Susannah Touchandgo, and by inference that of Peacock himself. Mill's discussion of whether the opulent classes have more to fear from a population educated or uneducated is the leading concern of the satiric side of Peacock's novel, dominated by Dr Folliott. Peacock's dinner-table discussions illustrate Mill's condition of intellectual anarchy. Thus far *Crotchet Castle* conveys a picture of the state of England in 1831 which resembles the conception of Peacock's younger colleague at the India House. What remains to be examined is the topic lightly touched on in the last chapter of *Crotchet Castle*, the possible solution offered by the Saint-Simonian collectivism with which John Stuart Mill was flirting between 1830 and 1831.

The real-life insurrection Peacock alludes to in his final chapter was taken seriously enough: as in 1817–19, there was genuine fear of violent revolution. Disquiet was such that on 8 November 1830 the King's visit to the City of London had to be cancelled: Wellington's government was so unpopular that it could not guarantee quiet. Rumours of planned insurrections were rife, and the Home Office 'was deluged with warnings and advice'. The radical leader Joseph Hume actually received a letter inviting him to take part in a rising. 'Eighty thousand men were believed to be ready to rise in the north, and twenty thousand might march from Kent.' Meanwhile in London the seasoned radical Richard Carlile organised lectures most evenings of the week in his hall in Blackfriars Bridge Road. 'Though advocating pressure by moral, rather than physical, force, the lecturers preached a class war and a contemptuous hatred of the aristocracy, which its objects found difficult to distinguish from downright sedition.'[93]

Faced with a crisis of this dimension, re-enacted by the mob's attack on Chainmail Hall, neither MacQuedy nor Folliott, the political economist and the Tory, comes off very well. Much more sympathetic is Mr Chainmail, who makes an observation for once apparently free of Peacock's habitual irony. Comparing the unrest of the twelfth century with that of the present, Mr Chainmail observes: 'The cause is the same in both: poverty in despair.'[94] It is at this point that the reader becomes fully aware how little Chainmail is merely a collector of old objects, like S. R. Meyrick.[95] Earlier in the book, he described himself to his co-hero, Fitzchrome, as a fellow-artist: 'you being picturesque, and I poetical; you being for the lights and shadows of the present, and I for those of the past.'[96] Artists in Peacock's work are properly always sincere people, truth-tellers. Here they are also, as Fitzchrome's name perhaps confirms, for fine shades, 'lights and shadows', as opposed to the over-clear definition of the ideologues.

Though the walls of Chainmail's hall are decorated with the armour that it was fashionable for antiquarians to collect, the principle of life in the hall is its attempt to revive the social cohesion of life in feudal and Catholic times. 'I understand you live *en famille* with your domestics', says Fitzchrome;[97] and Christmas at Chainmail Hall demonstrates that the members of this wider family are meant to eat together and to enjoy themselves together. As his attitude to Susannah has revealed, and his remarks about his tenants confirm, Chainmail's notion of communal living is a hierarchical one – though his watchwords, 'beef and ale', are comically material compared with the spirituality of Saint-Simonianism.[98] So far he appears to stand for the radical solution proposed originally by the French group, but as it was modified for the English by John Stuart Mill.

The threat of actual revolution throws liberal intellectuals, in the satire as in life, into confusion. When Mr MacQuedy tries to argue with Dr Folliott about the causes of present discontent, he falls distractedly into agreeing with him. Peacock bestows upon MacQuedy a damaging line of reasoning which actually appeared in a liberal newspaper, the *Morning Chronicle*: 'Discontent increases with the increase of information.'[99] Afterwards, in conversation with Chainmail, he further gives the game away:[100]

MR. MACQUEDY.

You are e'en suffering from the sins of Sir Simon Steeltrap, and the like, who have pushed the principle of accumulation a little too far.

MR. CHAINMAIL.

The way to keep the people down is kind and liberal usage.

MR. MACQUEDY.

That is very well (where it can be afforded), in the way of prevention; but in the way of cure, the operation must be more drastic. (*Taking down a battle-axe.*) I would fain have a good blunderbuss charged with slugs.

MR. CHAINMAIL.

When I suspended these arms for ornament, I never dreamed of their being called into use.

MacQuedy panics, and deserts his reformist principles in favour of the defence of the existing interest, by force of arms. Dr Folliott was of course never in favour of the populace, but when he is told that the baronial hall stands for collectivism his support of ancient ways also fails the test.[101] Chainmail's attitude seems more promising as a social solution, especially if modified in the direction proposed by the Owenite Mr Toogood:[102]

THE REV. DR. FOLLIOTT.

No more of the twelfth century for me.

MR. CHAINMAIL.

Nay, doctor. The twelfth century had backed you well. Its manners and habits, the community of kind feelings between master and man, are the true remedy for these ebullitions.

MR. TOOGOOD.

Something like it: improved by my diagram: arts for arms.

Here, with Dr Folliott calling for a punch-bowl, overt discussion of the topic of revolution ends. But reading the events of the entire last chapter, rather than the self-contradictions of its theorists, or their equally inconsistent sallying forth with weapons, we may feel that Peacock has said considerably more than first appears.

What Mr Chainmail intended, in setting up his hall, should have prevented violence. He wanted a genuine community, governed by mutual respect and interdependence. But Peacock has shown Chainmail already in retreat from some of his cherished feudal notions, and now he has to face up to the fragility of the entire experiment. The collectivist ends, like the other progressives, in a resolute and self-interested defence of private property. One implication is that John Stuart Mill's idealisms are inconsistent. Another is that in a society ruled by selfish wealth, and riddled with desperate poverty, individual attempts at a solution are bound to be cranky and impracticable. This does not altogether undercut what is admirable about the younger Mill or about his incipient socialism. Just as Mill felt afterwards that the social ideal had at least an educational value, so Peacock seems to have believed when he made the scene at Chainmail Hall his climax. Chainmail, as a poet and idealist, is, for all his absurdity, one in the series of Peacock's crusading heroes.

These seem large conclusions to draw from the characters' brief discussions, but then the book is not over with the retreat of the rioters. Peacock's almost cursory treatment of the hungry mob has seemed baffling or unpleasant largely because so many readers have mistaken not merely the viewpoint but the topic of *Crotchet Castle*. It is not a satire on the March of Mind from a Tory point of view; it is a satire on the rich governing classes, landed and commercial, and their new philosophy of wealth – the practice and theory of materialism, seen from the viewpoint of a humanist. If confirmation is needed that Peacock felt as deeply on this topic as Mill, it comes, once again, from his journalism.

The culling of biographical sources, even other writings, for insights into literary works is a practice entirely disallowed by some critics, and it is right to be suspicious of material lifted out of one context into another. Yet knowledge of the continuity of a writer's thinking can act as a check on that type of unsupported, essentially subjective assertion which derives from the shallow reading of an isolated text. When Peacock writes on 'French Comic Romances' and 'The Epicier', some five years after *Crotchet Castle*, he is not concerned, any more than in the satire, with the rights of the masses. His subject is, once again, the illiberality of a system ruled by wealth and by the mercantile interest, a system which he evidently finds unchanged by the 1832 Reform Act in England, and if anything confirmed by the July Revolution of 1830 in France.

The bourgeoisie is represented in these two essays by an archetype, the sordid, grasping, Balzacian figure of the *épicier.* Peacock sketches him with a ferocity which almost all critics have agreed to be beyond his range. (He 'lacked the anger, the conviction of his own rightness, and the didactic urge that go to make up a major satirist.')[103] The *épicier* is neither monarchical nor republican. He has no principles, and no motive for action except his own commercial advantage. Benjamin Constant, the veteran of the earlier French Revolution, and a leading figure of the July Revolution, lived long enough, according to Peacock, to recognise that what he had achieved was to transfer power into the hands of the *épicier*:[104]

> He had dreamed of popular power – great, majestic, beneficent: he had seen it little, abject, ridiculous, selfish. The reality stared him in the face: he closed his eyes, and died. He who has lost his last illusion, who has used up his ideality, has nothing to do but die.

The class that rules in France rules in England, and culturally the consequence for each society is the same: the death of intellectual life, of the critical spirit which both liberals and radicals uphold. In the past, Peacock would have claimed that it was the function of the artist to keep intellect alive; above all, it was the function of the satirist. In 1836, considering the fate of the great French satiric tradition, he writes almost wearily, as a sociological critic of literature who sees that for the moment the battle is lost. Why were the writings of de Kock, the most popular of contemporary French novelists, so unlike those of his predecessors, in being divested of opinion?[105]

> The answer, we think, is twofold: first, there is no demand for the commodity amongst the great body of his readers; second, it does not fall under his view as an observer of a particular class of society. ... An age which demands free inquiry, pushed without fear or compromise to its legitimate conclusions, turns up an Epicurus or a Hobbes. In one which likes to put up at a half-way house, there will be no lack of a Dugald Stewart, or a

Mackintosh, to provide it with comfortable entertainment.

So with literature. Among a people disposed to think, their everyday literature will bear the impress of thought; among a people not so disposed, the absence or negation of thought will be equally conspicuous in their literature. Every variety of mind takes its station, or is ready to do so, at all times in the literary market; the public of the day stamp the currency of fashion on that which jumps with their humour. Milton would be forthcoming if he were wanted; but in our time Milton was not wanted, and Walter Scott was. We do not agree with the doctrine implied in Wordsworth's sonnet,

Milton! thou shouldst be living at this hour:
England hath need of thee.

England would have been the better for him, if England would have attended to him, but England would not have attended to him if she had had him. There was no more market for him than for Cromwell. ... Pigault le Brun lived in the days of the Rights of Man, Political Justice, and Moral and Intellectual Perfectibility. Paul de Kock lives in the days of the march of mechanics, in the days of political economy, in the days of prices-current and percentages, in the days when even to dream like a democrat of the Constituent Assembly, would be held to qualify the dreamer for Bedlam: in short, in the days of the *épicier*.

In view of the content of John Stuart Mill's thought about France and her Revolution, and his hope that a critical age would give way to an organic age, this historical account is expressive. Though the analysis of the current state of French (and English) society owes much to Mill, Peacock reverses the tendency of Mill's Comtean thinking. He agrees that the past has been a critical age, but that, he believes, is its glory. The critical and sceptical habit of the eighteenth century still seems preferable to anything the nineteenth century has produced to put in its place. Peacock reads the present and the future not as a co-operative age, but as a period of money-making and mindlessness, because the *épicier* demands nothing else.

Somewhere between 1833 and 1835 Peacock began a tale, 'The Lord of the Hills', which shows him ready to make pleasant satire out of the high hopes induced by successive French revolutions, and their equally regular disappointment. It was abandoned, probably because promotion at the India House made him too busy;[106] but the fact of its existence shows how central to him in these years was the preoccupation he shared with Mill and so many intellectuals, with social tension, class interest and potential revolution as the largest and most urgent of modern issues. The difference is that Peacock is sceptical of organicist and visionary solutions. Though he refrains from offering answers, his personal values remain unmistakably within the tradition of liberal individualism.

The concerns are all present, or all alluded to, in *Crotchet Castle*. The society of the first half of the book is already that of the *épicier*, a world of systematic profit-making, illustrated in practice by young Crotchet, and expressed by MacQuedy as a science, or even as a creed. Equally, the real indifference to ideas, the illiberalism, of the so-called radical party is exposed when popular unrest threatens the middle-class interest. Though Grey's administration, which would clearly put through the Reform Bill, was already in power as chapter xviii was being written, Peacock does not mention it. In the light of his pessimism about the omni-present *épicier*, it is easy to see why a mere Act promised no solution. But it would have been too clear a departure from Peacock's lifelong principles to end a work of art with anything like total despair. What he proffers are the merest hints, in certainly the least confident of his resolutions; but he does not leave his imaginary world in the hands of the *épicier*.

The solution he gives is as stylised, as notional, as he can make it. The rioters driven off, the characters assembled in Chainmail Hall listen to three songs which all have an application to the situation. The first two are adapted from medieval fabliaux. Susannah sings a version of the contest between Florence and Blancheflor, who love, respectively, a knight and a clerk, and accordingly dispute over the merits of the two professions. It is in the end Blancheflor's clerk, or rather his advocate at the court of the birds, who wins the dispute:[107]

> The nightingale prevailed at length,
>   Her pleading had such charms;
> So eloquence can conquer strength,
>   And arts can conquer arms.

It is a gentle correction of Susannah's own lover – who, though really a poet, has an erroneous belief in weaponry and in fighting for his own – and it confirms Mr Toogood's point, that the way ahead lies with arts rather than with arms.[108] The second of the fabliaux makes a fool of a cleric not unlike Dr Folliott. The third, sung by the repentant Clarinda, exalts a concept of love which is simpler and more sincere than the modern habit, by which 'Love is bought and sold'.[109] The songs bring together, with Peacock's characteristic lightness and elegance, the underlying moral themes of his two plots. Arts, or intelligence: sincere feeling, or humane rather than commercial values; these are ideals which survive only fraily, perhaps, in the actual world of the *épicier*, but they may stand as some kind of inspiration on the page of the satirist.

Opinions have divided violently about *Crotchet Castle*. For some, it is Peacock's best book, largely perhaps on account of its witty and engaging scapegraces, Folliott and Lady Clarinda. But it has also been singled out for attack. Though most of the objectors are surely mistaken in thinking of Peacock as the equivalent of his own Dr Folliott, a pedant, a sybarite, and a Tory who dislikes ideas, their misreading is at least in part Peacock's fault. In its detail, *Crotchet Castle* contains some of the best things in his satires. The dialogues are often excellent. The contrast between the two halves, different in principal characters as well as in setting, has all Peacock's characteristic elegance of form. The voyage, that beautiful idea, is hard to match elsewhere. But when due credit is given for the skilful plan, the execution still leaves something to be desired. The debates of the first half are not very well separated or differentiated, and the continuous flow of dialectic becomes somewhat monotonous. Subjects for conversation and satire accumulate, as though Peacock has a list. The syntax of the chapter-heading, 'Science and Charity', seems symptomatic: why science *and* charity? Is there a connection? Is there a connection when in the second half Peacock calls a chapter, 'The Lake. The Ruin'? It seems not. He thought he would get both topics in.

A rich fund of satiric material is squeezed into the first half, and it looks as though the pastoral and narrative second half has been spun out somewhat to compensate. Neither the strict logic nor the elegant variety of Peacock's other arrangements has room to operate. The previously all-expressive structure here dictates the content, and the first and last chapters, and the two central ones: elsewhere in the book there is a sense of the desultory, of less than perfect control. Part of Peacock's trouble may arise from an increased naturalism. The principal characters are certainly more developed than those that inhabit the satire of his earlier period. But here too the result is a crop of fresh problems. The more important personages of *Crotchet Castle* seem quite frequently to speak out of character. The underlying reason for this is that two figures especially, Crotchet and Folliott, are spokesmen for more *kinds* of argument, progressive and reactionary, than any two real-life individuals would be at all likely to employ. But we are troubled by the sense of improbability, precisely because we are more conscious than ever before of what each character is supposed to be like. Singly any one of these small surprises might signify an admirable and imaginative flexibility; together they have to be construed as inattention. Of course, it could be Peacock's subtlety that it is Folliott, the defender of ancient learning, who pours scorn on Oxford, while Mr Crotchet innocently seems to defend it. The unexpected reversal of roles might imply that Oxford's classicism is defunct even by Folliott's pedantic standards. But how apt is Folliott's choice of words for a man who has spoken of the charm of the outside of books? 'I run over to myself the names of the scholars of Germany, a glorious catalogue! but ask for those of Oxford – Where are they?'[110] The dart was too well directed for Peacock to resist it, but the outlines of his satire would have been distinctly clearer if he had not thus separated the clergyman from the very party which elsewhere in the book he represents. Similarly, even though Mr Crotchet is a good utilitarian in his love of discussion, there seems no cogent reason why his quest for knowledge should take him to Greek statues, to Plato's doctrine of love, or to Byron's view of cant.[111] Real incongruities of this kind do not occur in the other satires – at least not to major characters. Nor do flat passages of naturalistic dialogue, such as the three pages in which Dr Folliott tells the others about the new mistress of Chainmail Hall, a sequence which must certainly rank among the feeblest Peacock ever published.[112]

It is by Peacock's own normal standards that such details appear clumsy, as blemishes upon the complete work. The lack of real concern for consistency of character, the readiness to seize instead any passing opportunity for satire, has certainly been a factor in the persistent misreading of *Crotchet Castle*. But the medal has, clearly, its reverse side. Ideas have been preferred to character precisely because Peacock cares passionately for ideas, and exalts the comedy of ideas above the comedy of character.[113] *Crotchet Castle* is difficult essentially because it tackles the largest and most intractable subject Peacock has faced, and does so with intellectuality.

In one of his deliberately sly and misleading half-statements about his work, Peacock afterwards claimed that 'I have endeavoured to be impartial, and to say what could be said on both sides.'[114] Though this has been taken to mean he had no strong preferences, it is an impression that will not hold for any of the earlier satires. *Headlong Hall* and especially *Nightmare Abbey* are brilliant because they are incisive: though free of the warped partisanship, the wretched personality-mongering of the period, they have a vigorous liberal point to make, and the illiberal are not allowed more than a decent fig-leaf of intellectual dignity. *Crotchet Castle* is different. The running dialogues between Folliott and MacQuedy, or between Folliott and Crotchet, are very nearly detached dramatisations of contemporary controversies, in tone more or less equally unfavourable to both. It is no longer a case of demonstrating that one faction, or ideology, is benighted. A subtler point is being made: Peacock is trying to sift what is genuine in liberal ideals from the large accretion of hypocrisy, self-interest and pseudo-science. For virtually all his readers, he has not succeeded, since his meaning remains remarkably unclear. But the failure is that of a man struggling to adjust to a new era, and to its new intellectual aberrations. An unthinking and shallow liberalism may be a more insidious orthodoxy than the Toryism he battled against in his earlier writing life.

It is difficult to make a clear choice in favour of one or other half of Peacock's satiric career. The literary satire so cleverly expressed in *Nightmare Abbey* is timely and, for a literary reader, of special importance. But then the subject of *Crotchet Castle* is, in its wider way, of quite peculiar importance too. It is no less than a survey of the range of cultural attitudes, the ideology, of the new commercial ruling classes. Virtually every major writer of the next thirty years is to struggle to find artistic expression for an analysis, a critique, of the mores and morals of this very middle class: Carlyle, Dickens, Thackeray, Arnold, Browning, Ruskin, George Eliot. Peacock had his own style, his own genre. Judging him not by those who followed, but by the standards of elegance and control he set himself elsewhere in his very best work, and by his aim of influencing opinion, he may be said relatively to have failed. But this is a matter of artistic execution, not of intellectual grasp of the subject. As a critic, an analyst, Peacock can be very impressive. His work around 1830 – the two satires, *The Misfortunes of Elphin* and *Crotchet Castle,* and the handful of review articles, from the discussion of *The Epicurean* to that of Paul de Kock – shows him, surely, at the height of his formidable powers. In print he is never in the end less than essentially serious. He despises those who are, from writers like Moore to entire journals like the *Edinburgh Review,* 'that shallow and dishonest publication'.[115] He is intellectually responsible, and he has a penetrating grasp of what the social, or socio-literary, critic ought to be saying. Following the elegant satire on Tory delays, *The Misfortunes of Elphin,* the more flawed *Crotchet Castle* attempts an impression of current social values, which is a subject of more lasting importance. It is the mark of the writer of real creativity, and major talent, that he thus so consistently in one sense or other excels himself. Anticipating his own essay 'The Epicier', with *Crotchet Castle* Peacock marks the birth of a new, post-revolutionary world.

Chapter 7

The Satisfied Guest:
Gryll Grange

As men who leave their homes for public games,
We leave our native element of darkness
For life's brief light. And who has most of mirth,
And wine, and love, may, like a satisfied guest,
Return contented to the night he sprang from
       Alexis: *Tarantini* (Peacock's epigraph
            to *Gryll Grange*, chapter xxiii)

In the 1840s, that great decade for the English novel, Peacock wrote almost nothing for publication. The busy opera reviewing and literary essays of the years up to 1836 gave way at first to little and, after 1838, to nothing more in print until the 1850s. In 1842, however, he wrote a poem which shows that his verse might have matured in strength and grace, just as the satires did. Within walking distance of his home at Halliford were the ruins of Newark Abbey, a favourite haunt since, at the age of twenty-two, he had been there with the first girl he loved, Fanny Faulkner. Little is known of Fanny Faulkner, except that she became engaged to Peacock in 1807, when she was eighteen, but, after the intervention of a relative, married someone else and died in the following year. Peacock's contained but moving lyric is a wholly characteristic poem, with its discipline, its understated but sincere grief, its absence of flamboyance, its eighteenth-century derivation:[1]

I gaze, where August's sunbeam falls
Along these gray and lonely walls,

Till in its light absorbed appears
The lapse of five-and-thirty years.

If change there be, I trace it not
In all this consecrated spot:
No new imprint of Ruin's march
On roofless wall and frameless arch:
The hills, the woods, the fields, the stream,
Are basking in the self-same beam:
The fall, that turns the unseen mill,
As then it murmured, murmurs still:
It seems, as if in one were cast
The present and the imaged past,
Spanning, as with a bridge sublime,
That awful lapse of human time,
That gulph, unfathomably spread
Between the living and the dead.

For all too well my spirit feels
The only change this scene reveals:
The sunbeams play, the breezes stir,
Unseen, unfelt, unheard by her,
Who, on that long-past August day,
First saw with me these ruins gray.

Whatever span the Fates allow,
Ere I shall be as she is now,
Still in my bosom's inmost cell
Shall that deep-treasured memory dwell:
That, more than language can express,
Pure miracle of loveliness,
Whose voice so sweet, whose eyes so bright,
Were my soul's music, and its light,
In those blest days, when life was new,
And hope was false, but love was true.

It is perhaps simplest to account for so prolonged a literary silence in the circumstances of Peacock's life. In 1833 his mother died, depriving him of his best critic and, he declared, of much of his personal pleasure in writing.[2] Since his wife Jane was now an invalid, who was probably insane, he was also left with the responsibility for two surviving daughters and a son. In 1836, on the death of James Mill, Peacock succeeded to the senior position, the post of Examiner of Correspondence, in the office which dealt directly with the administrators out in India. He held this post, which carried with it the very substantial salary of £2000 a year, until his retirement in March 1856. Though Peacock was henceforth very busy, he never exercised the real influence over Indian policy of his predecessor. James Mill was an ideologue, who wrote his *History of British India* (1817) without ever going there; he believed that the happiness of Indians was best served by an efficient, modern, authoritarian government, imposed by the British from above. Mill and his disciples had a profound influence on the judiciary and on taxation, two areas of policy on which the social and economic future of British India would turn. But in 1834 the East India Company lost its commercial functions, to become instead something more like an ordinary branch of the Civil Service, and the accompanying internal reorganisation of the India House weakened the influence of the Examiner. Besides, after a period of expansion, and an enthusiastic campaign for 'progress' (which in effect meant the anglicisation of Indian society) by utilitarians and evangelicals alike, the foundations of British policy in India, in law, revenue, and the form of government, were for the time being settled. The next twenty years – Peacock's period as Examiner – was an era of consolidation in some parts of India, frontier war in others.[3]

Both by situation and by temperament, Peacock was more of an executive civil servant, and certainly less of an ideologue, than James Mill had been. He did not write about the problems of governing India, as both Mills did, although he applied himself briskly and effectively to an important administrator's problem – that of better communications, both between England and India, and within India itself. He seems to have proved capable at supervising the building of ships, and at defending the Company's policy, on this topic and others, before various committees. He also seems to have been well liked at the India House, as an amusing raconteur, and a man kind to his subordinates, though he was a more aloof and idiosyncratic figure than his successor, John Stuart Mill. Beyond this, he has left less mark in the history books than other colleagues of comparable eminence. It is only indirectly that one gathers what his opinion was of the more ambitious hopes of assimilating India, commercially, religiously, culturally, to European norms. Before one committee, he commented briefly but significantly on such aspirations: 'I am not aware that it would be any benefit to the people of India to send Europeans among them.' Consistent to his satirist's preference for 'ancients' over 'moderns', and nicely inverting the assumptions of Evangelical missionaries, he added that such a course might have a sinister effect on the 'morals and domestic habits' of the Hindus.[4]

Administration took up his time, or his creative energy, or both. In the 1850s, when his family were grown up, he was not too busy to begin writing again: the article with Mary Ellen on 'Gastronomy and Civilisation', the first two parts of a three-part article on Greek drama,[5] two fragments of stories are tentatively dated from this time.[6] There was a further, unexplained gap in his output for several years. Perhaps the likeliest explanation is that Peacock enjoyed writing when he had a partner to work with. After his mother's death in 1833, he found little incentive to begin again until Mary Ellen was living nearby, and willing to take her grandmother's place; but after a time Mary Ellen's unhappiness with Meredith made her restless and took her away from home. It may have been her new relationship with Wallis, or simply the increased leisure of retirement, that made it possible for Peacock to write again, in three rich years of productivity. They began with more literary fragments[7] and long review articles, of which the most important became the first part of his *Memoirs of Shelley*.

Though the review articles are characteristically rich in learned asides, anecdotes, wit and snatches of translation, at first glance they might appear desultory. Peacock's criticism, when discussed at all, has been quickly passed over as the chance reflections of a clever and amusing man, rather than the sustained, philosophical approach to literature and life of a major critic. But in its context Peacock's literary output of the 1850s looks more important. He is a writer who is never trivial. Unlike most of us, if he has nothing to say, or something he is not quite willing to say, he is simply silent. 'No man is bound to write the life of another. No man who does so is bound to tell the public all he knows.'[8] Everything Peacock did publish was the genuine, if partial, expression of a coherent philosophy of life and art; and it is finally given full expression in the book which brings together all the writing of his last years. Sardonic reflections on his times – appreciations of wit, lyricism, fantasy, and comment on the comedy of the past – aspersions on prudery and puritanism – consideration of the link between gastronomy and civilisation – contemplation of the life of Shelley – all find their way into the richest, most ambitious and complete of his satires, *Gryll Grange*.

Though first published in *Fraser's* in nine monthly instalments between April and December 1860, *Gryll Grange* was surely conceived and written as a whole. There are none of the usual traces of a book being written part by part – haste, an altered plan, the sudden introduction of the enlivening character, or the big scene which takes precedence over the general design. It is a finely articulated performance, which resembles *Melincourt* in its epic ambitiousness of scale, and *Nightmare Abbey* or *The Misfortunes of Elphin* in its polish and assurance. The artistry alone would suggest that *Gryll Grange* took time to devise; but it is also exceptionally complex in its thought, and wide in its range of reference. It has three main motifs, or asks three large questions: What is present-day England like? What is, or ought, art to be like? How, between the real or ideal worlds, should the individual choose to live? All three questions, and the answers to them, had been separating and coalescing in Peacock's mind since 1851.

Like all Peacock's books, *Gryll Grange* is dense with allusion to current controversy; a glance at the periodicals and newspapers he read shows that his time-scale was effectively the whole of the 1850s. He had of course never shown the journalist's concern for up-to-the-minute topicality. The controversies he picked out were amusing in themselves, and also illustrated some wider principle. There was no need in addition for them to sell his books. Thus *Headlong Hall* employed disputes about landscape gardening which were in the air before 1809, when Peacock first mentioned them in a letter[9]: that is, fully seven years before *Headlong Hall* appeared. Though the subsequent books tended to be more topical, if only because Peacock used up examples of the ludicrous as he went along, he was content in *Crotchet Castle* to describe an experiment with a cat which happened at least nine years earlier, and to draw heavily on areas of controversy – education, for example, and Scott's novels – which were liveliest three to six years before his book appeared. Perhaps he kept a commonplace book, or a scrapbook of cuttings; perhaps he liked re-reading old journals. Immediacy mattered less to him than finding a range of satiric targets which fitted coherently together, while yet seeming sufficiently varied to evoke the frenetic intellectual activity of the day.[10]

The satire of the last book is directed at two large targets: religious bigotry and acquisitiveness. Educated men and women were considerably less fervent when they discussed religious matters in the time of *Gryll Grange* than they had been in the 1840s. A comparison between the novels of Charlotte M. Yonge written in the 1840s and those of Anthony Trollope in the 1850s illustrates the increasing urbanity of tone: the former are proselytizing, dogmatic, the latter merely use a clerical setting in order to explore character and motive.[11] But in the public discussion of religion a bitterly polemical tone survives into the 1850s. In the winter of 1850–1, for example, after the Papal Bull which created Roman Catholic bishops in England, the Prime Minister, Lord John Russell, initiated an anti-Catholic campaign. Russell wrote an open letter dated November 1850, which alluded to Roman practices as 'the mummeries of superstition'. Afterwards he devised a Bill against 'Papal aggression', which he presented to the House of Commons in February 1851 and, after a four-day debate, carried by an enormous majority. Peacock, the veteran of the campaign for Catholic Emancipation in the late 1820s, now riposted in private with a satirical poem, 'A Goodlye Ballade of Little John', and in public with his three articles for *Fraser's*.[12] The latter, whatever their nominal subjects, in fact celebrate the un-puritanical pleasures of food, drink, and laughter, and, with typical indirection, advance the claims of the alternative creed of Bacchus.

Peacock's fondness throughout the decade for Bacchus is in part an allusion to the campaign for teetotalism, which he also mentions with distaste in *Gryll Grange*.[13] Though alcoholism was a serious evil, preaching against it could readily acquire the sanctimony of middle-class snobbery towards the pleasures of the poor. The same objection could be made against strict Sabbatarianism, which often made it harder for the poor to enjoy their scant free time in their own way. In 1855 a Bill was introduced into Parliament for the suppression of Sunday trading, including the sale of beer. London working men saw this as a class measure, and on successive Sundays demonstrated against the wealthy enjoying *their* favourite amusement of riding in the Park — after which the Bill was withdrawn. Earlier, probably in 1837, Peacock wrote a poem called 'A Bill for the Better Promotion of Oppression on the Sabbath Day', which anticipates the rioters' point of view:[14]

> Forasmuch as the Canter's and Fanatic's Lord
> Sayeth peace and joy are by me abhorred;
> And would fill each Sunday with gloom and pain
> For all too poor his regard to obtain;
> And forasmuch as the laws heretofore
> Have not sufficiently squeezed the poor;
>
> Be it therefore enacted by Commons, King
> And Lords, a crime for any thing
> To be done on the Sabbath by any rank
> Excepting the rich. No beer may be drank,
> Food eaten, rest taken, away from home,
> And each House shall a Sunday prison become. ...

In disputes between Protestants and Catholics, Peacock always inclined to the Catholic side. He took pleasure in a hostile newspaper reference to anti-Catholic polemic. 'I send you', he wrote to Mary Ellen, 'a *Morning Post*, containing a very good article on Mr Spurgeon and his audience, under the head of *Transpontine Preachments*.'[15] Following the Papal Bull which in December 1854 promulgated the doctrine of the Immaculate Conception, both Mariolatry and virulent preaching and writing against it were in full spate. Ever since his *Maid Marian*, Peacock had revealed an interest in the Virgin Mary, whom he seems to have equated with a pagan goddess, and St Catharine — the favourite of Falconer, the hero of *Gryll Grange* — is another such figure.

Peacock's attitude to religion, now as in the days of Shelley, is subtle and idiosyncratic. Superficially *Gryll Grange* makes it look as though he was flirting with Catholicism, but this is probably a tease. Peacock has Dr Opimian wonder if Falconer is secretly a convert, but Falconer assures him that he is not a Catholic, and not tempted to become one.[16] And, indeed, what clues to Falconer's religion can be pieced together do not suggest any kind of Christianity — as a contemporary reviewer sensed when he called the book, and its author, pagan.[17] Falconer may appear to incline to Catholicism, but this is because that faith, with its individual saints, goes some way to preserve the ancient world's divinities for each particular mood, moment and place. Peacock thus mischievously accepts the Evangelical charge that Popery is nearly allied to paganism — and takes it as a compliment to Catholicism, since it is paganism rather than any kind of Christianity that attracts him.

From the time of *Rhododaphne* and *Maid Marian*, Peacock associated paganism with a healthy acceptance of the body and the body's pleasures, and Christianity with a dualism that linked sexuality with sin and shame. He brought up Mary Ellen unconventionally in this respect; neither she, nor her father on her behalf, subscribed to the view that one is morally obliged to remain monogamous. Whether Peacock remained faithful to his own wife, who was insane for twenty-five years, will presumably never be known. Whatever he felt or did on his own account, the 1850s, with their raking up of the Shelley scandal, and their blows to the social standing of Mary Ellen, were years which kept alive his dislike of the Christian churches' personal ethic — and especially in relation to sexuality. Some time during this period, Peacock wrote a poem in Greek, a commentary on Matthew 10,v.34 ff:

> Think not that I am come to send peace on earth: I came not to send peace, but a sword.
>
> For I am come to set a man at variance against his father, and the daughter against her mother, and the daughter in law against her mother in law.
>
> And a man's foes shall be they of his own household.
>
> He that loveth father or mother more than me is not worthy of me: and he that loveth son or daughter more than me is not worthy of me.
>
> He that taketh not his cross, and followeth after me, is not worthy of me.

In 1862, after Mary Ellen's death, Peacock sent the poem to a printer, and told L'Estrange about it. When in 1873 the latter was preparing Peacock's works for publication, he enquired after the

Greek poem, and Edith Nicolls produced some printed copies; but, after L'Estrange had translated part for her, they decided that it was too controversial for publication. The poem itself is lost, supposedly destroyed by Edith, but L'Estrange's translation of the final lines survives:[18]

> Oh, all ye who use your utmost exertions to avoid all false worship, and to hate all teachers of falsehood, if truthlovingly and unremittingly ye lift up your mind to wisdom, come now in a body and dash in pieces, strike, shake, beat, cut down, drop in pieces and overthrow the cursed imposter, the soul-destroying son of Erebos, a false prophet, who, a causer of death, like a THIEF at midnight, came to throw on the sad Earth 'Not Peace but a Sword' — not peace — but a sword defiled with blood newly shed: and to make hateful what is dearest to all mortals, and to all delights. — Break in pieces, hurl down him who is a seller of marvels, him who is hostile to the Graces, and him who is abominable to Aphrodite, the hater of the marriage-bed, this mischievous wonder-worker, this destroyer of the world, CHRIST.

Nothing in *Gryll Grange* is as heterodox as this; yet there is a strong underlying movement in the book, as we shall see, towards exalting the physical, human and social pleasures, while the conventional Christian connection between asceticism and virtue, solitariness and idealism ('he that taketh not his cross, and followeth after me') is steadily denied.

A further dimension is added to the satire on contemporary religious excesses by the Aristophanic comedy performed at Gryll Grange. The early 1850s had seen a rage for table-turning and spirit-rapping, which had become curiously associated with the ultra-Protestantism Peacock particularly disliked. The link was spelt out in a long review article in the *Quarterly* in 1853, which Peacock is likely to have seen and absorbed. The reviewer first gives an account of each pretended psychic phenomenon. In spirit-rapping, a medium answers unspoken questions, or puts her clients in touch with the illustrious dead. Table-turners sit in a circle, concentrating, and the table on which their hands are placed appears to move without human agency. Individual reactions to these psychic phenomena depend largely upon religious preconditioning. The *Quarterly* reviewer's sympathies are with G. H. Lewes, who had ridiculed the claims of the best-known medium, an American called Mrs Hayden, and had even got her to rap the answer 'Yes' to his question, 'Is Mrs Hayden an imposter?' On the other hand, two clergymen, the Rev. N. S. Godfrey and the Rev. E. Gillson,[19] believing that each phenomenon was a genuine manifestation of the supernatural, concluded that they were the work of Anti-Christ.

The *Quarterly*'s contributor is a rationalist and a believer in scientific explanation. He includes in his review a discussion of recent work on the nervous system, and suggests that many so-called wonders are accounted for by auto-suggestion and fantasy. One common fantasy of the day, as the two clergymen illustrate, is religious mania, fanned by bigotry:[20]

> In all ages, the 'possession' of men's minds by dominant ideas has been most complete, when these ideas have been *religious* aberrations. The origin of such aberrations has uniformly lain in the preference given to the feelings over the judgment, in the inordinate indulgence of emotional excitement without adequate control on the part of the rational will. No one, who is as yet untainted by kindred sentiments, can read the productions of Mr. Godfrey and Mr. Gillson, without perceiving that they have abandoned their sober judgment, if ever they possessed any, to the tyranny of their abhorrence of Papal aggression and their dread of Satanic agency, as completely as the biologized 'subject' gives up the guidance of his thoughts to the direction of the operator. .... Such persons are no more to be argued with, than are insane patients. They cannot assent to any proposition, which they fancy to be in the least inconsistent with their prepossessions; and the evidence of their own feelings is to them the highest attainable truth. ... We would save from this pseudo-religious pestilence those who are yet unharmed by it ... many of the victims of these delusions have become the subjects of actual Insanity. Mr. Gillson himself confesses to have heard of one such case, which might, he admits, have been caused by excitement, though, he adds, 'I think it more probable that a spirit entered in and took possession'. What kind of spirits they are, which thus take possession of credulous and excitable minds,

we hope that we have made sufficiently plain. They are
Dominant Ideas.

The reason the writer gives for disliking religious hysteria is in
keeping with the general current of mid-Victorian individualism,
and also with the rational humanism to which Peacock had
adhered since *Headlong Hall*:[21]

> We have seen in the various phenomena we have been
> discussing how largely the Will is concerned in all those higher
> exercises of the reasoning powers, even on the most common-
> place subjects, by which our conduct ought to be governed; and
> how important it is that the automatic tendencies, of whatever
> nature, should be entirely subjugated by it.

In his *Memoirs of Shelley* (1858–60), Peacock is deeply interested
in Shelley's repeated claims, or fantasies, that his father, uncle and
others had designs on his life or liberty; implicitly these make a
parallel to Shelley's sincere conviction that his first wife Harriet
was a whore.[22] The reasons Peacock gives for refusing to believe
Shelley's stories, and the explanation he offers – auto-suggestion –
seem to reflect the rational and scientific scepticism of the
Quarterly's approach in 1853.[23] Though modern scholars have been
inclined to suggest that Peacock may have been too prosaic, and
that Shelley may really have been attacked by, for example, some
of his Welsh neighbours at Tan-yr-allt in February 1813, Byron's
old friend Lord Broughton strongly backed Peacock's opinion that
Shelley imagined this episode. After Peacock had published the
main part of his *Memoirs*, Broughton even thought of a possible
source for Shelley's fantasy: Rousseau (who has always been
suspected of paranoid delusions, especially in later life) describes in
his *Confessions* a remarkably similar episode, when in 1765 his
house at Motiers in Neuchâtel was attacked at night by a gang of
murderous peasants:[24]

> Do you recollect about the pretended attack on Shelley's house?
> you and I had some talks on that queer subject at Corsham – but
> I forgot at the time that exactly the same trick was played by
> Rousseau and I have little doubt that Shelley copied that obscene
> worthy.

Even without this interesting hypothesis, Peacock's narrative is consistently, and notoriously, rational and scientific. At first sight it seems perverse, therefore – and perversity is another, often not unreasonable, charge against Peacock – that so many of the jokes in *Gryll Grange* are apparently at the expense of science.

One of the book's leading characters, Lord Curryfin, is made amiably ridiculous for his inventions, his lecturing, and his membership of the newly-formed Pantopragmatic Society (the Social Science Association). The Chorus of the Aristophanic comedy places the modern characters in an unflattering context when he alludes to 'your steam-nursed, steam-borne, steam-killed, And gas-enlightened race'.[25] Yet there is plenty of biographical evidence that Peacock felt no animus against science in general, or steam in particular. He had, after all, on the East India Company's behalf, initiated research into a quicker, more modern, route to the East – that wholly characteristic scientific achievement of the second quarter of the nineteenth century. Apparently he took the leading part in the Company's early commitment to steamships. He personally superintended the building and trials of the steamships *Pluto* and *Proserpina* ('my iron chickens').[26] Just as his attitude to Shelley's fantasy-life is that of a man with a scientific interest in the mind, so his professional actions are those of a man interested in technology. The problem Peacock notes in *Gryll Grange* is not science, but an uncritical, or exploitative, attitude to science. His strategy is the classic one of the satirist, to cast doubt upon anything in which his contemporaries seem inclined to put too much trust.

As far back as 1830 Peacock had written an article for the *Westminster Review* on the new London Bridge, in which, as far as the subject and the sobriety of the journal permitted, he allowed himself the free play of the satirist. Two kinds of problem are liable to beset the wonders of modern technology. One is that in defiance of the new sophistication they will not work:[27]

The old London Bridge was begun in 1176, and finished in 1209. It was built on such unscientific principles, that it ought to have been carried away before it was finished, when it was finished, and at any given time subsequently; but partly by the awkward contrivances of barbarous men, partly by its own obstinacy, it has stood six centuries and a quarter, amidst the perpetual prophecies of disinterested engineers that it could not stand any longer: while one bridge after another, on different parts of the same river, in which no son of science has espied a flaw, has wilfully tumbled to pieces, by the sinking of the piers, or the yielding of the abutments, in despite of the most mathematical demonstrations of the absurdity and impropriety of such a proceeding.

The second problem is implied by the word 'disinterested', which Peacock uses of the engineers in the passage above. There is a danger that the prevailing spirit of commerce − more of a god even than technology − will make out of scientific achievements a handsome profit:[28]

> The whole affair [of the proposed new London Bridge] is an instructive specimen of the way in which public business is done, and public money expended. Evidence is collected, and conclusions are drawn in the teeth of it. Plans are collected, and it has been predetermined whose plan shall be adopted. Tenders are called for, and the contractors have been already chosen. Estimates are prepared, and the expense doubles, triples, quadruples, in the progress of the work. Millions are thrown away in buildings, in colonies, in baubles and incumbrances of all kinds, in order to put a few thousands into the pockets of favoured individuals.

Much of what Peacock has to say against science in *Gryll Grange* makes the same two points, against complacency and profiteering. The 1850s was a decade in which persistent efforts were made to get public health measures on to the statute books, and to see that once on they were enforced. Filth bred disease; industrial processes polluted the air and the rivers. Dr Opimian, the clergyman in *Gryll Grange*, complains for example of the industrially polluted Thames, which flows directly past the inactive legislators:[29]

> Between them [Parliamentary Wisdom, and Science] they have poisoned the Thames, and killed the fish in the river. A little further development of the same wisdom and science will complete the poisoning of the air, and kill the dwellers on the banks.

A further real-life threat to public health was the frequency of cases of poisoning, many of which were accidents due to the ease with which poisons were bought and to the absence of labelling. Even commoner were instances of illness or death caused by manufacturers' adulteration of food. Thanks largely to an energetic campaign conducted by the medical journal the *Lancet*, in 1855 a parliamentary committee was set up, and its report eventually led to the Adulteration Act of 1860. But the new law was still insufficiently rigorous: its loopholes were not closed until the 1870s. Meanwhile scandalous reports appeared in the newspapers: the worst, in 1858, described the Bradford sweet-seller whose poisonous lozenges killed eighteen people and left over two hundred ill, with seven or eight unlikely to recover.

Another controversial issue of the 1850s was the high level of industrial accidents. The *Annual Register* shows that a large proportion of all such accidents reported in the late 1850s were caused by the explosion of steam boilers in collieries, iron works, dockyards, factories, ships and locomotives. The loss of life and injury had become so serious that the *Annual Register*, like many another journal, demanded government inspection. Peacock had in fact already intervened publicly on the subject of exploding steam boilers. When superintending the building of the East India Company's steamships, he had seen to it that they were fitted with the safer low-pressure steam-engines, rather than the high-pressure ones. In September 1854 he wrote to the *Spectator*, using the pseudonym Carebus, to point out the advantages, in terms of safety, of these vessels built for the East India Company by Messrs Laird. Not surprisingly, the references in *Gryll Grange* to accidents caused by steam have the ring of authenticity. Dr Opimian is scientifically accurate when he speaks of explosions: 'Explosions of powder-mills and powder-magazines; of coal-gas in mines and in houses; of high-pressure engines in ships and boats and factories'.[30] Equally, when Gryllus complains, apparently blimpishly, that many such accidents are caused by the reckless desire for speed, he is speaking what Peacock knew to be the truth. For trains and especially cargoships, a quick journey was a profitable one, and their owners did accordingly demand speed, regardless of the increased risk to human life. Part of the problem was that design and technology lagged behind the expansion of trade in the new era of steam, but it was at least arguable – and reformers did argue –

that with legal safety standards the casualty rates would be brought down. The modern reader takes it for granted that Opimian's speech, or Gryllus's visions of accidents by land and sea, are exaggerations, an aspect of both characters' eccentricity. But Eric Robinson, the modern historian of science who has examined the topical references in *Gryll Grange*, calls one of Dr Opimian's speeches 'an abstract of the chief accidents that occurred in the 1850s':[31]

MRS OPIMIAN.
If the world grew ever so honest, there would still be accidents.

THE REV. DR. OPIMIAN.
But honesty would materially diminish the number. High pressure steam boilers would not scatter death and destruction around them, if the dishonesty of avarice did not tempt their employment, where the more costly low pressure would ensure absolute safety. Honestly built houses would not come suddenly down and crush their occupants. Ships, faithfully built and efficiently manned, would not so readily strike on a lee shore, nor go instantly to pieces on the first touch of the ground. Honestly made sweetmeats would not poison children; honestly compounded drugs would not poison patients. In short, the larger portion of what we call accidents are crimes.[32]

It is interesting that Peacock has somehow the reputation of being a Tory in *Gryll Grange*; while Dickens, so much the better-known campaigner of the period, is certainly regarded as a radical. Actually there is a very large overlap in the causes they take up, and where there are differences, they hardly confirm Dickens as the more dedicated radical. Comparing the handling of science by the two — Peacock in *Gryll Grange*, Dickens in his novels and in *Household Words* — Dr Robinson concludes that it is Peacock who shows the more serious interest in reforming abuses. Dickens is at best an erratic champion of a cause, both because he is a muddled thinker, and because, for all the world like a man of his time, he cannot resist making capital for himself out of any subject in hand. His reservations about progress are compromised by his excitement at speed; his baroque imagination is more gripped by the psychology of the criminal than by an activity which killed more people, the adulteration of food. When, in *Little Dorrit* (1857), Dickens has a house fall down — an event straight out of contemporary newspapers — he gives his description more atmosphere, and less significance, by insisting that Mrs Clennam's house is old; the point in real life was that so many of the houses that fell down were new. Jerry-built homes and tenements in the new slums of industrial cities were collapsing on their inhabitants, because of the get-rich-quick methods of their speculative builders, who remained, at this date, beyond the reach of the law.

It is what Peacock gives Opimian to say; and in the 1860s, when these issues were very live ones, the point would be correctly taken. When Peacock died in 1866, the *Atheneum* assumed that his viewpoint was too plain to call for elaborate discussion:[33]

> Rated as a satirist who shot Folly as it flew, and could exhibit the philosophies and paradoxes of the time with an epigrammatic keenness, and withal a genial recognition of all that is best, highest, and most liberal, he demands no common praise, and will hold no common place whenever the story of ultra-liberal literature shall come to be written.

Peacock was not described as a Tory satirist until George Saintsbury suggested the idea, in his introductions to the novels of 1895–7, three decades and many parliamentary Acts later.

And yet a striking difficulty still remains: Peacock's friend and correspondent of later years, John Cam Hobhouse, Lord Broughton, also described him as by then 'in politics a strong conservative'.[34] Broughton's opinion is supported by a number of sallies in Peacock's letters to him. Peacock reports for example on the classical reading he has done on his regular train journey between Weybridge and London — 'I have lately read through the *Iliad*, the *Odyssey* and Aeschylus: the result of this confirms me in the opinion, that the March of Mechanics is one way, and the March of Mind is another.'[35] It sounds like the very tone of Dr Folliott; and more than a decade later the letters still hardly suggest the ardour of the would-be reformer of public health:[36]

> I think there are some miracles in store for us: at least, I hope so, when I think of the Government Board of Works, the Metropolitan Board of Works, and the Sanitary Commission. If

they do not breed a pestilence between them, it will be a clear manifestation of Special Providence.

Broughton was evidently familiar with his friend's grumbles against modernity, and would half-humorously expostulate: 'but what do you think of printing? what of steam? what of gunpowder? Indeed what of any art of which very mischievous use has been made more frequently than any good use?'[37]

In the very act of exchanging opinions, of dialogue, surely lies the secret of Peacock's later whimsicalities. Hobhouse was in youth a radical, and later a Liberal President of the Board of Control for two periods between 1835 and 1852. He must have made a good sparring partner for Peacock, since what was true of the late 1820s was even truer of the middle of the century: in the absence of any centre of opposition to a dominant liberalism, intellectuals who wished to challenge orthodoxy (like Mill, Peacock, and later Arnold) had to adopt some strange postures.[38] Besides, the 1850s and 1860s were an interlude of relative political stasis, between two periods of social unrest and very strong pressure for reform. The air of cynicism and disengagement which is reflected in *Gryll Grange* – and, from what one knows of it, in Peacock's conversation – is typical of these years, and has no precise political colouring, although to a committed and active liberal it would have seemed like conservatism. On other occasions and to other interlocutors Peacock was prepared to avow that he did not think of himself as either a Tory or a Conservative:[39]

If I have said lately nothing about the Tories, it arises from my considering them to be as completely extinct as the Mammoth. Their successors, the Conservatives as they call themselves, appear to me like Falstaff's otter, 'neither fish nor flesh'; one knows not where to have them. I could not, in a dialogue, put into the mouth of one of them the affirmation of any principle which I should expect him to adhere to for five minutes.

It is in fact possible to recognise in *Gryll Grange* a broadly coherent social satire, though it has no political end in view. Other observers of the period, like Dickens and Thackeray, see Britain in the 1850s in similar terms. They identify the same contradiction: a society that is obsessively acquisitive, and complacent about its material, technological progress, and, at the same time, earnestly enforces a religion which specifically denies the things of this world. The phrase of Edward Oliphant neatly sums up the inherent problem with so much mid-century exhortation − 'worldly holy' and 'wholly worldly'.[40] The quiddity of Peacock's manner masks a viewpoint which must to educated contemporaries have seemed non-doctrinaire and moderate. The attitudes are those of the pragmatic, experienced public servant. An underplayed but persistent animus against the commercial vested interest is, meanwhile, fully in keeping with Peacock's earlier satiric vein.

However, one campaign in *Gryll Grange* does appear to set its face against a proposed change: Peacock persistently makes fun of the decade's important proposals to reform the Civil Service. In 1853, the Northcote−Trevelyan Report advised that entry to the higher strata of the Civil Service should henceforth be by competitive examination, rather than by the old system of patronage. Since Peacock himself won his place at the India House late in 1818 as the result of an admirable performance in an examination ('Nothing superfluous and nothing wanting', said the examiners' report), his sustained ridiculing of the idea in *Gryll Grange* seems virtually inexplicable, the whimsicality of an elderly eccentric. In his Aristophanic play, he stages a parody of a competitive examination, in which a succession of youths, all future practical men (Hannibal, Richard Coeur de Lion, Oliver Cromwell), are tried and fail. Earlier the Rev. Dr Opimian has directed an apparently Folliott-like invective at examinations:[41]

THE REV. DR. OPIMIAN.

Questions, which can only be answered by the parrotings of a memory, crammed to disease with all sorts of heterogeneous diet, can form no test of genius, taste, judgment, or natural capacity. Competitive Examination takes for its *norma*: 'It is better to learn many things ill than one thing well;' or rather: 'It is better to learn to gabble about everything than to understand anything.' This is not the way to discover the wood of which Mercuries are made.

The Northcote−Trevelyan Report was written with the kind of doctrinaire assurance which can irritate in reforming literature. It was followed by a great deal of public comment adverse to the old

Civil Service, of which Dickens's Circumlocution Office in *Little Dorrit* is an example. But the accusations of inefficiency and jobbery were not entirely fair, or even themselves necessarily disinterested. Sir James Stephen and Rowland Hill, who rose to the top of the Civil Service in the first half of the nineteenth century, were energetic, high-minded, and not a bit like the Tite Barnacles. Between 1855 and 1860, the voice of existing civil servants began to be heard, complaining against the assumption that young amateurs, trained in Latin, Greek and Sanskrit at one of the older universities, would necessarily turn into better administrators than the existing breed.

Anthony Trollope of the Post Office thus defended his profession against the appointment of outsiders to top positions, and claimed that the old circumstances of appointment actually made for many of the right attitudes. A young man was put into a vacancy by his family because an early income had to be found for him. Compared with other occupations, the Civil Service was not lucrative: the recruit knew this, but expected to find his satisfaction in work that was gentlemanly, responsible, useful, and relatively independent.[42] What was true for older branches of the Civil Service was also true for the India House, which came under direct government authority only in 1858. The East India Company had a policy of recruiting men of first-class ability and integrity, like the two Mills, Peacock, and Macaulay. It is not surprising that a former Examiner should want to point out the difference between academic promise and actual achievement – particularly in 1860, at the end of a decade when the Indian Mutiny had brought down a torrent of criticism on the existing administrators. If he felt pride in the achievements of his own generation, so too did his successor John Stuart Mill, who wrote a dignified and spirited state paper petitioning Parliament against the abolition of the East India Company:[43]

> Your Petitioners ... do not seek to vindicate themselves at the
> expense of any other authority; they claim their full share of the
> responsibility of the manner in which India has practically been
> governed. That responsibility is to them not a subject of
> humiliation, but of pride ... the Government in which they have
> borne a part has been not only one of the purest in intention, but
> one of the most beneficent in act, ever known among mankind.

Peacock and Mill might well wonder – as others certainly did – whether the civil servant was being made a whipping-boy, by interests adverse to the encroachments of central authority, and by politicians anxious to deflect criticism from themselves.[44]

Gryll Grange's satire on recruitment by examination implicitly seconds Trollope's and Mill's defence of the existing administrators. In taking this line, Peacock testifies to the self-respect of a caste that already thought of itself, independent of class origins, as the public service. It is one of the fascinations of a long literary career in changing times, that a writer who begins by admiring *philosophes* like Rousseau and Monboddo should end by testifying to the emergence of a new intellectual aristocracy, the professional servants of the modern centralised state.

The presentation of the satiric material in *Gryll Grange* is by a method new to Peacock. He has given up his characteristic crowd of pedants and cranks. The contemporary world does not appear dramatised through a host of personae. The characters who assemble at *Gryll Grange* in chapter xiii are not satiric types but genial friends, who, like Mr MacBorrowdale, decline to display their foibles. This does not mean that the outer world is kept at bay. It is always present in the minds of the leading characters, as is firmly established in the opening chapter, where the book's satiric targets are rehearsed by Dr Opimian and Mr Gryll.

Gryll Grange is not less aware of social evils than the earlier books, but it has a more personal perspective. How the right-minded individual should act in such a world becomes the leading preoccupation. Themes like the nature of idealism or of art, and the idealist's duty to the actual, take what is formally the central position, relegating the satire for once to the margin. The reality from which Lord Curryfin has come remains shadowy, while the literary alternatives are in the foreground, vividly etched.

The entire book dramatises the most familiar of all Peacockian conflicts, the 'ancient' versus the 'modern', which it sees in fresh terms, as an elaborate confrontation between ideality and reality. Peacock so arranges the satire that the reader, like the characters, forever moves between the two ideas. Just as the topic of science, or modern learning, recurs in conversation, so too does art, or ancient learning, and the two are placed with conscious symmetry. After the satiric, anatomising conversation with which the book opens, the Squire, his niece and Dr Opimian move (via the modern 'art-form', the lecture) to the medieval *tenson*, and Aristophanic comedy; and the same deliberate conversational polarities are maintained throughout, until they reach a final expression in dramatic form, in the contrasts offered by the inset Aristophanic play. But it is hard to appreciate the richness of Peacock's treatment of art from his dialogue alone. Already in *Crotchet Castle* he firmly established his romantic plot as the principal vehicle for his meaning. It is even more necessary to approach *Gryll Grange* as an action, which turns upon Falconer's choice of a solitary way of life, and his subsequent decision to leave it for marriage with Morgana.

The plan of the book helps to emphasise that it is about Falconer's mental progress from one choice of life to another. His first decision has been to pursue the ideal. He has withdrawn from society to an isolated Tower, where he studies and surrounds himself with art and music. He is served by seven maidens, who are at once Vestal Virgins, or priestesses of his cult, and the Arts, or Graces. Peacock's idea for them must derive from the Pleiades,[45] the seven daughters of Atlas by one of the Oceanides, who after death formed a constellation in the heavens. In classical literature the seven maidens are sometimes given alternative names: Vergiliae, from *ver*, the spring, or Hesperides, from the garden which belonged to their father, Atlas. Peacock retains some associations with spring, and with the mythical garden, but above all he gives his seven the otherworldliness of their starry originals. A secondary association of the word Pleiades is with two different groups of artists: at the Alexandrian court, the group which included Theocritus and in sixteenth-century France, Ronsard and his friends. The link with the arts is further developed when Peacock, with fantastic elaboration, gives the girls names recalling the seven notes of an octave on the diatonic scale – which Algernon Falconer himself completes. Afterwards, he makes their seven suitors (led naturally by the next note, H, personified in Harry Hedgerow) equally representative of the same scale in the lower register. The original Pleiades all (except Merope) married immortals. Peacock's marry men who 'are all something to do with the land and the woods; farmers, and foresters, and

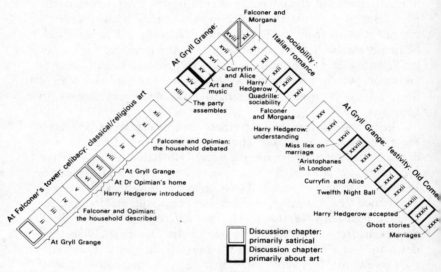

Figure 3 Gryll Grange

nurserymen'.[46] But, like the male half of an operatic chorus, they will not shatter the harmony of the Pleiades, but enrich and complete it.

Falconer's scheme is to live life on the Homeric plan, in accordance with the value of equality, simplicity, and the pursuit of tranquil happiness. His life is comfortable and satisfying to the senses, but it is also religious. Each day closes with a hymn to St Catharine, the personification of purity. The issue raised in the first 'Book' of *Gryll Grange* – that is, its first movement, of twelve chapters – is whether such an ideal is perfect. Thus, though the location of this section of *Gryll Grange* is mainly the Tower, it is not exclusively so, for as always Peacock proceeds not descriptively but dialectically. There are two substantial passages, of equal length, at the Tower, but each is framed by a shorter, introductory passage, placed away from the Tower in a more worldly, or at least a more social, context. Thus the first two chapters are set at Gryll Grange, and both the world and the alternative ideals of the Grange are shown before we are introduced to Falconer's Tower (in chapter iii). Four chapters there are followed by another two elsewhere. In chapter vii, the commonplace Mrs Opimian evokes the outside world of everyday with her prudish suspicions of a Bachelor's Abode of Love.[47] Chapter viii returns to the more sympathetic atmosphere of the Grange, which nevertheless is governed by ideals distinct from those of Falconer. The final four chapters at the Tower – or, as it is alternatively known, the Folly – are thus firmly established in a framework of scepticism. Even when in Falconer's company, we do not see his idealism as he does. All eight chapters at the Tower are mediated through the consciousness of that amiable and well-disposed onlooker, Dr Opimian, who is aware that Falconer's life is not for him. 'I never pretended to this sort of spiritualism. I followed the advice of St Paul, who says it is better to marry – MRS OPIMIAN. You need not finish the quotation.'[48]

Opimian's meetings with Falconer all fall into the same pattern, a good-humoured questioning of Falconer's choice of ideal. To some extent – when we meet Mrs Opimian, for example – our sympathies are with the hero. But never entirely so, any more than we think Desdemona 'right' when she discusses marriage and human nature with the coarser Emilia. 'Vows of celibacy, and inward spiritual grace' are idealisms, but the first of them has its drawbacks. When Dr Opimian meets the love-lorn Harry Hedgerow, longing for Dorothy at his hearth, and pitying his father, who has no grandchildren, the Doctor wants to help his courtship. He returns to the Tower from Gryll Grange with the intention of asking Falconer to help with the Aristophanic comedy, a ploy to draw him into the ambit of Gryll Grange and Morgana. Opimian already knows that the two ideals, the two gardens, cannot co-exist. 'It is like an enchanted palace ... Miss Gryll might fancy herself in the dwelling of her namesake, Morgana. But I fear she would be for dealing with it as Orlando did with Morgana, breaking the talisman and dissolving the enchantment.'[49] From now on, Dr Opimian is not only Falconer's amiable opponent in debates about, for example, celibacy versus marriage, but the real enemy of his idyll. And the gods are evidently on Opimian's side, for one of Jove's thunderbolts causes the carriage accident which brings both Morgana and the concupiscent Harry Hedgerow inside the virginal household at the Tower.

On a grand scale, the structure of *Gryll Grange* reproduces the strophe and antistrophe of the Greek dramatic chorus. Peacock also continually employs the same dialectic pattern in his detail, in the conversational combats and, more literally, in the pastiche of Old Comedy which occupies chapter xxviii, 'Aristophanes in London'. But the structural pattern, though it resembles the tripartite arrangement of *The Misfortunes of Elphin*, and more especially of the longer *Melincourt*, is in fact more finely dialectical than either, since the three books represent statement, counter-statement, and resolution.

The middle book of the three, set at Gryll Grange, offers an idyll which is opposed to that of Falconer's Tower. Both are enchanted ground; but where Falconer presides over a pure little world – significantly, an enclosure, an exclusive and faintly forbidding place – Morgana's garden at the Grange is all sociability and joyousness. She is perceived throughout in such terms. The beautiful passage from Boiardo which she offers Falconer as an approximation of their courtship portrays 'Morgana, all with joy elate ...',[50] and Peacock's heroine, like her literary prototype, epitomises delight. The household of which she is the mistress is entirely different in atmosphere from the Tower. Falconer professes a wish to surround himself with kindred spirits, but in fact as a bachelor he is prevented by Victorian convention from inviting women to his home. The second Book begins 'A large party was assembled at the Grange ...', and all its scenes are dedicated to the ideal of mutual enjoyment, represented by a large company over dinner, or by two lovers *tête à tête* and delighting in one another's company.

The Symposia over dinner, which are always among the chief features of Peacock's satires, in *Gryll Grange* occur in the main in this central Book. Because Peacock's idea here is to illustrate sociability, he makes the discussions far less disputatious than in any earlier book. The characters do not stand for discrete, opposed points of view. Some of them overlap: Dr Opimian is certainly not easy to distinguish from his genial host, Mr Gryll. In earlier books, Peacock portrayed his crowd of pedants as incapable of learning from, or even hearing, another point of view.[51] The discussions at Gryll Grange are more rewarding mutual exchanges (rather like Shelley's conversation, as Peacock had recently recalled it, with its 'freedom and calmness ... good temper and good feeling ... quiet and gentle toleration of dissent').[52] They are defined, characteristically, by balance and contrast. Within the book's twelve chapters, a conversation begun in the second chapter (xiv) about art balances one in the penultimate chapter (xxiii) about social pleasures such as dancing and card games. Similarly, at the very centre of the Book (and thus at the centre of *Gryll Grange*), a satirical chapter on the anti-social London fad of lecturing (xviii) is complemented by another satirical episode, chapter xix, on the follies of the day.

But the central Book, at Gryll Grange, exists not so much to discuss the social virtues as to enact them. Its first page introduces the secondary hero, Lord Curryfin, who is the foil to Falconer. In all obvious respects he is Falconer's very opposite. Where Falconer is withdrawn, Curryfin is a busy man of the contemporary world: a scientist and inventor, restlessly employing the new technology; a faddist, lecturing on the latest enthusiasm. He is 'a young gentleman who forces his mind into a receptacle for a chaos of crudities'.[53] Thus far he is a comic figure, and much in need of the spell of the enchanted garden. There his Science will be schooled by Miss Niphet's Art, by her gift of repose, and by her unfashionable refusal to force her voice, or her nature, into unsuitable channels.

But Curryfin has positive qualities, and if he has much to learn he has also something to teach. Everyone likes him, not only because he is a lord, and eligible. 'In the promotion of social enjoyment, he has few equals.'[54] Miss Niphet, who is shy and often silent, is drawn by him into sociability, and she is grateful to him:[55]

I have also seen a whole company all willing to be pleased, but all mute from not knowing what to say to each other; not knowing how to begin. Lord Curryfin would be a blessing to such a party. He would be the steel to their flint.

He takes his place naturally as a leader at Gryll Grange, the initiator of games and amusements, and (in the third, festive Book) both stage-manager of the play and master of ceremonies at the ball. Falconer is a by-stander during the second Book, and Curryfin becomes, for the time being, the acting hero.

All the while the courtship of Falconer and Morgana is in some enchanted, dream-like abeyance, and what we actually see in the second Book is the more vigorous and earthly wooing of Curryfin and Alice Niphet. Sub-plots have great technical uses, not least in letting the leading characters keep their simplicity, or mystery. Peacock briefly introduces the traditional comic plot of confused relationships between two pairs of lovers,[56] so that Curryfin's courtship can appear to give some stimulus, and complication, to Falconer's. Jealousy at least appears to give Falconer something to think about, while Curryfin's activities are really pulling the diverse threads of the book together. Curryfin's experiences at Gryll Grange serve to bring the satire on science into focus. He is already social, but Miss Niphet transforms his understanding of the social, giving it a calmer, more humane meaning. She arrests his attention when she sings a ballad, with appropriate naturalness and feeling. The Art which she presents to his Science is thus not any art, and certainly not an art of technical complication and pretentiousness that would merely duplicate the errors of his kind of science. Opimian defines the difference between ancient and modern taste. 'Simple beauty – of idea in poetry, of sound in music, of figure in painting – was their great characteristic. Ours is detail in all these matters, overwhelming detail.'[57] Alice Niphet's singing illustrates the ancient taste, especially in the superiority of the human element – feeling, expressiveness, meaning – over technical virtuosity. She is like her singing, 'a person of very deep feeling, which she does not choose should appear on the surface'.[58] 'The artificial, the false, in any degree, however little, is impossible to her.[59] Though subordinate protagonists in terms of the deepest moral issue of the book – the choice between two versions of the good – at a more familiar level Lord Curryfin and Miss Niphet are central in their enactment of its oppositions. Because humanism is one of the polarities, Alice in particular is given an almost surprising degree of physical presence for so intellectual and stylised a book.

She especially bestows on the notion of love a physical reality which the ethereal Falconer and the fleeting Morgana would not do. Falconer and Morgana court in the most indirect manner imaginable, by invoking the precedent of Orlando and the other Morgana, in the pages of Boiardo. But Curryfin and Miss Niphet have a succession of scenes together which are unusually clearly defined for Peacock, in visual and emotional detail. Both are active people, graceful and energetic. Over and again they are seen delighting, as the ancient Greeks did, in bodily exercise: at first alone, he taming a horse, she running like Atalanta; then in unison, skating, dancing, playing at battledore and shuttlecock. Of course, by the standards of the novel, especially the twentieth-century novel, these love scenes are hardly sensual. The conversations of the two will not strike most readers as passionate:[60]

> The next morning, Lord Curryfin said to Miss Niphet: 'You took no part in the conversation of last evening. You gave no opinion on the singleness and permanence of love.
>
> MISS NIPHET.
> I mistrust the experience of others and I have none of my own.
>
> LORD CURRYFIN.
> Your experience, when it comes, cannot but confirm the theory. The love which once dwells on you can never turn to another.
>
> MISS NIPHET.
> I do not know that I ought to wish to inspire such an attachment.
>
> LORD CURRYFIN.
> Because you could not respond to it?
>
> MISS NIPHET.
> On the contrary; because I think it possible I might respond too well.
>
> She paused a moment, and then, afraid of trusting herself to carry on the dialogue, she said: 'Come into the hall and play at battledore and shuttlecock.'

And yet, measured by their formal, stylised setting, these dialogues are – like the sports – unusually direct and communicative. 1860 is not a year for advocating the free love of *Rhododaphne*, still less for hints *à la* Payne Knight about Priapus. But *Gryll Grange*'s love scenes are nevertheless perhaps the only occasion in all Peacock's fiction where he is primarily interested in the inter-action between two of his characters. He uses the two to convey the pleasure of mutuality, of complementariness, which includes physical attraction and frank delight in the body. Gryll Grange is a place dedicated to the pleasure people find in one another, and they cannot all be the pleasures of a party.

Appropriately, then, the final Book is festive. The personal solutions, the marriages, are postponed to the end of the season. What comes first is the communal celebration of Christmas, very clearly still a semi-pagan feast, with its traditional ball (in which children — it is not clear whose — and the old have their part), its play, and its ghost stories. In the first Book, Harry Hedgerow anticipates the third by alluding to the year's end: he imagines his father comforted for the loss of his mother by seeing grandchildren at his knee.[61] Towards the end of the second Book the same half-choric character brings up the subject of the most popular and universal of festivals: he imagines the still larger party all seven sisters might have together.[62] The thought provokes Opimian's reverie, that in past ages, Homeric Greece and pre-industrial England, the Christmas feast was not, indeed, merely the gathering of the nuclear family — 'the life and joy of the old hall, when the squire and his household and his neighbourhood were as one.[63]

In all such fiction, the tell-tale compression of the pages speaks of lovers coming together. Though much less ironic than in his earlier satires, Peacock, as in *Newark Abbey*, touches romance with the bitter-sweet. In his epigraphs, in Miss Ilex's reminiscences, in some of the ghost-stories, he reminds the reader of happiness missed. But the coupling is as satisfactorily complete as in a dance, or in the familiar tradition of stage comedy. More stylised than virtually any comedy is the matching of the starry Pleiades and their seven men of the earth, who come to an understanding in the first chapter of the third Book, and confirm it in chapter xxxiii. 'With the accordance of the young gentleman as keynote, [the] two heptachords ... harmonize into a double octave.'[64] Lord Curryfin and Miss Niphet become engaged in chapter xxx, and with the inevitable agreement between Falconer and Morgana in chapter xxxv – which needs only to be briefly stated – all nine couples can be married. Gryll Grange, with its social ideal, is completely victorious. Falconer's Tower is forsaken, his household broken up. The weighing of one notion of life against another is not left as an unresolved issue, but decidedly settled in favour of mutuality.

At first sight, Peacock endows the existence of the hermit of the Tower with a quaint, idyllic beauty, giving it most of the good things he seems to have sought for himself in old age – a study full of old and rare books, a good table and cellar, art, the countryside, and an idiosyncratic religion which brings the immaterial into the material world. But Peacock's book implies that though these things are good in themselves, they are not good enough for the young. The Tower resembles the Garden of Epicurus, but it does not resemble it perfectly. The virgin St Catharine is a 'beautiful ideality', but a virgin is a sterile thing, and the young have something better to do, if they can, than die.

The hero's misanthropic retreat to a Tower in *Gryll Grange* resembles that of *Nightmare Abbey*, except that it is more kindly presented. It follows that in each book the heroes have much in common with the idealistic young poet Peacock knew and argued with – Shelley. In the very years when *Gryll Grange* must have been evolving, 1858–60, Peacock was reading accounts of Shelley's life, and composing his own reply to them. The first part of his summary of Shelley as a poet and intellectual has much relevance to the presentation of Falconer:[65]

So perished Percy Bysshe Shelley, in the flower of his age, and not perhaps even yet in the full flower of his genius; a genius unsurpassed in the description and imagination of scenes of beauty and grandeur; in the expression of impassioned love of ideal beauty; in the illustration of deep feeling by congenial imagery; and in the infinite variety of harmonious versification. What was, in my opinion, deficient in his poetry, was ... the want of reality in the characters with which he peopled his splendid scenes, and to which he addressed or imparted the utterance of his impassioned feelings. He was advancing, I think, to the attainment of this reality. It would have given to his poetry the only element of truth which it wanted.

But Falconer is no more a portrait of Shelley than is Scythrop. Both are types, literary presentations of the young poet at the outset of life. The literary echoes are stronger than the real-life biographical ones, and Falconer has perhaps more in common with the Milton of the Early Poems than with the actual figure of Shelley. His Tower is the one Milton imaged for himself:[66]

Or let my lamp of midnight hour
Be seen in some high lonely tower,
Where I may oft outwatch the Bear,
With thrice great Hermes, or unsphere
The spirit of Plato to unfold
What world or what vast regions hold
The immortal mind that hath forsook
Her mansion in this fleshly nook.

His religious idealism, his exalted and spiritual notion of virginity, his attempt to make a life, with the Pleiades, that half belongs to a starry sphere, could be echoes of *Comus*. Falconer recalls Milton before he entered the service of the Commonwealth, where – for the Milton of the prose, as for Peacock – the race was to be run for, not without dust and heat.

If this were all, the quaint figure of the poet-idealist in his Tower would be an introverted literary conceit, thrown up by Peacock's complex recollections of Shelley, and hence reverting back to an earlier stage of his own career. Almost certainly there is a new element, and Falconer also stands for a contemporary figure, a Shelley of the present day. *Gryll Grange* appears to contain an elaborate series of allusions to the poetry and public statements of a modern idealist, a classicist, and, imaginatively, a hermit – Matthew Arnold.

Through his essays and lectures, Matthew Arnold was to become a spokesman for the classical position in a fully social rather than narrowly aesthetic dimension. But when *Gryll Grange* was appearing in 1860, almost all Arnold's best criticism – *On Translating Homer* (1861), *Essays in Criticism* (1865 and 1888), *Culture and Anarchy* (1869) – remained to be written. Peacock, like the rest of the educated public, already knew Arnold as the champion of classical literature, but not through the large and generous definitions of Greek 'culture' he wrote in his maturity – 'to see the object itself as it really is', or 'it reminds us that the perfection of human nature is sweetness and light'. The classicism which Arnold stood for at the end of the 1850s was expressed by tragic dramatic poems like *Empedocles on Etna* (1852) and *Merope* (1858), and by Arnold's prose comments, especially on the former, which appear in the well-known Preface to his *Poems* of 1853.

The youthful Arnold was a very learned writer. The syllabus at both Winchester and Rugby, the two schools he attended, was of course dominated by the classics, and even before he went to Oxford Arnold had done (especially by twentieth-century standards) a prodigious amount of classical reading. But at his father's school, Rugby, where Matthew spent the years from fourteen to eighteen (1837–41), the classical syllabus had been somewhat modified to meet Thomas Arnold's tastes. Arnold senior was impatient with the old approach to Greek and Latin literature, which emphasised verse-writing and parsing. His own interest was in philosophy and history, especially that of the Greeks, with Aristotle and Thucydides pre-eminent. He believed in the value of studying Greek civilisation as an ethical training for living in the present. He saw in Thucydides' *History* 'a living picture of things present, fitted not so much for the curiosity of the scholar, as for the instruction of the statesman and citizen.'[67] The recently modified Oxford syllabus ('Lit. Hum.') again gave pride of place to the culture of Periclean Athens, and to Greek philosophy, history and tragedy. This was a distinctly different classical grounding from Peacock's, much graver and more moral, much less concerned with poetry, and hardly at all with satire. Understanding of the classics had been profoundly affected by new modes of historical thinking, and by the religious revival, both of which contributed to Matthew Arnold's approach of modish gloom.

Matthew Arnold's very paganism is deeply religious. His poetry, the product of his twenties and thirties, is profoundly introspective, altruistic in its goals but virtually despairing of their fulfilment. Having inherited his father's ethical imperatives, he preaches (in poems like 'Sohrab and Rustum' and 'Balder Dead') stoicism in the face of personal suffering. But the poems which seemed, and still seem, most characteristic, are those which reject a degenerate social world: '... this strange disease of modern life/With its sick hurry, its divided aims.'

'The Scholar Gipsy' idealises the way of the hermit – 'But fly our paths, our feverish contact fly.' The central character of *Empedocles on Etna* is a religious philosopher who has lived on into times of doubt – modern times. 'The dialogue of the mind with itself has commenced.'[68] Empedocles' solution, to withdraw from the world, and to plunge into the crater, is not precisely commended, in a work that sets itself up as an open-ended dialectic; and yet Empedocles, high on the mountain, is clearly for Arnold a nobler and profounder character than the cheerful lyrist Callicles, the alternative kind of artist, facilely celebrating the beauties of nature in the valley below.

Arnold himself had ethical reasons to feel troubled by the implications of *Empedocles*, which he demonstrates in his Preface, and they led him to drop it from his *Poems* of 1853:

> it is not enough that the Poet should add to the knowledge of men, it is required of him also that he should add to their happiness. 'All Art', says Schiller, 'is dedicated to Joy, and there is no higher and no more serious problem, than how to make men happy. The right Art is that alone, which creates the highest enjoyment.' ... In presence of the most tragic circumstances, represented in a work of Art, the feeling of enjoyment, as is well known, may still subsist. ... What then are the situations, from the representation of which, though accurate, no poetical enjoyment can be derived? They are those in which the suffering finds no vent in action; in which a continuous state of mental distress is prolonged, unrelieved by incident, hope, or resistance; in which there is everything to be endured, nothing to be done. In such situations there is invariably something morbid. ... To this class of situations, poetically faulty as it appears to me, that of Empedocles, as I have endeavoured to represent him, belongs.

Peacock nowhere refers directly to Arnold (though Arnold afterwards knew Peacock as 'a man of keen and cultivated mind').[69] Nevertheless, Peacock must have been aware of Arnold, and have reacted to him for some years with the keenest interest. Here was a young man who had argued the case for the classics in poetry, urgently and polemically. Made Professor of Poetry at Oxford, he had delivered in 1857 an inaugural lecture which compared the manners of the Elizabethans and the literature of the Romans unfavourably with the culture of Periclean Athens. In the journals which were Peacock's perennial reading matter, Arnold's writings and Arnold's opinions were among the controversies of the decade. The fact that he argued (in connection with *Empedocles*) for a classical subject-matter, and with *Merope* actually wrote a Greek tragedy, must have interested Peacock deeply: Arnold was an 'Ancient', who had successfully brought the classics into play. And yet it was in a version deeply uncongenial to Peacock.

From Peacock's last phase of writing a characteristic and coherent view of the classics emerges, which defines itself in contradistinction to that of Arnold. If *Gryll Grange* is not a direct answer to Arnold, it is uncannily *à propos*. Perhaps, indeed, Arnold's choice of one classical Merope, the tragic one, as a heroine[70] led Peacock to allude so fantastically to the other Merope – that one of the Pleiades who ended with a harmonious part to play in the cosmos, within a constellation of stars. Certainly Falconer's initial choice of life is that of the hermit, of Empedocles and the Scholar Gipsy. A scholar, an idealist, a religious man – like Arnold in real life, and like his best-known personae – Falconer acts on the belief that the sensitive, cultivated course is retreat. In Arnold's versions, withdrawal is given a responsible ethical colouring; similarly, Falconer does not see himself as running away from the world's problems, but as seeing truly and presumably offering some kind of notional corrective:[71]

MR. FALCONER.

It is not my own world that I complain of. It is the world on which I look 'from the loopholes of retreat'. I cannot sit here, like one of the Gods of Epicurus, who, as Cicero says, was satisfied with thinking, through all eternity, 'how comfortable he was'. I look with feelings of intense pain on the mass of poverty and crime; of unhealthy, unavailing, unremunerated toil, blighting childhood in its blossom, and womanhood in its prime; of 'all the oppressions that are done under the sun'.

It sounds very fine, and certainly sincere; but the action of *Gryll Grange* challenges it, and proposes, as an alternative, a wholly different classicism from Arnold's practice – a classicism in which sociability is substituted for solitariness, joy for gloom, and comedy for tragedy.

Much of Peacock's time during his last years was spent in the contemplation of classical literature, especially of comedy. His earliest essays on the classical drama were the efforts of a learned amateur, interested in describing and translating two texts which were not generally known: a Roman comedy of the third century, and the *Phaethon* of Euripides.[72] These two essays were published in 1852, which means that they pre-date the observations on the classics of Matthew Arnold. Now Peacock had a genuine scholarly interest in heterogeneous works of ancient literature, and in 'Julia Procula' adapted another story he found in a late Roman comic author.[73] But it is noticeable that when later in the decade he resumes his series of general reflective essays on classical literature, they have a new edge and, however idiosyncratically expressed, a new appositeness. It is in the third essay, written in 1857, that he begins to establish a clear system of values, and to insist on the relative greatness of comedy; above all, the comedy not of Rome but of Athens, and especially of the Athenian Golden Age – of Aristophanes and his predecessors. Peacock's argument is amusing, but it is a great deal more amusing if it is thought of in the context of Arnold's veneration for Periclean Athens, and of his penchant for tragedy. There are three reasons, according to Peacock, for awarding the palm to 'Old Comedy': its nearness to festive, Bacchic origins; its poetic quality and inventiveness; and its satiric, indeed directly political content. The first two qualities he sees as interdependent. The Father of Comedy, Cratinus, was a devotee of Bacchus. Peacock, anxious to thrust a lance at Puritan teetotalism, adds characteristically that 'the Father of Tragedy [Aeschylus] was no less so'.[74] 'The inspiration of lyrical poetry by wine might be amply illustrated by the theory and practice of its greatest masters, from Alcaeus downwards.'[75] 'The Middle Comedy was less poetical than the Old, and the New than the Middle; and with these we descend progressively into a more and more temperate region.'[76] What most of us think of as the 'classic' comedy of the Romans and the Italian Renaissance, a love-intrigue staged against an urban setting, is to Peacock a tradition in decline. Comedy in the age of Aristophanes had been 'the most wonderful combination the world has ever seen of splendid imagery, exquisite versification, wit, humour, and moral and political satire.'[77]

The decorative qualities delighted him, but without the ideas, the involvement in society, there would have been no greatness. Paradoxically, it is a kind of seriousness which is lost in the transition from Old Comedy to new:[78]

> The political characters of the old comedy, leaders and
> misleaders of the people, with its infinitely diversified chorus,
> Cloud-Nymphs, Stygian Frogs, City-building Birds, disappear
> from the scene. Gods and Demi-Gods, Bacchants and
> Bacchanals still lingered in the middle comedy, but they too
> passed away, and in their place came the lover and his mistress.

And so it progressed, through a catalogue of familiar comic types – parents and children, the faithful nurse, the cunning slave, the boastful soldier – many of whom survive into the comedy of the Renaissance. It is very comparable with the transition Peacock describes when he writes of the decline from the older French satiric manner to that of Paul de Kock – from comedy of ideas to comedy of character.[79] In the middle of the nineteenth century, the rejection of the idea of character is challenging. Peacock is writing in the very age of the literature of character – of the great novels, the verse portrait-sketch, the critical absorption with Shakespeare's central figures. Again, the point of view implies a fundamental dissent from a basic tenet of Matthew Arnold's poetry so far – that poetry, as well as employing character, is concerned with the personal perspective.

Reviewing the general *History of Greek Literature* by Müller and Donaldson in 1859 gave Peacock an even better opportunity to analyse what was, for him, the essence of the classics:[80]

> It is claimed for [Cratinus] ... that from jokes, which had aimed
> only at exciting laughter, he took to lashing public and private
> vice in all its forms, and administered his flagellations with more
> justice than mercy. The Old Comedy thus became a mighty
> instrument of moral and political censure, and the satiric rod
> was wielded most effectively by Cratinus, Eupolis, and
> Aristophanes, whom both Horace and Persius cite as their three
> great precursors in the poetical denunciation of rascals. The Old
> Comedians had, in fact, an unlimited lawful authority to say

whatever they pleased of anybody; they spared neither gods nor man; and they exercised, during about sixty-four years, a very salutory control over profligates and demagogues, till the license degenerated into abuse; or, in other words, became obnoxious to parties in the State who had sufficient power to coerce it.

The heirs of Aristophanic Comedy were thus not other stage writers, because these fell victim to censorship, and thereafter became content to reflect society rather than to criticise it. The true tradition passed instead to the non-dramatic verse and prose satirists. In their different styles, Horace and Persius, Lucian, Rabelais and Voltaire inherit what is essential in Old Comedy: its gaiety, its fancifulness, and its political commitment. In the scholars whose *History* he is reviewing, Peacock detects a grudging note against Lucian and Voltaire, the imputation that a writer is not quite of the highest rank if he is negative. A few pages earlier, Peacock has already dropped into his discussion his own, arresting judgment: 'Dr Donaldson explains Plato's positive doctrines as well as they can be explained; but it is in negation that Plato shines most, – in the exposure of the errors of others. The Academy is essentially sceptical.'[81]

This highly significant observation is not as quirky as it sounds. The philosophical radical George Grote, the great historian of Greece, shared Peacock's view of Plato, although Grote's book on Plato was not published until shortly before Peacock's death. Plato, who had been banished from the curriculum of Oxford and Cambridge, was now gradually making headway as a potential rival to Aristotle, because the received view of him, as an idealist, was very much in keeping with mid-century religious feeling. Grote may have been influenced by a traditional Platonic canon in which views hard to reconcile with one another appeared in various places. It seems more likely that, as a utilitarian belonging in the same tradition as Peacock, he admired the critic and iconoclast rather than the idealist. 'Above all he was impressed by the fact that the Greek thinker appeared often to be more concerned in Socratic fashion about the mere exercise of the dialectical faculty than about any particular conclusions at all.'[82]

It is possible that in addition Peacock had been irritated twenty years earlier by the most substantial review of his own satire to appear in his lifetime, in which James Spedding, that characteristic early Victorian, expressed worry at Peacock's apparent lack of 'deeper purposes', but in the end resolved to give him the benefit of the doubt. 'Naked scepticism', asserted Spedding, '... is an uncertain succession of fleeting partialities; vain, querulous, discontented, full of quarrel and unquietness, full of spite and favouritism, full, above all, of itself'; therefore so serenely poised an author as Peacock *must* have 'within a deeper and more substantial faith to repose on than any which he allows to appear'.[83] Whether or not Peacock has himself in mind when he writes of Lucian and Voltaire, his name can be substituted for theirs in all that he has to say of them:[84]

> That 'the results of the efforts of both against false religion and false philosophy were merely negative;' that they had 'nothing tangible to substitute for what they destroyed,' is open to observation. To clear the ground of falsehood is to leave room for the introduction of truth. Lucian decidedly held that moral certainty, a complete code of duty founded on reason, existed in the writings of Epicurus; and Voltaire's theism, the belief in a pervading spirit of good, was clear and consistent throughout. The main object of both was, by sweeping away false dogmas, to teach toleration. Voltaire warred against opinions which sustained themselves by persecution. The case of Calas alone attests with what self-forgetting earnestness he followed up this, the main purpose of his life.
>
> The account of Lucian's work is unexceptionably good, and we fully concur in the concluding remarks:-
>
> 'As a writer of pure and elegant Greek, which was neither vernacular with him, nor spoken and written by the most highly educated men of his day – as a humorist whose gaiety and fancy are inexhaustible – as an honest hater of shams and dishonest bigotry – as an educational reformer, whose exertions were not the less praiseworthy because they were not perfectly successful – Lucian of Samosata stands forth in favourable contrast to all the so-called sophists of his age, and we are among the number of those who think that his merits can hardly be over-estimated.'

It can be argued that all Peacock's books, being satirical and more or less political, approach to the condition of Old Comedy. But – most probably because he wanted to make an emphatically comic point in reply to the exaggeratedly gloomy Matthew Arnold – *Gryll Grange* more unmistakably suggests Aristophanes than do the others. This is not simply because an Aristophanic comedy is acted in it, but because it is joyous and celebratory in spirit, and witty, inventive and fanciful in its imaginative conception. *Gryll Grange* occupies the same position in Peacock's œuvre as *The Clouds* in that of Aristophanes: both seem less directly political than usual because the author's approach is oblique and fantastic, almost surreal. When Peacock praised the ingenuity and variety of the Chorus of Old Comedy,[85] he must already have been evolving his own imitation, the quaint device of the seven sisters and their seven round-faced suitors. Once complete, with Harry Hedgerow as their leader and spokesman, they fulfil the true Aristophanic function: as earthy, commonsensical and corrective (where Falconer is concerned) as the idea of them seems initially perverse and extraordinary.

The Chorus is one reason why *Gryll Grange*, more fully even than *Nightmare Abbey*, succeeds in establishing Peacock's point – long ago, and in memory still, a point against Shelley – that comedy is the complete art-form. In music, Mozart is perfection;[86] in literature, Aristophanes comes near it. And he is genial, inclusive: all kinds of beautiful and airy conceptions – for example, Boiardo's – are encompassed within the tradition of which he and Cratinus are forerunners. Thus the two heroines of *Gryll Grange*, who teach their suitors gaiety and humanity, grace and feeling, add a depth to the book's meaning that is not within the scope of *Nightmare Abbey*. But even they would seem insufficient, in Peacock's conception, were the book not destined to end at Christmas – the social and communal time of ritual, 'Pagano-Popish' festivity. The ideal of love and romance which the heroines represent takes its place within the Bacchic celebration of life as a whole. The wider context is epitomised – indirectly and through art – when one life-style is contrasted with another in the Aristophanic comedy. The play shows what a work of art should be like: it brings the characters together in the performance; it is amusing, inventive, and engaged with existing society. In fact, though at a double remove, it is the only scene of Peacock's published satire that purports to be set in London.[87] Thus it brings back to our attention what has so long seemed the third, subordinate element, far removed from the two enchanted gardens: the contemporary world, of pseudo-science and pseudo-religion; the world which needs the balance and wholeness of the Greek.

The Aristophanic play, Falconer's reason for coming to the Grange, is also the goal of his intellectual journey. It marks the replacement of his over-refined aestheticism and religiosity with a more whole and thoroughly human philosophy of life. When Opimian remembers the remark Cicero attributes to Terence's Chremes (a reference phrased by Peacock with characteristic precision) that nothing human is alien to himself, he rebukes Falconer (as Peacock rebukes the romantic idealists Shelley and Arnold) for an attitude towards humanity that is unreal and so, despite their good intentions, evasive. The romantic Morgana, though she drives St Catharine from Falconer's mind, would probably not have seemed enough to teach him this, any more than the unspiritual Dr Opimian could persuade him of it in discussion. It takes Harry Hedgerow, the representative of the common and everyday, to supply the element wanting in Falconer's idealism, as it is wanting in Shelley's. Equally, it takes the lightness, the inventiveness, and the consistency of Peacock's created world in *Gryll Grange* to correct an Arnoldian idea of the classical that tends to be solemn, pedantic, subjective, and (in Peacock's view) tainted by religious ardour.

Comparison between Peacock's two Tower-dwellers, Scythrop and Falconer, suggests minor modification, rather than wholesale revision of his principles. From first to last, he rejects the way of the Wordsworthian Solitary: the Good Life, and Good Art, are social. It is not a question of forsaking a lofty idealism in order to come to terms with mediocre reality. Peacock's Greek-taught ideal is that man rightly lives in harmony with nature and with his kind, and art is the expression of that ideal harmony. There is, accordingly, no idealism without harmony: life in Scythrop's Tower is absurd, in Falconer's attenuated and delusory. Both hermits in the end stand rebuked by a notion of art, and the ideal, that paradoxically insists on bringing them out into the world.

At the technical level, the difference in design and approach is clear warning not to read the two books as examples of a linear development, as sketch and painting. Earlier, when Peacock was using the prose satirists as his models, he deliberately aimed at an effect that contained discordant, unresolvable elements – notably, the disputatious pedants who could never be brought to agree. They are gone from *Gryll Grange*. Basing himself on the poetic Aristophanes, he weaves discord, and disparate themes, into a fabric designed from the start to seem harmonious. *Gryll Grange* realises its own conceptions: it moves towards Old Comedy as an ideal, and all the while it is one. But to see *Nightmare Abbey*, with its sustained contrasts, its deliberate angularity, as somehow falling short of *Gryll Grange*'s synthesis, must surely be perverse. There will in fact always be readers prepared to come to a different conclusion: to see some decline from the clear and forceful partisanship of *Nightmare Abbey*. *Gryll Grange* proposes a rich humanism, and conveys it through an elaborate pattern of action and motif. Paradoxically, the involvement of *Nightmare Abbey* with actual people on a real-life scene will always make it, for some, the more human book of the two.

How high one rates *Gryll Grange* in Peacock's *œuvre* depends on how one rates his goals, as set out in his later critical remarks on comedy, and as epitomised in all the rest of his work. Peacock took the function of the satirist to be the correction of society, which in *Gryll Grange* he attempts in two ways: by satirising the mania for science and for religion; and by proposing, in ascending order, three idealisms, or alternative ways to live. Of these two methods of conveying his moral point, the second is the more important in *Gryll Grange*, though elsewhere in his books, with the partial exception of *The Misfortunes of Elphin*, the positive alternative plays a negligible part.

Perhaps James Spedding had carried his point with Peacock, despite the latter's stalwart defence of Lucian and Voltaire for being 'negative'. For once, Peacock himself is not negative; and many have found great pleasure in the amiable imaginative worlds he successively realises. He will, then, gratify those who do not like the harshness of great satire – as Victorians seldom did like Voltaire, or Swift, or their kind. But if a man is known by his friends, a book is to some extent known by its admirers, and this kind of admiration is suspect. Logically it is hard to find fault with *Gryll Grange*, since its genial positives are given definition by negatives which, if less to the fore, are nevertheless distinct.

Aesthetically speaking, it is one of Peacock's most assured successes. But is it effective satire? The suggestion already made, that it does not, after all, feel very human, can be supported by a second point for concern: that, Aristophanes notwithstanding, it does not feel very critical. The harshness and grotesquerie characteristic of much satire is there for a purpose — to stimulate thought. So too is the dialectical openness, the shunning of agreement, which is typical of Peacock's earlier work. Just as it is possible to admire *Crotchet Castle*, despite its imperfections, for the large thoughts it encourages, so it is possible to suspect *Gryll Grange*, despite its perfection, for an air of finality.

The compensations are real. *Gryll Grange* is not impersonal, if one may think of it (as this least egotistical of writers never invites one to do) in the context of Peacock's own life. It is the last satire of a man of seventy-five who had lost his wife, two of his children, most of his best friends, and the political goals of his youth. His favourite daughter was unhappy, and already ill. He wrote about living life in a spirit of celebration. *Gryll Grange* is a serious book, which introduces pertinent comments on society, religion and art, but above all it proclaims the virtue of urbanity, which denies that life and art are solemn. Compared with Matthew Arnold's literary practice to date, it has the merit of consistency, and of bringing its ideals to literary life. Whether in the long run Peacock's notion of classical was better or worse than Arnold's is a larger topic. In essence, when Arnold's prose criticism was written, these two advocates for Athens were often to prove alike.[88] Arnold's manner had the very great virtue, in the age of the 1867 Reform Bill, of intelligibility to the middle-class readership, and applicability in a coming age of mass suffrage. But it is surely also true that, as a judgment of what is more valuable in the European cultural inheritance, Peacock's classicism has some strengths that Arnold's does not. For Arnold's High Seriousness, Peacock has Old Comedy: a conception rich enough to include the eighteenth-century satiric poets — to whom Arnold was notoriously blind — as well as Rabelais and Bacchus.[89]

> The Old Comedy was in its origin essentially lyrical, and never lost sight of its Bacchic birth; and though the personal history of many of its brightest ornaments is obscure, yet, as far as positive evidence goes, there is not a single water-drinker among them.

Chapter 8

The Negative Voice:
Peacock as Critic

> To clear the ground of falsehood is to leave room for
> the introduction of truth.
>
> Peacock on Lucian and Voltaire

The English poets of the early nineteenth century are not,
comparative critics tell us, in the front rank as thinkers. 'Without
him [Coleridge], we would feel that English Romanticism –
glorious as its poetry and prose is in its artistic achievement –
remained dumb in matters of the intellect.'[1] The two poets of the
period we probably most admire today, Wordsworth and Keats, are
intensely private men, whose remarks on the poetic craft are
primarily commentaries on their own efforts to write, and at that
fitfully intelligible. In matters intellectual they seem to leave the
field to Coleridge – with the unfortunate result that Coleridge's
historical importance becomes inflated. Coleridge made a large
contribution to the religious revival of the 1820s and 1830s, and he
made England aware of German metaphysics and aesthetics, at
least in his version of them. These are important matters, but they
do not justify the assumption that, among the poets of the first two
decades of the nineteenth century, Coleridge as a theoretician holds
a central place. It is curious that on the basis of so very little
evidence he has become the spokesman for 'English Romanticism',
a 'movement' which is held to embrace Byron, Shelley and Keats;
instead of the atypical, not to say obnoxious, figure he actually
seemed to the younger writers concerned.

The axiom that English poetry of the early nineteenth century failed to supply its own critical commentary is the conclusion of a later date. At the time it seemed that criticism had never been so plentiful, nor so powerful. The critical spirit and style indeed survived for a while, and quite prestigiously, in verse:[2] a vogue which could attract a Byron was hardly *passé*. But more influential than the verse satires and even better witness to the critical Spirit of the Age was the format and quality of the great new Reviews, especially the *Edinburgh* and the *Quarterly*.

At the height of its success, in 1814, the *Edinburgh* was printing 13,000 copies, and the *Quarterly* about the same, but this conveys no notion of their domination over the reading public. Jeffrey estimated that at least three people saw every copy, so that the journals had a readership of several times their actual circulation. Besides, before 1817 their rivals did not print really sustained, serious literary criticism. Then as now, the successful journal was designed for a particular market. The *Monthly Review* was aimed at a middle-class, perhaps provincial reader, with a practical and scientific bent. Similarly, the sectarian journals were designed for a middle-class public often suspicious of art: the Evangelical *Christian Observer* and the Dissenting *Eclectic Review* readily gave space to history and biography, but tended to notice the imaginative writing only of established figures. The *Christian Observer* seldom considered novels at all. Leigh Hunt's *Examiner* and *Indicator* were unusual in their efforts to bring poetry, and avant-garde poetry at that, to the notice of a middle-class reader. Shelley and Keats must have been grateful for his sympathy; it was only unfortunate that a favourable mention by Hunt tended to bring down on a writer the much more influential disfavour of the *Quarterly*. In these circumstances, and until the founding of *Blackwood's Edinburgh Magazine* in 1817, the *Edinburgh* and the *Quarterly* exercised the cultural influence of near monopolists. Jeffrey, Croker and Hazlitt may not have slain with a review, but it is not surprising that contemporaries thought them capable of it.

Francis Jeffrey, editor of the *Edinburgh*, could be described by his first biographer, Lord Cockburn, without qualification as 'the greatest of British critics'.[3] This is not a claim given much weight in modern literary histories. But contemporaries would probably not often have challenged Jeffrey's pre-eminence, at least among living critics, and since it is generally more important for the scholar to know what people thought than what they ought to have thought, it is useful to consider what the centrality of Jeffrey implies. He was, above all, a Scotsman: Edinburgh-born, a lawyer and son of a lawyer. The schoolmaster who first taught him Latin had taught Walter Scott in the previous class, and was to teach Henry Brougham in the next one. The *Edinburgh Review* was founded by two Scottish lawyers, Jeffrey and Francis Horner, together with the English clergyman, Sydney Smith – and thereafter was largely sustained by contributions from yet another Scottish lawyer, Brougham. Its rival, the *Quarterly*, was initiated by a splinter group which included Scott. *Blackwood's* was the inspiration of another group of young Scotsmen. The most essential fact about 'English' criticism of the period is, therefore, that it is predominantly Scottish. Understanding the cultural assumptions inherited from the Scottish Enlightenment is a precondition to understanding the common language of English writers in the early nineteenth century.

It would be highly misleading to force Scottish thinking into party-political moulds, as Whig and Tory were understood at that time. Edinburgh threw up redoubtable Whigs, but some of its most brilliant sons – Hume, Scott, the more dubious figure of Lockhart – were avowed Tories. In practice, Scotland was Tory in politics – it was one great rotten borough at this time, expertly run by Henry Dundas. Despite this, the weight of Scottish influence in the early nineteenth century was felt on the liberal side, and ultimately went to support liberal causes. The tradition inherited from Scotland's intellectual Golden Age was empirical, scientific, modern-minded: driven by a passion to understand man and his world, and impatient with *a priori* assumptions (such as religion offers). The two most influential teachers in Scottish universities in the 1790s – John Millar at Glasgow and Dugald Stewart at Edinburgh – were professed liberals. Jeffrey, though forbidden by his Tory father from formally enrolling in their classes, fell under their general influence, and early became, like Horner and Brougham, a liberal Whig. Stewart especially became a mentor and in some instances a lifelong friend to a succession of future politicians: Lord Henry Petty (afterwards Lord Lansdowne), J. W. Ward (Lord Dudley), Palmerston, and Lord John Russell. William Lamb, the future Lord

Melbourne, was meanwhile a pupil of Millar's. Most of these young English aristocrats would probably have finished their education on the Continent rather than in Scotland, had the European cities not been closed to the English by the war. Circumstances thus conspired to increase the importance of Edinburgh as an intellectual centre at this time; or, rather, what is not quite the same thing, to enhance its intellectual prestige and influence in London. Even without the war, something of the kind must have occurred, since the Scottish universities, with their empirical science, their political economy, their independence of the Church of England, had long been an intellectual inspiration to the ablest of the English manufacturing class. As the 'commercial interest' rose rapidly in wealth and more gradually in power, it brought into increasing favour the Scottish intellectual movement known broadly as utilitarianism.

The 'Scotch reviewers' lampooned in 1809 by Byron are thus simultaneously a handful of individuals with too much power, and the legitimate spokesmen for a dominant movement of ideas. Jeffrey deserves his reputation for pre-eminence among them, not merely because in the first two decades of the *Edinburgh*'s life he reviewed more of the literary books than anyone else, but because he clearly conveys in his reviewing the general precepts of his cultural tradition. Had he been required to give a theoretical account of his procedure as a working critic, he would no doubt have referred the enquirer to a book by an Edinburgh friend of his: Archibald Alison's *The Nature and Principles of Taste* (1811).[4] Alison approaches the question of what makes an object beautiful from the viewpoint of the psychologist: objects are beautiful not in themselves, but as they suggest certain associations to the mind. The implication of such a line, for a working critic like Jeffrey, is that there is no point in dwelling on the aesthetic properties of a work, since his judgment of these must be relative. He is encouraged to try to place the literature of the past in its historical context, in order to determine why it has the qualities it has. When he considers the literature of the present, the most relevant questions are again contextual, virtually sociological: not, how good is the work in itself? (an impossible point to determine, since the critic's personal reaction, of pleasure or disgust, cannot be shown to have general validity), but, how will it be received? And perhaps thereafter, what social end will it serve?

Indeed, the impression left by reading the prefaces, essays and reviews of the period is that, after all, its critics are ultimately historians, not aestheticians at all. They are conditioned by the great eighteenth-century Scottish works of history or anthropology – by Hume, Ferguson, Adam Smith and Robertson – into seeing the arts as the by-product of a society in a particular phase of its culture. Research into the literature of the past is a growing subject, with a two-way charge: information about a society is employed to account for its literature; the literature in turn affords insight into the society, and into the minds of the men and women who made it up. The literary scholar is driven by the same motive as any other intellectual, to establish the facts about man; and, when he comes to consider the literature of his own period, he generally expects the artist also to make a contribution to human knowledge, as an observer of man's mind, or his manners, or his natural environment. The literature of the past is valuable largely because it supplies this kind of insight. Scott exemplifies the approach, which might be described as sociological rather than aesthetic, in his introduction to *The Minstrelsy of the Scottish Border* (1803), a fine piece of historical criticism which must be coupled with Wordsworth's Preface to the *Lyrical Ballads* by those interested in identifying the spirit of the age.

It is misleading to think of either Wordsworth or of contemporary German critics as the more modern, and hence somehow necessarily better, than Francis Jeffrey. They may be better, but modernity is not the reason. All are equally heirs of the Enlightenment, and moreover generally still writing within an Enlightenment tradition. Wordsworth in his Preface is a scientific and psychological critic, and his universal, almost populist aspirations are far more characteristic of the Enlightenment than of Romanticism. Herder and the Schlegel brothers are as much cultural historians as Scott and Jeffrey. It could even be said that the crucial differences that develop between the Germans and the Scotsmen during the Napoleonic War period largely derive from political circumstances. With the French armies victorious on the Continent, it was in the German critics' interest to evoke their own cultural consciousness – a mystical sense, through literature, of national unity. Jeffrey had the less grandiose task of defending

English national security in wartime. Hence his dislike of Wordsworth's simple style and popular subject-matter in the *Lyrical Ballads*, which strikes him, while danger threatens from a 'jacobin' enemy, as subversive. From about 1809, the external danger seemed to recede, and Jeffrey came to feel that there was less to fear from France than from internal High Tory reaction.[5] It is unfortunate for Jeffrey's reputation that, as he became freer to profess liberalism, so Wordsworth became more Tory, because this makes it appear as if Jeffrey was obstinately bent on damning the greatest poet of his age; while actually the critical principles which emerge in his handling of Wordsworth are consistent and coherent. Above all, they are general principles. He conceives that writing for the public (as both he and Wordsworth are) is a social activity, and that the needs of society are appropriate standards to judge it by.

The common run of criticism in Peacock's day is, of course, adversely affected by dire, inveterate partisanship. Especially in the second decade of the century, party feeling leads to automatic pre-judgment, and to spiteful assaults on individuals. But when it comes to personality-mongering, Hazlitt is a much worse offender than Jeffrey, and the egregious Lockhart less palatable than either. In his day, Jeffrey was, quite correctly, ridiculed for just the opposite tendency, his serious-minded habit of moving from the particular instance to the general law – 'our Scotch manner of running everything up to elements, and explaining all sorts of occurrences by a theoretical history of society.'[6] Jeffrey's real fault surely arises from the demands put on him by a large non-specialist audience: he has to make his criticism lively, and so he frequently tries to pass off what actually is an attack on principle as something else, something smarter and more amusing. Time and again, he makes fun of Wordsworth's manner – his 'namby-pamby' affectations, or his unintelligibility. There were general principles behind the assault, but Jeffrey, in his anxiety to make 'things level to the meanest capacities',[7] became increasingly reluctant to spell them out. Though an able man, and according to his lights an honest one, he set his sights on the middle-brow public, and so in the end inevitably lost caste among his fellow-intellectuals.

If this is true, it is not a weakness of his critical system, but of the limits within which he elected to put it into practice. One of the best critiques of Jeffrey was written from within his own philosophical tradition by James Mill, who complained not that Jeffrey was a utilitarian, but that he was not enough of one. Mill's powerful case in the *Westminster Review*[8] against the cultural influence of the *Edinburgh* (which is largely a case against Jeffrey) is that the *Edinburgh* has taken an unnecessarily narrow, class-based, and thus in the end illiberal, view of art. Its literary tastes have been those of the Whig aristocracy. Ultimately, whether Tories or Whigs are in office, the government has been drawn from the same ruling oligarchy; and it has been in the interests of this class in every sphere to discourage disputatiousness, or any kind of radical thought. Accordingly the art that they prefer is decorative and fanciful rather than vigorous and intellectual. Jeffrey has thus achieved his purpose, of promoting the art which socially and politically he favours. But, Mill concludes, he has not seen his function disinterestedly, as the genuine philosopher would have done. Though he believes in serving society, it has become plain that he and the *Edinburgh* serve no-one so well as the Whigs.

Peacock grew up on the *Edinburgh Review*, but treated it as an anthology of contemporary opinions rather than as a model to follow. When he passes general judgment upon the *Edinburgh* – as 'that shallow and dishonest publication' – it is for reasons similar to Mill's: he condemns it for trivialising, and for implicitly bringing aid and comfort to the powers that be.[9] But this is not surprising, since Peacock's self-education led him to share the very same general utilitarian principles to which both Mill and Jeffrey would have subscribed. However, like Mill but not like Jeffrey, he was prepared to do without drawing-room success.

The congruence between Peacock's aesthetic ideas and Jeffrey's is established when one notes that Peacock's Archibald Alison – his favourite aesthetician – was Richard Payne Knight. After the turn of the century, Knight forsook the vein of social criticism of rich landowners that had made him notorious in the 1790s.[10] His *Analytical Enquiry into the Principles of Taste* (1805) takes up the more philosophical and less controversial issue of the criteria of beauty. Like Alison, he concludes that there are no absolute criteria, but that beauty is related to function – or, as he puts it, to utility. Knight's treatise is thus another example of the typical contemporary procedure which subordinates literature to social circumstance, and makes of literary criticism a historical and sociological enquiry.

Precisely because the approach of the period to literary matters is not primarily aesthetic, it would be unrewarding to try to understand Peacock by way of Knight's outmoded terminology. It is more important to recover the general mood and purpose of the education-by-reading to which he submitted himself in the first decade of the nineteenth century. Why was he attracted to certain writers? What qualities did he see in them? *Headlong Hall* suggests that he approved of Malthus, who criticised Godwin's optimism, and of Monboddo, who criticised contemporary materialism.[11] He also admired Drummond, who was both a popular synthesiser of the work of other philosophers, and an often sharp-edged critic of them.[12] It is possible to discern common characteristics in these three figures, as in Knight. All are themselves identifiably writing within the British tradition inherited from the Enlightenment. None advances a new system; they write as the revisers of a current idea, or panacea. Each can be seen, in a word, as a critic.

Peacock's satires have already been shown to value criticism as an activity to a remarkable degree. Their genuine heroes are their philosophers – heirs of Socrates, from Escot on – who challenge the commonplace intellectual assumptions of the day. The Socratic dialectic is a medium of criticism; one recalls Peacock's significant observation, that 'it is in negation that Plato shines most, – in the exposure of the errors of others.'[13] Without an adequate intellectual history of this period in England, it is hard to establish how universal the habit of negation, of revisionism, actually was; the impression left by books and reviews, and by private correspondence, is that the visionary 1790s were succeeded by a decade and a half of wariness, of sharply reduced claims. It is interesting that, of Peacock's favourite modern authors, all except Monboddo begin publishing after the reaction against revolutionary optimism has set in. Malthus in 1798 uses arguments of a typically historical, scientific type to debunk Godwin's perfectibilarian hopes for the future. A number of Peacock's favourite books – those of Drummond and Knight, but also of Horne Tooke and Forsyth[14] – appeared in 1805, when progressives had had time to digest two deeply unpalatable truths: England was

279

at war with France, the state which before had seemed the inspiration of mankind; France had betrayed its own Revolution, temporarily perhaps in the Terror, but now more profoundly by bowing the knee to a military dictator.

Mr E. P. Thompson has depicted the English liberal intellectual after 1794 as a rather pitiful creature. He calls the religion that overtook some former radicals 'the chiliasm of despair',[15] and represents as a similar failure of nerve the increased emotionalism and introspection of Godwin, the sharp falling away of radical writers after the great age of Paine. A historian interested in working-class political movements rightly sees Godwin, even at his most ardent, as essentially middle-class, a writer for other intellectuals and not much of an influence upon the masses, through whom, in the end, the radical changes would come. Though the 1793 edition of *Political Justice* is, at its theoretical level, a relatively bold book, it is certainly not aimed at the lower orders, nor intended as a rallying-call to actual revolution; and Peacock, who in tone and temper is so characteristic a product of the next generation – he came of age during the first decade of the nineteenth century – could be charged with taking to a further extreme the same sterile intellectuality. Whatever the moral message of his work, according to this view, a style which is at once learned and polished must be read as élitist, and thus innocent of any real commitment to political action. Shelley's writing, so radical in its meaning, so difficult in its manner of conveying it, is open to precisely the same line of criticism.

But such strictures are, when all is said, ultimately unreal. They ignore the historical circumstances, that throughout Europe, in all intellectual matters, including philosophy and the arts, conservatism, refinement, consolidation and reflection were much stronger tendencies after 1800 than the innovation which had prevailed in the last quarter of the eighteenth century.[16] With all allowance for personal talent and temperament, the liberal student of Peacock's generation and Shelley's was led towards the careful, dispassionate intellectualism of a Malthus, or, a few years on, a John Stuart Mill.

Often it is not a period's heroes who illuminate its perplexities for us, but more commonplace minds. Peacock had in Robert Forsyth a contemporary whose very ordinariness serves to throw the plight of the war-time progressive into sharp relief. In the 1790s, as a young Scottish advocate, Forsyth was so notorious for his association with 'the friends of the people' that he found it difficult to get briefs. After the turn of the century he looked, like Payne Knight, to more theoretical issues, and his book, *The Principles of Moral Science*, is another typical product of its era. The line of descent from Godwin's *Political Justice* is still discernible. Godwin, even at the beginning, had argued that political justice could be achieved only with the spread of moral enlightenment; revolution is in the hands of the philosopher, not the political agitator. Forsyth never implies that he has a political change in view at all. Nevertheless, though the cultivation of Mind is (at least for the time being) a goal for attainment by individuals, a society made up of such individuals would necessarily be a libertarian one. In political hard times, Godwin's anarchic individualism could not openly be canvassed.[17] What takes its place, temporarily divorced from the political context, is the strenuous intellectuality so typical of the utilitarians. Later, with the emergence of the group known as Philosophic Radicals, the connection between intellectualism and political reform would come out again into the open. In Forsyth it has to remain implicit:[18]

It appears to me ... that the great object which the human race ought to pursue, and the attainment of which they ought to regard as the business of their lives, is not to produce happiness, pleasure or felicity, in themselves or others; but that, on the contrary, the end for which they were formed, and which alone they can pursue with success, is the improvement of their whole intellectual faculties, whether speculative or active. In one word, it is the business of man in this world to endeavour to become an excellent being, possessing high powers of energy and intelligence. This is his chief good; and ought to be the great and ultimate object of his pursuit, to which every other consideration ought to be sacrificed.

If this principle, that intellectual excellence, or the perfection of mind and of its rational powers, is the most important and valuable object of human pursuit, can be clearly established, it will follow, that those actions are good, and right, and best, which produce, not happiness or pleasure, but the greatest portion of knowledge, ability and intellectual perfection in the world; and that those actions are the worst, which produce, or have a tendency to produce, not suffering, but the greatest degree of ignorance, of stupidity, and of intellectual weakness and degradation. It will even follow, that the rulers of nations (though they are seldom so well employed) do actually misapply their labour, and mistake their duty, when they imagine that their proper business consists in conferring felicity upon their fellow-creatures.

I shall here endeavour to prove, that the great task, to the performance of which the existence of every man ought to be devoted, consists of two branches: first, to produce the individual improvement of his own individual mind and character; and, secondly, to produce the improvements of the minds of other rational beings.

Peacock first read Forsyth in 1809, but his work in 1818 is again full of references to him.[19] Forsyth indeed says plainly what Peacock conveys with irony and indirection over a lifetime. As a formal ethical creed, it no doubt has its limitations. Philosophers are professionally obliged to view one another's books as though they were written as academic exercises, and in a historical vacuum − rather than for a clearly defined readership, in a community and at a specific moment in time. Forsyth makes no mark on the history of ethics, but he does try to convey a message to the beleaguered, study-bound radical in England or Scotland in 1805. The point taken by Peacock, and through Peacock by Shelley, is that self-cultivation need not be a poor alternative to political campaigning − still less, a withdrawal inward. The man who through his own reason brings about reason in others will be, after his own fashion, an activist. The doctrines to be resisted are those which induce passivity in the public − and here it is possible to see that, for all his bromide vagueness, Forsyth's message has political implications. It is interesting to re-read the passage on the pursuit of the perfection of mind, in order to try to sense which he is more anxious to assail: the philosophical principle, that the rational society pursues the greatest happiness of the greatest number, or the pervasive current practice, the Churches' attempt to preach contentment to the people? It is a truism in English wartime journalism of all shades of opinion, that the population of France has been degraded by centuries of autocracy, and is now proving it by its servility to Napoleon Bonaparte. But the strategy proper to the liberal in response to this situation is very different from that of the Tory: it is to seek to create, in England at least, a population that is sceptical, rational, *critical* – and so, in a literal sense, ungovernable.

The reason why Peacock's stock as a commentator is low is easy to see. Irony is a dangerous weapon for a critic, and his most polished performance, *The Four Ages of Poetry*, has been found – to put it bluntly – too hard to understand. But in addition the modern reader is hampered by certain preconceptions about what the 'Romantic' critic should be saying, and a wholesale prejudice against what the Enlightenment critic actually is saying. Peacock's utilitarianism, his historicism, his intellectuality are all matters of reproach. At least we need not think them the whims of an isolated eccentric, still less of an antiquarian with a bias against modernity: Peacock stands foursquare in a powerful intellectual tradition. Whether this alone entitles him to respect as a critic depends on what he succeeds in doing with it.

Peacock's prose criticism is not a large *oeuvre*. Only two pieces date from the 'Romantic' period proper, a fragment written in 1818 on 'Fashionable Literature', and the essay published in 1820 as *The Four Ages of Poetry*.[20] In the 1820s Peacock wrote a handful of reviews and general articles, in which the comments on Hunt, Byron and Moore, in particular, apply rigorous intellectual standards, and the criterion of utility, to what Peacock sees as meretricious writing of a characteristic contemporary kind.[21] In the 1830s, in addition to his opera reviewing, he published the two interesting articles on French Comic Romance, which place satire in the context of the society capable of producing it. The 1850s yield more orthodox 'literary' writing than the rest of his career put together – an entire series of articles on classical and theatrical subjects, and an appreciation of the seventeenth-century French writer Chapelle. No-one ever employed Peacock to review new creative writing, for the reason, surely, that he was too obviously a philosopher – more inclined even than Jeffrey to return to principle, and less willing to disguise the fact.

The first two pieces are obviously of special interest to anyone concerned with Romantic criticism. They are, as their titles proclaim, social rather than narrowly literary criticism: an age, a culture, is being defined in terms of its total literary output. Of the two, the incomplete and unpolished 'Essay on Fashionable Literature' is a much easier performance, a fact which has led one modern scholar to suppose it the better essay.[22] This is not really so: *The Four Ages* is better written, better organised and better thought through. Nevertheless, the 'Essay on Fashionable Literature', on which Peacock worked in the very summer in which he finished *Nightmare Abbey*, is a useful index to his thinking about the arts, and an invaluable commentary on the most literary of all his satires.

The essay begins more elegantly than it continues, with a thumb-nail sketch of the reading public – the idle leisured classes, for whom the great enemy is Time. At night the fashionable assail Time 'in battalion'; at operas and exhibitions, routs and concerts, dinners at midnight and suppers at sunrise. In the morning they are compelled to encounter him single-handed, and then the weapons they call on are 'light and easy books which command attention without the labour of application, and amuse the idleness of fancy without disturbing the sleep of understanding'.[23]

The literature which will satisfy such a special need is emphemeral and superficial. It may appear more brilliant than comparable writing of a generation earlier: periodical journalism certainly appears to have become much more sophisticated. In fact is has cultivated qualities which are only for show, without real depth.[24] An occasional writer may appear to instruct, as Scott does, but he conveys information about manners, which is material for the philosopher without being philosophy itself. 'Information, not enquiry – manners, not morals – facts, not inferences – are the taste of the present day. If philosophy be not dead, she is at least sleeping in the country of Bacon and Locke.'[25]

Peacock puts a sinister interpretation upon this sleep of the understanding. He sees in contemporary England a society in which, for all the superficial differences between the fields of enquiry, and all the appearance of political cut and thrust between Whig and Tory, there is in fact no real debate at all:

XXII. There is a common influence to which the periodical press is subservient: it has many ultras on the side of power, but none on the side of liberty (one or two *weekly* publications excepted).[26] And this is not from want of sufficient liberty of the press, which is ample to all purposes; it is from want of an audience. There is a degree of spurious liberty, a Whiggish moderation with which many will go hand in hand; but few have the courage to push enquiry to its limits.

XXIII. Now though there is no censorship of the press, there is an influence widely diffused and mighty in its operation that is almost equivalent to it. The whole scheme of our government is based on influence, and the immense number of genteel persons, who are maintained by the taxes, gives this influence an extent and complication from which few persons are free. They shrink from truth, for it shews those dangers which they dare not face. The *legatur* of corruption must be stamped upon a work before it can be admitted to fashionable circulation.[27]

The two nominal rivals among the journals, the Whig *Edinburgh Review* and the Tory *Quarterly Review*, are really on the same side, because each tacitly upholds the System. The literature which the Establishment favours falls by general consent within a restricted category — 'the best recommendation a work of fancy can have is that it should inculcate no opinions at all, but implicitly acquiesce in all the assumptions of worldly wisdom. The next best is that it should be well-seasoned with *petitiones principii* in favor of things as they are.'[28] Occasionally the journals will almost state as much: reviewers will for example stupidly pretend of works that are original or intelligent that they are too difficult to understand.[29] This implicit consensus requires literature to ask nothing of its readers, while letting their intelligence sleep. It finds one dissenting voice at least in Peacock, as he indicates in a rare flight of enthusiasm:

XXV. Fancy indeed treads on dangerous ground when she trespasses on the land of opinion. ... But she is a degenerate spirit if she be contented within the limits of her own empire, and keep the mind continually gazing upon phantasms without pointing to more important realities. Her province is to awaken the mind, not to enchain it. Poetry precedes philosophy, but true poetry prepares its path. — See Forsyth. —[30]

XXVI. Cervantes – Rabelais – Swift – Voltaire – Fielding –
have led fancy against opinion with a success that no other
names can parallel.[31]

This passage contains a statement, without irony, of Peacock's
desired ideal, a campaigning literature of ideas, a comic vehicle
conveying a wholly serious purpose. Presumably it is the early
version of the more finished paragraph he published eighteen years
later, in his essay 'On French Comic Romances':[32] so much,
indeed, for the frequently expressed view that there is some total
change in Peacock's aesthetic and political views between one date
and the other. As usual, Peacock found support in the attitudes of
the ancient Greeks for his belief in engagement. He made a laconic
entry in his diary for Sunday 26 August 1818, the month when he
was writing the essay – 'Rd. the life of Solon. Noticed in C.VI the
law by which Solon declares infamous and banishes any person
who takes neither part in political discussions.'[33] Peacock agrees
with Solon – that silence is the negation of citizenship. And in
condemning the literature of his day for its effective silence on
public matters, he anticipates the cultural radicalism of the
Benthamite *Westminster Review*; of James Mill, in the first number,
in particular.

But Peacock's best critical achievement outside the satires, and
surely the cleverest essay ever to put the orthodox utilitarian
position, is *The Four Ages of Poetry*. Its meaning has been obscured
by its irony and allusiveness, and for clarification it needs to be set
beside its principal source – the fourth chapter, 'Of Taste', in the
first part of Forsyth's *Principles of Moral Science*. Here, in the best
Enlightenment manner, which could owe ultimately as much to
the German J. J. Winckelmann as to any Scotsman, Forsyth offers a
historical survey of the arts as products of successive periods of
civilisation. It is the goal of man as a moral being to perfect the
powers of his own intellect. In this ceaseless endeavour of the
individual and the race, literature has historically played a part, but
always a subordinate one. It is not admirable for its own sake, but
as an aid to education, and once a nation (for example, modern
Scotland) has arrived at a certain state of advancement, its need for
the fine arts is ended. At such a point of cultural evolution, by
implication, the arts may become worse than an irrelevancy; they
may be a distraction, or a soporific:[34]

All the efforts of the fine arts are addressed to the passions. It is necessary they should be so to excite the attention of barbarians. They have only an indirect tendency, therefore, to render mankind rational. They foster and soothe the passions of love, ambition, and vanity; but they also teach men to admire skill and ability, and to take delight in something else than war, gaming, gluttony, and idleness, which are the vices of all savages. As succeeding artists improve upon each other, their countrymen become more discerning and skilful, till at last a great proportion of mankind learn to take delight in the exertion of thought, and in the pursuits of literature and of knowledge. When this object is accomplished, the fine arts have done their duty; and an important duty it is, seeing they are the means of alluring the human race to the pursuit of intellectual improvement. In themselves, however, and without regard to this object, they are of little real value; for a man is not a more excellent being when his ears are tickled by music than when he hears it not; and we derive no greater improvement from an important truth, when it is conveyed to us in rhyme, than when it is conveyed in prose.

Peacock's version is more complex than Forsyth's, and much more elegant and witty. But underlying his argument in *The Four Ages* is the same perfectly serious historical framework as Forsyth uses in his *Principles* (or indeed Scott in his *Minstrelsy of the Scottish Border*, or, before all three of them, Hume, Robertson, Monboddo, *et al.*). The perspective places little value on an artist's originality, or on the characteristics most personal to him, such as style. The tendency of the philosophical historian to trace art back to its primitive origins tends to reduce its status – even as other theorists of the period are exalting both art and the artist to a wholly new, semi-religious importance. And Peacock sets out to exploit the tendentious possibilities of historicism, because by 1820 theories about art and culture have become both topical and controversial. What is a dispassionate and rather routine survey in Forsyth becomes in *The Four Ages* a piece of Voltairean iconoclasm, a very deliberate outrage:[35]

> The natural desire of every man to engross to himself as much power and property as he can acquire by any of the means

which might makes right, is accompanied by the no less natural desire of making known to as many people as possible the extent to which he has been a winner in this universal game. The successful warrior becomes a chief; the successful chief becomes a king; his next want is an organ to disseminate the fame of his achievements and the extent of his possessions; and this organ he finds in a bard, who is always ready to celebrate the strength of his arm, being first duly inspired by that of his liquor. This is the origin of poetry, which, like all other trades, takes its rise in the demand for the commodity, and flourishes in proportion to the extent of the market.

And yet, for all his cynicism, and his deflationary tone, Peacock has his own ideals for the artist. Like Forsyth, he considers that the poet participates in the highest of all human pursuits. He deeply admires the poetry of the age of Homer, when 'the whole field of intellect is its own'.[36] It is in fact the intellectual he admires, not the narrower specialist, the poet, and if, like Forsyth, he demotes poetry, it is only to insist that the moral leadership of mankind still rests with its thinkers:[37]

This state of poetry [the Silver Age, the period of greatest stylistic refinement] is however a step towards its extinction. Feeling and passion are best painted in, and roused by, ornamental and figurative language; but the reason and the understanding are best addressed in the simplest and most unvarnished phrase. Pure reason and dispassionate truth would be perfectly ridiculous in verse, as we may judge by versifying one of Euclid's demonstrations. This will be found true of all dispassionate reasoning whatsoever, and of all reasoning that requires comprehensive views and large combinations. It is only the more tangible points of morality, those which command assent at once, those which have a mirror in every mind, and in which the severity of reason is warmed and rendered palatable by being mixed up with feeling and imagination, that are applicable even to what is called moral poetry: and as the sciences of morals and of mind advance towards perfection, as they become more enlarged and comprehensive in their views, as reason gains the ascendancy in them over imagination and feeling, poetry can no longer accompany them in their progress, but drops into the background, and leaves them to advance alone.

Thus the empire of thought is withdrawn from poetry, as the empire of facts had been before.

By an inevitable evolutionary process, the poets of the modern period have lost what ancient poets genuinely possessed, the intellectual leadership of the community. What is culpable in them (Peacock thinks) is that they have ceased even to aspire after the highest qualities of intellect and reason. Those who have not simply settled for earning a living have become content with a feeble alternative, an obvious refuge – feeling. Seen in the full context of their culture, the artists of 1820 divide into categories: the purely frivolous, who set out to entertain (into this category go mere narrative and descriptive writers, including Moore, Scott, and, presumably, Hunt and the immature Keats); the more serious, who, however, irresponsibly avoid public themes (the Lake poets); the wholly serious and well-intentioned, who try to direct moral truths at the public, but are not understood (Shelley).

But of all contemporary schools of poetry, it is the Lakists who most attract Peacock's sarcasm, because they have made a positive cult of the subjective and the feeling:[38]

> They wrote verses on a new principle; saw rocks and rivers in a
> new light; and remaining studiously ignorant of history,
> society, and human nature, cultivated the phantasy only at the
> expense of the memory and the reason; and contrived, though
> they had retreated from the world for the express purpose of
> seeing nature as she was, to see her only as she was not,
> converting the land they lived in into a sort of fairy-land, which
> they peopled with mysticisms and chimaeras.

Peacock contrasts his own conception of the philosopher, engaged and intellectual, with his modern rival, the poet:[39]

> The philosophic mental tranquillity which looks round with an
> equal eye on all external things, collects a store of ideas,
> discriminates their relative value, assigns to all their proper
> place, and from the materials of useful knowledge thus collected,
> appreciated, and arranged, forms new combinations that
> impress the stamp of their power and utility on the real business

of life, is diametrically the reverse of that frame of mind which poetry inspires, or from which poetry can emanate. The highest inspirations of poetry are resolvable into three ingredients: the rant of unregulated passion, the whine of exaggerated feeling, and the cant of factitious sentiment.

Though the argument is in keeping with the themes of the two most relevant satires, *Melincourt* and *Nightmare Abbey*, Peacock's play of wit seems to have made his later readers afraid to take him seriously. The safest, or at least the commonest, guess has been that he is writing in a vein of such eccentricity and whimsicality that the issue of meaning hardly arises. 'It is idle to inquire about the exact boundaries between the serious and the playful in this witty essay.'[40] One different and ingenious recent notion is that Peacock 'impersonate[s] a bigoted Utilitarian ... engaged in attacking the (equally bigoted) subjectivism and primitivism of contemporary Romantic poetry. ... He uses one prestigious intellectual position as a satiric norm against which to measure another, without committing himself to either.'[41] The proposition that, on the contrary, Peacock puts the genuine utilitarian case — though it is in a deliberately provocative and extreme form — rests on three kinds of evidence: internal (analysis of the text); external (comparison with Peacock's other work, and with favourite authors like Forsyth); and the conduct of Shelley's essay in reply. For it is surely apparent that when in *A Defence of Poetry* Shelley answers Peacock, he is addressing himself with perfect seriousness to a utilitarian.

Shelley's essay is considerably longer than Peacock's, and occasionally discursive, but essentially it constitutes a 'defence of poetry' against what seem to Shelley profoundly serious charges: that it has become selfish, or ornamental, and thus marginal or useless to mankind. To begin with, Shelley has to challenge some of Peacock's factitious distinctions. He declares that Imagination is a faculty of the mind complementary to Reason, rather than opposed to it, and that its insights are of at least equal value. He considers the real relationship between poetry and philosophy, and concludes, first, that many of those whom we normally designate 'philosophers' are essentially, in their appeal to the imaginative faculty, poets; second, conversely, that one 'philosophical' element in literature, the overtly ethical or didactic, is detrimental to it. One significant feature of this part of Shelley's discussion is that it does see the different powers of the mind as complementary, and by no means allows that unchallenged primacy – which we have come to expect of the 'Romantic' – to the creative Imagination. Though Shelley may appear to be advancing the claims of Imagination, and Poetry, over those of Reason, and Philosophy, he is trying to restore an equilibrium disturbed by Peacock; Shelley is careful, in fact, not to be exclusive.

The greatest part of *A Defence of Poetry* is taken up with a historical survey of European literature, in the genuine tradition of eighteenth-century philosophical history. But Shelley is also a son of his own age, and he addresses himself to the task of qualifying and refining the over-simple account of evolution which Peacock has given. He accepts the central proposition, that the role of poetry in every age has been social: to inspire, and to promote enlightenment. But it achieves this best, he argues, when it is most imaginative. Following the line of argument that he took up after *Nightmare Abbey*, and first expressed in the Preface to *Prometheus Unbound*, he suggests that poetry is least effective when it follows the course Peacock advocates, and confuses itself with prose.

Shelley's re-definition of what poetry is makes an ingenious answer, which turns the tables on Peacock, because it demonstrates that the agreed vices – selfishness, ornamentation, uselessness to mankind – are those not of the poets but of the enemies of poetry. On selfishness Shelley writes with witty evenhandedness. 'The extinction of the poetical principle' which characterised the Dark Ages was 'connected with the progress of despotism and superstition': men became 'insensible and selfish'.[42] So much for the Germanists, and their claim that the religious intensities of the feudal period inspired the highest kind of art. But the age of Charles II was also selfish – and impoverished in literature – because it was self-interested, and calculating.[43] So much for that side of utilitarianism that concerns itself with material enrichment. Shelley neatly argues that while the progressive in politics or science has been usefully employed upon such tasks as 'banish[ing] the importunity of the wants of our animal nature, the surrounding men with security of life, the dispersing the grosser delusions of superstition', great poets have been utilitarians in a profounder sense. 'Whatever strengthens and purifies the affections, enlarges the imagination, and adds spirit to sense, is useful.'[44]

Peacock accepted the essence of Shelley's argument, as his next book, *The Misfortunes of Elphin*, shows.[45] And no wonder, since for all its emotional tone Shelley's essay is a Defence of Poetry on classic utilitarian grounds. There is no attack on reason, on prose, or on science, as anyone might assume who read the essay out of the context of *The Four Ages*.[46] Instead, there is the valid warning against too narrow and illiberal an understanding of the possibilities of poetry. Shelley approaches the question of what poetry is via the traditional eighteenth-century routes. He is concerned with its immediate source in the unconscious mind of the poet, and with its more generalised origin in the spirit of the age. He outflanks Peacock, and proves more of a utilitarian than the utilitarian, when he argues that modern poetry is great precisely because it is, and must be, the product of a whole society. Individual poets may be personally fallible, or corrupt, or unenlightened. Such criticisms of the private vices of poets of former ages — of Spenser, for example, or of Bacon — now seem supremely unimportant in relation to their central achievement. For, if poetry is ultimately the voice of a culture at a certain stage of evolution, it emerges in spite of the characteristics, or opinions, of single writers. Peacock should have known better than to have launched an attack on the Lake School, or any other individuals. He should have gone back to his own first principles, and seen that the energies released in an age of revolution must find their expression in an exalted literature. The peroration of *A Defence* insists, logically, upon seeing the living English poets in Peacock's own impersonal and historical perspective:[47]

> For the literature of England, an energetic development of which has ever preceded or accompanied a great and free development of the national will, has arisen as it were from a new birth. In spite of the low-thoughted envy which would undervalue contemporary merit, our own will be a memorable age in intellectual achievements, and we live among such philosophers and poets as surpass beyond comparison any who have appeared since the last national struggle for civil and religious liberty. The most unfailing herald, companion, and follower of the awakening of a great people to work a beneficial

change in opinion or institution, is poetry. At such periods there is an accumulation of the power of communicating and receiving intense and impassioned conceptions respecting man and nature. The persons in whom this power resides may often, as far as regards many portions of their nature, have little apparent correspondence with that spirit of good of which they are the ministers. But even whilst they deny and abjure, they are yet compelled to serve, the power which is seated on the throne of their own soul. It is impossible to read the compositions of the most celebrated writers of the present day without being startled with the electric life which burns within their words. They measure the circumference and sound the depths of human nature with a comprehensive and all-penetrating spirit, and they are themselves perhaps the most sincerely astonished at its manifestations; for it is less their spirit than the spirit of the age.

Shelley's elevated tone is intended to convey by rhythm and association – that is, by poetic means – the excitement, the imaginative reality, of literature. It has misled most interpreters into assuming that he is carried away by mindless enthusiasm, or confusedly rifling the stranger reaches of his reading ('neo-Platonism', for example) in a 'Romantic' protest against the mechanical. It would give a more accurate notion of Shelley's opinions if we regarded the excited tone and the exalted, abstract imagery as the tools of a rhetoric designed to support an argument, which, after assuming common ground in Forsyth and Peacock, thereafter develops what is in its context an appropriate kind of answer. Shelley's *Defence* is anything but the confused *mélange* of incompatible opinions it has been represented.

Taken together, as they ought to be, the two essays by Peacock and Shelley make a philosophic dialogue, the significance of which for the literature of their period has never been recognised. The utilitarian movement was to run into such storms in the next generation, and the mediocre mass of its spokesmen were to utter such stupid and rigid barbarisms, that all its positions on art have tended to become discredited. What was to happen to others later should not lead us to pre-judge the cultural issues of 1818–21. Peacock and Shelley staged a civilised and elegant rehearsal of a conflict that was genuinely to divide their successors. Both were historical critics; both were practising imaginative writers; they

293

argue as friends, sharing many important assumptions, and this is what gives their disagreement its good humour and its subtlety. It is certainly interesting to compare their literary merits with the shortcomings of the essayists and reviewers who in the next decade tried to hammer out a utilitarian aesthetic. 'Had the intellectual seriousness of the Benthamites been accompanied by a more educated taste and sensibility,' a modern critic has remarked, 'the *Westminster* might have proved an important check to the excesses of Romanticism.'[48] But it is worth determining whether the efforts of Shelley and Peacock do not represent a check to certain 'excesses of Romanticism' in their own generation.

Before turning to the larger question, what of *The Four Ages* in the light of Shelley's criticism of it? It is hard to take the essay as Peacock's complete, or usual, view of the potential role of poetry. Its harsh literalness cannot be reconciled with his feeling for Renaissance romance in *Melincourt* or classical romance in *Rhododaphne*, or, indeed, with his descriptive writing in his later satires. Howard Mills deduces that he had become aware of the limit of his own talent, a discovery followed by partial alienation from Shelley and by his decision to enter the East India Company.[49] But this conclusion is based on what is surely a misreading of the tone and intention of *The Four Ages*, and Peacock's correspondence with Shelley in Italy hardly supports it. A more plausible guess at his short-lived readiness to take Forsyth's proposition to extremes would be his irritation with the ambience of Leigh Hunt, in which the Shelleys' departure for Italy had left him high and dry. Peacock, sceptical, tough-minded, rational, engaged in immediate contemporary satire, had no taste for what he considered to be Hunt's aestheticism and escapism. To Peacock, the literature of classical Greece and the Renaissance represented an intellectualist tradition. Hunt and his 'followers', Keats and Barry Cornwall, appeared bent on exploiting its decorative otherworldliness, which they saturated with their own nostalgia. In Hunt's 'The Nymphs', for example, published in *Foliage* (1818), hints seem to survive of *Rhododaphne* – that pointful allegory – but they are lost in a luscious and nauseating day-dream:[50]

> And towards the amorous noon, when some young poet
> Comes there to bathe, and yet half thrills to do it,
> Hovering with his ripe locks, and fair light limbs,

And trying with cold foot the banks and brims,
They win him to the water with sweet fancies,
Till in the girdling stream he pants and dances.

Byron is said to have quizzed *Foliage* immoderately,[51] but Peacock (who no doubt remembered that Hunt failed to print Shelley's review of *Rhododaphne* in the *Indicator*) may be forgiven for a certain tartness. 'We know that there are no Dryads in Hydepark nor Naiads in the Regent's Canal.'[52] In private, Peacock does not write that he despairs of *all* modern poetry. The poetry being written in Italy, by Shelley and by Byron – now that the latter has given up his *Childe Harold* posture, and taken up satire with *Don Juan* – in fact elicits his praise.[53] It is in reaction to the writing and the writers he is exposed to in England that he writes *The Four Ages*, and exclaims furiously to Shelley against the state into which poetry seems to be declining:[54]

> If I should live to the age of Methusalem, and have uninterrupted
> literary leisure, I should not find time to read Keats's 'Hyperion'.
> ... Considering poetical reputation as a prize to be obtained by a
> certain species of exertion, and that the sort of thing which
> obtains this prize is the drivelling doggrel published under the
> name of Barry Cornwall, I think but one conclusion possible,
> that to a rational ambition poetry is not only not to be desired,
> but most earnestly to be deprecated. The truth, I am convinced,
> is, that there is no longer a poetical audience among the higher
> class of minds; that moral, political, and physical science have
> entirely withdrawn from poetry the attention of all whose
> attention is worth having; and that the poetical reading public,
> being composed of the mere dregs of the intellectual community,
> the most sufficing passport to their favour must rest on the
> mixture of a little easily-intelligible portion of mawkish
> sentiment with an absolute negation of reason and knowledge.
> These I take it to be the prime and sole elements of Mr. Barry
> Cornwall's *Madrigals*.

As an *oeuvre*, Peacock's work has its own integrity. The pessimism of *The Four Ages* is accountable for in its immediate context, but it is not typical. Taken together with the satires, the critical essays advance a humanistic, positive conception of the role of the intellectual in society. The issue is thus not whether the prose essays and reviews stand up as an achievement on their own; but whether Peacock, who in all his writing poses as a critic, has ultimately something valid to say about society and literature.

It is characteristic of his type of critic, and his period, that he should deal very little with the style of the contemporaries he discusses. His opera reviewing of the 1830s is, necessarily, concerned with manner, and with details of execution at a particular performance.[55] It is not till the 1850s that he discusses another writer in these terms.[56] In the period of the so-called Romantics, he concerns himself with the content of the new books he reads and with their meaning at the time of their appearance. The two essays and the two most 'literary' of the satires depict the living poets in relation to one another, to contemporary ideologies, and to the society that produces them.

All criticism, however apparently untheoretical, rests on broad aesthetic assumptions. Most modern writing about poets who are Peacock's contemporaries is either 'critical' – that is, concerned with stylistic matters, with the way the poet handles words; or biographical; or, very commonly though not always confessedly, a mixture of both. These approaches, alone or in combination, rest upon assumptions about literature that one might call post-Romantic. Poetry emanates from the creative imagination, or subconscious, of the individual poet. The poem, once created, is an organism with a life independent of its original context. These post-Romantic tenets are not applied in their full rigour to pre-Romantic poetry. *The Dunciad* is not usually discussed as though it emanated solely from Pope's subconscious, or existed independent of its context, or lacked a meaning which can be stated, not too reductively, in prose. Pope's own poetic, in short, is allowed to influence our understanding of his poetic practice. If we habitually discuss the poetry of, say, Shelley and Keats without making this kind of historical allowance, and indeed without reference to the society in which the poets lived, it is because we judge it appropriate to do so, in terms of their 'Romantic' beliefs about poetry and the creative process. A most important feature of Peacock's criticism, taking the satires and the essays together, is that it opens the question, of how much we really know about the common literary principles of the younger English Romantics, and above all whether we have been justified in letting Coleridge be their spokesman.

Peacock's judgment of Wordsworth and of Coleridge is not a judgment of their whole *oeuvre*. Where Coleridge, writing about Wordsworth in the *Biographia Literaria*, had turned his attention largely to the *Lyrical Ballads*, Peacock thinks of Wordsworth as the author of *The Excursion*, and, to a lesser extent, as a public figure supporting the Tory administration. Coleridge is the currently prolific journalist: in the *Lay Sermons* the apologist for aristocratic and hereditary government, the champion of old-established religion against modern science, commerce, free-thinking and egalitarianism; in the *Biographia Literaria*, the advocate of literature that is sound in its conservative values, and intended for an élite. The satire in *Melincourt* and *Nightmare Abbey*, and the remarks on the Lake School in *The Four Ages*, are an accurate description from a political opponent of the content of the work of these two writers between 1814 and 1818. Peacock, an exact and honest critic, never purports to be talking about anything else. When he accuses Wordsworth of childishness,[57] he may be making a sidelong glance at Jeffrey's old jibe against the diction of the *Lyrical Ballads*, but he justifies the charge specifically by arguing that Wordsworth's intellectual posture *now* is regressive and infantile. Unlike Moore, he does not pretent that, because Coleridge is currently opposed to democracy, *Christabel* as a poem does not make sense.[58] Peacock deserves some credit for genuinely returning to first principles. If his criticism is not distorted, nor is it necessarily unfair. Though selective, he has taken what is manifestly an important part of the *oeuvre* of both writers. Whatever the modern judgment of *The Excursion* may be, Wordsworth himself in his prefatory remarks gives it a central place in his life's work.[59] The *Lay Sermons* and the *Biographia Literaria* represent, equally, Coleridge's arrival at maturity as a national figure, a sage. These are the texts which set out to explain, in (relatively) connected style, his concept of the hierarchical state, sanctioned by religious institutions, and reflected in an exalted philosophy and art. When Peacock observes that Wordsworth stands both in his life and in his writing for introspection, he can hardly be said to travesty him. Where *The Iliad* and *Paradise Lost* were social, national, even universal, Wordsworth's central achievement – provocatively to have been called *The Recluse* – was confessedly autobiographical. In *Nightmare Abbey*, Peacock suggests that for Coleridge, preferences in philosophy and literature are contingent upon his over-riding zeal for a religious, traditional society. Peacock's depiction of the new German Romanticism, for which Coleridge made himself the English advocate, as a proselytizing reactionary movement, is a true observation of the second decade of the nineteenth century, and therefore of special significance in interpreting the position of the younger so-called English Romantics.

Peacock's satires, begun in 1815, illuminate the moment when Wordsworth and Coleridge are rejected by the next generation of poets, on ideological grounds, as literary leaders; when Byron, Shelley and Keats take over as, in Shelley's terms, spokesmen for the spirit of the age. Peacock's work offers a unique commentary on the extent and nature of that literary revolt. Through it, the splendid literary flowering of 1816–22 defines itself as in the first instance a literature of reaction against the mode of Wordsworth and the theory of Coleridge. Byron's career, viewed purely from Byron's own point of view, seems to lack any sort of coherence, to jump, arbitrarily, from self-advertising intensity to comic objectivity. His failure to account even to himself for such a volte-face seems to justify Arnold's later stricture, that Byron is a man without ideas. Seen in the wider intellectual context which Peacock's work illuminates, there is every reason why, at a time of ideological tension in England, the liberal Byron should abandon the gloomy, Germanic, 'Romantic' style for which he was celebrated up to 1817, to turn instead with *Don Juan* to a social epic, after a model from Renaissance Italy.[60] *Don Juan* is, after all, an explicitly ideological poem. The dedication denouncing the Lake School might almost have been inspired by *Melincourt* – which Byron had read, and in which, as the hero Forester, he thought he saw himself.[61] Actually there is no evidence that Byron owed a direct literary debt to *Melincourt*, or was teased into changing his ways by *Nightmare Abbey*. But Peacock does supply what Byron does not: a connected, general explanation, why an English liberal poet felt the need in 1818 to reject the manner, along with the opinions, of Wordsworth and Coleridge, and to develop in conscious reaction a medium that is not personal but extrovert, not feeling but comic and critical.

The case of Keats appears at first sight to be very different. Keats, perhaps largely on account of social embarrassment, stood rather aloof from the upper-class Shelley. He was not to be wooed by Leigh Hunt's enthusiasm for both poets, or by Shelley's overtures of friendship. He referred almost as rudely to Peacock's writing as Peacock wrote of his.[62] If only because of his lower-middle-class origins and his relative lack of education, he was personally tempted by Wordsworth's autobiographical mode. The fact remains that in all the sensitive technical choices in this period of highly politicised poetry, Keats aligned himself with the liberal group of poets. He was perceived by his first critics as obviously a member of a party. As G. M. Mathews observes, all the early criticism of his poetry was politically motivated.[63] One symptom betraying his sympathies was the idiomatic, 'Cockney' diction associated with Leigh Hunt, which, like Wordsworth's ballad-style a generation earlier, was taken for an effort to democratise literature. An equally significant clue was his choice of setting — either classical or Italian — coupled with his debt to authors of the Renaissance (Dante, Boccaccio, Chaucer, Spenser, Shakespeare, Milton). While this separated him from the neo-classical century, 'French' and traditionally liberal, it also marked him off from those owing imaginative allegiance to the cloudy, religious Middle Ages. Keats's inclination to one cultural polarity looked evident, and it was underlined by his choice of forms. He liked to tell a story; alternatively, he used a genre — the sonnet, the ode, — which was a well-established Renaissance kind. A number of points potentially were made by this. Keats joined a pre-existent culture, neither created by nor centred on himself. The sense of objectivity was enhanced by frequent allusions to literature, generally of the distant past, and to faraway lands. Keats was not 'correct', in the neo-classical tradition — and about this time classicism was one way of denoting a liberal. All the same, his literariness must have looked, in 1817–20, very unlike the personal, confessional, autobiographical style of the great apologist for religion and tradition, Wordsworth. Even if it was in the privacy of his letters, Keats implied disapprobation of this style when he coined the phrase for Wordsworth, 'egotistical sublime'.

Peacock was certainly premature in writing off Keats for what he took to be self-indulgence and emotionalism, in Hunt's worst manner, for Keats in his later poetry moved steadily nearer in line with the liberals. His 'Ode to Psyche' (written April 1819) and *Lamia* (written June–September 1819), both of which read as though they owe a debt to Peacock's *Rhododaphne*, seem even more strongly affected by the polemical paganism of the young intellectuals against the Christian proselytizing of their elders. 'Psyche' after all proposes to set up an external cult of Love, and links it to an inward process, 'Soul-making' – much as Peacock was doing in *Rhododaphne* and *Maid Marian*. *Hyperion* is an attempt at the most objective of forms, epic. It takes as its model not *The Excursion* but Milton's *Paradise Lost*, yet Milton's Christian cosmology is pointedly replaced by an evolutionary, necessitarian vision of historical change.[64] In the 'Fall of Hyperion', Keats has added a highly significant examination of the role of the poet, in which the more classical concept of the physician and humanist is preferred to that advanced by Coleridge in the *Lay Sermons*, the *Biographia Literaria*, and the lectures of 1818, of the religious prophet ('the fanatic' and 'the dreamer'). Proper illustration of Keats's most subtle and interesting response to the principles of his liberal contemporaries must await a fuller account elsewhere. His development perhaps owes a little, but not much, to Peacock's poetic practice, and nothing to his theory. If he has a mentor influencing him against the Coleridgean poetic, it is Hazlitt. This does not lessen the value of Peacock's critique, as again affording a general insight into the rationale behind Keats's evolving attitudes. It is not a source that is wanted, but a representative, or spokesman, a critic more disinterested than Hazlitt and nearer than Coleridge to the younger generation of writers.

So far the movement incorporating the younger 'Romantic' poets has seemed defined, if it is definable at all, in terms of a negation. Much more markedly after 1818 than before, Byron and Keats appear to adopt themes, settings, styles, that are everything that the practice of Wordsworth, and the theory of Coleridge, are not: they become, in a confined though strictly precise sense, anti-Romantic. For a positive understanding of this poetic generation it is necessary to consider the career of the member of it most often considered as a law unto himself – Shelley. More serious than Byron, more learned than Keats, Shelley focusses for us the intellectual pressures felt by both.

Already Shelley's work has figured many times in these pages, since his career and Peacock's are inseparably intertwined. Though the manner of each seems distinctive, they evolve intellectually by a process of reciprocation, of real-life dialogue. The first shared experience of their friendship was Shelley's rediscovery, with Peacock's encouragement, of the classics. For Shelley as for Peacock, ancient Athens came to stand for republicanism and an ideal of citizenship, for Voltairean iconoclasm and intellectuality. 'The Academy is essentially sceptical.'[65] Nor do they differ in their general allegiance to the philosophical traditions of the Enlightenment. Though Shelley's intellectual position refines itself continually, from first to last (as *A Defence of Poetry* illustrates) his method is essentially the empiricist one inherited from Hume: that the best means of understanding experience is through analysis of the workings of the mind. His insistence that the external world is illusory – so often cited as evidence of his neo-Platonism – is more plausibly explained in terms of the Enlightenment's preference for careful scientific observation over received ideas – 'All things exist as they are perceived.'[66] In literature the decisive moment of Shelley's early career, as of Peacock's, is his reading of *The Excursion*, and his gradual formulation of the intellectual position which would define him in his maturity as the poet comprehensive enough to challenge Wordsworth.

The necessary, negative first steps are inseparably involved with Peacock's *Melincourt*. In *Alastor*, Shelley rejects Wordsworth's doctrine of privacy; in 'Verses Written on Receiving a Celandine' he attacks Wordsworth frontally, for deserting the cause of freedom; in 'Mont Blanc', he proposes a necessitarian alternative to Wordsworth's Christian explanation of the universe. But *Alastor* and 'Mont Blanc' are still Wordsworthian kinds of poem. With the allegorical Renaissance epic, *Laon and Cythna*, and the classical drama, *Prometheus Unbound*, Shelley offers a public statement in an impersonal mode; it is the decisive step in freeing himself from Wordsworth, the development of a form and a rhetoric that owe nothing to Wordsworthian introspection.

It seems that the reaction against Wordsworth's cult of the Solitary helps to provoke in Peacock and Shelley their interest in the social virtues, and especially in the highest of them – love. It was, as we saw, in 1817, the year of *Laon and Cythna*, that the two began their discussion of sexuality. While on Peacock's side the literary products included *Rhododaphne* and the unfinished 'Sir Calidore', Shelley in 1817 began 'Prince Athanase'; in 1818 translated Plato's *Symposium* and wrote an expository essay, 'A Discourse on the Manners of the Ancient Greeks Relative to the Subject of Love'; in 1818–19 gave love the central role in his revision of the Prometheus myth; and in 1820 brought his ideas together in 'Epipsychidion'. It is of course possible to read Shelley's writings on love in the context of his own marriages, and his temporary infatuation with Emilia Viviani; but his debate over several years with Peacock raises other issues. When the writings of the two friends are combined, it becomes clear that the topic holds the key to their thinking about man. This entailed, first, a rejection of the Christian tradition. Christian theology separated soul and body, idea and matter. Shelley and Peacock wanted a more organic philosophy, or religion, in which the loved one's body, instead of falling under the ban of a taboo, becomes an aspect or expression of an ideal such as Beauty or Love.

Peacock does not often sound like a profoundly religious man, though Shelley does. Both are looking for some faith whereby the physical and the ordinary become spiritualised. However indirect, fanciful, or comic his expression of this search, Peacock is consistent in it. *Maid Marian*, mostly written in 1818, is rich in hints of an immanent natural religion; so, at the end of his career, is *Gryll Grange*. Sexual pleasures, food, drink and sociability are not distractions from virtue, but have their place in the good life. Playing their part in this same collective meditation are Shelley's remarks to Peacock about the social life and religion of the Greeks, as he saw them exemplified at Pompeii:

> It seems as if from the atmosphere of mental beauty which
> surrounded them, every human being then caught a splendour
> not his own. ... The houses have only one story [sic]. ... A great
> advantage arises from this, wholly unknown to our cities. The
> public buildings, whose ruins are now, forests as it were of white
> fluted columns, and which then supported entablatures loaded
> with sculpture, were seen on all sides over the roofs of the
> houses. This was the excellence of the ancients. Their private

expenses were comparatively moderate. ... But their public buildings are everywhere marked by the bold & grand designs of an unsparing magnificence. ... Another advantage too is, that in the present case the glorious scenery around is not shut out, & that unlike the inhabitants of the Cimmerian Ravines of modern cities the antient Pompeians could contemplate the clouds & the lamps of Heaven could see the moon rise behind Vesuvius, & the sun set, in the sea, tremulous with an atmosphere of golden vapour, between Inarime & Misenum. ...

This scene was what the Greeks beheld. (Pompeii you know was a Greek city.) They lived in harmony with nature, & the interstices of their incomparable columns, were portals as it were to admit the spirit of beauty which animates this glorious universe to visit those whom it inspired. If such is Pompeii, what was Athens?

From his fresh and literal insight into the wholeness of ancient life, Shelley passes at once to the topic never far from his mind: art, as the translation, the embodiment, of this best of all ideals:[67]

I now understand why the Greeks were such great poets, & above all I can account, it seems to me, for the harmony the unity the perfection the uniform excellence of all their works of art. They lived in a perpetual commerce with external nature and nourished themselves upon the spirit of its forms. Their theatres were all open to the mountains & the sky. Their columns that ideal type of a sacred forest with its roof of interwoven tracery admitted the light & wind, the odour & the freshness of the country penetrated the cities ... O, but for that series of wretched wars which terminated in the Roman conquest of the world, but for the Christian religion which put a finishing stroke to the antient system; but for those changes which conducted Athens to its ruin, to what an eminence might not humanity have arrived!

Shelley's letters lack the emotional dimension, the personal glamour, of Keats's, who discovered his manhood, his genius and his fatal condition all within the same short period. But intellectually Shelley's letters are of crucial importance, for they illustrate as nothing else does the task of the poet in this second phase of English 'Romanticism': to participate in universal culture, in the objective and inevitable movement of history, through a medium, literature, that by now is perceived to speak first to the emotions and the senses. Byron's play of wit and intelligence, Keats's intensity and vitality, make their letters the splendid personal documents they are. The virtue of Shelley's lies in his disinterested dedication to the problem posed in his time for his craft. It is a devotion illustrated, for example, when (prompted by Schlegel) he learns Spanish in order to read Calderon, the ultra-Catholic; and, with typical openness to literary idealism, of no matter what party colouring, succeeds in learning even from him.[68]

If the wholeness of life was one major topic of discussion in talk and letters between Peacock and Shelley, another was how this wholeness could be revived in the art of the modern period. Beginning, again, from rejection of Wordsworth's example, the way of the recluse, the two argued about the role of poetry and of the poet. The point of *Melincourt* and, supposedly, *Alastor* is the anti-Wordsworthian one, that poetry ought to be social, *engagé*. Continental politics, emanating from Vienna, and Coleridge's intervention in support of German intensity, and tragedy, helped to confirm Peacock's conviction that art also ought to be comic. Shelley's reaction to this proposition is a complex one, too difficult perhaps to express adequately in anything short of a full-scale study of his *oeuvre*. But it surely needs stressing that the case for Comedy, as opposed to Tragedy, is in some respects the case for polish, stylisation, conscious artistry, against a literary mode that can be turned into an unartful and self-indulgent cry of pain. To this extent, Shelley would seem largely to have accepted the case against 'Tragedy'. Here, paradoxically, he was relatively in line with German theorists on the subject, who admired the truly 'dramatic': that is, a literary form that was controlled, externalised, objective. When it comes to drama, Shelley is out of step only with some popular current English notions: the intensely subjective acting style of Edmund Kean, for example, or the equally intense critical response of Kean's admirer Hazlitt. Shelley's dramas – *Prometheus, The Cenci, Swellfoot the Tyrant* and *Charles I* – are all essentially intellectual in their interest. In no case is the audience encouraged to dwell vicariously upon the sufferings of the protagonist. His deliberate detachment as a dramatist has much in common with the contemporary German interest in irony. But it marks off his plays from those of his English contemporaries, who were more strongly influenced by a subjective reading of Shakespearean tragedy – from Wordsworth's *Borderers*, Coleridge's *Remorse*, Byron's *Manfred*, and Keats's *Otho the Great*.

It may, even so, seem almost perverse to suggest that Shelley approaches Peacock's position in the case of comedy. His taste for serious literature never wavers; Scythrop only inadvertently plays his part in a scene from *A School for Scandal*. But in a characteristically subtle sense Shelley is after all won round. He comes to see the virtue, indeed the necessity, of a classical tradition we might designate 'serious comedy'. After his initial surprise, he is convinced of the legitimacy of Byron's new enterprise, *Don Juan*. He pays it the compliment, in fact, of imitation. His finest translation, of Homer's 'Hymn to Mercury', and one of his most beautiful poems, 'The Witch of Atlas', both use the stanza of *Don Juan*. Each is, moreover, about a comic spirit. Mercury and the Witch are light, joyous, essentially counterparts for one another. Though in the latter poem, at least, there is a sad consciousness of human suffering, the theme is the truly classical one, that from the gods' eye view life is an occasion for laughter rather than tears, and thus properly matched by the poet with comedy.[69] If as an outcome it seems unexpected, in reality it is the point at which Shelley's thinking as a poet, about technique, fully catches up with his classicism as a general intellectual position. The aptness, and at the same time the imaginativeness, of his poetic experiments are what make him so impressive a figure. He is the largest-minded of all the so-called Romantics, and writes no more than the truth to Keats when he claims that as a poet, in his approach to form and style, he has steered clear of narrow party orthodoxies – 'In poetry *I* have tried to avoid system and mannerism.'[70]

But it is also highly significant that he does come down decisively on one side in the two crucial aesthetic decisions of his immediate period. He decides that poetry has a social responsibility (which means, in the context, to intervene on the liberal side); and that it should be, if not comic, at least stylized and objective. Because poetry is not the voice of the individual poet, but the voice of the age, its content cannot be personal, nor should its texture aim to re-enact the special quality of one man's experience. Its subject-matter is man in history – all our experience – which can be conveyed not through stories about particularised individuals, but only through the great myths common to our culture. Where Wordsworth is an innovator in being private and exclusive, Shelley pointedly develops another style, which is public and inclusive. To call him a traditional poet would be absurd, because a new historical situation has prompted him to combine traditional materials in entirely new ways. Nevertheless, he will deliberately emphasise his place in the whole European tradition by his eclectic range of allusion; by writing dramas on the Greek and Elizabethan models; by memorialising Keats in a highly figured ode in the Renaissance manner; by employing in *Alastor*, *Laon and Cythna*, *Prometheus Unbound* and 'The Triumph of Life' that most unspontaneous and literary of devices, allegory. The thoroughness of his reaction against Wordsworth and High Romanticism, and what they both stand for, has made him neo-classical, or, if the term is pre-empted, truly and consciously classical, in his own and Peacock's understanding of the term: a humanist and a critic, as well as a creator. Shelley is properly the central figure among the three younger Romantic poets, in that he identifies for himself, and articulates for us, the alternatives confronting all three. The entire, invaluable intellectual process is largely carried out, and always furthered, in discussion with Peacock. What is clear in retrospect is that despite his wit and apparent eccentricity, what Peacock represents for Shelley (from *Melincourt* to *The Four Ages*) is a hard-thought rational position, a kind of radical orthodoxy: a liberal utilitarianism, a discriminating scepticism, a scientific and historical perspective. Peacock helps Shelley to a firm intellectual foundation upon which Shelley's brilliantly idiosyncratic poetic experiments can be raised.

Peacock's importance to literature is inseparably bound up with Shelley's, but our judgment of him must ultimately depend on what he wrote himself, the accuracy and centrality of the content of his criticism, and the fineness of its artistic expression. It has often been suggested that Peacock's career breaks into two, according to whether his main targets are 'Romantics' or 'Utilitarians'. On the whole it seems sounder to think of it as unified, because he is always the satirist of society: the arts, even if singled out for attack, are always presented as the by-product of a civilisation at a distinctive stage of development. Nevertheless, the first three books, beginning with *Headlong Hall*, are full of references to specific contemporary artists; the second and third, *Melincourt* and *Nightmare Abbey*, to the major poets Wordsworth, Coleridge, Byron and Shelley. It may be on this account that the earlier group seems to be rather more read, at least by literary readers,[71] than the later ones, and that a reaction to them – as a 'critique of Romanticism' – has often coloured the modern response to the whole *oeuvre*.

One consequence of reading Peacock only in part (and especially this part) may be to under-rate his skill. The four earlier satires, those written essentially in the 'Romantic' period of 1815–18, are not on the whole as sophisticated as the later three. Of the four, only *Nightmare Abbey* seems an outright success, a perfectly judged achievement. Among the later three there are no failures, unless *Crotchet Castle* is counted one – that rich, even profound, book, which is as far above *Melincourt* in technique and knowledge of the world, as it is beneath *Gryll Grange* in cohesion. Technically, Peacock continues to grow; and he also grows in worldly experience. *Headlong Hall* has some large truths to convey, but it is occasionally crudely farcical, and seldom particularly lifelike, in its representation of country house conversation. (It is interesting that though most of Peacock's satires are set in country houses, he may never have stayed in one before he wrote *Crotchet Castle*.) Similarly, *Melincourt* takes the view of politics of a political outsider, a member of the newspaper-reading public. *Nightmare Abbey* seems a decided advance, because it depicts the relations between the upper classes and literature with a new sharpness of focus. It is not a question of sketching individuals from the life, since Peacock does not deal in this sense in personalities. It is a matter of the increased assurance which comes from first-hand knowledge of the world. Because he henceforth came to know and understand society better, by strict and legitimate standards he became in later years a fine social satirist, better-informed, more accurate, in a serious sense more true.

But what of the message he wished to convey to intellectuals? The earlier satires are, for all their balanced tone and personal detachment, essentially polemical. Peacock detests the Tory administration of 1815–18. He suspects the motives of its supporters, both as individuals and as a class. He is totally decided in his view of the proper duty of the artist in these circumstances. This means that he is harshly unsympathetic to the current attitudes of Wordsworth and Coleridge, but it also means that he is prepared openly to advocate a positive role for the liberal intellectual.

The philosophers of his first two satires convey his approval of strenuous dialecticians, like Rousseau, Malthus and Monboddo. After this phase of his career, it may seem at first sight that he becomes more introverted, more idiosyncratic, and more negative. Independent of Peacock's own evolving techniques as a satirist, there were reasons why his mode was bound to change, which have to do both with the world he was describing, and with the public for whom he was writing. Peacock himself is, as so often, the acutest critic of his life and times, when he argues in his essay on 'The Epicier' that the era of the old type of satire – the comedy of opinion – has by the 1830s gone by. All art is produced for a certain historical situation, and for a public. The comedy of opinion – the tradition of Rabelais and Voltaire – arises in circumstances where there is autocratic government, and ideological resistance to it: that is, in pre-revolutionary conditions. Its public is highly educated, but out of office, the upper reaches of a typical aristocratic society. In early nineteenth-century Europe a social revolution was in progress, but it was gradualist and piecemeal. The accommodation being arrived at in England and France between the aristocracy and the bourgeoisie was dissipating the public for learned radical literature. The liberal-classical reaction against, or resistance to, Romanticism was a more specialised and historically more upper-class mode than the emotional and autobiographical vein of a Wordsworth or a Coleridge: Shelley had severer trouble than either in finding an audience. What Peacock said of Milton, in the new age, was equally true of Shelley, of Voltaire, and of himself – 'there was no more market for him than for Cromwell.'[72]

When in his last years Peacock was discussing Shelley's difficulty in writing about, and for, real people, he added a rider which implied his own growing disappointment with humanity as a cause:[73]

> He was advancing, I think, to the attainment of this reality. It
> would have given to his poetry the only element of truth which

it wanted; though at the same time, the more clear development of what men were would have lowered his estimate of what they might be, and dimmed his enthusiastic prospect of the future destiny of the world. I can conceive him, if he had lived to the present time, passing his days like Volney, looking on the world from his windows without taking part in its turmoils; and perhaps like the same, or some other great apostle of liberty (for I cannot at this moment verify the quotation), desiring that nothing should be inscribed on his tomb, but his name, the dates of his birth and death, and the single word,

'DESILLUSIONNE'

But he was speaking here about his own hopes for social progress, equality, enlightenment, the alleviation of poverty and suffering, and the rule of reason. In later life these goals seemed further off to Peacock than they had done in youth, and the cynicism which pervades his portrait of England in *Gryll Grange* seems in its way more despairing than the righteous anger of *Melincourt*. Yet, strangely enough, an important feature of Peacock's intellectual position, which in itself is a symptom of liberal idealism, remains constant in his work to the end. From *Nightmare Abbey* on, he uses the device of a representative hero, comic and fallible because he is over-impulsive, who is yet depicted as essentially right-minded. Scythrop, with his radicalism, his stylistic perversity, and hence his ineffectuality, alludes clearly to Shelley. (Taliesin is not perhaps one of the sequence at all, since he has no comic characteristics, and does not appear to refer to a real-life individual; he is, on the other hand, the perfect type of the poet-intellectual.) Chainmail in *Crotchet Castle* has a strong family resemblance to Scythrop, and contains a reference to another real-life enthusiast, currently acting like something of a crank – John Stuart Mill. Falconer in *Gryll Grange* looks back to Scythrop and to Shelley, but also has a link with a contemporary idealist, the Matthew Arnold whose persona is the Scholar Gipsy.

The presence of these heroes is not enough to counter a sense of increasing privacy in the later work. But it ought to forestall any simple judgment that Peacock gradually became conservative, escapist or self-indulgent. The real generic fault of the later work, if it has one, is its air of not being written for any conceivable audience. By most conventional standards, it ought to be judged

better than the work written between 1815 and 1818. It is more
elegantly written, more carefully planned, more detailed –
superior, therefore, in every sphere in which the individual artist
has it in his power to determine the quality. But his earlier work is
more forceful, more hopeful about society and culture, more
generally inspiriting. The satiric formula he evolved from the
dialogue, from the comedy of manners, and from Mozart, was the
product of a particular culture; when the culture broke up,
something – life, even – could no longer be evoked within the same
literary frame.

Because Peacock's original dialectical form belongs to its period
does not mean that his criticism itself goes out of date. The real-life
men he chose to celebrate in his heroes – most notably Shelley,
Mill, and Arnold – were genuine champions of liberalism,
humanism, and precision of thought. All were associated, like
Peacock himself, with intellectual traditions which evolved from
the Enlightenment, such as classicism and utilitarianism. The latter
two, J. S. Mill (born 1805) and Arnold (born 1822) are in a sense
alter egos for Peacock, each nearly twenty years younger than his
predecessor. They are political liberals, but afraid of liberalism's
unpleasant tendency to harden into orthodoxy. Becoming
proselytes of a sect, declared John Stuart Mill, 'is a character above
all to be avoided by independent thinkers';[74] and, 'the very idea of
progressiveness implies not indeed the rejection but the questioning
of all established opinions.'[75] Matthew Arnold speaks for the same
tradition of intellectual dissidence, when he satirises the Philistine
notion of liberalism:[76]

> let us have a social movement, let us organise and combine a
> party to pursue truth and new thought, let us call it *the liberal
> party*, and let us all stick to each other, and back each other up.
> Let us have no nonsense about independent criticism, and
> intellectual delicacy, and the few and many. ... If one of us
> speaks well, applaud him; if one of us speaks ill, applaud him
> too; we are all in the same movement, we are all liberals, we are
> all in pursuit of truth. ...
> To act is so easy, as Goethe says; to think is so hard! It is true
> that the critic has many temptations to go with the stream, to

make one of the party movement, one of these *terrae filii*; it
seems ungracious to refuse to be a *terrae filius* when so many
excellent people are; but the critic's duty is to refuse, or, if
resistance is vain, at least to cry with Obermann: *Périssons en
résistant.*

Mill, with his consistent rigorous interventions on the political
scene, his mental activity from early youth to old age, his warnings
against the tyranny of the majority, is the most celebrated
champion of the genuine liberal tradition. But he is also one of a
type, more numerous probably in England, and certainly more
influential, than the bohemian intellectual of Romantic mythology.
On the Continent too, it is easy to overestimate the universality of
Romanticism: France had its Sainte-Beuve, and Russia its Tolstoy.

Within the field of aesthetic criticism, which was the more
special interest of Peacock's earlier work, the battle also outlasted
the generation in which it was fought, and the aristocratic
Voltairean form in which Peacock cast his contributions to it. Here
Peacock, the older man, appears at first sight more obdurate than
Mill or Arnold. Mill, after all, spoke of resolving the two traditions
his generation inherited, of the eighteenth and nineteenth centuries,
of Bentham and Coleridge. Arnold's classicism was invaded by
Romantic despondency. Yet it is interesting that afterwards, in his
criticism, Arnold reflects severely on the English Romantic
generation, which, he thinks, wanted 'a critical effort behind it'.
The stir of the French Revolution did not in itself produce great
works of literature; it had too practical and political a character:[77]

> The movement, which went on in France under the old *régime*,
> from 1700 to 1789, was far more really akin than that of the
> Revolution itself to the movement of the Renascence; the France
> of Voltaire and Rousseau told far more powerfully upon the
> mind of Europe than the France of the Revolution.

He too demanded, with Peacock, that the artist should fulfil a social
role, on the liberal side, that he should be 'the true apostle of
equality. The great men of culture are those who have had a
passion for diffusing, for making prevail, for carrying from one end
of society to the other, the best knowledge, the best ideas of their
time.'[78]

If the two distinct traditions in cultural life could be perceived in Mill's and Arnold's day, they are there still. A liberal consensus, not very favourable to dissidence or to independent thinking, on the whole prevails in English public life. Not that automatic opinion is the special vice of the political sphere. Intellectuals in all walks of life — and academics perhaps above all — like the dogmas of a generation, or of a school of thought. Peacock's comic impression — of a society of enthusiasts, deaf to other theories, and to argument — is hardly less valid now than in the early nineteenth century. Thus avant-garde art cuts itself off, not only from the world of money-making, but from other kinds of intellectual endeavour; it is no more enamoured of the rational, critical intelligence than it was in the day of *Nightmare Abbey*. Students of literature are taught to think more highly of introspection than of objectivity, to isolate works of art from their social context, and to give them a high and special kind of value. Students of politics meanwhile study institutions inherited from the Enlightenment. Publicly our society's behaviour is regulated by eighteenth-century assumptions about human nature, for example that men are free, equal, and innately well-disposed towards one another, which more recent thinking has actually done much to disparage. The same benevolent fallacies govern the concern of parliaments for justice and rights, and of the press for the truth. The hold of the liberal eighteenth century on our public life has been a striking historical phenomenon, matched by the steady advance over the same two centuries of science and technology. And yet, in literature and the other arts, in some fields of philosophy and psychology, in many less formalised social attitudes, we see a deep dislike both of science and of politics in its ordinary liberal form. The early nineteenth-century irrationalist reaction — Romanticism — is a current movement still.

Peacock's *oeuvre* is one of the best hostile accounts of what the cult of the irrational might mean. In England at the close of the Napoleonic Wars, Romanticism was perceived to encourage indifference to contemporary politics, or to offer outright aid to illiberal governments. A literature that is concerned with style, and with feeling, rather than with intellect and reason, may be merely decorative; in relation to practical affairs, it will almost certainly be passive. Later, in the mid-nineteenth century, Peacock observes the march of science. But the point he makes in *Gryll Grange* is not that a prosaic, mechanistic science is in competition with imagination and the spirit. On the contrary, in mid-Victorian society the cults of science and religion not only co-exist, but resemble one another, for they are equally mindless and superstitious. What has happened is that with the departure of rationalism and humanistic ideals from the literary culture, a vacuum is left, to be filled by any passing fad or self-indulgence. Without the critical faculty, moreover, a technological society's pursuit of profit goes unchecked. It is typical of the critic who belongs to the classic phase of humanism to assail *both* the Romantic and the mechanistic; solipsistic introspection and bland confidence in social progress.

To the degree that our literary ideas continue to be coloured by High Romanticism, they remain open to Peacock's charges. The humanist critic of today tends to argue that it is actually the emotional content of literature that strikes a posture of dissent in a technological age. It is a comforting doctrine, but not always a convincing one. There is scant force in the dissent that leaves science and the public arena to another type of thinking, and another type of human being. Equally, iconoclasts among the structuralists are hardly radical, if in essence their theory still proclaims that art is made for art's sake.

Peacock has great importance for the literary critic and historian, since he asks that we should reassess Romanticism as an English phenomenon. But he is also of live interest, because he addresses himself as a critic to a world still identifiably our own. Part of his timeliness is that he is a bridge-builder, a man of two cultures, and a sceptic about both. Like Plato, Peacock probably would not have wanted the artist as magus in his Republic, but he would have welcomed the artist as critic. We are stunned by reiteration into believing that what the world wants is positive thinking. Peacock makes out a case, illustrated by Voltaire, for negative thinking, and its attendant virtues of challenge, self-doubt, mutual acceptance and toleration.

Since Coleridge we have been fond of the artist-prophet, and the art-work which is monologue, or confession, or even opium dream. Peacock, whose art is based on the dialogue, has waited a long time for his turn to be heard.

Notes

I have used the *Halliford Edition of the Works of Thomas Love Peacock*, edited by H. F. B. Brett-Smith and C. E. Jones, 10 vols, London, 1924–34, which has the definitive text, a biographical introduction, and bibliographical notes. Unfortunately it is hard to come by, having been printed in a limited edition of 675 sets. I have accordingly made references to the novels as full as possible, by giving the chapter and the title of the chapter in most of the cases where Peacock supplies one. The Halliford volume-number is given after a colon, in small roman numerals: see, e.g., nn. 9 and 10 to ch. 1, below.

1 'A Strain too Learned': Introduction

1 F. R. Leavis, *The Great Tradition*, London, 1947, p. 18n.
2 *Edinburgh Review*, lxviii (1839), 438.
3 These are J.-J. Mayoux's substantial *Un Epicurien anglais: Thomas Love Peacock*, Paris, 1933, and Lionel Madden's monograph, *Thomas Love Peacock*, London, 1967. Each investigates aspects of the intellectual background, though neither goes on to represent the satire as the product of a coherent or consistent attitude. For the other books on Peacock, see Bibliography.
4 Introduction by J. I. M. Stewart to J. B. Priestley, *Thomas Love Peacock* (1927), reprinted London, 1966, p. xvii.
5 J. W. Draper, quoted in Madden, op. cit., p. 30.
6 A. E. Dyson, *The Crazy Fabric*, London, 1965, pp. 58, 61. For a similar note of exasperation, cf. Douglas Hewitt, *The Approach to Fiction*, London, 1972, pp. 147–60.

7   R. Glynn Grylls, *Mary Shelley*, London, 1938, especially the last two
    chapters.

8   It was Jane, together with her husband, the poet's only surviving son
    Sir Percy Florence Shelley, who encouraged T. J. Hogg to write his
    Life of Shelley, 2 vols, 1858. She disapproved of his version, and with
    Richard Garnett produced her own *Shelley Memorials: from Authentic
    Sources*, 1859. Although some of his detail incurred Lady Shelley's
    displeasure, Hogg was no less concerned than she to present an
    innocuous portrait of the poet.

9   'Moore's *Letters and Journals of Lord Byron*', *Westminster Review*, xii
    (1830): ix. 76.

10 'Jefferson's *Memoirs*', *Westminster Review*, xiii (1830): ix. 168.

11 TLP to Claire Clairmont, 12 May 1858: viii. 249. The first part of
    Peacock's *Memoirs of Shelley* appeared in *Fraser's* in June 1858 as a
    review of the recent publications by Hogg, Trelawny and Middleton.
    Part II of Peacock's *Memoirs* appeared in *Fraser's* in January 1860,
    Lady Shelley's *Shelley Memorials* having come out in the interval. His
    Supplementary Notice, resuming the subject of Harriet Westbrook's
    marriage, appeared in *Fraser's* in March 1862.

12 Walter Coulson to Leigh Hunt, cited in G. L. Nesbitt, *Benthamite
    Reviewing*, New York, 1934, p. 122.

13 See p. 241.

14 E.g. Howard Mills, *Peacock: his Circle and his Age*, Cambridge, 1968,
    pp. 56 ff, and, briefly, Eleanor L. Nicholes, in her life of Peacock
    contributed to *Shelley and his Circle*, ed. K. N. Cameron, Oxford,
    1961, i. 106–7.

15 See his statement to his next father-in-law, annotated by J. T.
    Vulliamy, quoted by Diane Johnson, *The True History of the First Mrs.
    Meredith and Other Lesser Lives*, London, 1973, p. 153. My account of
    the Meredith marriage, and of Peacock's attitude to it, is indebted to
    the previously unpublished documents and to the commentary in this
    imaginative biography.

16 H. F. B. Brett-Smith, Biographical Introduction to the Halliford
    edition: i. cxc–cxci.

17 Letter of 16 August 1861. Cf. another, the same to the same, in early
    October – 'there neither is, nor has been since the beginning of
    August, a day on which I could say to myself, "I can now leave home
    with a quiet mind." ' Johnson, op. cit., pp. 142–3. The
    correspondence of TLP with Lord Broughton is in the British
    Library. Add. MSS. 47225, ff. 1–177b.

18 See pp. 238–9.

19 Quoted in Johnson, op. cit., p. 153.

20 See pp. 105–7 and p. 239.

21 PBS to TLP: *Letters of P. B. Shelley* (hereafter Shelley's *Letters*), ed.
    F. L. Jones, 2 vols, Oxford, 1964, ii. 192.

22 Mary Shelley to Maria Gisborne, 13 October 1835: *Letters of Mary
    Shelley*, ed. F. L. Jones, Oklahoma, 1944, ii. 106.

23 TLP to Lord Broughton, 22 February 1862: vii. 256.

24 TLP to T. J. Hogg, 20 March 1818: *New Shelley Letters*, ed. W. S.
    Scott, London, 1948, p. 108.

25 The recollections of Sir Edward Strachey and Sir George Birdwood:
    quoted in Halliford edition, i. cxxx, clxvii.

26 See pp. 99–100, and R. Holmes, *Shelley: The Pursuit*, London, 1974,
    pp. 221–3, 238.

27 PBS to Leigh Hunt, 24 August 1819: Shelley's *Letters*, ii. 113.

28 Leigh Hunt to PBS, July 1819: *Shelley and Mary*, privately printed for
    Sir Percy and Lady Shelley, 4 vols, 1882, ii. 390.

29 TLP to Jane Gryffydh, 28 November 1819: viii. 217.

30 PBS to T. Hookham, 3 December 1812: Shelley's *Letters*, i. 334.

31 'Your sentiments on the awful subject of Religion I trust are
    changed.' Jane Gryffydh to TLP, 30 November 1819: viii. 477.

32 Halliford edition: i. cxxviii.

33 Ibid., p. ccvi.

34 S. Sassoon, *Meredith*, 1948, p. 21.

35 TLP to Lord Broughton, 7 March 1859: British Library Add. MSS
    47225, f. 94.

36 See p. 233.

37 *Reminiscences*, ed. J. A. Froude, 1881, i. 221–2.

38 See pp. 186–7.

39 Carl Van Doren, *The Life of Thomas Love Peacock*, London and New
    York (1911), reprinted 1966, p. 275.

40 Peacock, *Memoirs of Shelley*: viii. 70–1.

41 'Lord Byron told Captain Medwin that a friend of Shelley's had
    written a novel ... founded on his bear ... but assuredly, when I
    condensed Lord Monboddo's views of the humanity of the Oran
    Outang into the character of *Sir Oran Haut-ton*, I thought neither of
    Lord Byron's bear nor of Caligula's horse.' Annotation by TLP to
    'Unpublished Letters of P. B. Shelley', *Fraser's*, March 1860: viii.
    500–1. For the identification of Shelley with Scythrop, see pp. 125ff.

42 *U. S. Magazine and Democratic Review* n.s. xvi (June 1845), 578. This
    article may be an unacknowledged reprint of a review previously
    published in an English journal.

43 Medwin's assertion, that Peacock 'seized on some points of Shelley's
    character', occurs in a revised passage, unpublished at his own death
    in 1869 (Medwin's *Life of P. B. Shelley*, ed. Buxton Forman, London,
    1913, p. 194). Buchanan claimed the story was 'well known'

('Peacock: a Personal Reminiscence', *New Quarterly Magazine*, iv. 1875).

44 Halliford edition: viii. 497. Cf. Shelley's *Letters*, ii. 98, 100, 105, 244.
45 'French Comic Romances', *London Review*, ii (1836): ix. 257–61.
46 *Shelley and his Circle*, ed. K. N. Cameron, Harvard and Oxford, 1961, i. 108–9.
47 For a clear and accurate summary of the scope of Peacock's reading, see Van Doren, op. cit., pp. 18–24.
48 'Letter to Maria Gisborne' (1820), ll. 240–7.
49 Thomas Taylor, *Mystical Initiations*, 1787, p. 13.
50 E. V. Lucas (ed.), *Works of Charles and Mary Lamb*, 7 vols, London, 1903–5, ii. 21.
51 Prospectus: 'Classical Education', n.d. (written after his visit to the Lakes with Shelley in October 1813): viii. 429–31.
52 L. E. A. Eitner, quoted by Hugh Honour, in his foreword to the catalogue to the Arts Council of Great Britain Exhibition, *The Age of Neoclassicism*, 1972, pp. xxv–xxvi. My discussion is indebted both to the prefatory matter by several scholars in the catalogue, and to Hugh Honour's *Neoclassicism*, Harmondsworth, 1968.
53 See p. 113.
54 See pp. 266ff.
55 PBS to T. J. Hogg, 22 September 1815: Shelley's *Letters*, op. cit., i. 432. Shelley's admiration for Lucretius, as the opponent of orthodox religion and of the political establishment, was also at its height about this time. *Queen Mab* (1813) has an epigraph from Lucretius, and 'Mont Blanc' is notably Lucretian in spirit.

2 *Experiments with Form:* Headlong Hall

1 Peacock's best long poem, *Rhododaphne* (1818), though much more genuinely expressive of its author's attitudes (see pp. 106–7), can still chime disconcertingly with echoes of Scott. For example, Rhododaphne's song in the first canto, beginning 'What ails thee, stranger? Leaves are sear,/And flowers are dead, and fields are drear ...' strongly recalls the opening of *Marmion* –

  November's sky is dull and drear,
  November's leaf is red and sear ...

2 Halliford edition: vi. 117.
3 Peacock did however have 'pleasant associations with' George III, whom he long afterwards recalled seeing as a child in the neighbourhood of Windsor. It was a favourable opinion which had, as

he said, nothing to do with politics. TLP to Thomas L'Estrange, fragment, n.d. [1860s]: viii. 254–5.

4 Halliford edition: vi. 118–19.

5 PBS to Thomas Hookham, 18 August 1812: Shelley's *Letters*, i. 325. In this letter, Shelley also makes his first explicit statement that he is working on *Queen Mab*. (What has been taken for a reference to this poem, on 23 November 1811: Shelley's *Letters*, i. 189, is actually more equivocal.) Shelley may have been stimulated by reading Peacock's didactic poetry to do better.

6 TLP to Edward Hookham, 28 November 1808: viii. 162.

7 This would appear to be Peacock's sincere view on slavery. See p. 93.

8 TLP to Edward Hookham, 6 June 1809: viii. 172–3.

9 TLP to Edward Hookham, 28 November 1808: viii. 162. The dates at which the comedies were written are uncertain. Their most recent editors, H. F. B. Brett-Smith and C. E. Jones, suggest they were composed 'not long after his first visit to Wales in 1810, but before the inception of *Headlong Hall*, in which he drew upon both of the discarded comedies for speeches and names of characters.' Scholars agree that *The Three Doctors* is the later of the two (Halliford edition: vii. 527).

10 Richard Payne Knight, *The Landscape*, 1794, Bk I, note to l. 57.

11 He was to develop the aesthetician's case later, in his *Analytical Enquiry into the Principles of Taste*, 1805. See p. 278.

12 He began the attack in Dialogue I, 1794, n. to l. 128, and Dialogue II, 1795, ll. 149–56 n. Passing references to Knight are common in subsequent editions.

13 *The Progress of Civil Society* is parodied as 'The Progress of Man', *Anti-Jacobin*, 1798: *Poetry of the Anti-Jacobin*, ed. Charles Edmonds, London, 1854, pp. 83–91, 109–15.

14 E.g., Knight on Brown, '... whose innovating hand/First dealt thy curses o'er this fertile land.' Knight, op. cit., Bk I, ll. 287–8. Cf. Price's censure of Kent as 'mannerist', in his 'Reply to Repton', *Works*, 1810, iii. 92.

15 *The Landscape*, Bk I, l. 159n.

16 Repton, pp. 94–5.

17 *Edinburgh Review*, vii (1806), 307–8.

18 U. Price, *Works*, 1810, iii. 119–26. James's powder was a much-advertised patent medicine.

19 'A Letter to H. Repton, Esq.': U. Price, *Works*, 1810, iii. 87–8.

20 *Headlong Hall*, ch. viii, 'The Tower': i. 86.

21 See p. 278.

22 TLP to Edward Hookham, 22 March 1810: viii. 183. His letters of the previous year have several eager enquiries after the landscape

controversy – 'Are Knight and Price still at issue respecting the distinct characters of the picturesque and the beautiful?' (TLP to Edward Hookham, 10 February 1809: viii. 164).

23 'Payne Knight is fond of paper war …' TLP to Edward Hookham, 18 August 1810: viii. 188.

24 E.g., Knight picks up much of the original dispute with Repton in the second edition of *The Landscape*, where Peacock probably found it, and alludes sarcastically to earlier critics of *The Progress of Civil Society* in his *Analytical Enquiry*, 1805, pp. 249–52.

25 PBS to Thomas Hookham, 17 December 1812, and to Clio Rickman, 24 December 1812: Shelley's *Letters*, i. 342, 344–5.

26 *Academical Questions*, 1805, i. xiii–xv.

27 John Horne Tooke (1736–1812), a supporter of Wilkes and of the American colonists, was one of the radicals tried for high treason and acquitted in 1794.

28 *Diversions of Purley*, rev. ed. R. Taylor, 2 vols, London, 1829, ii. 5–6.

29 Ibid., ii. 21.

30 PBS to William Godwin, 29 July 1812: Shelley's *Letters*, i. 318.

31 Many quotations from Rousseau and Monboddo are italicised and annotated by Peacock himself.

32 *Headlong Hall*, ch. iv, 'The Grounds': i. 34–5. Cf. N. A. Joukovsky, 'A Critical Edition of TLP's *Headlong Hall* and *Nightmare Abbey*', thesis submitted at Oxford, 1970, MS D Phil. d. 5154.

33 Thomas Malthus, *An Essay on the Principle of Population*, 1798, ch. i: ed. Anthony Flew, Harmondsworth (Pelican Classics), 1970, pp. 69–72.

34 Ibid., ch. i: pp. 68–9.

35 *Edinburgh Review*, xxiv (1815), 491.

36 Letter to Mrs F. Edgeworth, 8 April 1844: *Maria Edgeworth: Letters from England*, ed. Christina Colvin, Oxford, 1971, pp. 610–11. The Rev. Richard Jones (1790–1850) was, like Malthus himself, a professor of political economy at Haileybury; John Frederick Herschel (1792–1871) was an astronomer, like his father, Sir William. Maria Edgeworth met Malthus on a number of occasions and described him vividly: cf. especially Colvin, op. cit., p. 331.

37 *Headlong Hall*, ch. i, 'The Mail': i. 10–11.

38 Mr Escot's theoretical disapproval of marriage may not be derived uniquely from Godwin, but it was an attitude which in England at this date was more closely associated with the Godwin of *Political Justice* than with any other thinker. *Headlong Hall*, ch. xv, 'The Conclusion': i. 151–4.

39 *Headlong Hall*, ch. ii, 'The Breakfast': i. 16; cf. Monboddo, *Antient Metaphysics*, 1784, iii. 129–70.

40 David Garnett and Dr Joukovsky 'place' Headlong Hall at Thomas Johnes's beautifully landscaped estate at Hafod, Cardiganshire (now Dyfed). Johnes, a cousin of R. P. Knight and a friend of Uvedale Price, must indeed have interested Peacock if he met him. Peacock does occasionally use real places in Wales; the anecdotes in *Headlong Hall* about the magician Huw Llwyd certainly derive from the Merioneth locale he knew best. However, his sources are far more characteristically extrapolations from books than from personal experience, and the incident at Powis Castle (p. 34) serves as a warning against guesses at real-life topography.

41 *Headlong Hall*, ch. viii, 'The Tower': i. 87–9.

42 Ibid, ch. vii, 'The Walk': i. 77–8. It is hard to know whether this passage derives from Peacock's observation (and he had after all in 1810–12 walked in North Wales, where such factories were to be seen), or is another literary allusion. Certainly it resembles Southey's *Letters from England*, 1807, Letter xxvi, and Wordsworth's *Excursion*, 1814, viii. 117 ff; but not with Peacock's usual textual fidelity to a conscious source. His description has much fresh detail not in the other two.

43 *Headlong Hall*, ch. v, 'The Dinner': i. 47.

44 See pp. 272ff.

45 *Headlong Hall*, ch. v, 'The Dinner': i. 48.

46 Ibid., ch. xiv, 'The Proposals': i. 144–5.

47 Ibid., ch. ii, 'The Breakfast': i. 18.

48 Ibid., ch. vii, 'The Walk': i. 79–80.

49 Ibid., i. 81.

50 Ibid., ch. x, 'The Skull': i. 103.

51 Godwin to PBS, 4 March 1812: Shelley's *Letters*, 1. 261n.

52 *Headlong Hall*, ch. iv, 'The Grounds': i. 32, and ch. viii, 'The Tower': i. 86 (quoted, p. 34).

53 Entry for 16 September 1814: *Mary Shelley's Journal*, ed. F. L. Jones, Oklahoma, 1947, p. 15.

54 Their book appeared in French under the title *Anatomie et Physiologie du Système Nerveux en général, et du Cerveau en particulier; avec des Observations sur la Possibilité de reconnoitre plusieurs Dispositions intellectuelles et morales de l'Homme et des Animaux par la Configuration de leur Têtes.* Par F. J. Gall et G. Spurzheim (other works of reference give Spurzheim's initials as J. K.).

55 *Edinburgh Review*, xxv (1815), 227. For a rival account, equally hostile but somewhat less lively, see *Quarterly Review*, xiii (1815).

56 *Edinburgh Review*, xxv (1815), 251.

57 *Headlong Hall*, ch. iv, 'The Grounds': i. 30.

58 The connection between Cranium's lecture and Stevens's is

established by Joukovsky, op. cit.

59 *Headlong Hall* appeared in December 1815, though it has 1816 on the titlepage. No information about the date of its composition has survived: Brett-Smith assumes that it was written in the summer and autumn of 1815, while Peacock was living at Marlow (Halliford edition: i. lxii–lxiv).

60 *Critical Review*, cxlii (January 1816), 70.

61 Northrop Frye, *Anatomy of Criticism*, Princeton, 1957, p. 309.

3 *Satire and Romance*: Melincourt

1 *Odes to his Royal Highness the Prince Regent, His Imperial Majesty the Emperor of Russia and His Majesty the King of Prussia, 1814.* This publication was followed by *Carmen Triumphale, for the commencement of the year 1814*, which is in the same vein.

2 See pp. 112–13.

3 See pp. 90, 117–19.

4 See pp. 148–9.

5 See p. 117.

6 William Cobbett, *Political Register*, 2 November 1816 (from 'Address to the Journeymen and Labourers': this was the first number to be simultaneously published as 'twopenny trash').

7 *Courier*, Letter no. 1, 7 December 1809: *Essays on his Times*, ed. Sara Coleridge, 3 vols, 1850, ii. 594. Cf. Wordsworth's 'On the Convention of Cintra', which first appeared in the *Courier*, December 1809, and Coleridge's 'Letters on the Spaniards', written December 1809, which were originally intended as an accompaniment to Wordsworth's essay.

8 The first 8 vols, published in Paris 1809 and not yet translated from French, were reviewed in the *Quarterly Review*, vii (June 1812), 357–374. *De la littérature du Midi de l'Europe* was reviewed in the *Quarterly Review*, xi (April 1814); its English translation (by Hazlitt) in the *Edinburgh Review*, xxv (1815). Consideration of the later literary volumes led to comparison with the *Italian Republics*, which was agreed to be the greater book.

9 See pp. 110–12.

10 *Quarterly Review*, vii (June 1812), 362–3.

11 Ibid., pp. 357–8.

12 Cf. M. Butler, 'One Man in his Time', *E in C*, xxviii (1978), 52–60.

13 Evidence for these dates has been recently surveyed in the article on the 'Ahrimanes' fragments by Eleanor L. Nicholes, *Shelley and his Circle*, ed. K. N. Cameron, Oxford, 1963, iii. 211–44.

14 'Shelley and Ahrimanes', *MLQ*, iii (1942), 295.
15 C. P. Brand dates the heyday of Italian literary influence in England, and the popularity of Italian as a language, from 1815 to 1830 (*Italy and the English Romantics*, Cambridge, 1957, ch. 1). But girls were often taught Italian in fashionable schools in the second half of the eighteenth century, and boys who knew Latin well found it easy to pick up a reading knowlege. Both Peacock and Shelley taught themselves in this way.
16 See J. Hoole (trans.), *Jerusalem Delivered*, 2 vols, 1797, i. viii–ix.
17 *Melincourt*, ch. xv, 'The Library': ii. 163–4.
18 Ibid., ch. vi, 'Sir Oran Haut-ton': ii. 63. According to the romance, English versions of which include a ballad in Percy's *Reliques*, twin brothers were abandoned in the woods in infancy. Valentine is brought up at the court of King Pippin or Peppin, while Orson grows up in a bear's den to become a wild man of the woods, until he is defeated and tamed by Valentine. As companions they take the castle of a wicked giant, where they rescue an imprisoned lady who proved to be a queen and their mother. Peacock lightly finds equivalents in *Melincourt* for many essentials of this story.
19 *Melincourt*, ch. x, 'The Torrent': ii. 109, and ch. xlii, 'Conclusion': ii. 453–4.
20 Cf. the *Shorter Oxford Dictionary*'s definition of satyr:

> 1. *Myth*. One of a class of woodland gods or demons, in form partly human and partly bestial, supposed to be the companions of Bacchus; also *fig.* as the type of lustfulness. 2. A kind of ape ...; in mod. use, the orang outang; *Simia satyrus* (rare) late ME.

21 *The Excursion*, ix. 338–9.
22 Ibid., ix. 336–62.
23 Ibid., iv. 917–94.
24 Ibid., ix. 351–3.
25 Ibid., Preface to the edition of 1814.
26 Entry for 14 September 1814: *Mary Shelley's Journal*, ed. F. L. Jones, Oklahoma, 1947, p. 15.
27 Peacock, *Memoirs of P. B. Shelley*: viii. 100.
28 Mary Shelley, *Frankenstein*, 1818, ch. xviii.
29 PBS to TLP, 17 July 1816: Shelley's *Letters*, i. 489.
30 Ibid., i. 490.
31 See p. 316, n. 41.
32 *Melincourt*, ch. xxiv, 'The Barouche': ii. 264.
33 Ibid., ch. xiv, 'The Cottage': ii. 150.
34 Ibid., ch. xxxv, 'The Rustic Wedding': ii. 366.
35 Peacock was not in fact to praise Malthus in print again. A year or

two later, at least, Shelley was to declare himself passionately against him: allusively in the first book of *Prometheus Unbound* (1818–19), more coarsely with the 'sow-gelder' of *Swellfoot the Tyrant* (1819). Peacock was sending *The Political Register* to Shelley in Italy, and its animus against Malthus was very marked at this period.

36 The intellectual relationship between Monboddo and Rousseau, and the wider, more moralistic aspects of Monboddo's contribution to eighteenth-century controversy, were illuminatingly discussed by Dr Robert Wokler, of the Department of Government of Manchester University, in a paper delivered at Oxford in May 1978.

37 Johnson visited him on his Scottish travels in 1773, as Boswell records in his *Tour to the Hebrides*. See Boswell's *Life of Johnson*, etc., ed. Birkbeck Hill, rev. ed. L. F. Powell, 6 vols, Oxford, 1950, especially ii. 74 ff and v. 74 ff. The outline in A. Chalmers's *Biographical Dictionary*, 1813, vii. 389–93, makes use of other sources, which it cites, including the *Memoirs of Lord Kames* by A. F. Tytler (Lord Woodhouselee).

38 A. F. Tytler, *Memoirs of Lord Kames*, 2nd ed., 3 vols, Edinburgh, 1814, i. 249n.

39 Cf. Forester's dispute with Sir Telegraph Paxarett on keeping a carriage, particularly in *Melincourt*, ch. xxiv, 'The Barouche': ii. 271–4.

40 A. Chalmers, *Biographical Dictionary*, 1813, vii. 390.

41 E.g., Monboddo, *Antient Metaphysics*, 6 vols, 1779– , i. viii, and *The Origin and Progress of Language*, 6 vols, 1773– , i. 161 ff. Shelley's poetry written about the time of *Melincourt*, e.g., 'Hymn to Intellectual Beauty', 1816, sounds as though it might have been influenced by this side of Monboddo's thought. For hints of it in Forester's speeches, see ch. xl, 'The Hopes of the World'.

42 *Melincourt*, ch. xvi, 'The Symposium': ii. 173.

43 Ibid, ch. xxi, 'The City of No-Vote': ii. 228–9.

44 Scott, '*Emma*', *Quarterly Review*, xiv (1815), 200.

45 *Melincourt*, ch. ii, 'Fashionable Arrivals': ii. 21–3.

46 Burke, *Reflections on the Revolution in France*, *Works*, London, 1826, v. 149.

47 Byron, *Childe Harold*, Addition to the Preface, London, 1813.

48 *Melincourt*, ch. viii, 'The Spirit of Chivalry': ii. 85.

49 Ch. xxxix, 'Mainchance Villa', alludes in a footnote to a speech of Canning's of 29 January 1817, and pervasively to an article in an issue of the *Quarterly* which, although dated October 1816, in fact appeared on 11 February 1817. (H. and H. C. Shine, *Quarterly Review under Gifford*, Chapel Hill, N.C., 1949, p. 53.) In addition, Coleridge's *Statesman's Manual*, satirised in ch. xxxi ('Cimmerian

Lodge') was not published until December 1816. For a fuller
discussion of this problem, see N. A. Joukovsky, 'A Critical Edition
of TLP's *Headlong Hall* and *Nightmare Abbey*', thesis submitted at
Oxford, 1970, MS DPhil. d. 5154.

50 Biographical Introduction, Halliford edition: i. lxix–lxxi.

51 For a discussion of authors' consciousness of volume in the period,
and printers' frequent non-co-operation, see M. Butler, 'Disregarded
Designs: Jane Austen's Sense of the Volume', *Annual Report of the
Jane Austen Society*, 1978.

52 It is tempting to think the electoral 'battle' may have been suggested
by the abortive assault on Jerusalem which similarly occupies the two
central books of Tasso's twenty-book epic. But in general Peacock's
structure seems more indebted to the commoner division of classic
epic into twelve books: though the electoral centre-piece stands apart,
each volume of *Melincourt* seems otherwise to divide into four distinct
sections.

53 Cf. for example the openings of chapters xxxvii to xl – 'The
mountain-roads being now buried in snow, they were compelled, on
leaving Mainchance Villa, to follow the most broad and beaten track,
and they entered on a turnpike road which led in the direction of the
sea.' (Ch. xl, 'The Hopes of the World': ii. 420).

54 *Lay Sermons*, ed. Derwent Coleridge, 3rd ed., 1852, p. 23.

55 Ibid., pp. 15–16.

56 Ibid., p. 28.

57 Ibid., p. 7.

58 Ibid., p. 110.

59 Quoted in J. Colmer, *Coleridge: Critic of Society*, Oxford, 1959, p. 133.

60 *Lay Sermons*, p. 116.

61 Ibid., p. 16.

62 Ibid., p. 116.

63 *Melincourt*, ch. xxxvi, 'The Vicarage': ii. 365–6.

64 Ibid., ch. xxxi, 'Cimmerian Lodge': ii. 338–9. Cf. *Lay Sermons*, op.
cit., pp. 73–4; p. 22; p. 82 (notably the last, where Coleridge
exclaims, 'Man of Understanding, canst thou command the stone to
lie, canst thou bid the flower bloom, where thou hast placed in thy
classification?').

65 *Edinburgh Review*, xxvii (December 1816), 454.

66 Ibid., p. 451.

67 Carl Van Doren, *The Life of Thomas Love Peacock*, London and New
York (1911), reprinted 1966, p. 102.

68 *Melincourt*, ch. xxxix, 'Mainchance Villa': ii. 396.

69 E. Halévy, *History of the English People in the Nineteenth Century ii: the
Liberal Awakening*, 1961, p. 20 n 3.

70 *Selections from Cobbett's Political Works*, ed. John M. Cobbett and James P. Cobbett, 6 vols, 1835–7, iv. 507.
71 *Quarterly Review*, xvi (October 1816), 257–8.
72 Ibid., p. 255.
73 Ibid., p. 272.
74 H. and H. C. Shine, *The Quarterly Review under Gifford: Identification of Contributors, 1809–1824*, Chapel Hill, 1949. Hazlitt attacked Southey by name for the article, in the *Examiner* of 30 March 1817.
75 *Melincourt*, ch. v, 'Sugar': ii. 41–51.
76 Ibid., ch. xxxix, 'Mainchance Villa': ii. 403.
77 Ibid., ii. 276.
78 Ibid., ii. 273–5.
79 Cf. Shelley's description of the people of Switzerland, PBS to TLP, Chamonix, 23 and 25 July, 1816: Shelley's *Letters*, i. 358 and 360.
80 *Melincourt*, ch. xxxvii, 'The Mountains': ii. 386–7.
81 Ibid, ch. xl, 'The Hopes of the World': ii. 422.
82 Ibid, ii. 428. But cf. Carl Dawson, who thinks that the attitude of passive acceptance which both philosophers here reject is actually advocated by Peacock. Dawson claims that the old man in 'The Deserted Mansion' speaks for the author when he says 'I eats my beef-cake and drinks my ale, and lets the world slide' (ii. 350). 'Despite the ... political tirades, this essentially is the resolution in *Melincourt*' (*His Fine Wit*, London, 1970, p. 205).
83 *The Four Ages of Poetry*: viii. 17–18.
84 *Melincourt*, ch. xl, 'The Hopes of the World': ii. 430–1.
85 Ibid., ch. v, 'Sugar': ii. 43 ff., and ch. xxiv, 'The Barouche': ii. 262 ff.
86 Ibid., ch. xvi, 'The Symposium': ii. 177 ff.
87 See pp. 111, 199–200, and Peacock's review of Moore's *The Epicurean*, *Westminster Review*, viii (1827): ix. 3–67.
88 *Monthly Magazine* (1 June 1817), 453. Cf. the admiration, mildly tempered, of the *Monthly Review*, (July 1817), 322–3.
89 *British Critic* (October 1817), 430–42.
90 PBS to Leigh Hunt, Marlow, 8 December 1816: Shelley's *Letters*, i. 518.
91 PBS to TLP, Pisa, 8 November 1820: Shelley's *Letters*, ii. 244.
92 PBS to TLP, Ravenna, [? 10] August 1821: Shelley's *Letters*, ii. 331.
93 PBS to Harriet Shelley, Troyes, 13 August 1814: Shelley's *Letters*, i. 392. See also p. 12.
94 PBS to T. J. Hogg, 26 November 1813: Shelley's *Letters*, i. 380.
95 PBS to Mary Godwin, 4 November 1814: Shelley's *Letters*, i. 418. Cf. PBS's observation to Maria Gisborne, Florence, 13 or 14 October 1819, that TLP 'is a nursling of the exact and superficial school in

poetry' (Shelley's *Letters*, ii. 126). This is an observation about Peacock's critical ideas, and is lightly made, without the distinct personal disapproval of the earlier comments.

96 PBS to Leigh Hunt, Marlow, 8 December 1816: Shelley's *Letters*, i. 518.

4 *The Critique of Romanticism:* Nightmare Abbey

1 A total of five reviews of the first edition have been traced by Bill Read and W. S. Ward (see Bibliography). Among the journals which noticed the book, the liberal *Monthly Review* was quite widely read. Otherwise, it is noticeable that Peacock failed to attract the attention of leading reviews, and that in the first phase of his career his reputation did not grow. *Headlong Hall* had been discussed in the respected Nonconformist *Eclectic Review*, and *Melincourt* in the Tory organ, *The British Critic*.

2 Timothy Webb, *The Violet in the Crucible: Shelley and Translation*, Oxford, 1976, p. 65.

3 Ibid., quoted p. 66.

4 PBS to T. J. Hogg, 8 May 1817: Shelley's *Letters* i. 542.

5 Ibid., editor's note. The dates are significant, for Peacock was writing *Rhododaphne* that November, and Mary transcribed it for him in early December. See pp. 106–7.

6 PBS to T. J. Hogg, 6 July 1817: Shelley's *Letters*, i. 545.

7 Hunt, *Autobiography*, ch. xv.

8 Hunt to Hogg, 22 January 1818: ed. W. S. Scott, *New Shelley Letters*, London 1948, p. 106. Hunt also wrote two essays on ancient religion: 'On the Household Gods of the Ancients', *Indicator*, 10 November 1819, and 'The Spirit of Ancient Mythology', *Indicator*, 19 January 1820.

9 The possibilities are reviewed in N. A. Joukovsky, 'A Critical Edition of TLP's *Headlong Hall* and *Nightmare Abbey*', thesis submitted at Oxford, 1970, MS D Phil. d. 5154: Appendix C, 'The Date of "Calidore" '. Whether or not Peacock planned to write it earlier, it seems likely that he actually did write it in March 1818. On 20 March 1818 he wrote to Hogg, 'I intend to pass the interval between Easter & Christmas ... in writing a novel of which the scene will be in London' (Scott, op. cit., p. 109; and cf. p. 112). On 2 April 1818, however, Peacock wrote to Shelley, by now in Italy, to tell him of his plan to write *Nightmare Abbey* instead (see p. 329 n. 69).

10 It is a comic version of the situation in the abandoned epic 'Ahrimanes'. See p. 66.

11 Halliford edition: viii. 334.

12 See p. 268.

13 *Rhododaphne*, Canto III: vii. 30. The standard view of the poem, as unsatisfactory and lacking meaning, is expressed by Douglas Bush, *Mythology and the Romantic Tradition*, New York, 1937, p. 113.

14 Ed. D. L. Clark, *Shelley's Prose*, Albuquerque, 1966, p. 311.

15 See p. 115.

16 Especially in his poem 'The Nymphs', for which see pp. 294–5.

17 Quoted in W. J. Bate, *John Keats*, Cambridge, Mass., 1963, p. 265.

18 René Wellek, *A History of Modern Criticism: The Romantic Age*, London, 1955, p. 5.

19 Ibid., p. 1.

20 See pp. 64–5.

21 *Edinburgh Review*, xxii (October 1813), 213.

22 Ibid., 232. For Peacock on the subject of Epicureanism, see pp. 95–7 and p. 325 n. 87.

23 *Edinburgh Review*, xxii (October 1813), 234–5.

24 Ibid., 235.

25 The second *Lay Sermon* has an extended diatribe against the demagogues on the English scene. Cobbett and Hazlitt, among others, are readily identifiable. *Lay Sermons*, ed. D. Coleridge, 3rd edn., 1852, pp. 155–87.

26 Ibid., p. 191.

27 R. Wellek, *Kant in England*, London, 1935, p. 135.

28 Unfortunately, the editor of the most convenient recent English edition of the *Biographia* (Dent, Everyman), Mr George Watson, has left out this chapter, as a makeweight and no part of Coleridge's original intention. This is a pity in the present context, since Peacock's satire of Coleridge turns upon the latter's admiration for one kind of German literature, and rejection of another.

29 *Biographia Literaria*, ed. J. Shawcross, Oxford, 1907, i. 99.

30 *Nightmare Abbey*, ch. vii: iii. 74.

31 Ibid., ch. vi: iii. 49–50. For Coleridge's praise of enthusiasm, and of geometry, see *Lay Sermons*, op.cit., pp. 24–5 and pp. 108–9.

32 *Nightmare Abbey*, ch. viii: iii. 74.

33 Ibid., iii. 73.

34 H. House, *Listener*, xlii (8 December 1949), 998.

35 *Nightmare Abbey*, ch. vi: iii. 51–3. Cf. *Biographia Literaria*, ii. 192–3. For further verbal resemblances between the two works, see Coral Ann Howells, '*Biographia Literaria* and *Nightmare Abbey*', *NQ* (February 1969), 50–1.

36 Peacock's method is illustrated by Flosky's remark in ch. xii (iii. 120), 'I can safely say I have seen too many ghosts myself to believe in their

external existence'. After one of his Shakespeare lectures, Coleridge, asked by a lady if he believed in ghosts, replied, 'No, Madam, I have seen too many to believe in them' (C. R. Leslie, *Autobiographical Recollections*, 1860: quoted Brett-Smith, Halliford edition: lxxxvii).

37 'An Essay on Fashionable Literature': viii. 289. For the authorship of the review, see E. Schneider, 'The Unknown Critic of *Christabel*', *PMLA*, lxx (1955), 417–32.

38 *Examiner* (2 June 1816), 348–9.

39 *Edinburgh Review*, xxvii (December 1816) and xxviii (August 1817).

40 *Examiner* for 6, 13 and 20 April, 1817. The reference is not clearly to Coleridge but to the author of an anonymous anti-Bourbon book. Allusions to Coleridge are, however, frequent.

41 *Yellow Dwarf*, 21 February 1818, in reply to note in *Courier* of 9 February 1818: *Centenary Edition of Hazlitt's Works*, ed. P. P. Howe, 1930–4, xi. 418.

42 *Nightmare Abbey*, ch. i: iii. 10–11.

43 *Mill on Bentham and Coleridge*, ed. F. R. Leavis, London, 1950, p. 40; cf. also pp. 102–3.

44 Though Peacock's own catalogue of Byron's recent imitators seems full enough in *Nightmare Abbey*, he might for example have added Scott's *Black Dwarf* (December 1816). Other remarkable instances of the fashion had still to appear. *The Bride's Tragedy* (1822), by the nineteen-year-old Thomas Lovell Beddoes, was as black and bilious as Mr Flosky could have desired.

45 *Nightmare Abbey*, ch. viii: iii. 72.

46 Ibid., iii. 48–50 (quoted p. 115).

47 Ibid., ch. v: iii. 39.

48 See below, p. 298.

49 *Nightmare Abbey*, ch. xi: iii. 103.

50 Ibid., iii. 105.

51 Ibid., ch. v: iii. 38.

52 PBS to Godwin: Shelley's *Letters*, i. 569.

53 *Mandeville*, 3 vols, London, 1817, i. 47–8.

54 Ibid. i. 50–1. Peacock's use of detail from Godwin is too frequent to list, though naturally much appears in the descriptive first chapter. Some points are too subtle to read like parody; Flosky's wilful preference for a candle at noon (ch. viii: iii. 72–3) is based on actual necessity at Mandeville's house, which 'for a great part of the year' was 'involved in thick fogs and mists' (i. 50).

55 *Mandeville*, i. 111; cf. *Nightmare Abbey*, ch. i: iii. 8.

56 *Nightmare Abbey*, ch. viii: iii. 77, where Mr Flosky tells Marionetta that the most approved methods of getting at secrets 'as recommended both theoretically and practically in philosophical novels, are

eavesdropping at key-holes, picking the locks of chest and desk ...'.

57 In *Political Justice*, 1793, Godwin argued that *because* society determines character, it is necessary to change society in order to achieve man's moral advancement – a much more positive creed.

58 See e.g. [J. Mackintosh] 'Godwin's Lives of Milton's Nephews', *Edinburgh Review*, xxv (June 1815), 489.

59 See p. 72.

60 *Nightmare Abbey*, ch. v: iii. 41.

61 Ibid., ch. ii: iii. 14. Cf. T. J. Hogg, *Memoirs of Prince Alexy Haimatoff*, 1813, p. 173.

62 *Nightmare Abbey*, ch. ii: iii. 17.

63 Ibid., ch. iii: iii. 24.

64 See p. 115. The character and role of Mr Listless, and indeed the syllogistic effect of the structure of *Nightmare Abbey*, are further elucidated by comparing them with the 'Essay on Fashionable Literature': see p. 284.

65 E.g. Carl Van Doren, op. cit., pp. 118–20, and Halliford edition: i. lxxxvi.

66 *Nightmare Abbey*, ch. iii: iii. 21.

67 See p. 284.

68 'We shall see whether Thalia or Melpomene – whether the Allegra or the Penserosa – will carry off the symbol of victory', *Nightmare Abbey*, ch. iv: iii. 33. For the use of a comparable idea in *Gryll Grange*, see pp. 254–6.

69 PBS to TLP, 20 April 1818: Shelley's *Letters*, ii. 6 (see p. 326). It is worth noting that Peacock's earlier plan, if it was 'Sir Calidore', has much in common with *Nightmare Abbey*. A joyous Greek civilisation, pagan and Bacchic, is clearly to be compared with the joyless Christian England, represented in the surviving chapters by the shipwrecked missionary. It even seems possible that scenes of gloomy London life (Mr Toobad? Mr Listless?) originally intended for 'Sir Calidore' have been utilised in *Nightmare Abbey*.

70 A. W. Schlegel, *Dramatic Art and Literature*, trans. J. Black, 1815: Bohn's Standard Library ed., London, 1902, pp. 24–5.

71 PBS to William Godwin, 7 December 1817: Shelley's *Letters*, i. 574.

72 PBS to Byron, 17 December 1817: Shelley's *Letters*, i. 584.

73 PBS to Byron, 9 July 1817: Shelley's *Letters*, i. 547. But cf. PBS's later letter, of 24 September 1817, where he says it is Leigh Hunt's view that *Manfred* 'administers to a diseased view of things', and not his own. Shelley's *Letters*, i. 557.

74 PBS to TLP, 25 July 1818: Shelley's *Letters*, ii. 27.

75 PBS to Leigh Hunt, 2 March 1811: Shelley's *Letters*, i. 54.

76 PBS to TLP, ?20–1 June 1819: Shelley's *Letters*, ii. 98.
77 See pp. 280–3.
78 Robert Forsyth, *Principles of Moral Science*, Edinburgh, 1805, i. 290.
79 Ibid., pp. 291–3.
80 Cf. his fairly practical and moderate *Proposals for Putting Reform to the Vote*, and his ability, consistently, to write practical business letters.
81 See p. 17.
82 Asturias is a wayward, contradictory character, rather like Cranium in *Headlong Hall* (see above, pp. 54–5). Joukovsky (op. cit., pp. 213–24, 226–8) illustrates very fully how his speeches anthologise examples of gullibility and superstition in a number of eighteenth century scientists.
83 *Nightmare Abbey*, ch. vii: iii. 66.
84 Ibid., ch. xi: iii. 105–10.
85 Ibid., iii. 106. Mr Sackbut, Southey, makes no direct appearance in *Nightmare Abbey*, but as Poet-Laureate recurs shadowily as an allusion. He is needless to say the 'honest friend' of Mr Flosky (iii. 106).
86 *Memoirs of Shelley*: viii. 81–2.
87 Ibid., p. 83.
88 Paulina Salz, 'Peacock's Use of Music in his Novels', *JEGP*, liv (1955), 370.
89 Ibid., p. 372.
90 'Musical Glasses of Peacock', quoted in Salz, op. cit., p. 370.
91 A. H. Able, *George Meredith and Thomas Love Peacock*, 1933: quoted in Salz, op. cit., p. 375.
92 Ibid., p. 376.
93 See p. 220 and pp. 254–5.
94 PBS to TLP, ?20–21 June 1819: Shelley's *Letters*, ii. 98.
95 Quoted in R. Wellek, *A History of Modern Criticism: The Romantic Age*, London, 1955, p. 10.

5 *The Good Old Times*: Maid Marian *and* The Misfortunes of Elphin

1 Halliford edition: viii. 43. Fifteen of the eighteen chapters were written this autumn, before he joined the India House in January 1819. The remaining three were added shortly before publication in 1822. See Peacock's prefatory note to the first edition, which appears between the title-page and the text.
2 TLP to PBS, 29 November 1818: quoted in Halliford edition: i. xci.
3 *Common Sense*, (first published 1776), ed. R. Carlile in Paine's *Political and Miscellaneous Works*, 1819, i. 16.

4 C. Hill's summary of Paine's argument in 'The Norman Yoke', *Puritanism and Revolution*, 1968, p. 106, an article which most usefully surveys the long radical campaign against the Norman kings and the idea of legitimacy – though it omits *Maid Marian*.

5 E.g., in his *Romische Geschichte*, 3 vols, 1827–8 (though the first two volumes were originally published in 1812), Niebuhr brought ideas of race and a new understanding of myth to his interpretation of the early history of the Roman republic.

6 For Sismondi and his favourable reception, see pp. 64–5. The English history classic of these years was Henry Hallam's *A View of the State of Europe during the Middle Ages*, 1818, which has been variously described as soundly Whiggish, Tory, and superior to the polemical tendency of the period.

7 See pp. 286–95; and cf. Shelley's historical perspective in *A Philosophical View of Reform* [1819], as well as in historical plays like *The Cenci* and *Charles I*.

8 Joseph Ritson, *Robin Hood*, 2 vols, London, 1795, i. vi.

9 Ibid., i. 9.

10 Ibid., i. xi–xii.

11 *Maid Marian*, ch. ix: iii/2.84. (Vol. iii of the Halliford edition contains both *Nightmare Abbey* and *Maid Marian*, just as vol. iv contains *The Misfortunes of Elphin* and *Crotchet Castle*. In each case, pagination of the second novel begins again at p. 1.)

12 Ibid., iii/2.86.

13 See pp. 67–8, 86.

14 *Maid Marian*, ch. xi: iii/2.100.

15 Richard Price (1723–91) preached a famous sermon, 'On the Love of Our Country', at the Meeting-house in the Old Jewry on 4 November 1789, which rejoiced at the Fall of the Bastille – 'I could almost say, Lord, now lettest Thou thy servant depart in peace, for mine eyes have seen Thy salvation' – and advanced the constitutional claims of the people above those of kings. Burke replied with tremendous vehemence in the *Reflections on the Revolution in France* of the following year.

16 *Maid Marian*, ch. xi: iii/2.100–1.

17 Ibid., iii/2.101.

18 Ibid., iii/2.102.

19 See p. 63.

20 *Examiner* (29 September 1816): *Complete Works of William Hazlitt*, Centenary Edition, ed. P. P. Howe, 1933, xix. 164. *The Times*'s chief leader-writer was Dr John Stoddart, 'the Doctor', 1773–1856, the brother of Hazlitt's wife, Sarah. Stoddart's hatred of Napoleon earned him many jibes from his brother-in-law at this time.

21 *Maid Marian*, ch. xviii: iii/2.172–3.
22 Ibid., ch. ii: iii/2.33.
23 Ibid., ch. xi: iii/2.108.
24 Ibid., ch. xvii: iii/2.160.
25 Ibid., iii/2.161–2.
26 Ibid., ch. xviii: iii/2.171.
27 See pp. 237 ff.
28 Carl Van Doren, op. cit., p. 261. See also pp. 238–9.
29 See pp. 104–9, 302–3, and T. Webb, *Shelley: a Voice not Understood*, Manchester, 1977, especially pp. 171 ff, 231 ff.
30 Diane Johnson, *The True History of the First Mrs Meredith and Other Lesser Lives*, London, 1973, p. 199.
31 The lady of the castle in ch. xiv wears a miniature of her absent husband. Drinkers, passim, favour Madeira, though these islands were not discovered by the Portuguese for another century. Peacock's nineteenth-century editor, Richard Garnett, annotates this type of 'error', apparently under the impression that it is committed through ignorance.
32 Both cited in Halliford edition: i. cxxxvii. Strachey had a special insight into the antiquarian side of Peacock: his father Edward Strachey (see p. 15) was an Assistant in the Examiner's Department at the India House until his death in 1831, a genial and satirical man in Peacock's own style, and a great lover of Chaucer. See p. 335 n. 3.
33 Herbert Wright, 'The Associations of T. L. Peacock with Wales', *Essays and Studies*, xii (1926), 34–46, and David Garnett in the notes to his edition of TLP's novels, 1948.
34 *Westminster Review*, viii (1827), 351: ix. 3.
35 Both quoted in John Cannon, *Parliamentary Reform, 1640–1832*, Cambridge, 1972, pp. 182, 245.
36 Both quoted in E. Halévy, *History of the English People in the Nineteenth Century*, ii: *The Liberal Awakening*, 1961, p. 262 n.
37 'Hallam's *Constitutional History of England*', *Edinburgh Review*, xlviii (1828), 96–169.
38 Ibid., xlvi (1827), 264–7; see p. 161.
39 It was reviewed on the whole respectfully, especially in *The Athenaeum*, which referred to the esteem in which Peacock was held by the thinking portion of the reading public: the remainder being put off, the reviewer suggested, by the element of 'philosophical speculation' in his books (*Athenaeum* (6 May 1829), 276–8). But *Misfortunes of Elphin* did not go into a second edition and was not included in the one-volume Bentley's Standard Novels edition of Peacock in 1837.

40 'The Present Administration', *Edinburgh Review*, xlvi (1827), 264–7.
41 *Misfortunes of Elphin*, ch. iii: iv. 27.
42 Ibid., ch. ii, 'The Drunkenness of Seithenyn': iv. 15.
43 Ibid., ch. xi, 'The Heroes of Dinas Vawr': iv. 97.
44 *Speeches of George Canning*, ed. R. Therry, 6 vols, 1828, iv. 334–43.
45 Ibid., p. 356.
46 Ibid., p. 373.
47 See also p. 167
48 *Misfortunes of Elphin*, ch. ii, 'The Drunkenness of Seithenyn': iv. 15–17.
49 See pp. 60, 91–2, 147.
50 *Misfortunes of Elphin*, ch. ii, 'The Drunkenness of Seithenyn': iv. 10.
51 Ibid., ch. vii, 'The Huntings of Maelgon': iv. 63–4.
52 Ibid., iv. 63.
53 Ibid., iv. 66.
54 Ibid., ch. xiv, 'The Right of Might': iv. 125. Cf. Canning's speech defending England's policy of *de facto* recognition of the S. American republics, on the ground that it was a quite different issue for England than for the mother country, Spain. 'The other state [England] simply acknowledges the fact, or rather its opinion of the fact ... there is nothing more plain and easy than the act of acknowledging a fact.' (Therry, op. cit., v. 299–300).
55 *Misfortunes of Elphin*, ch. xiv; 'The Might of Right': iv. 131.
56 James Mill, *Essays on Government, Justice, Liberty of the Press and the Law of Nations*, London, n.d.
57 Mill, *Essays on Government*, etc.: 'On the Law of Nations', p. 4.
58 Ibid., p. 8.
59 See *Works*, vii. 244–5. Each squib, 'A Speech in Embryo' and 'When John of Zisca went to Kingdom Come', lampoons an anti-Catholic speaker during the Parliamentary debates on Emancipation in February 1829.
60 *Misfortunes of Elphin*, ch. vi: iv. 54–60.
61 See p. 157.
62 Preface, p. vi.
63 *Misfortunes of Elphin*, ch. vi, 'The Education of Taliesin': iv. 56, 61.
64 Ibid., ch. xi, 'The Heroes of Dinas Vawr': iv. 89.
65 Articles on 'Moore's *Fables for the Holy Alliance*' and 'Vocal Music', *Westminster Review*, i (January 1824): quoted G. L. Nesbitt, *Benthamite Reviewing*, New York, 1934, pp. 100–1. Nesbitt has an excellent discussion of the controversy over the utilitarians' hostility to literature, pp. 96–127.
66 For Peacock's criticism, see pp. 283 ff.
67 Review of Washington Irving's *Tales of a Traveller*, *Westminster*

Review, ii (October 1824), 334 ff: quoted in Nesbitt, op. cit., pp. 102–3.

68 'The Utilitarian Controversy', the *Atlas*, 19 July 1829: quoted in Halliford edition: ix. 402–3. This appendix surveys Peacock's career as an opera-critic, which belongs to the 1830s. See E. D. Mackerness, 'Peacock's Musical Criticism', *The Wind and the Rain*, iv (1948), 177–87.

69 For Peacock's discussion of this topic with Shelley in 1820–1, see pp. 286–95.

70 *Misfortunes of Elphin*, ch. i, 'The Prosperity of Gwaelod': iv. 6.

71 Ibid., ch. ix, 'The Songs of Diganwy'; iv. 80–1. Cf. Edward Davies, *The Mythology and the Rites of the British Druids*, 1809, p. 535.

72 *Misfortunes of Elphin*, ch. vi, 'The Education of Taliesin': iv. 52. Peacock used this Welsh slogan – Y Gwir yn Erbyn y Byd – as an epigraph when he came to write his defence of Harriet Shelley (see pp. 6–7).

73 *Misfortunes of Elphin*, ch. xv, 'The Circle of the Bards': iv. 144.

74 Ibid., ch. vi, 'The Education of Taliesin': iv. 57.

75 Ibid., ch. xii, 'The Splendour of Caer Lleon': iv. 102.

76 *Misfortunes of Elphin*, London (Macmillan), 1897, p. xiii.

77 *Misfortunes of Elphin*, ch. i, 'The Prosperity of Gwaelod': iv. 9. Cf. Canning's speech on the constitution, quoted above, p. 164.

78 See pp. 215 ff.

79 Ch. vi, 'The Education of Taliesin', and more specifically ch. xii, 'The Splendour of Caer Lleon': iv. 111–12.

80 Ibid., ch. vi, 'The Education of Taliesin': iv. 51 and 59–60.

81 Carlyle to J. S. Mill, 24 September 1833: *Letters of Thomas Carlyle to John Stuart Mill, John Sterling and Robert Browning*, ed. A. Carlyle, 1923, p. 71.

82 Probably 'Sir Calidore'; see pp. 105–6.

6 The March of Mind: Crotchet Castle

1 TLP reviewed Moore's *Letters and Journals of Lord Byron*, 1830, and took the opportunity to associate with it Hunt's *Lord Byron and Some of his Contemporaries* (1828), both men having proved in his view 'varieties of the small Boswell or eavesdropping genus.' *Westminster Review*, xii (1830): ix. 76. See p. 6.

2 Benjamin Collins Brodie (1783–1862) was professor of Comparative Anatomy and Physiology at the Royal College of Surgeons. He was created a baronet in 1834. Maria Edgeworth was told the tale of his experiments with the cat when she stayed with Joanna Baillie in

Hampstead. (ME to Lucy Edgeworth, 12 January 1822: Christina Colvin (ed.), *Maria Edgeworth: Letters from England*, Oxford, 1971, pp. 316–17.)

3 David Garnett suggests another candidate for Mr Chainmail, the future Sir Edward Strachey, though he admits that he was only eighteen when *Crotchet Castle* was written. It is perfectly possible that one of the Stracheys, the father or the son, expressed views in conversation which matched those attributed to Mr Chainmail by Lady Clarinda (ch. v, 'Characters': iv. 60). Otherwise Meyrick (1783–1848) seems the likelier allusion. He was author of a book on arms and armour (1824) as well as his *History of Cardiganshire* (for which see p. 156). The press noticed it when Meyrick was called in to advise on the arrangement of the royal collection of armour at Windsor; he was also reported to be building a house, Goodrich Court in Herefordshire, to contain his own collection of armour (*Gentleman's Magazine*, xcviii, pt 1 (1828), 463).

4 See pp. 204, 220.

5 A. E. Dyson, *The Crazy Fabric*, London, 1965, pp. 65, 67. Cf. Douglas Hewitt, *The Approach to Fiction*, London, 1972, pp. 158–9 and (rather less hostile) Howard Mills, *Peacock, his Circle and his Age*, Cambridge, 1969, pp. 19–39.

6 Mountstewart E. Grant Duff, *Notes from a Diary*, 1897, i. 60 (entry for 10 November 1853).

7 TLP to Lord Broughton, 13 September 1859 and 1 May 1860: BL Add. MSS. 47225.

8 E. Halévy, *The Growth of Philosophical Radicalism*, trans. M. Morris, 1929, p. 276.

9 See pp. 172–4.

10 'The Present System of Education', *Westminster Review*, iv (July 1825), 147 ff.

11 'Mill on Government', *Edinburgh Review*, xlix (March 1829): reprinted in *Complete Works of Lord Macaulay*, (Albany edition), 12 vols, London, 1898, vii. 329.

12 Ibid., p. 330.

13 Ibid., p. 365.

14 *Crotchet Castle*, ch. x, 'The Voyage Continued': iv/2.127. (In the Halliford edition, *Crotchet Castle* appears in the same volume as *Misfortunes of Elphin*, but pagination begins again at p. 1.)

15 'Southey's *Colloquies*', *Edinburgh Review*, li (January 1830): Macaulay's *Complete Works*, vii. 493.

16 *Crotchet Castle*, ch. iii, 'The Roman Camp': iv/2.37–8.

17 John Ramsay McCulloch (1789–1864) was at this time the *Edinburgh Review*'s most regular contributor on matters connected with

economics, and in 1828 had become London University's first Professor of Political Economy. Peacock's MacQuedy is more than an inflexible bigot: he is also the arch-priest of materialism, a fact probably to be connected with McCulloch's views, particularly his wages fund theory, which he expounded in his *Essay on the ... Rate of Wages and the Condition of the Labouring Classes*, 1826.

18 See p. 45. It has been suggested to me, by the economist Mr David Bensusan Butt, that Mr Crotchet has many points in common with David Ricardo – who was also a London financier of Jewish descent, and became a country squire when he bought Gatcombe Park in Gloucestershire. There is also a story that Ricardo collected statues, but I have not been able to confirm it.

19 *Crotchet Castle*, ch. ii, 'The March of Mind': iv/2.22.

20 Both anecdotes are related in Halliford edition: i. cxxx–i.

21 *Westminster Review*, i (January 1824), 43 ff.

22 'The Education of the People', *Westminster Review*, vii (April 1827), 314–17. Macaulay's strictures on the utilitarian style (see p. 189) may have seemed snobbish, but it would be hard to find an equally badly written passage in the *Edinburgh Review* under Francis Jeffrey.

23 'The Scientific Education of the Upper Classes', *Westminster Review*, ix (April 1828), 361.

24 Brett-Smith produces evidence to show that fragments of the finished book, which have to do with Susannah Touchandgo and her father, already existed in January 1829, a month before *The Misfortunes of Elphin* was published. (*The Paper Money Lyrics*, written in the winter of 1825–6, are trial runs for much more of the satire on financiers.) The last chapter of *Crotchet Castle*, with its topical references to the Capt. Swing riots, cannot have been finished until December 1830 (see p. 220); Halliford edition: i. cxlv.

25 Edward William Grinfield (1785–1864), was minister of Laura Chapel, Bath, and a schoolfellow of De Quincey.

26 *Edinburgh Review*, xlii (April 1825), 206–7. The attribution to Brougham is by the Wellesley Index.

27 Ibid., p. 207.

28 Ibid., pp. 207–8.

29 Ibid., p. 213. The quotation is from p. 14 of Grinfield's pamphlet.

30 *Edinburgh Review*, xlii, 213.

31 Ibid., p. 219.

32 Ibid., xlviii (1828), 526 and 530.

33 See p. 199.

34 *Lay Sermons*, ed. D. Coleridge, 3rd edn, 1852, i: *The Statesman's Manual*, p. 45.

35 *Crotchet Castle*, ch. xviii, 'Chainmail Hall': iv/2.204.

36 'Southey's *Colloquies*', *Edinburgh Review*, li (January 1830): Macaulay's *Complete Works*, 1898, vii. 492.

37 A. Aspinall, *Lord Brougham and the Whig Party*, Manchester 1927, p. 188.

38 *Crotchet Castle*, ch. ii, 'The March of Mind': iv/2.13.

39 Ibid, iv/2.19.

40 Ibid., ch. vi, 'Theories': iv/2.83–4.

41 Ibid., iv/2.76.

42 Ibid., ch. vii, 'The Sleeping Venus': iv/2.95–7. For the last speech, substantially adapted from sentiments of Byron, see pp. 202, 337 n. 49. In real life the lady who sat naked to the sculptor was Napoleon's sister, Pauline Borghese.

43 TLP, 'Moore's *Epicurean*', *Westminster Review*, viii (1827): ix. 67. Though some critics repeatedly use the word 'Epicurean' to describe Folliott (e.g. Carl Van Doren, pp. 194, 201), he could hardly be further from the definition of the term provided by Peacock in this article.

44 Quoted in Halliford edition: i. cxlvii.

45 *Crotchet Castle*, ch. v, 'Characters': iv/2.66.

46 Ibid., ch. vii, 'The Sleeping Venus': iv/2.92.

47 Ibid., ch. iv, 'The Party': iv/2.48–9.

48 Ibid., ch. ii, 'The March of Mind': iv/2.16–17.

49 'Moore's *Letters and Journals of Lord Byron*, Vol. 1,' *Westminster Review*, xii (1830): ix. 69–139.

50 Halévy argues that the typical liberal wishes to make government as complex as possible, preferring a system of checks, safeguards and delays, in order, essentially, to disperse power. Bentham was never a liberal in this sense, but a centralist whose ideal system was an enlightened despotism (Halévy, op. cit., pp. 375 ff.).

51 'Memoirs of Thomas Jefferson', *Westminster Review*, xiii (1830): ix. 179 (written by Jefferson in 1787, and quoted from his *Memoirs*, ed. T. J. Randolph, 4 vols, Charlottesville, Va., 1829, ii. 84).

52 Ibid., ix. 174 (written by Jefferson in 1813, and quoted from his *Memoirs*, iv. 236).

53 Ibid., ix. 185.

54 Carl Dawson, *His Fine Wit*, London, 1970, p. 266.

55 *Crotchet Castle*: iv/2.85.

56 See p. 217, and J. S. Mill, *The Spirit of the Age*, ed. F. A. Hayek, Chicago, 1942, p. 13.

57 See p. 48.

58 Much later in his life, Peacock expressed his great admiration for the charming and lyrical travels of this title by the seventeenth-century French writers, Chapelle and Bachaumont (*Fraser's* (April 1858): x, 91–118. See p. 347 n. 56). Despite a certain sympathy of tone with his

own work, there is no reason to suppose he had this *Voyage* in mind in *Crotchet Castle*.

59 TLP to PBS, 15 December 1818: viii. 211.

60 PBS to TLP, 17 July 1816: Shelley's *Letters*, i. 490.

61 *Crotchet Castle*, ch. v, 'Characters': iv/2.58.

62 Ibid., iv/2.56.

63 Ibid., ch. x, 'The Voyage, Continued': iv/2.130–2.

64 Frances Trollope, *Domestic Manners of the Americans*, 1832.

65 Peacock's picture of Touchandgo's banking exploits in America copies the ideas and occasionally the phrases of Jefferson, who writes of 'a paper promise', 'the dominion which the banking institutions have obtained over the minds of our citizens', and his fear that

> we shall plunge ourselves into inextinguishable debt, and entail on our posterity an inheritance of eternal taxes, which will bring our government and people into the condition of those of England, a nation of pikes and gudgeons, the latter bred merely as food for the former (Halliford edition: ix. 176–7: quoted from Jefferson's *Memoirs*, 1829, iv. 251).

66 *Crotchet Castle*, ch. xi, 'Correspondence': iv/2.138.

67 Ibid., iv/2.137.

68 In his critique of James Mill's *Essay on Government*, Macaulay complains that 'Mr. Mill seems to think the preservation of property is the first and only object.' If this were true, a society in which *life* is perpetually at risk, such as one in which it is the practice to fight 'wanton and sanguinary duels' would equally well 'accomplish the end of its institution'. (*Edinburgh Review*, xlix (1829): Macaulay, *Complete Works*, vii. 332–3.) In *Crotchet Castle* Peacock neatly develops this criticism, by applying it both to his portrait of America, and to J. S. Mill's still orthodox utilitarian views about property.

69 See pp. 215 ff.

70 *Crotchet Castle*, ch. xi, 'Correspondence': iv/2.141.

71 *Edinburgh Review*, xlix (March 1829): Macaulay's *Works*, vii. 353–4.

72 Ibid., ch. xvii, 'The Invitation': iv/2.192.

73 Ibid., ch. v, 'Characters': iv/2.59.

74 Ibid., ch. iii, 'The Roman Camp': iv/2.41.

75 Quoted from Rabelais, *Gargantua*, Bk 5, ch. 7.

76 *Crotchet Castle*, ch. xviii, 'Chainmail Hall': iv/2.195.

77 Ibid.

78 For the designs of J. S. Mill and Macaulay, as well as Carlyle, to write histories of the French Revolution, see p. 180.

79 Social relations at the India House appear to have been somewhat formal and remote – although the evidence for this comes from P. A.

Daniel, who was only a junior in the Examiner's Office during
Peacock's later years there (Van Doren, op. cit., p. 223.)

80 For Peacock's view, see pp. 172–4; Mill's is given in his
Autobiography, first published 1873, Oxford, World's Classics (with
Introduction by H. Laski), 1924, pp. 94–6, 121 ff.

81 See above, p. 190, and Mill's *Autobiography*, pp. 133–6. The younger
Mill had been developing reservations about the sufficiency of a view
of human nature based upon economic self-interest. He wrote an
important essay enshrining his new opinion in 1829 or 1830, 'On the
Definition of Political Economy', though its first publication was in
the *Westminster Review* of October 1836. This article points out that
political economy *is* a science, 'of the laws which regulate the
production, distribution, and consumption of wealth'; the feelings
called forth by other human beings – the affections, the conscience,
etc. – are the province of another portion of mental philosophy,
morals or ethics. *Early Essays of J. S. Mill*, 1844, p. 122 and p. 130.
Peacock's lifelong scepticism about Macaulay's stature was recorded
in a letter to Broughton of 13 January 1860, when he reflected on
Macaulay's interment in Westminster Abbey – 'our greatest
historians [Hume and Gibbon] are not there, because they were the
foes of superstition.' (BL Add. MSS 47225).

82 After writing five opera notices for the *Globe* (under the editorship of
his friend Walter Coulson) in 1830, Peacock seems to have written
fifteen articles on opera for the *Examiner* between February 1831 and
the end of 1834 (see Halliford edition: ix. 405 ff.). In 1834 Peacock
was specially recruited by the Philosophic Radicals for their new
London Review: Mill himself, in asking for Fonblanque's support, told
him that they had everyone worth asking except Bulwer, and he
included Peacock in the list (Van Doren, op. cit., p. 204).

83 'The Epicier', *London Review*, ii (January 1836): Halliford edition: ix.
300–11. See 223–5.

84 J. S. Mill to G. d'Eichthal, 15 May 1829: *Earlier Letters of J. S. Mill*,
ed. Francis E. Mineka, Toronto, 1963, p. 31.

85 Mill to d'Eichthal, 1 March 1831: Mineka, op. cit., p. 71.

86 J. S. Mill, *Autobiography*, Oxford, 1924, pp. 141–2.

87 Ibid., pp. 140–1.

88 Hayek, op. cit., p. 33.

89 J. S. Mill to G. d'Eichthal, 30 November 1831: Mineka, op. cit.,
p. 88.

90 Mill to John Sterling, 20–22 October 1831: Mineka, op. cit.,
pp. 83–4.

91 For Mill's views on the Catholic Church, see his review of 1844 of
Michelet's *History of France* (*Dissertations and Discussions*, 1859, ii.

155–6). He commented later that the Coleridge article made him appear 'too far on the contrary side' from Bentham, and in the *Autobiography* accounts for this by saying that Radicals and Liberals need to have the writers of a different school set before them in the best light (I. W. Mueller, *J. S. Mill and French Thought*, Urbana, Ill., 1956, p. 14).

92 J.S. Mill, *Autobiography*, pp. 144–6.

93 J. R. M. Butler, *The Passing of the Great Reform Bill*, 1914, London, pp. 100–3.

94 *Crotchet Castle*, ch. xviii: iv/2.199.

95 See p. 184.

96 *Crotchet Castle*, ch. xiii, 'The Lake – The Ruin': iv/2.149.

97 Ibid., 146.

98 See p. 216.

99 *Crotchet Castle*, ch. xviii: iv/2.200.

100 Ibid., iv/2.201–2.

101 Ibid., iv/2.204: quoted p. 197.

102 Ibid., iv/2.204.

103 R. Wright, introduction to *Nightmare Abbey and Crotchet Castle*, Harmondsworth, 1969, p. 16. Wright quotes approvingly J. J. Mayoux's opinion that Peacock was incapable of holding a position without perceiving the force of its contrary position (*Un Epicurien anglais*, Paris, 1932, p. 606).

104 Peacock 'The Epicier', *London Review*, ii (January 1836): Halliford edition: ix. 306.

105 Ibid., ix. 292–5.

106 See p. 233.

107 *Crotchet Castle*, ch. xviii: iv/2.208.

108 See p. 222.

109 *Crotchet Castle*, ch. xviii: iv/2.210.

110 Ibid., ch. ix, 'The Voyage': iv/2.114. See pp. 200, 206.

111 See p. 202.

112 *Crotchet Castle*, ch. xvii, 'The Invitation': iv/2.188–191. These pages may have been added at speed, as a link to the last chapter, which cannot have been completed before late December 1830. Publication was on 15 February 1831.

113 TLP's important critical statement on this subject, from the article of 1835, 'French Comic Romances', is quoted pp. 17–18.

114 TLP to Thomas L'Estrange, 11 July 1861: viii. 253.

115 'Letters and Journals of Lord Byron', *Westminster Review*, xii (1830): ix. 128.

7   *The Satisfied Guest:* Gryll Grange

1   'Newark Abbey, August 1842. With a reminiscence of August, 1807': vii. 252–3.
2   Halliford edition: i. xix.
3   E. Stokes, *English Utilitarians in India*, Oxford, 1959, ch. i. Information on Peacock at the India House is hard to come by in printed sources; reminiscences of colleagues and valuable details about the steamship navigation were collected by Van Doren and by Brett-Smith.
4   Carl Van Doren, *The Life of Thomas Love Peacock*, p. 218. For evidence that Peacock was no believer in centralised power, a fact which may be of significance in relation to his attitudes to India, see p. 202.
5   The article on Gastronomy first appeared in *Fraser's*, xliv (December 1851): the dramatic articles in vol. xlv (March and April 1852). The third and last part finally appeared in vol. lvi (October 1857).
6   'Julia Procula' and 'A Story Opening at Chertsey'. For the texts and a discussion of dates, see Halliford edition: viii.
7   'A Story of a Mansion among the Chiltern Hills' and 'Cotswold Chace', both of which contain detail in common with *Gryll Grange*.
8   Peacock, *Memoirs of Shelley*: viii. 40.
9   See p. 318, n. 22.
10 Among these very minor topics of satire, that odd topic of conversation, human hair and its relationship to beauty, may have been suggested by a long, urbane, almost Peacockian review-article in the *Quarterly*, which purported to discuss a medical book about hair and its diseases (*Gryll Grange*, chs. iv and xxix; cf. *Quarterly Review*, xcii (1853), 305 ff.). Dr Opimian is inclined to attribute the blame for some misconceptions on female baldness in ancient times to inferior classical dictionaries: again, a batch of these were reviewed in 1854: *Gryll Grange*, ch. xxix: v. 294–5; *Quarterly Review*, xcv (1854). The electric telegraph was discussed in another article of the same year and ridiculed, as a characteristically overrated modern discovery, in *Gryll Grange*, ch. xi: v. 87–8; cf. *Quarterly Review*, xcv (1854).
11 J. E. Baker, *The Novel and the Oxford Movement*, Princeton, 1932.
12 See above, p. 341 n. 5. The poems, together with evidence for their dates, are published in vol. vii of the Halliford edition.
13 *Gryll Grange*, ch. xiv: v. 135–7. Like all Peacock's satires except *Nightmare Abbey* and *Maid Marian*, *Gryll Grange* is supplied with titles for its individual chapters. About half are in the familiar format ('Misnomers', 'The Seven Sisters', and so on). But the titles of the more conversational chapters are in effect résumés of the topics

covered, and here the running-titles may change several times. In this instance only, therefore, it seems least confusing to give the number of the chapter without its title.

14 Halliford edition: vii. 236.

15 16 August 1857: i. 246. Cf. also the review of sermons and books against the new dogma, *Quarterly Review*, xcvii (June 1855).

16 *Gryll Grange*, ch. ix: v. 78–80.

17 *Saturday Review* (16 March 1861), 274–5.

18 'Translation of An Anapaestic Ode to Christ: Matthew, X, 34': D. Johnson, *The True History of the First Mrs. Meredith and other Lesser Lives*, London, 1973, p. 86. Cf. Halliford edition: viii. 465–6, where Brett-Smith tells the story of the Ode under 'Lost' Works, but omits to give the translation, though he has evidently seen it.

19 Godfrey was author of *Table-moving tested, and proved to be the result of Satanic Agency* (1853), and *Table-turning, or the Devil's Modern Masterpiece* (1853); Gillson of *Table-telling: Disclosures of Satanic Wonders and Prophetic Signs* (1853).

20 *Quarterly Review*, xciii (September 1853), 557.

21 Ibid., p. 556. See pp. 49 ff.

22 See pp. 5–7.

23 *Memoirs of Shelley*: viii. 66–9, 100–4.

24 Broughton to TLP, 2 May 1860: BL. Add MSS 47225, f. 110 (one of two versions of this letter: cf. f. 108).

25 *Gryll Grange*, ch. xxvii: v. 286.

26 Van Doren, op. cit., p. 219.

27 'London Bridge', *Westminster Review*, xiii (October 1830): ix. 193.

28 Ibid., ix. 218.

29 *Gryll Grange*, ch. i: v. 4–5.

30 Ibid., ch. xix: v. 186–7.

31 Eric Robinson, 'Thomas Love Peacock: Critic of Scientific Progress', *Annals of Science*, x (1954), 69–77. My discussion of the satire on science is much indebted to this article.

32 *Gryll Grange*, ch. vii: v. 61.

33 *Athenaeum* (10 February 1866): quoted in Halliford edition: i. ccx.

34 *Recollections of a Long Life*, ed. Lady Dorchester, 1911, v. 184.

35 TLP to J. C. Hobhouse, 6 October 1843.

36 Ibid., 10 December 1856.

37 Broughton to TLP, 22 October 1854.

38 See pp. 215–20, 260–4, 309–11.

39 TLP to Thomas L'Estrange, 26 July 1861: viii. 254.

40 Quoted in W. L. Burn, *The Age of Equipoise*, London, 1964, p. 99.

41 *Gryll Grange*, ch. xix: v. 200–201.

42 Four lectures, 'The Civil Service as a Profession', privately printed, 1861.

43 Quoted in William Foster, *The East India House, its History and Associations*, London, 1924, pp. 220–1.
44 W. R. Greg, *The Way Out*, 1855; cited in Burn, op. cit., p. 144.
45 Dr Opimian compares them with the Pleiades in, for example, ch. vii: v. 43 and 56.
46 *Gryll Grange*, ch. xxii: v. 226.
47 Ibid., ch. vii: v. 55–7.
48 Ibid., v. 55.
49 Ibid., ch. vi: v. 48.
50 Ibid., ch. xx: v. 204.
51 See especially the discussions of *Headlong Hall*, pp. 46 ff, and *Crotchet Castle*, p. 204.
52 *Memoirs of Shelley*: viii. 104.
53 *Gryll Grange*, ch. xv: v. 148.
54 Ibid., ch. xxvi: v. 265.
55 Ibid.
56 Peacock's translation of the Italian play *Gl'Ingannati (The Deceived)*, was published in 1862. It is a dramatisation of what is essentially the *Twelfth Night* story, first performed at Siena in 1531, and interesting for its comparable handling of the two central couples.
57 *Gryll Grange*, ch. xiv: v. 132–3.
58 Ibid., ch. xvi: v. 154.
59 Ibid., v. 155.
60 Ibid., ch. xix: v. 302.
61 Ibid., ch. vi: v. 50.
62 Ibid., ch. xxii: v. 227.
63 Ibid., v. 230.
64 Ibid., v. 231.
65 *Memoirs of Shelley*: viii. 130–1.
66 ll. 85–92. Falconer quotes the first four lines in ch. iii: v. 26.
67 Quoted in W. D. Anderson, *Matthew Arnold and the Classical Tradition*, Ann Arbor, 1965, p. 8.
68 Preface, 1853.
69 'Shelley', *Essays in Criticism*, 2nd ser., 1888: *Complete Prose Works of Matthew Arnold, xi: The Last Word*, ed. R. H. Super, Ann Arbor, 1977, p. 313.
70 Arnold's Merope married Cresphontes, King of Messenia, by whom she had three children. Her husband and two children were murdered by Polyphontes, who attempted to force her to marry him; but Aepytus, her third son, avenged his father by assassinating Polyphontes. For Peacock's entirely different Merope, see p. 252.
71 *Gryll Grange*, ch. xi: v. 92.
72 'Horae Dramaticae, Pts. I and II', *Fraser's*, (March and April, 1852): x. 3–68.

73 See p. 341 n. 6.
74 'Horae Dramaticae, Pt. III', *Fraser's*, (October 1857): x. 78–9.
75 Ibid., x. 78.
76 Ibid., x. 82. For Peacock's dislike of temperance campaigns, see pp. 236–7.
77 Review of Muller and Donaldson's *History of Greek Literature*, *Fraser's*, (March 1859): x. 201.
78 Ibid., x. 203.
79 See pp. 17–18, 223–5.
80 'Horae Dramaticae, Pt. III': x. 76–7.
81 *'A History of Greek Literature'*: x. 212. See chapter 8.
82 Article, 'George Grote', by George Croom Robertson, *Dictionary of National Biography*, viii. 732. Cf. Peacock to Broughton, 20 June 1861, where the former defines the spirit of ancient philosophy: 'The dialogues of Plato and Cicero are made up of discussions among persons who differed in opinion'. They would not 'have been content to pass eternity in the company of persons who merely thought as they did. They were enquirers. They did not profess to have found truth' (BL Add. MSS 47225).
83 'Tales by the Author of *Headlong Hall*', *Edinburgh Review*, lxviii (1839): reprinted in *Peacock: the Satirical Novels: a Casebook*, ed. Lorna Sage, London, 1976, pp. 64–5.
84 *'A History of Greek Literature'*: x. 225–6. The quotation from Muller and Donaldson is from iii. 229.
85 See p. 265.
86 See p. 135.
87 An earlier attempt, probably one and the same with 'Sir Calidore', was abandoned in 1818. See p. 326 n. 9.
88 See pp. 310–12.
89 'Horae Dramaticae, Pt. III': x. 78.

8 The Negative Voice: Peacock as Critic

1 R. Wellek, *Kant in England*, London, 1935, p. 139.
2 See p. 52.
3 H. T. Cockburn, *Life of Jeffrey*, 2 vols, Edinburgh, 1852, i. 1.
4 Reviewed by Jeffrey in *Edinburgh Review*, xviii (May 1811). For fuller consideration of the link between Alison's aesthetics and Jeffrey's, see Byron Guyer, 'Francis Jeffrey's *Essay on Beauty*', HLQ, xiii (1949–50), 71–85, and 'The Philosophy of Francis Jeffrey', MLQ, xi no. 1 (1950), 17–26.

5 Jeffrey to Francis Horner, 26 October 1809: Cockburn, op. cit., i. 195–7.

6 Jeffrey to Horner, 5 January 1813: Cockburn, op. cit., ii. 139.

7 Ibid. Both quoted John Clive, *Scotch Reviewers: the 'Edinburgh Review', 1802–1815*, London, 1956, p. 54.

8 *Westminster Review*, i (January 1824).

9 See pp. 230, 285.

10 See pp. 30–1.

11 See pp. 42–6.

12 See pp. 38–9. Shelley describes Drummond as 'the most acute metaphysical critic of the age'. PBS to the Editor of the *Examiner*, 3 November 1819: Shelley's *Letters*, ii. 142.

13 See p. 266.

14 See pp. 38 ff.

15 E. P. Thompson, *The Making of the English Working Class*, Harmondsworth, 1968, p. 411.

16 See p. 21.

17 Forsyth's book is, however, incomplete. In the first and only volume he has dealt with Private Duties; Public Duties were reserved for volume ii, which never appeared.

18 Robert Forsyth, *Principles of Moral Science*, Edinburgh, 1805, i. 9–10.

19 TLP to Edward Hookham, 13 March, 1809: viii. 165, and above pp. 129 ff., 285.

20 First published in *Ollier's Literary Miscellany*, i (?November 1820), 183–200 (the only number of the periodical ever issued).

21 See pp. 6, 157.

22 Howard Mills, *Peacock, his Circle and his Age*, Cambridge, 1968, p. 31.

23 Halliford edition: viii. 263. In beginning by sketching the fashionable reading public, and going on to the writers who serve it, Peacock echoes the formal arrangement of *Nightmare Abbey* (see p. 125). The relationship between the content in the two versions is correspondingly close.

24 Ibid., viii. 267.

25 Ibid., viii. 275.

26 Presumably Cobbett's *Political Register* and the Hunt brothers' *Examiner*.

27 'An Essay on Fashionable Literature': viii. 273.

28 Ibid., viii. 274.

29 The two examples of this kind of reviewing which most affronted TLP were in the *Edinburgh*: the review of Drummond's *Academical Questions*, *Edinburgh Review*, vii (1805), and of Coleridge's *Christabel*, ibid., xxvii (1816). For the latter, see p. 117; and cf. 'Essay on Fashionable Literature', viii. 275 ff.

30 See pp. 129 ff.
31 Halliford edition: viii. 274–5.
32 See pp. 17–18.
33 Halliford edition: viii. 437.
34 Forsyth, op. cit., pp. 160–1.
35 *The Four Ages of Poetry*: viii. 4. The resonance of this passage in Peacock's later work is strong: cf. the allusion to Southey in *Maid Marian*, ch. ix: iii/2.88, and above, pp. 145–6, 175–6.
36 Halliford edition: viii. 9.
37 Ibid., viii. 11.
38 Ibid., viii. 18.
39 Ibid., viii. 21.
40 M. H. Abrams, *The Mirror and the Lamp*, Oxford, 1953, p. 126. Professor Abrams regards *The Four Ages* relatively kindly, as a good parody, at least, of Wordsworth's tenets. Harsher opinions of Peacock's essay are recorded by R. Wellek, *A History of Criticism: the Romantic Period*, London, 1957, p. 127, and W. K. Wimsatt and C. Brooks, *Literary Criticism: A Short History*, New York, 1964, pp. 416–17.
41 Lorna Sage, *Peacock: the Satirical Novels: a Casebook*, London, 1976, pp. 14–15.
42 *A Defence of Poetry, Prose Works of P. B. Shelley*, ed. R. H. Shepherd, 2 vols, London, 1888, ii. 22.
43 Ibid., ii. 16.
44 Ibid., ii, 28.
45 See pp. 172–8.
46 From the first it was too easy to read it out of context, owing to its publication history. Shelley wrote it for *Ollier's*, specifically as an answer to Peacock; it was apparently full of phrases alluding to him and to his case. When that journal folded, *A Defence* was offered to the *Liberal*, and John Hunt struck out the references to Peacock in preparing it for publication. The *Liberal* in turn died, and *A Defence* was ultimately published by Mary Shelley in 1840, from Hunt's text – 'a defence without an attack', as Peacock called it (Halliford edition: viii. 500).
47 *A Defence of Poetry*: *Prose Works*, ii. 38.
48 R. G. Cox, 'Nineteenth-century periodical criticism', unpublished Cambridge PhD thesis (1935), p. 182: quoted in Mills, op. cit., p. 44.
49 Ibid., pp. 47–56.
50 Leigh Hunt, 'The Nymphs' (first published in *Foliage*, 1818), ll. 205–10.
51 PBS to Mary Shelley, 23 August 1818; Shelley's *Letters*, ii. 37.
52 *The Four Ages*: viii. 19.

53 TLP to PBS, 28 February 1822: viii. 228.

54 TLP to PBS, 4 December 1820: viii. 219–20. Shelley comments in reply: 'I received at the same time your printed denunciations [i.e., *The Four Ages*] against general, and your written ones against particular, poetry; and I agree with you as decidedly in the latter as I differ in the former'. (PBS to TLP, Pisa, 15 February 1821: Shelley's *Letters*, ii. 261.)

55 See p. 334 n. 68.

56 Peacock's essay of 1858 on Chapelle (x. 91–118) is largely though not exclusively stylistic, an interesting index to the 'Romanticisation' of English aesthetic ideas in the two decades since his essay 'On French Comic Romance'.

57 See pp. 97, 289.

58 See pp. 116–17.

59 See pp. 69 ff.

60 See pp. 108–23.

61 See p. 316 n. 41.

62 See p. 295, and Keats to B. R. Haydon, [14] March, 1818 – 'Peacock has damned satire': Keats's *Letters*, ed. M. B. Forman, 3rd ed., London, 1947, p. 119.

63 G. M. Mathews, *Keats, the Critical Heritage*, London, 1971, p. 2.

64 *Hyperion*, Bk II, ll. 173–243. Cf. the letter which treats of revolution and historical change, JK to George and Georgiana Keats, [18] September 1819: Keats's *Letters*, pp. 406–7.

65 See p. 266.

66 *A Defence of Poetry: Prose Works*, ii. 34.

67 PBS to TLP, 23–4 January 1819: Shelley's *Letters*, ii. 72–5.

68 E.g., PBS to TLP, 21 September 1819: Shelley's *Letters*, ii. 120.

69 Since writing this passage, I have found that Timothy Webb has developed similar points in more detail in *Shelley: A Voice Not Understood*, Manchester, 1977, especially pp. 249 ff., and 'Shelley and the Religion of Joy', *Studies in Romanticism*, xv (1976), 357–82.

70 PBS to JK, 27 July 1820: Shelley's *Letters*, ii. 221. Shelley continues, 'I wish those who excel me in genius, would pursue the same plan' – a reference probably to Byron and possibly to Wordsworth.

71 However, Peacock is a writer with an unusually large following (in England, at least) among those who do not study English literature. The economists, historians, philosophers, and well-read citizens who regularly return to him often seem to prefer *Crotchet Castle*.

72 See p. 225.

73 *Memoirs of Shelley*: viii. 131.

74 J. S. Mill to G. d'Eichthal, 8 October 1829: Mill's *Earlier Letters*, ed. Mineka, Toronto, 1963, pp. 37–8.

75 J. S. Mill, 'The Church', delivered at the Debating Society, 1829: published as Appendix to edition of *Autobiography* by Harold Laski, Oxford (World's Classics), 1924, p. 322.
76 'The Function of Criticism at the Present Time'. *Complete Prose Works of Matthew Arnold, iii: Lectures and Essays in Criticism*, ed. R. H. Super, Ann Arbor, 1962, p. 276.
77 Ibid., pp. 261–4.
78 Matthew Arnold, *Culture and Anarchy*, 1869; *Complete Prose Works*, v. 113.

Bibliography

Editions

Brett-Smith, H. F. B. and Jones, C. E. (eds), *Halliford Edition of the Works of Thomas Love Peacock*, 10 vols, London, 1924–34.
Garnett, David (ed.), *The Novels of Thomas Love Peacock*, 2 vols, London, 1948.

Secondary Works

Able, A. H., *George Meredith and Peacock: a Study in Literary Influence*, Philadelphia, 1933.
Abrams, M. H., *The Mirror and the Lamp: Romantic Theory and the Critical Tradition*, New York, Oxford, 1953.
Bush, Douglas, *Mythology and the Romantic Tradition in English Poetry*, Cambridge, Mass., 1937.
Cameron, K. N. (ed.), *Shelley and his Circle, 1773–1822*, Oxford, 1961–(8 vols projected). Contributions on Peacock by E. L. Nicholes in vols i and iii.
Campbell, Olwen W., *Thomas Love Peacock*, London, 1953.
Dawson, Carl, *His Fine Wit*, London, 1970.
Dyson, A. E., 'Peacock', in *The Crazy Fabric*, London, 1965.
Freeman, A. Martin, *Thomas Love Peacock, a Critical Study*, London, 1911.
Frye, Northrop, *The Anatomy of Criticism*, Princeton, 1957.
House, Humphry, 'The Works of Peacock', *Listener*, xlii (8 December 1949), 997–8.
Jack, Ian, 'Peacock', *English Literature, 1815–32*, Oxford, 1963.

Bibliography

Johnson, Diane, *The True History of the First Mrs. Meredith and Other Lesser Lives*, London, 1973.
Joukovsky, N. A., 'A Critical Edition of Peacock's *Headlong Hall* and *Nightmare Abbey*', thesis submitted at Oxford, 1970, MS D Phil. d.5154.
Mackerness, E. D., 'Peacock's Musical Criticism', *The Wind and the Rain*, iv (1948).
Madden, Lionel, *Thomas Love Peacock*, London, 1967.
Mayoux, J.-J., *Un Epicurien anglais: Thomas Love Peacock*, Paris, 1933.
Mills, Howard W., *Peacock, his Circle and his Age*, Cambridge, 1968.
Nesbitt, G. L., *Benthamite Reviewing: the first twelve years of the Westminster Review, 1824–36*, New York, 1934.
Nicholes, see Cameron.
Praz, Mario, *The Hero in Eclipse*, London, New York and Toronto, 1956.
Priestley, J. B., *English Comic Characters*, London, 1925.
Priestley, J. B., *Thomas Love Peacock*, London, 1927.
Read, Bill, 'The Critical Reputation of Thomas Love Peacock, with an Annotated Enumerative Bibliography of Works by and about Peacock from February 1800 to June 1958', thesis submitted at Boston, 1959.
Read, Bill, 'Thomas Love Peacock: an Enumerative Bibliography', *Bulletin of Bibliography*, xxiv (1963–4), 32–4, 70–2, 88–91.
Robinson, Eric, 'Peacock: Critic of Scientific Progress', *Annals of Science*, x (1954).
Sage, Lorna (ed.), *Peacock: the Satirical Novels*, London, 1976. A Selection of Critical Essays (Casebook series).
Saintsbury, George, *Essays in English Literature, 1780–1860*, London, 1890. See also his Prefaces to his edition of the novels, London, 1895–7.
Salz, Paulina, 'Peacock's Use of Music in his Novels', *JEGP*, liv (1955), 370–9.
Scott, W. S. (ed.), *New Shelley Letters*, London, 1948.
Shelley, The Letters of P. B. Shelley, ed. F. L. Jones, 2 vols, Oxford, 1964.
Stewart, J. I. M., *Thomas Love Peacock*, London, 1963 (Writers and their Work, no. 156).
Van Doren, Carl, *The Life of Thomas Love Peacock*, London and New York (1911), reprinted New York, 1966.
Ward, W. S., 'Contemporary Reviews of Peacock: a Supplementary List for the years 1805–20', *Bulletin of Bibliography*, xxv (1967).
Wellek, René, *A History of Criticism: the Romantic Period*, London, 1957.
White, N. I., *The Unextinguished Hearth: Shelley and his Contemporary Critics*, Durham, NC, 1938.
Wilson, Edmund, 'The Musical Glasses of Thomas Love Peacock', in his *Classics and Commercials*, New York, 1951.
Wright, Herbert, 'The Associations of Peacock with Wales', *E & S*, xii (1926).

350

Index

351

Index

Roebuck, John, 191
Romanticism, *see* chapters 4 and 8,
    passim; Coleridge; Wordsworth;
    Germany
Rome, 23, 24, 64
Ronsard, Pierre de, 252
Roscoe, William, *Life of Lorenzo de
    Medici*, 64; *Life and Pontificate of Leo
    the Tenth*, 64
Rosewall, Mary, 15
Rossini, 150
Rousseau, Jean-Jacques, viii, 22, 30,
    71, 80, 207, 250, 308, 311;
    Confessions, 241, *Discours sur les Arts
    et les Sciences*, 41, 75; *Discours sur
    l'origine et les fondements de l'inegalité
    parmi les Hommes*, 41, 75–6; *Julie, ou
    la Nouvelle Héloise*, 126
Rugby School, 261
Ruskin, John, 230
Russell, Lord John, 163, 236, 274
Russell, William, Lord Russell, 63

Sage, Lorna, *Peacock: the Satirical
    Novels*, 346 n. 41
Saint-Beuve, Charles Augustin, 311
St Pierre, Bernardin, *Paul et Virginie*,
    207
St Simonians, 215–20
Saintsbury, George, 18, 178, 246
Salz, Paulina June, 135–6,330 n. 88
Sassoon, Siegfried, *Meredith*, 316 n. 34
Schiller, F. von, 262; *Ghost-Seer*, 124
Schlegel, A. W., 109, 276, 304;
    Dramatic Art and Literature, 127, 134
Schlegel, Friedrich, 109, 139, 276
Schneider, E., 328 n. 37
Scott, Walter, 27, 172, 181, 225,
    235–6, 274, 284, 289; *Black Dwarf*,
    328 n. 44; *Marmion*, 317 n. 1;
    Minstrelsy of the Scottish Border, 276,
    287; review of *Emma*, 80; *Waverley*,
    59, 102
Scottish influence, 274 ff.
Selden, John, 89
Senancour, Etienne Pivert de,
    Obermann, 311

Shakespeare, 201, 265, 299, 305; *As
    You Like It*, 147, 152, 207; *Twelfth
    Night*, 343 n. 56; *Winter's Tale*, 59
Shaw, Bernard, 2
Shelley, Harriet (*née* Westbrook), 5–7,
    10, 16, 99, 125, 241, 315 n. 11, 334
    n. 72
Shelley, Mary Wollstonecraft (*née*
    Godwin), 4–5, 7, 11–12, 103–4,
    125, 206; editions of Shelley's
    poems, 4; *Frankenstein*, 72, 123
Shelley, Percy Bysshe, 3–7, 142, 206,
    241, 300–6; 'Adonais', 306; *Alastor*,
    4, 71–2, 100, 104, 124, 206, 301,
    306; *Cenci, The*, 304, 331 n. 7;
    Charles 1, 304, 331 n. 7; *Defence of
    Poetry*, 142, 174, 290–4, 301;
    'Discourse on the Manners of
    Ancient Greeks Relating to the
    Subject of Love', 302;
    'Epipsychidion', 302; 'Hymn to
    Intellectual Beauty', 323 n. 41;
    'Hymn to Mercury', translation,
    104, 305; *Laon and Cythna*, or
    Revolt of Islam, 66, 100, 103, 127,
    301, 306; 'Letter to Maria
    Gisborne', 1, 20; *Letters*, 303–4;
    'Mont Blanc', 71, 301, 317 n. 55;
    Philosophical View of Reform, 331
    n. 7; 'Prince Athanase', 104, 302;
    Prometheus Unbound, 4, 25, 100,
    301–2, 304, 306, 323 n. 35; *Proposal
    for Putting Reform to the Vote*, 103,
    330 n. 80; *Queen Mab*, 40, 45, 100,
    317 n. 55, 318 n. 5; *Refutation of
    Deism*, 40; review of *Rhododaphne*,
    107–8; *Swellfoot the Tyrant*, 304, 323
    n. 35; 'Triumph of Life', 306;
    'Verses Written on Receiving a
    Celandine', 71, 301; 'Witch of
    Atlas', 305; allusions to in
    Peacock's work, 7, 17, 40, 73, 125,
    127–39, 174, 241, 259, 309;
    comments on Peacock, 1, 12, 20,
    28, 99–101, 107, 128–31, 137,
    290 ff., 325 n. 95; debates with
    Peacock, 28, 37–8, 70–3, 100,

Index

103–8, 128–39, 290–5, 347 n. 54;
for intellectual friendship with
Peacock, *see* Peacock, T. L.
Shelley, Sir Percy Florence, 5, 315 n. 8
Sheridan, Richard Brinsley, *School for Scandal*, 133–5, 305
Shuttleworth, Philip Nicholas, 196
Sidney, Algernon, 63
Sismondi, J. C. L., *History of the Italian Republics*, 64–5, 111, 321 n. 8
Skelmersdale, Lord, 159
Smith, Adam, 276
Smith, Horace and James, *Rejected Addresses*, 52
Smith, Sydney, 274
Soane, Sir John, 23
Socrates, 24, 39–40, 45, 46, 200, 266
Solon, 286
Southey, Robert, 20, 31, 59, 61, 90, 92–4, 146–9, 178, 218; *Colloquies*, 190, 197; *Letters from England*, 320 n. 42
Spain, 63, 66, 148
Spedding, James, 1–2, 266, 270
Spenser, Edmund, 99, 187, 292, 299; *Faerie Queene*, 66–9, 86, 100
Spurgeon, Charles, 237
Spurzheim, J. K. (or G.), 52–5
Stephen, Sir James, 249
Sterne, Laurence, 57
Stevens, George Alexander, 'A Lecture on Heads', 55
Stewart, Dugald, 224, 274
Stewart, J. I. M., 314 n. 4
Stillingfleet, Edward, 89
Stoddard, John, 149, 331 n. 20
Stokes, Eric, *English Utilitarians in India*, 341 n. 3
Strachey, Edward, 15, 332 n. 32
Strachey, Sir Edward, 15, 155, 316 n. 25, 332 n. 32
Sun, 91
Swift, Jonathan, 57, 89, 93, 186, 270, 286; *Gulliver's Travels*, 138, 166
Swing, Captain, 213, 220–1
Switzerland, 23, 71, 72–3

Taliesin, 156 ff., 176–8
Tasso, 71, 82, 324 n. 52; *Jerusalem Delivered*, 67–8, 146
Tatton Park, 32
Taylor, Charles, 159
Taylor, Jeremy, 89
Taylor, Thomas, 19–21; *Mystical Initiations: or Hymns of Orpheus*, 20
Tennyson, Alfred Lord, 119
Terence, 269
Thackeray, W. M., 230, 247
Theocritus, 252
Thompson, E. P., *The Making of the English Working Class*, 280
Thomson, James, 27; *Ode to Liberty*, 23
Thucydides, *History of the Peloponnesian War*, 261
Tillotson, John, 89
Times, The, 91–2, 149
Tolstoy, Count Leo, 311
Trollope, Anthony, 236, 249–50
Trollope, Frances, 208
Turgot, Anne Robert Jacques, 160–2, 174
Twain, Mark, 2

Unitarianism, 88
University College London, 192
Utilitarians, 172–4, 176, 186–94, 211, 216, 223, 281, 290–4, 310, 336 n. 22

Valentine and Orson, 69, 322 n. 18
Van Doren, Carl, *Life of Thomas Love Peacock*, 316 n. 39, 317 n. 47, 324 n. 67
Venice, 23, 64
Venus (Aphrodite), 199, 239
Virgil, *Aeneid*, 25, 89, 108
Viviani, Emilia, 302
Volney, Constantin François Chasseboeuf, 36, 309
Voltaire (François-Marie Arouet), 49, 68–9, 78, 191, 266–8, 270, 286–7, 308, 311, 313
Vulliamy, J. T., 10

360